THE LIFE COURSE

The Life Course

A Sociological Introduction

Second Edition

Stephen J. Hunt

First edition 2005
This edition published 2017 by
PALGRAVE MACMILLAN

Palgrave in the UK is an imprint of Macmillan Publishers Limited, registered in England, company number 785998, of 4 Crinan Street, London, N1 9XW.

Palgrave Macmillan in the US is a division of St Martin's Press LLC, 175 Fifth Avenue, New York, NY 10010.

Palgrave is a global imprint of the above companies and is represented throughout the world.

Palgrave® and Macmillan® are registered trademarks in the United States, the United Kingdom, Europe and other countries.

ISBN 978–1–137–52196–5 hardback
ISBN 978–1–137–52195–8 paperback

This book is printed on paper suitable for recycling and made from fully managed and sustained forest sources. Logging, pulping and manufacturing processes are expected to conform to the environmental regulations of the country of origin.

A catalogue record for this book is available from the British Library.

A catalog record for this book is available from the Library of Congress.

Printed and bound by CPI Group UK Ltd, Croydon, CR0 4YY

Brief Contents

Contents

List of Tables and Boxes

TABLES

BOXES

Introduction

This is the second edition of *The Life Course: A Sociological Introduction*, published by Palgrave Macmillan. In the first edition (2005), I contended that few specialised sociological textbooks addressed the subject of the life course in a comprehensive yet accessible way. My supplementary observation was that in many respects such a deficiency was not to be anticipated. This was particularly so given that the contemporary life course had increasingly attracted academic interest, was accordingly widely taught in institutions of higher education and constituted an integral part of the vocational training of the 'caring professions'. The initial volume thus endeavoured to rectify such a discrepancy by 'filling the gap' and in doing so employed a number of broad objectives, not least to connect with contemporaneous theorising and empirical research. This updated second edition tackles the continued scarcity of texts analysing the life course. As before, it does so from a sociological perspective which nonetheless recognises the contribution of additional disciplines at a time when interdisciplinary approaches are progressively more welcomed.

Put succinctly, the focus of this edition, as with the first, is to explore the experiences of human life from the beginning to end within contemporary Western societies. This invariably means surveying significant social-cultural transformations and some of the contentious debates, public as well as academic, which accompany them as the twenty-first century progresses. Many of these changes have occurred at a time when lifespans continue to lengthen in 'advanced' industrial nations and indeed are, in part at least, consequences of this. Here might be cited the example of trends in the USA, which are not dissimilar to those elsewhere in the West. According to the Centers for Disease Control and Preventions' Health Statistics in 1900 the average life expectancy was 46.3 years for men, 48.3 for women; in 1950 65.6 for men, 71.4 for women; and in 2012 had risen to a high of 78.8 years (women averaging at 81.2 years, men 76.4 years). The causes of death in later life remained the same as they had for several decades, including such major illnesses as heart disease, cancer, strokes, Alzheimer's disease, diabetes, pneumonia and kidney disease (the report nonetheless noted that the death rates for heart disease and cancer, the two leading causes of death, accounting for 46.5 percent of all deaths, had been falling since 1999).

While the US media has continuingly expressed concern that the nation's life expectancy was ranked only 36th in the World Health Organization's list of countries in 2012, practically all of those placed higher were to be found in the Western world. Additional tendencies are also observable in such 'developed' nations. Using the example of the United Kingdom, by way of marking increase in longevity, in 1951 there were only 271 centurions (people aged 100 and over), while according to the Office for National Statistics Report (2013) their number was estimated to be 13,780 in 2013; of these, 710 were approximated to be aged 105 or older. By the year 2030, there may well be 30,000 people living beyond their hundredth birthday.

There is some conjecture as to the underlying reasons behind this progressive gain in the lifespan, although broadly speaking they are undeniably related to improved environmental conditions and, to a lesser extent, medical advances which have virtually eliminated infectious diseases in Western societies. What cannot be doubted, however, are the *consequences* of longer life duration. One consideration is that Sociology is obliged to reconsider the familiar 'stages' of life, raising such profound questions as to what exactly constitutes the onset of 'old age'. Is it 65, 75 or 85 years old? As will continuingly be discussed throughout this volume, at the same time as life expectancy increases, the age categories which once formed a primary basis for structuring the life course are arguably disintegrating. At the very least some categories are increasingly shortened, others lengthened, raising further questions such as when does childhood end?; when does mid-life begin?; and indeed, is 'old age' a meaningful 'stage' in the contemporary life course at all? Given these questions, the sociological tendency has been to practically abandon concepts related to the 'stages' of life. Plausibly they are now better designated as 'phases' or 'transitions' of life, often lacking coherence or direction and open to considerable negotiation.

These developments have, in turn, enforced a growing sociological emphasis on embracing a social constructionist approach that is concerned with deconstructing how such concepts as 'stages' have come to be forged in the first place and what the implications are for designating people into categories such as 'youth', 'mid-life' or 'old'. Nonetheless, it would probably be erroneous to entirely discard these age categories, even if they no longer comprehensively provide guides to life encounters. They do, for the most part, permit a point of departure for discussion over a number of crucial subject matters. That acknowledged, there is little doubt that these categories are increasingly void of their more deterministic qualities and provide only broad signifiers of life course experiences.

If these 'phases' of life are deemed as a starting point for analysis, it is clear that a number have been subject to a radical change. Others, or at least some aspects of them, have endured in fairly time-honoured tradition. The undertaking of this volume, as before, in investigating both change and continuity, is to consider the ongoing deliberations about the repercussions. These deliberations are of more than sociological interest, since they also inform current policy discourses surrounding such topics as the implications of an ageing population, sexual diversity and ethics circumscribing various emergent technologies. It is these discourses which, if a generalisation can be made, inform competing views of the socio-cultural trajectories associated with the life course, literally from (if not before) the cradle to the grave.

While the so-called stages of life might be transformed, how individuals envisage and negotiate them is impacted by the anticipation that, all things being equal, life expectancy will extend into at least the late 70s/early 80s. This is almost certain to influence reflexive thinking in the present. In short, what is unique about Western culture is not just the prevalence of modes of individualism and individual responsibility, but the way in which many people plan ahead and navigate future life and major life events. In this sense, the life course may have become more meaningful and more subjective. Yet, at the same time, the life course now seems less predictable and pre-determined, more infused with calculations of risk and anticipations of possible repercussions of discontinuity.

If such reflexive thinking and life experiences signify a profound shift in how the life course is appraised and comprehended, then this tilt has been accompanied by some notable economic, technological and cultural developments associated with what has come to be alternatively known as late- or postmodernity. The rise of the so-called new technologies, and the move to an economy of consumption rather than production – one accompanied by a distinct culture of choice – have all forged novel modes of social experience and encounter. It follows that the sociological enterprise has attempted to identify and account for the implications which, in turn, have generated fresh theoretical perspectives clearly building upon the growing distinction between the 'life-cycle' and the 'life course', the latter being the current preferred operational framework. As a result, notions of a coherent and inevitable 'life-cycle' are largely redundant and make little sense in a changing world where, as tentatively already noted, the once assumed 'stages' of life and what they entail for life events are no longer so 'fixed' and predictable.

Yet, it is probably true to say that sociological theory is now betwixt 'n' between. New theories are not quite universally accepted and continue to be ardently deliberated, while older paradigms are by no means entirely redundant. There is still scope to apply conventional sociological suppositions. Many of these are concerned with such issues as structured social inequalities which continue to inform life course chances – class, gender, ethnicity and, of course, age – demographic categories scarcely rendered superfluous by acute changes observable at the end of the twentieth century and the beginning of a new millennium.

To be sure, recent sociological work has thrown light on how social inequalities and demographic variables may have a cumulative impact on the life course and life experiences. In turn, these factors not only impinge on life chances, but forge the very nature and structure of the 'phases' and crucial transitions throughout the life course. Simultaneously, Sociology has come to understand the importance of 'historical generations'. In short, that life experiences are influenced by the historical periods in which an individual's life course takes place. Yet while such factors invariably shape life course experiences, there is increasing recognition that human beings, through conscious personal agency, attempt to make sense of and act in response to situations in which they find themselves. This recognition in respect of the importance of personal agency would seem to be of increasing relevance in a social context that is subject to considerable change and variation.

If it can indeed be claimed that contemporary societies are undergoing rapid change, then what precisely may they be compared to? Although this is far from its principal aim, another concern of this volume is to present a measure of historical and cross-cultural approaches to the life course, since an understanding of its major features today can only be fully grasped with a degree of contrast with Western societies in previous centuries and non-Western societies – past and present. Clearly, a comparative dimension has the merit of permitting an appreciation of how much of the life course is forged in any given societal context. In this respect, there are undoubtedly marked cultural similarities, as well as departures, between societies not only observable through the 'stages' of life, but also the way biological and psychological processes, not least of all the process of ageing, are perceived. Just as importantly, are the differences in the life course to be found in contrasting forms of society today – a dissimilarity generated by numerous socio-economic variables which, in an increasingly globalised world, produce infinite possibilities underpinning life experiences.

At the same time, this volume is concerned with possible future 'trends', although notions of 'trends' are now radically challenged by contemporary sociological theorising, suggesting that little – be it economic, technological or cultural – can be viewed as long term or predicted with any certainty. Nonetheless, there are observable important current demographic developments which are more undeniably certain in their future impact, most notably the increasing population size of those of retirement age compared to younger age categories. That profound consequences for the generations to come will be forthcoming cannot be doubted. Later on in the twenty-first century, there will be weighty problems related to the dependency ratio. In short, there will be increasingly more dependents and fewer people of working age to economically support them. This is a dilemma being grappled with by emerging social agendas, however unpopular their implications undoubtedly will be. For instance, the USA, much like the rest of the world, is an ageing society. Between 2000 and 2050, the proportion of the population over the age of 65 will increase from 12.7 per cent in 2000 to 20.3 per cent in 2050. Over this time period, the proportion of the population that is aged 85+ will rise from 1.6 per cent in 2000 to 4.8 per cent. This will clearly put substantial strain on publicly funded health and long-term and income support programmes for older people (Wiener and Tilly 2002).

Other future developments are less clear. Sociology may come to the aid here. As a discipline that examines and explains social trends, it plausibly has a predictive element which may aid government and welfare agencies in policy-making. This is Sociology's practical side. However, the reality is that the discipline has a rather mixed track record in predicting the future. Sometimes its exponents have been impressively accurate and, at other times, lamentably mistaken. With the onset of modernity, or in some cases when it was well under way, early and pioneering sociologists such as Emile Durkheim and Max Weber outlined, accounted for and anticipated future possibilities. Not all of their predictions came true. Perhaps in the present day, however, sociologists may be permitted to set down their excuses well in advance, since forecasting social trends is perhaps more arduous than ever.

Uncertainty and lack of predictability, so theorists of late/postmodernity would maintain, are among the major hallmarks of the contemporary world. What is also lost, they frequently argue, is the declining faith in progress as an inevitable evolutionary process. Thus, the optimism of the founders of the discipline appears to have receded, suggesting that any notion of 'progress' should be jettisoned. The world is teeming with an assortment of hazards and it is clearly evident that there is much uncertainty about what the future holds in the face of potential disasters: global economic recession such as that commencing in 2008 or environmental catastrophes remain strong possibilities. Individuals and communities are faced with numerous hazards in what Ulrich Beck refers to as the 'risk society' (Beck 1992): the likelihood of unemployment, family breakdown and relentless challenge of negotiating rapid technological transformations and their social implications.

If much indeed appears unpredictable, it is also impossible to know whether anticipated social change will be for the better. Presently, individuals may make only particularistic judgements as to the merits of a world where long-established social structures appear to be disintegrating. Such structures are not just those related to communities and the family, but plausibly also include class, ethnicity and gender. All have previously impacted on the life course as a source of belonging and community. If these structures are dissipating (and there is considerable debate as to whether this is the case), then they are arguably being replaced by increasing pluralism and social diversity, cultural fragmentation, pick 'n' mix lifestyles and a society that is finely graded by people's ability to participate in the consumer marketplace. At the same time, the possible decline of these social structures will have implications for concepts of 'self'. After all, it was community, class, gender and so on which once gave individuals, for better or for worse, a sense of identity. Now individuals are faced with the prospect of creating their own identity in a largely consumerist society, while at the same time being challenged to forge a sense of belonging.

Given all these above developments associated with the life course, some articulating change and others continuity, a critical analysis would therefore seem to be warranted. This second edition seeks to refresh the gaze. This is not an easy task and perhaps the most obvious difficulty for a volume of this kind is related to how the chapters could plausibly be organised. Given the flexibility and unpredictability associated with the 'phases' of life, it might be unjustifiable to use them as chapter headings. Yet, to reiterate, even transformations within late/postmodernity have not yet rendered them entirely invalid and they at least present starting points from which to begin a meaningful survey.

There also remains a certain logic in commencing with the beginning of life and ending with its close – from birth to death. Hence, the chapters loosely follow the 'phases' of biological growth. This does not mean, however, that the structure of the volume simply reflects what might be designated 'a sociology of ageing'. Rather, commentators increasingly utilise terms such as 'middle childhood' and 'early adulthood' to conceptualise human life from beginning to end. These 'phases' have become adopted as the life course approach continues to develop. Such an approach is particularly constructive since 'phases' suggests the association between crucial life events and transitions of childhood, youth and adulthood (Newman and Aptekar 2007; O'Rand 1996).

At the same time, this volume seeks to unearth not only how the 'phases' of the life course are exposed to considerable social construction and elaboration, but how they continue to be shaped by social inequalities. Indeed, the significance of social constructs, alongside societal determinants of the life course, constitutes the major subject matter of the first three chapters, which seek to explore key dominant theoretical frameworks. These frameworks are brought to bear on subsequent chapters related to birth, infanthood, childhood, youth, adulthood, later life and death. Organising the volume in this way has hopefully contributed to both its accessibility and relevance. However, departing from the first edition, this second edition has substantially revised the progression and content of a number of chapters. This reorganisation is not only due to the social transformations which they seek to account for and describe, but also to the constructive comments of reviewers of this volume. I would like to thank them for undertaking this task.

Finally, this volume aims not merely to produce a reader for students of Sociology. The discipline as a whole, not least its account of the contemporary life course, lends itself to the interests of professions working in health, social work and other human services. The volume is mindful of the requirements of these professions, noting the importance of how the theorising may translate to a practical level and recognises the significance of differing epistemological stances such professions may embrace. For these reasons, and those outlined above, this second edition attempts to be of sufficient scope and penetration of principal sociological concerns as to inform a wide readership.

FURTHER READING

Elder, G. (1985) *Life Course Dynamics*, Ithaca, NY: Cornell University Press.
Elder, G. and Giele, J. (eds.) (2009) *The Craft of Life Course Research*, New York: Guildford Press.

Elder, G., Kirkpatrick, M. and Crosnoe, R. (2003) *The Emergence and Development of Life Course Theory*, in T. Mortimer and M. Shanahan (ed.), *Handbook of the Life Course*, New York: Springer.

Featherstone, M. and Hepworth, M. (1989) 'Ageing and Old Age: Reflections on the Postmodern Life Course', in B. Byetheway, T. Keil, P. Allat and A. Bryman (eds.), *Becoming and Being Old*, London: Sage.

Frost, E. and McClean, S. (2013) *Thinking About the Life Course*, Basingstoke: Palgrave Macmillan.

Giddens, A. (1991) *Self-Identity, Self and Society in the Late Modern Age*, Cambridge: Polity Press.

Giele, J. and Elder, G. (1998) *Methods of Life Course Research: Qualitative and Quantitative Approaches*, Thousand Oaks, CA: Sage.

Green, L. (2010) *Understanding the Life Course: Sociological and Psychological Perspectives*, Oxford: Polity.

Howe, D. (2011) *Attachment Across the Lifecourse: A Brief Introduction*, Basingstoke: Palgrave Macmillan.

Katz, S. (1995) 'Imagining the Life-Span. From Pre-modern Miracles to Post-Modern Fantasies', in M. Featherstone and A. Wernick (eds.), *Images of Ageing: Cultural Representations of Later Life*, New York: Routledge.

Kohli, M. (1988) 'The World We Forgot: A Historical View of the Life Course', in V. Marshal (ed.), *Later Life: The Social Psychology of Ageing*, London: Sage.

Mayer, K. (2009) 'New Directions in Life Course Research', *Annual Review of Sociology, 35*: 423–24.

Pilcher, J. (1995) *Age and Generation in Modern Britain*, Oxford: Oxford University Press.

Riley, M. (ed.) *Sociological Lives. Social Change and the Life Course*, Newbury Park, CA: Sage.

Chapter 1

From life cycle to the life course: theoretical accounts

The introduction to this volume advanced the merits of sociological analysis as applied to the life course. It was suggested that the discipline aims to survey continuities and change, and even predict possible future societal trends. This objective constitutes no easy undertaking. Clearly, today Sociology finds itself in a condition of theoretical flux and engaged in considerable speculation as to where its central focus should settle. Undoubtedly, such a tendency is at least partly due to the rapidly transformative nature of that which it endeavours to describe and scrutinise – the human experience in a collective setting. This observation particularly stands in regard to the life course in contemporary Western societies.

Emerging theoretical perspectives require a measure of primary exploration. This chapter and Chapters 2 and 3 are largely concerned with shaping up a number of analytical remits for a study of the life course, raising some key issues, and developing a broad framework by which to aspire towards an understanding of both change and continuity. The following chapter will excavate late/postmodern theorising at some length since these remain the current dominant paradigms offering a broad understanding of the contemporary social world, and thus the major features which shape contemporary social life. This will lead to an exploration of how these paradigms have brought a radical challenge to the way in which life course studies have previously been approached.

Chapter 3 will consider the importance of social differentiation in generating what can be broadly termed 'inequalities' and their significance by way of forging the principal contours of the life course. Particular attention will be given to considering the degree to which they are relevant in the late/postmodern context. The impact of the variables of social class, gender, ethnicity and indeed age categories now appear to be less certain than they once were. Nonetheless, they remain central to the relevant sociological literature as well as government and other agencies' report findings in terms of the 'hard facts' about the impact of social inequalities and demographics and the way they continue to inform life experiences and opportunities.

Before overviewing some of the recent broad theoretical innovations and central concerns of Sociology it is pertinent to briefly survey a few of the more specific themes long associated with the life course. Hence, this chapter will seek to explain the shift in sociological thinking and the emergence of more nuanced and effective methodological tools that have led to a preference for a life course rather than conventional life-cycle approach which previously dominated the discipline. It will become apparent that preference for a life course perspective points not only to a greater sophistication in applying sociological analysis but the imperative of taking into account profound social transformations.

THE SOCIOLOGICAL ENTERPRISE AND THE LIFE COURSE

Undoubtedly, contemporary societies, whether the complex post-industrial societies of the West or the vast variety of cultures which may be placed somewhat awkwardly under the rubric of 'emerging economies' or 'developing nations', are undergoing considerable transformations in a rising global order. Nonetheless, the sociological enterprise, despite changing conceptualisations and contextualisations, continues its erstwhile project in attempting to comprehend the human condition in terms of institutional settings or, as frequently preferred in late/postmodern theorising, the 'processes' which forge the lives of individuals and the life chances and opportunities of particular social constituencies.

These 'processes', be they economic, technological, cultural or political, endure in influencing life in many different respects, and for all of life. Considering the way they have changed in terms of the life course is an attractive one. There remains so much about the life course that is indicative of the nature of contemporary society, at least within the Western environment. Once it would have been almost obligatory to discuss the experiences of the life course, or the concept of the 'life-cycle' as previously preferred, primarily in terms of the impact of social institutions at particular 'stages' of life. This was principally so by way of those institutions which appeared to be universal and enduring. The family is arguably the most obvious human arrangement in this respect. Whether through the nurturing or early social-isation of the child or the institution of marriage and parenting that seemed to provide a marker of adult maturity and social responsibility, kinship structures have historically been central. Much no longer holds, however. The so-called decline of the family and increasing rates of marital break-down, coupled with the emergence of variations in family life, typified by the single parent and 'reconstituted' family, whereby children from previous relationships come together in a new household, ensure that generalisations and predictions regarding experiences of the family during the life course are at least problematic.

Variations in family structure, to which can be added the far-reaching changes in human relationships generally, also beg to be flagged up by the relevance of a social constructionist approach as an essential part of the sociological enterprise. Above all, the emergence of the post-industrial society provides a reminder that, sociologically speaking, nothing is inev-itable and the once taken-for-granted social arrangements are by no means universal. There are patent and palpable implications to be registered for the life course, suggesting that the key 'markers' of life have been subject to cul-tural variation, if not transmogrification. Here is an acknowledgement that transformations, including those identified with the family, should not neces-sarily breed apprehension merely because they are novel and unfamiliar.

Comparative sociological, as well as anthropological, works have long underlined the richness and variety of social life and the organisation (a term itself perhaps now redundant) of the life course. Research, whether contemporaneous or historical, proves that many of the experiences encoun-tered in life are imposed by social convention and are not, as often assumed, necessarily 'natural'. For instance, it is a typically Western idealistic view that finding a partner of the opposite sex, falling in love, getting married and raising children is desirable. Marriage in some societies is, however, 'arranged'. In a number of Muslim countries, for instance, a young girl (not infrequently as young as eight years old) will be betrothed for a dowry and know well in advance whom it is she will marry. Through such marriages families of relatively equal wealth and status will come together to further their common interests. Between these two poles, marriage arrangements are numerous alternatives where, to some degree or another, close relatives will have a say on who marries whom. Human experience of partner selection, as with many other aspects of social life is, therefore, infinitely varied, even if some widespread patterns are clearly observable.

Recent sociological writings have also pointed out that such conventions as marriage, once so central to the life course, are seemingly increasingly superfluous in the late/postmodern age. The social compulsion to marry appears to have declined. It is now more a matter of choice and lifestyle preference, less subject to socialising pressures. This exemplifies, at least in Western societies, how many of the once assumed certainties of life no longer appear so certain. There are an increasing number of alternatives to the conventional heterosexual marriage: the freedom to choose the single life, to cohabitate and now, in many countries, the legal liberty to marry a member of the same sex.

Perhaps, above all, current research has shown how in late/postmodernity the 'inevitability' of the so-called stages of life once associated with a 'life-cycle' approach is increasingly challenged. In doing so, Sociology verifies

Table 1.1 Marriage and Cohabitation (UK)

Cohabitation (in millions)								
1996	**1998**	**2000**	**2002**	**2004**	**2006**	**2008**	**2010**	**2012**
2.9	**3.5**	**4.0**	**2.3**	**4.7**	**5.0**	**5.4**	**5.6**	**5.9**

Source: adapted from the Labour Force Survey – Office for National Statistics, 2013, licensed under the Open Government Licence v.3.0.

Marriages England & Wales	
1997	272,536
1999	263,515
2001	249,227
2003	270,109
2005	247,805
2007	235,370
2009	231,490

Source: adapted from data from the Office for National Statistics licensed under the Open Government Licence v.3.0.

that contemporary society with its relativism and pluralism points to the social construction of such 'stages', whether 'childhood', 'youth' or 'old age'. The latter provides a more than adequate example. In this regard socio-logical accounts of popular perceptions of ageing, such as that of Andrew Blakie (1999), show that 'old age' has included varying connotations accord-ing to historical periods, and differs between cultures. This is not to imply that some factors, most notably a tendency for social marginalisation in later life, are no longer worthy of consideration. Nevertheless, it is clear that older people today do not constitute a homogenous age group. Differing life trajectories and life events, as well as varying levels of wealth, education and health, all ensure this is not the case.

Sociology has invariably sought to understand the implications of such recent socio-cultural change. Yet disagreements within the discipline are reflected in competing theories and an often poorly disguised ideological discourse as to how the subject should be approached, what methods should be utilised and subjective recommendations for how and why society should change. Theoretical diversity may suggest a lack of rigour and focus. However, Sociology can perhaps be forgiven for its theoretical and analyt-ical multiplicity. Social change, its speed and trajectories, are increasingly undermining sociological 'certainties' and long-cherished paradigms. This has proved to be so for the sociological account of the life course, which, in particular, has continuingly challenged concepts of a 'life-cycle' and pre-dictable 'cycle of life'.

BIOLOGICAL AND PSYCHOLOGICAL APPROACHES

Biological dimensions

So far reference to the 'life-cycle' has been discussed as if it is now a super-fluous concept. This needs a measure of substantiation. For many decades the life-cycle approach dominated sociological and anthropological think-ing and not infrequently grounded research studies. Much of the focus appeared to be associated with observations concerning biological and psy-chological processes and how these related to social experiences. This was perhaps understandable given that the 'biological cycle' of life would seem to be an inevitable one. Human beings are living organisms with observable biological patterns which are dictated by their physiological constitution. There are inevitable, if uneven, biological 'developments' which typically merge with socially constructed ideas of progression from infanthood into adult maturity and through to old age: growth and physical decline, and eventually death. All of these are universal human experiences, inevitable and unchanging processes. Variations are, of course, to be discerned, since historically speaking high rates of infant mortality have been common, and living 'three score years and ten' has proved to be by no means a foregone conclusion in many previous societies and for the greater number of people in the Majority World today. The ageing process can therefore be impacted, for good or for bad, by a range of social and environmental variables that interact with an array of biological factors responsible for differing rates of morbidity and mortality.

In simple terms, the 'life-cycle' can be reduced to a developmental model or models which outline the social, biological and psychological change encountered as an individual passes through what are frequently understood as the major 'stages' of life: childhood, adolescence, mid-life, old age and eventually death. Much of the early literature on the subject apparently reflected an underlying common-sense conviction that reduced behaviour and outlooks associated with these stages to the 'biological clock', in which ageing was seen as merely a 'natural' process. Although focusing upon inevitable biological development as the principal bedrock to the life-cycle, these changes were, and frequently still are, associated with psychological repercussions.

Table 1.2 Infant Mortality Rates 1915–2011, USA (per thousand births)

1915	100
1925	67
1935	58
1945	40
1955	28
1965	24
1975	18
1985	16
1995	8
2005	7
2011	4

Source: derived from National Vital Statistics Report, National Centre for Health Statistics, 2012.

In considering biological factors, there is also the importance of the human reproductive system. In the case of females, there will be the commencement of menstruation, the years when a woman is fertile and the time when her capacity to reproduce comes to an end. Yet even these biological 'stages' have long been subject to elements of social construction. In Western society this is perhaps most evident through the medicalisation of natural processes. Medicalisation may be best defined as the process by which human conditions and problems come to be understood as the domain of medical specialisms in their diagnosis, treatment and prevention. It is medicalisation which has frequently located natural processes into so-called inevitable stages of life. In many instances the feminist critique has identified this tendency as a reflection of patriarchy, for example, by associating the end of the reproductive capacity with the inevitable onslaught of menopause synonymous with mid-life and all of its perceived accompanying psychological maladies connected with the female sex.

On the 'plus' side, as already noted, medical science (in many respects at least), along with a better diet and environmental conditions, has aided the lengthening of the life-span through new technologies of scientific advance so that a relatively long life is now practically guaranteed given that life expectancy is twice what it was a century ago. Indeed, perhaps the most noteworthy aspect of adulthood in Western societies is that today people can look forward to living through several decades stretching right through to 'deep' old age, perhaps with the aid of a heart 'pace-maker' or 'spare-part' surgery. In pre-modern times, few could confront such a future with much confidence. Death through sickness and disease was far more common than it is today. Women in particular were at greater risk due to the high rate of mortality at childbirth. For example, the Registrar General Reports for the period between 1890 and 1900 in England and Wales reported that around 70 women per thousand died as a result of the birthing process (Chamberlain 2006). Today such occurrences are relatively rare and for this development the medical profession is generally given the credit.

Finally, we may note that in many historical societies biological processes were framed by culturally forged moralities and value appraisals and many of such seemed to accompany the different 'stages' of the life-cycle. A good number underpinned adult maturity and restrictions related to sexual activity. Such cultural viewpoints assumed that the family structure was based upon the relationship between one male and one female united by some form of marital arrangement. Another set of values was linked to socially informed age-related behaviour. For example, culture largely dictated how the young were expected to conduct themselves given that they had not yet reached maturity and adopted the responsibilities that this was believed to entail. Hence, in sexual matters many societies employed restriction around an 'age of consent' – and still do – where sexual behaviour is limited to those who have reached a specific age, typically informed by legal statute or social norms. This may vary considerably. For instance, in Angola the prescribed age of consent today is 12 years old, in China 14, in Iraq 18, while in the USA it differs from state to state between 16 and 18. A few countries, including Israel, the Netherlands and Switzerland, employ graduated ages of consent, implying that youth in the same age group are permitted to partake of consensual sex, but not with those outside of that age group. The same holds for gay consent, previously unheard of in most historical societies. For example, in South Africa there is an equal age of consent at 16 years old; Albania 14 for heterosexuals and lesbians, 18 for gay men; while over 70 nations around the world continue to criminalise consensual sexual acts between persons of the same sex.

It may be argued that in the contemporary West, and particularly within a globalised order, culture is changing so rapidly that it is now increasingly difficult for individuals, and indeed social collectives, to be sure of what their values are: what can be regarded as moral or immoral, desirable or undesirable norms of behaviour. For instance, in Western societies – and this is evident in legislation regarding so-called permissive issues such as the age of consent for young people – the boundaries as to what sexual behaviour is socially tolerable are increasingly being pushed back, but this is not without a great deal of public deliberation. Merely 50 years ago homosexuality in practically all Western societies was regarded as a serious offence, and such moral digression punishable by penal sentencing. Much has changed, but debates over what is permissible continue. Public discourse surrounding the lowering of the age of consent, for both heterosexuals and gays, is frequently based on notions of 'responsibility': whether young people can make informed choices given that they may not be sufficiently mature – physically, emotionally and socially. Here, it may be noted that, since 'responsibility' is often assumed to be a mark of adulthood, the lowering of the age of consent may be interpreted as indicating the earlier onset of adult maturity.

Psychological dimensions

It was once common in the disciplines of Sociology and Anthropology to speak at least loosely of psychological aspects of the 'life-cycle'. Some anthropologists had identified a psychological dimension most clearly at work in the rites of passage of tribal societies that took individuals (often as part of an age grouping) from one stage of life to another. Psychologically speaking, such rituals were interpreted as expressing the ambivalent attitudes of adults towards the generation making the transition from the stages of pre-adulthood to mature adulthood. The members of the younger generation were perceived as emerging to some degree as status rivals to the older age cohorts. In the future the young would replace their elders in positions of authority and the relationship of dependence would be reversed as their parents aged. Such was Thomas Beidelman's explanation (1966) for the origins of rites of passage, which often involve the humiliation, the infliction of pain upon and not infrequently the mutilation of the initiates by elders.

Initiation rituals could also be viewed as having educational functions based upon psychological manipulation. Initiates for adulthood might be taught to think and act as adults and to know what it was to take on adult roles in the community. Thus, the infliction of pain in many instances could be interpreted as a kind of 'shock tactic' designed to induce a psychological disposition of how to behave in an adult way in the years which lay ahead (Whiting et al. 1958). The rites of passage of the Mbuti people in North Zaire today may be cited, whereby boys around the age of 13 are put through 'Nkumbi', a ritual that symbolically represents the 'death' of the child. The boys are then 'reborn' socially as men, and are thereafter expected to behave as adults. Such rites typically involve permanent marking of the body. These appeared quite brutal acts, such as inflicting scarification or tattoos, or more subtle registration of status including painted decoration, wearing jewellery and ear piercing.

The seemingly multi-dimensional purposes of the rites of passage identified with pre-industrial cultures are just one of the psychological aspects observable in the conventional life-cycle approach. In Western society today, however, psychological features may be more pronounced and explicit. Medical science may still refer to the psychological upheaval of adolescence, which can have a profound impact upon the behaviour of the young. Similarly, 'mid-life' is often identified with a 'crisis' brought on by negative psychological responses to losing the vigour of youth, and which, in turn, are exacerbated by physiological changes. Then, it is frequently asserted that as individuals age they not only undergo inevitable mental and physical decline but find it psychologically more difficult to adapt to change: in short, older people grow into a conservative frame of mind. In many respects these assertions can be deconstructed as merely derived from cultural perceptions indicative of how later life is understood, generalised and forged by stereotypical images exemplified by various explicit or implicit expressions of discrimination or what is more commonly known as 'ageism'. Comprehending the dynamics of such social constructionism in this way thus allows the discernment of a strong cultural component in all of these supposed psychological maladies.

SOCIOLOGY AND THE LIFE-CYCLE APPROACH

Initially, sociological constructs of a life-cycle were frequently heavily influenced by Anthropology and its focus on 'traditional' societies: a loose, catch-all typology, one incorporating a vast range of social organisation from tribal to settled agricultural communities, to large-scale feudal orders. Compared to 'modern' industrial societies, pre-industrial societies displayed a less complex and relatively undifferentiated 'cycle-of-life' and typically involved merely pre-adult and adult 'stages' – a simple distinction that endured over the generations. This basic differentiation was marked out by the near-universal phenomenon of rites of passage.

Writings emerging from the Structural Functionalist school of Sociology and Anthropology enjoyed a noteworthy influence on the study of pre-industrial societies – one which accounted for such rites in social rather than psychological terms. Thus, Alfred Radcliffe-Browne (1939) examined what he called the 'ritual prohibition' of rites of passage. Such prohibition centred on behaviour subject to taboo and social boundaries, including people, places, objects, words or names, at times of crucial life transformation and stages. For Radcliffe-Browne, these rituals were essentially about emphasising social values and helped bind people together with a sense of community. Typical were rites surrounding marriage, since the institution generated a sense of social continuity and amplified social values. Other rites dealt with natural processes associated with danger. Thus, for example, among the Andaman Islanders of the Bay of Bengal, ritual avoidance surrounding childbirth – rituals which the Western mind would regard as so much unwarranted superstition. At this precarious time parents were forbidden to eat certain foods, while friends of the parents were prohibited from using the name of the parents in fear of bringing misfortune upon mother and child.

Each stage of the life-cycle in pre-industrial societies appeared to present characteristic problems and transitions that involved learning something new and unlearning familiar roles and routines. Anthropological studies of these societies, including such works of Gluckman (1963), Douglas (1966) and van Gennep (1908), proved particularly influential in providing insights into a fairly structured life-cycle. They indicated how rites of passage often related to biological changes and their social implications, as well as psychological adaptation to socially grounded institutions such as marriage. Religious significance and taboo status were frequently attached to these transitions, especially when they connected to what amounted to a 'life crisis'. These 'crises' were precipitated by a significant individual and collective feeling of uncertainty that resulted from natural processes like pregnancy and childbirth – events which required psychological and social adjustment. They have also been perceived as inherently dangerous, as van Gennep showed in his *The Rites of Passage* (1908), where rites were associated with boundaries, ambiguities and anomalies – in other words, things which were at the margins of established social categories, the transitions from one category to another or things which did not quite fit into established classifications. One example of this was rites associated with pregnancy: where the pregnant woman, in a sense, became temporarily two people, in the condition of carrying her child.

Seemingly justifying a life-cycle approach to pre-industrial societies was the observation that for a good part of human history clearly defined stages of life, and age categories, proved to be an important form of social stratification or at least the basis of expected norms of behaviour. Works such as Shmuel Eisenstadt's *From Generation to Generation* (1956) insisted that common to most societies were the different culturally defined expressions of behaviour anticipated at a particular age. In the past at least, as the individual grew older, s/he was expected to progress towards a series of roles and relationships according to particular cultural markers and perceptions of the biological changes which came with ageing. In pre-industrial or 'traditional' societies, as people grew older, they progressed through socially acknowledged status boundaries which were usually of much greater societal significance than in the West today. A particularly crucial stage of status acquisition occurred when an individual entered social adulthood and was allowed to indulge in activities that only an adult was permitted to undertake, such as marriage or to conduct warfare against neighbouring tribes.

In dealing with the relevance of age categories anthropologists in particular developed specific terms such as 'age group' or 'age set', which referred to a group of people differentiated from others according to the stage of life reached. The related term 'age grade' was commonly used to describe age groups which were clearly and formally established, especially in relation to tribal societies that rigorously stratified members according to age. Within a stringently structured life-cycle, the importance of age categories seemed central and indispensable. For instance, male aborigines throughout Australia traditionally graduate through the age grades of the hunter, warrior and eventually emerge as elders of the tribe. Here, age is best conceptualised in terms of the life-cycle if understood to mean those stages through which all who survive a full life-span pass. Significantly, such pre-industrial societies allocate status (and sometimes wealth) not according to merit or achievement (as is supposedly the case in Western societies), but to one's specific age category.

In age set societies, the change in status involved in growing older may not have a legal foundation, but is frequently institutionalised to such a degree that it often constitutes the very basis of political organisation. Age represents a form of social structure which impacts practically every aspect of life – stipulating what an individual is permitted to do or not to do. For instance, males who are ritually initiated together constitute an age set if they are roughly of the same age – perhaps 13–18 years old – and pass collectively through a series of age grades, performing tasks based on increasing levels of authority and status which cumulate in later life.

The importance of age sets can be seen in the example of the Galla-speaking tribal peoples of North East Africa (the largest ethnic grouping in the region). Males, in particular, traditionally progress through the age-linked roles in life in an orderly and predictable way: as bachelors, warriors, married family men, political leaders and judges, and religious ritual officials. Age sets are formalised into 'grades' – arranged on five-point cycles of eight years each. Sons are initiated into their generational set when their fathers are in the reigning grade, five stages and 40 years further on in the system. In observing how their fathers behave, the young are presented with the acquired mode of behaviour when they reached that age, while certain aspects of the life-cycle (such as marriage) for the younger generation are initiated at the designated time – sometimes in the form of 'mass' weddings.

Unlike Western societies, social structures and culture in pre-industrial societies are usually static or change very slowly. The generations that pass through structured age categories will invariably be subject to similar life experiences. Thus, a degree of predictability is likely; individuals know with assurance what age set they belong to in years to come. By contrast, in the contemporary West age or 'generational cohort' denote a generation born in the same historical period. Members of these cohorts might be subject to similar life experiences, but are likely to depart in such experiences when compared to earlier or later generations.

Life-cycle models

Although the sociological endeavour had identified patterns and processes common to most societies, different and contrasting models of the life-cycle eventually emerged. Among the most well-known frameworks was the eight-stage model of the life-cycle presented by Erik Erikson (1963). Erikson's model was typical in that it took a developmental form which attempted to present the maturational relationship between the biological, chrono-logical, psychological and social aspects of human progression through the life-cycle as a fairly universal phenomenon. For Erikson, the basic biological processes are probably more or less similar in all human societies, although crucially the rate and quality of biological change was subject to wide vari-ation in terms of how they were culturally perceived.

Erikson identified a central 'crisis' for the individual in major stages of the life-cycle. For instance, he regarded the period of adolescence as one which brought its own particular 'crisis' as the child slowly became an adult. In doing so, entering adolescence engendered specific and vital social relation-ships and wider implications for the community, as well as demanding psy-chological personal adjustments. The most important aspect of Erikson's model was, nonetheless, the emphasis placed on the social context by way of significant relationships and institutions in which individual development occurred at a given stage. In the first year of life, by way of illustration, the potential 'crisis' was whether the infant forged a bond of trust with its mother. In the next stage of life, the child must, he argued, develop the level of self-control insisted by a process of socialisation.

Erikson's model was always open to the charge of ethnocentricity since it seemed to venerate the alleged virtues of monogamy and the nuclear family that reflected Western cultural norms and institutions respectively rather than truly universal social arrangements, while his assertions regarding the 'crisis' in early life made generalised assumptions about mother–infant bonding as a 'natural' condition. Another charge was that the model took for granted the completion of the life-cycle which largely reflected experi-ences in Western societies. Thus, such models, then, were more applicable to developments of the life course largely synonymous with the rise of mod-ernity, developments which will now be addressed.

In terms of culture, politics and economics, modernity radically departed from pre-industrial society or what was often abstractly referred to as 'trad-itional society'. Modernity, in the view of 'classical' sociological work, typified by Emile Durkheim and Max Weber, emphasised a fundamental contrast to the traditional order and implied progressive economic and administrative rationalisation, growth of science and technology, urbanisation and differentiation of the social world. The developments which began first in the West included the emergence of capitalism, which was given generally to refer to an economic system of commodity production involving both a competitive products market and the commodification of labour power: processes which brought into being new social formations exemplified by the emergence of social classes. Also characterising modernity was the emergence of the nation state, which ushered in new forms of social control and contributed to the industrialised society through educational and welfare reforms, and by extending the rights of its citizens (although in different countries to various degrees) through democratic processes and institutions.

These changes, identified with modernity, profoundly impacted life experiences and brought a restructuring of human life in discernible and sometimes in less discernible ways. Such changes were perceived in sociological writings as establishing what could be called the 'modern life-cycle' of childhood, youth, young and later adulthood, mid-life and old age. Under the impact of industrialisation and the demographic changes of the nineteenth century a gradual differentiation in age groups and a greater specialisation in age-related functions began to emerge, although it was by no means complete by the end of the century. Many such age groups structured social roles and at least some of them came to be discerned as 'natural' – that of childhood and adolescence providing prime examples.

According to Martin Kohli (1988) this structuring of the life course of modernity through institutions and chronological age proved in its own way to be an effective form of social manipulation. Education in schools helped forge what came to be known as childhood, while clear career stages in the labour market and retirement – legitimated by deferred gratification – meant that individuals largely passed in an orderly and calculable way through life. Rather than life patterns being ascribed according to positions in family and community as in pre-industrial times, status and identity were increasingly achieved by successfully negotiating expectations related to education and career opportunities. The reality, however, was that this 'cycle' seemed static and predictable as long as the processes which forged them remained relatively stable.

In Western societies such models as that developed by Erikson, which outlined the stages of childhood, school, work, marriage, retirement and old age, were ones largely applicable only after the 1930s and became well-established as late as the 1970s for the bulk of the population. These models contrasted very markedly with life in mid-eighteenth century Europe by way of example. At that time some 60 per cent of the male population died between 25 and 65 years old. The child-bearing period for females lasted late in life until about 40 years of age as a result of almost continuous pregnancies and childbirth. Working life began in childhood and endured throughout the adult years. Then, slowly the life-cycle, as often described in sociological models, truly emerged; first among the middle-classes at the end of the nineteenth century and eventually filtering down to the working-classes. Increased life expectancy meant that the significance of the 'generations' grew, as three family generations (children, parents, grandparents) coexisting at the same time became more established.

In the West more events also began to occur in the early years of the individual's 'development' and new 'slots' in the life-cycle were created such as 'adolescence', which, in industrial society, emerged as a buffer between childhood and adulthood. Corresponding roughly to the teenage years, this was the stage of life when young people were expected to establish some independence and learn the responsibilities and specialised skills required for adult life. Moreover, increasing life expectancy extended the span over which such life transitions took place and, up to fairly recently at least, brought a greater orderliness to life experiences.

The age categories firmly established in the mid-twentieth century have by no means been extinguished. One legacy of modernity is that, culturally speaking, childhood is viewed, ideally at least, as a clear, distinct and 'natural' stage of life, perhaps broadly as the first 12 years before puberty, free from the burdens of the adult world. In retrospect, this construct of childhood might, however, prove to be a short-lived. Up to the beginning of the twentieth century, in most Western countries, children were expected to work at a very early age and for long hours, and in many other respects they were not regarded as significantly different from adults. Factory legislation and laws concerning the child's welfare and education were to become crucial in constructing a clear period that came to constitute what Western culture understood as childhood. Today debates rage as to whether such an idealised view of childhood, free from the exposure to the attributes of adult life, is being eroded and with accompanying detrimental consequences.

Three quarters of the way into the twentieth century, life-cycle models had developed into something of a finely tuned art. Some very elaborate models were contrived in order to outline developments in the Western world. One such model was developed by Levinson et al. (1978). It depicted the life-span as a series of critical 'transitions' (at least for a small sample of middle-class males) in some detail. Here, the period of childhood, adolescence and adulthood were sub-divided into 'early' periods, stages of transition and consolidation. For example, 'early adulthood' included early adult transition (12–22); entering the adult world (22–28); mature adult transition (28–33); and a 'settling down' period (33–40). In this model adulthood was viewed as that period where most of life's accomplishments typically began: leaving the family home, getting married, becoming a parent and maintaining a household and career.

This kind of model had parallels in common-sense perceptions held by the population at large. Evidence of such cultural expectations were to be found in a study published in 1965 by Neugarten et al. in the USA, which indicated a high percentage of adults who accepted certain age-related characteristics. The correlation for both men and women was high. For example, some 85 per cent of the population surveyed by Neugarten and her associates regarded a 'young man' or 'young woman' as someone between the age of 18 and 22; around the same percentage believed that the 'best age for a woman to marry' was between 19 and 24; 75 per cent that most men should be settled on a career between the age of 24 and 26; and just over 80 per cent maintained that most people should become grandparents. Other evidence of socially prescribed views of age norms are offered by Hockey and James (1993, 50) who suggest that indications of chronological age were often more subtle in the twentieth century than ever before. For example, in the inter-war UK, age status was discernible by dress: young boys under 14 wore short trousers, while females of this age were not expected to use facial make-up. In such ways 'children' were clearly separated from the adult world, a world to which they would nonetheless make a future transition.

Transitions, trajectories and life events

Notions of a coherent series of 'transitions' particularly related to becoming a mature adult were fairly popular in sociological literature up until at least the 1970s and seemed to be applicable to a modern life-cycle approach. Sociological frameworks, however, gradually became more intricate, allowing for complexities of various kinds and thus generating theoretical innovations around concepts of 'transition'. Much seemed exemplified by the work of Glasner and Strauss (1965). Building on the significance of rites of passage, Glasner and Strauss preferred the term 'life course', one which denoted a number of crucial transitions from one social state to the next involving a change in social status, identity and roles marking a profound departure from earlier ones – themes developed by other commentators (e.g. Elder and Kirkpatrick Johnson 2003; Hagestad 2003).

A 'transition' was understood to be a discrete life change or event within a 'trajectory', for example, from a single to married status. Many such transitions were identified within the context of family life: marriage, childbirth, divorce, remarriage, etc.. Each status passage was said to consist of a negotiated process in which both the nature of the passage and the understanding of each participant of what this would entail would vary. Among the key considerations in examining such transitions were whether they were voluntary, desirable, inevitable or reversible; whether or not the passage occurred with others; the degree of control over the process; whether the passage was legitimation by others; the importance of events for those involved; and the duration of passage.

Surveys of transitions from one 'phase' of life to another, as determined by age categories, noticed that in contemporary societies such transitions were becoming increasingly more variable. Sometimes they were reached earlier, sometimes later, than conventionally anticipated (Hagestad and Neugarten 1985). For instance, the time in which a young person leaves the family home (if they indeed opt to do so), and establishes their own, now varies considerably. Then there is the matter of reversibility such as a middle-aged person opting to attend college, a choice which offsets the norm that education is largely for younger people.

In the sociological understanding each passage of transition is said to entail a 'trajectory' – a demarcated phase of life which incorporates the chronological progression of life events and subsequent change in self-image, whereby the individual merges several social roles in order to forge their own 'life paths' (Glasner and Strauss 1965, 1–13). A 'trajectory' is generally deemed to be a sequence of connected conditions within a remit of behaviour or experience, perhaps of the family or within education or occupational careers. Because individuals and families live their existence in several spheres, their lives are inevitably constructed of numerous intersecting trajectories that can be designated as educational trajectories, family life trajectories, health trajectories and work trajectories. Increasingly, the acceptance of the notion of a 'trajectory' provided a means of comprehending how the life course was influenced by wider society and how it might entail long-term patterns of stability and change or involve multiple transitions (Elder et al. 2003; Heinz 2003). The concept of a trajectory, then, seemed to imply both the possibility of change and continuity that was compatible with the nature of contemporary society in the Western world.

The concern with 'transitions' and 'trajectories' as key to understanding the contemporary life course spurred interest into a number of other realms including significant 'life events' and how these related especially to 'turning points'. 'Life events' have been conceptualised as significant incidents that entail a sudden change in life which may engender profound and long-term implications for life trajectories (Settersten 2003). Perhaps most obviously, this would include marriage, starting a family, death of a close relative, change of job and decline in health status. Such events are often associated with stress or at the very least suggest some form of personal psychological adjustment including that of self-concept, beliefs, motivations and future expectations. Much may depend on whether life events are positive or negative, major or minor events, whether they are personally desirable or not, whether anticipated or unanticipated and whether the individual has a level of control over events as they unfold (Settersten and Mayer 1997, 246). Moreover, specific life events will undoubtedly be given different meanings by individuals and collectives, not least of all according to cultural mores (Hareven and Trepagnier 2008).

Important life events may constitute a 'turning point' in the life course trajectory which, in turn, entails a radical change in how a person views themselves in relation to others and the social world around them. A 'turning point' suggests an enduring change in life rather than an impermanent occurrence and its true importance perhaps only becomes manifest later in life (Rönkä, et al. 2003). It will also inevitably involve a negotiation of future risks and opportunities (Cappeliez et al. 2008; Ferraro and Shippee 2009). 'Turning points' may be related to life transitions under particular conditions. This includes whether a transition transpires at the same time that a life crisis is experienced or is followed by a crisis. Also significant is whether the transition is 'off-time' – meaning that it does not occur when anticipated at a particular stage in life. Another variable is whether the transition entails family discord connected with the needs and wishes of individuals and the broader requirements of family members. Important also is whether the transition is followed by unpredicted harmful repercussions, and whether the transition requires major personal adjustment (Hareven and Trepagnier 2008).

Because of such theoretical innovations related to 'transitions', 'trajectories' and 'life events', it became clear by the end of the twentieth century that the notion of a life-cycle was almost impossible to sustain, despite recognition of the complexities and variations involved in historical and cross-cultural analysis. Partly too this was due to a greater acceptance that the models produced were biased towards experiences in Western societies and even then were increasingly less easy to conceptually and practically apply. Furthermore, life-cycle models appeared to put far too much emphasis on age as a form of social stratification and marker of behavioural norms (Hagestad and Neugarten 1985). Other social variables, especially in contemporary society, also proved to have considerable impact, forging different experiences and variation in the life-cycle. This included structured inequalities such as social class, ethnicity and gender.

Next, in rejecting the life-cycle model sociologists began to display a greater acknowledgement that, although each stage of life is connected to the biological process of ageing, the life course is largely a social construction and earlier models were often forged by enculturated views of the world. Thus, people in one society may experience a stage of life quite differently from another, or not at all. This acceptance allowed for a greater cross-cultural approach and enhanced appreciation of the similarities and differences between societies. Finally, further differentiation was recognised in Western societies by the increasing chance of discontinuities in life and the complex variety of experiences of being an adult. In relationships there might be the possible experience of divorce, remarriage or cohabitation. Changes in the labour market structure, including redundancy, job retraining and varied age of retirement, similarly complicated the picture. This meant that transitions, trajectories and status passages were not simply linear but became ever more characterised by synchronicity (the coincidence of events) and even reversibility (Du Bois-Reymond 1998). Given the evidence, then, the notion of a life-cycle appeared increasingly superfluous. In contrast, that of the 'life course' enjoyed the attraction of being more flexible, more operationally workable. The term 'life course' does not, unlike that of 'life-cycle', assume a stable social system but one that is constantly changing, recognising that in Western societies, in particular, social transformations and variations in life transitions and trajectories are to be expected.

THE LIFE COURSE: FRESH APPROACHES

As a theoretical perspective, the 'life course' has been characterised as 'a sequence of socially defined events and roles that the individual enacts over time' (Giele and Elder 1998, 22). Whether or not this definition entirely captures the essence of what the concept amounts to remains open to contention. What cannot be doubted, however, is the increasing acceptance of the framework of a 'life course' and its apparent conceptual advantages.

At the very least it is able to account for the variety and complexity of 'trajectories' and 'transitions' in life experiences in Western societies. The matter of variety and complexity was suggested by Glen Elder (1994) who detected several prevailing and interrelated themes in the life course approach which point to its conceptual advantages: the interplay of human lives and historical time; 'timing of lives'; linked or interdependent lives; and human agency in making choices. Each of these will be briefly considered in this chapter. At the same time it might be said that a life course perspective allows for a greater historical and cross-cultural comparison, and this seems imperative given the radical changing global order.

Barbara Mitchell (2003) has explored how it is possible to trace the development of a life course approach which became more prevalent by the middle of the twentieth century. She notes that it by no means constituted a single sociological perspective, since a number of themes developed which also saw contributions from other social sciences. This remains the case today. Nonetheless, if any generalisation can be made, Mitchell maintains, it is plausibly that fresh perspectives focus on the importance of social change rather than continuity. This was certainly true of Western society, and the timing of the academic writings on the life course reflected the profound social transformations which were taking place.

The emphasis of the relevant studies varied considerably but the tendency was to throw light on the matter of social change and how it related to age, the cohort effect and the historical period in which the life course was experienced. Mitchell points to the work of Bernice Neugarten in particular who, as noted above, orientated her research to concentrate on the degree of deviation by people from the norms expected of their age group, including the time they decided to marry and begin a family. It was clear in Neugarten's findings that the time of marriage and the commencement of the family were open to numerous variations, and the choice not to engage in either was becoming increasingly commonplace.

It was probably not until the late twentieth century, as Mitchell records, that the life course approach came to be increasingly designated as an 'emerging paradigm' (Rodgers and White 1993) with both distinctive theories and methods. She pinpoints how Glen Elder, in particular, began to further the central principles of life course theory which he defined as 'a common field of inquiry by providing a framework that guides research on matters of problem identification and conceptual development' (Elder 1998, 4). Mitchell points out that such a paradigm became increasingly synthesised with other theories or disciplines and lists those such as family development, status attainment, family history, 'stress' theory, demography, gerontology and ecological fields of study.

Important too, as Mitchell emphasises, were specific discernible developments within the sociological discipline. From the 1950s until the 1980s, according to Giele and Elder (1998), the life course approach arose out of the confluence of a number of major theoretical streams of research concerned with integrating several sociological schools emphasising social structure, on the one hand, and individual agency, on the other. The developing life course perspective was a product of its time in that the approach sought to take into account *both* the 'social surroundings' of the individual and his/ her liberty to make conscious choices and reflect on their past, present and future. As far as the life course was concerned, individuals were deemed to be active agents able to mediate the impact of social structure, endeavouring to fulfil goals such as achieving economic security in the future, to seeking life satisfaction or avoiding negative life situations (Claessens and Ryan 2003).

The emphasis on human agency was to some degree inspired by the work of Albert Bandura (2002, 2006) who stressed the human capability of intentionally influencing their own life circumstances. They could most obviously do so by exercising their own individuality, especially by utilising their personal influence to shape the surrounding social environment ('Personal Agency'). People might also call upon the influence of others who have better resources to take action on their behalf in order to meet needs and accomplish goals ('Proxy Agency'), or partake of a group to act with other people to meet mutual needs and goals ('Collective Age'). Bandura nonetheless conceded that agency may be constrained by structural and cultural arrangements. However, his work did bring an acknowledgement that personal agency, in particular, could explain extensive individual differences in life course trajectories as individuals constructed plans and made choices between options they were confronted with.

The emerging recognition of the significance of both structure and agency clearly identified life course change as bi-directional. For example, societal values and institutions and informal groups conveyed pressures on a woman that were likely to influence her life patterns. The woman as a social actor may, in turn, conform to previous standards or attempt to change norms, institutional rules and social values related to, say, her reproductive capacity. By adopting such an approach, along with comparing the timing and occurrence of retrospective life histories across different birth cohorts, Giele (1988) was able to chart a clear modification in multiple roles over the generations.

Mitchell also draws attention to how, as noted above, the life course approach increasingly recognised the importance of stressful life events. This concern fed into the matters of structure and agency. For instance, the death of a family member was likely to have profound repercussions for family relationships, since it could activate patterns of stress and vulnerability or, by contrast, promote adaptive behaviours and family morale. Indeed, personality attributes of individual family members could also impact their coping styles, functioning and general well-being. Furthermore, family members were likely to synchronise or coordinate their own lives with respect to future planning and the anticipation of future life events. However, this could sometimes generate tensions and conflicts, particularly when individual goals varied from the requirement of the family as a collective group. In another example, Tamara Hareven (1996) explores how historically the timing of adult children's individual transitions (for example when to marry) could generate difficulties if it interfered with the demands and needs of ageing parents.

Giele and Elder also stressed the significance of 'time', along with that of 'place'. This factor took into account the general but unique repercussions of the individual's location in a historical period which forged personal experiences. Such experiences were inevitably socially and culturally moulded and endured throughout the life course (Giele and Elder 1998, 9–10). The virtue of this approach, in short, was that it had the advantage of bringing a greater recognition that people's life experiences varied according to when precisely in the history of any given society into which they were born. Hence, a 'cohort' was understood as a category of individuals with common characteristics, perhaps most significantly, their age. A 'generation' similarly denotes those born in the same period and who experienced particular social change/life events in a similar sequence and at the same age (Alwin and McCammon 2003) – and where a shared sense of identity aided in facilitating an awareness of belonging to a particular generation (Alwin et al. 2006). Cohorts differ in size and, along with distinct circumstances, may face different opportunities and challenges compared to other cohorts. For example, the Baby Boom Generation (1945–54) was a large cohort in competition for jobs later in life (Pearlin and Skaff 1996). In turn, this generation adopted particular strategies in response to economic challenges. In the case of the Baby Boomers by avoiding or delaying life events and transitions such as marriage or childbearing or having fewer children.

Age cohorts will most probably be influenced by the same economic and cultural trends. It follows that individuals of the same age will characteristically display comparable attitudes and values and relate similar experiences. The lives of those born early in the twentieth century, for instance, were forged by traumatic events of economic depression and two world wars. Another example, pertinent today, is that younger people are entering adulthood during a period of economic uncertainty which has dampened the optimism that characterised, by way of contrast, the generation coming out of the 1960s.

There was more to consider by way of historical timing. Glen Elder (1974), in exploring the vast negative consequences of the Great Depression of the 1930s, noted how it impacted both individual and family pathways throughout the life course. Elder consequently recommended an emphasis on historical events over the generations and how they plausibly influenced the individual's familial relationship, educational advancement and job opportunities. Further studies in social history, such as that of Tamara Hareven, who focused especially on the family, enforced this emphasis on historical events by pointing out how individuals and families exercised agency in their lives in order to acclimatise themselves to changing social conditions (Hareven 1996; Hareven and Trepagnier 2008).

The matter of 'timing of lives' was also deemed significant in as much as the assumed stages of life – childhood, adolescence and old age – included taken-for-granted assumptions regarding social status, roles and behavioural expectations of a particular era that could be extremely varied and complex (Hagestad and Neugarten 1985). Furthermore, Elder (1985) observed 'time' was significant in that unique social circumstances could influence the sequence of 'transitions' which are enacted over a historical period.

More recently, the focus has been on whether there is a trend towards a greater standardisation in age-graded social roles and statuses or towards greater diversification (Settersten 2003). Research has, however, tended to suggest a greater variability in the timing of young adult transitions (moving out of the parental home, marriage, becoming a parent) and later transitions to young adulthood because of the impact of globalisation, declining labour market opportunities and housing costs on young adults.

For sociologists developing the life course approach, this 'timing of lives' was not understood to be wholly deterministic and devoid of agency. There remained the capacity for individuals to entertain strategic adaptations to external events and consider the resources available to them. How and when a person accumulates or deploys his/her resources, such as wealth or education; embarks on employment; or commences a family are examples of various possible strategies. Nonetheless, for Giele and Elder the way in which all these elements may come together is largely a matter of timing. Using a contemporary example, the Millennial Generation (or Generation Y), refers to young people in the Western world who were between the ages of 10 and 20 years at the beginning of the twenty-first century. It is a generation that has grown up during a period of considerable technological advancement, not least of all digital technology and the on-line social media. However, it is also a generation that has experienced a time of major economic insecurities and quite likely without the resources necessary to embark on conventional markers of adulthood: secure employment, leaving the parental home and starting a family.

At the same time advocates of the life course approach recognised that individuals did not live in isolation. The cohort effect, according to Giele and Elder (1998, 9–12), was also likely to be influenced by a number of further variables, including 'linked social lives', that is, social integration with others through shared culture and via institutions. The significance of this was that an individual's social position and cultural backdrop could merge with familial and friendship networks, as well as personal agency through motivation to shape responses to life situations and events. This link was inevitably extraordinarily complex and could be cut across by discontinuities and periodic disruptions experienced through the spheres of the family, education and employment.

The life course perspective emphasises not only the connection between individuals but the interdependence between them and the ways in which their social relationships are reciprocal on various levels. Here was a recognition that such relationships both sustained and determined a person's behaviour. The family provides perhaps the exemplary example of linked lives over the decades even if the relation between family members may vary over time, for example in the obligation of providing for financial aid. These links may also change according to historical events such as economic recessions, perhaps shaping the major transitions in life, while discontinuities such as re-marriage may conflict with the requirements of children.

Finally, Mitchell, in her overview of the relevant literature, also relates how the life course approach came to recognise the significance of the past in shaping the present and future in such a way as to link lives. Early life course decisions, opportunities and conditions plausibly have consequences for later life outcomes as a kind of ripple effect. This can occur at various levels, including that of the cohort/generational and the individual/familial level. Here was an acknowledgement that one generation can transmit to the next the effects of the historical circumstances which shaped its life history such as living through war-time conditions or economic recessions. The timing and conditions under which earlier life events, such as becoming unemployed, and behaviours take place could generate a cycle of consequences impacting experiences for individuals and their families, for example, the reproduction of poverty over generations. The past can thus influence later life outcomes such as socioeconomic status, mental health, physical functioning and marital patterns. By embracing this long-term view which takes into account cumulative advantages, disadvantages or reversals, it became possible to comprehend the impact of social inequality on the future life course (O'Rand 1996).

Moreover, the sociological enterprise, in understanding the life course, was compelled to consider tracing people's life experiences and their biographical accounts of them – an approach that was close to the life history tradition advanced by the Chicago school of Sociology, including the utilisation of the work of Herbert Mead (1931) on socialisation and the growth of the self, resulting from social interaction in small groups and face-to-face, and the importance of internalisation of the perception and reaction of others as the individual developed. By adopting such an approach Sociology was able to combine the micro approach of understanding life as experience in daily interactions with understanding the significance of macro factors such as historical time and place of individuals in particular age cohorts.

METHODOLOGY

Giele and Elder (1998, 13–25) maintain that an integrated approach to the life course and the various dimensions that it was prepared to incorporate clearly lent itself to various modes of research, which took into account the complexities of social life in numerous ways and thus could embrace a range or mixture of methodologies both quantitative and qualitative. Common quantitative methodologies today include longitudinal studies over the life course; cohort, cross-generational and cultural comparisons; and detailed life event history analysis. By contrast, descriptive and qualitative approaches entail archival research, biographical approaches such as life history reviews, diary records, in-depth interviews, personal narratives and life stories. This methodological pluralism seemed to be advantageous in that it was consistent with the increasingly multi-disciplinary nature of the life course perspective and the recognition of the necessity to bridge macro and micro levels of theory and analysis.

A few of the most popular methodologies perhaps require greater attention since a fair number will inform research referred to throughout the chapters of this volume. This would include, first, historical demography via such means as family reconstructions, official records and other evidence that points to the significant economic and political factors influencing any given time period. This carries the advantage of throwing light upon the key demographic events which shaped everyday life experiences. Second, it includes a life history approach which permits the advantage of comparisons both historically and cross-culturally. This has proved particularly popular with what came to be known as the 'sociology of ageing', which moved from a focus on ageing as primarily concerned with the end of life to explore significant variations over time and place, and often this called upon archival research. For example, Uhlenberg-Mauve (1969) took this approach in order to provide evidence of life patterns of women before 1900 and discovered that in reality only a fraction ever married or bore children.

Initially taking their tone from Erikson's model mentioned earlier, one direction of the life history approach focused on maturation and development with particular emphasis on the impact of 'identity formation'. If the concern with identity formation is more sociological in emphasis, rather than biological and psychological dimensions, then this more probably will utilise such methods as in-depth interviews, personal narratives and life stories. Finally, sociological work can take the form of panel studies (an investigation of attitude changes over time using a constant set of people and comparing opinions at different times) and longitudinal survey data of age cohorts. These methods exploited the potential of showing the impact of social structure and human agency over a contracted period of time.

SUMMARY

This opening chapter has considered tangible historical developments and possible social trends which have led to a shift in sociological thinking about the factors that shape experiences and opportunities throughout life. This has essentially entailed a change from a spotlight on structured life-cycle models (noting the significance of biological and psychological factors some theoretical frameworks were prepared to integrate) to a life course perspective. Such an approach has not only come about with greater sociological sophistication but more than hints at a number of changes in life experiences, especially in Western societies. This includes the growth in life expectancy, the breakdown of clearly demarcated 'stages' of life, and the repercussions of such increasing occurrences as discontinuities and reversibility which make life trajectories unpredictable and subject to risk.

This chapter has also attempted to show how sociological studies of the present-day life course have also contributed to the understanding of the way social constructionism, particularly through historical and cross-cultural comparisons, illuminate how 'stages' or 'phases' of life are framed in a societal context. Such studies have highlighted the extraordinary social environmental variations that human beings encounter from the beginning of life to its end and how cultures shape and perceive major life events. This more nuanced sociological approach includes the challenge of integrating personal characteristics and social settings by emphasising the significance of both structure and agency.

Much of the discussion in this chapter additionally points to the importance of socio-historical location. In short, experience of the life course is embedded in the circumstances dictated by a historical period and its social repercussions. For some generational cohorts this can include economic cycles of booms and recessions, war or natural disasters. The matter of agency is bounded to one degree or another by such events. The integrated approach advanced by those such as Giele and Elder would seem to produce a more precise picture of how the individual's life is mutually shaped by personal characteristics and social environment; by structure and agency. It is an approach which clearly has merit, and many of the methods advanced continue to be constructively utilised.

The difficulty, however, is that in the last decades of the twentieth century onwards, socio-cultural change has proved so rapid that in order to understand the complexities of life course fresh, broader theoretical sociological paradigms needed to be adopted and adapted. As explored in the next chapter, popular sociological accounts of late/postmodernity have proved increasingly influential in this respect. While these paradigms do not always coherently focus on the subject of the life course, their broad observations and speculations have illuminated the wider socio-cultural settings, not to mention the historical 'time and place' in which the life course is now experienced. This will be the subject matter of the next chapter.

FURTHER READING

Allat, P., Bryman, A. and Bytheway, B. (1987) (eds.) *Women and the Life Cycle: Transitions and Turning Points,* Basingstoke: Palgrave Macmillan.

Becker, H. (ed.) (1991) *Life Histories and Generation,* Utrecht: Isor.

Bryman, A. Bytheway, B., Allat, P. and Keil, T. (eds.) (1987) *Rethinking the Life-Cycle,* London: Methuen.

Cohler, B. and Hostetler, A. (2004) 'Linking Life Course and Life Story. Social Change and the Narrative Study of Lives Over Time', in J. Mortimer and M. Shanahan (eds.), *Handbook of the Life Course,* New York: Springer.

Elder, G. (1985) *Life Course Dynamics,* Ithaca, NY: Cornell University Press.
  (1985) 'Perspectives on the Life Course', in G. Elder (ed.), *Life Course Dynamics: Trajectories and Transitions 1968-1980,* Ithaca, NY: Cornell University Press.

Elder, G. and Giele, J. (eds.) (2009) *The Craft of Life Course Research,* New York: Guildford Press.

Elder, G., Johnson, M. and Crosnoe, R. (2004) 'The Emergence and Development of the Life Course Theory', in J. Mortimer and M. Shanahan (eds.), *Handbook of the life Course,* New York: Springer.

Featherstone, M. (1995) *Undoing Culture: Globalization, Postmodernism and Identity,* London: Sage.

Frost, E. and McClean, S. (2013) *Thinking About the Life Course,* Basingstoke: Palgrave Macmillan.

Giele, J. (2002) 'Life Course Studies and the Theory of Action', in R. Settersten and T. Owens (eds.), *Advances in Life-course Research: New Frontiers in Socialization,* vol. 7, Elsevier Science.

Green, L. (2010) *Understanding the Life Course: Sociological and Psychological Perspectives,* Oxford: Polity.

Guillemard, A. (1997) 'Re-Writing Social Policy and Changes Within the Life Course Organization: A European Perspective', *Canadian Journal on Aging,* 16(3): 441–64.

Hutchinson, E. (2010) *Dimensions of Human Behaviour: The Changing Life Course,* London: Sage.

Katz, S. (1995) 'Imagining the Life-Span. From Pre-modern Miracles to Post-Modern Fantasies', in M. Featherstone and A. Wernick (eds.), *Images of Ageing: Cultural Representations of Later Life,* New York: Routledge.

Kotre, J. (1990) *Seasons of Life: The Dramatic Journey from Birth to Death,* Ann Arbor, MI: University of Michigan Press.

Mayer, K. (2009) 'New Directions in Life Course Research', *Annual Review of Sociology,* 35: 423–24.

Moen, P., Elder, G., and Lüscher, K. (eds.) (1995) *Examining Lives in Context: Perspectives on the Ecology of Human Development,* Washington, DC: American Psychological Association.

Pilcher, J. (1995) *Age and Generation in Modern Britain,* Oxford: Oxford University Press.

Riley, M. (ed.) *Sociological Lives. Social Change and the Life Course,* Newbury Park: Sage.

Chapter 2

The life course in late/postmodernity

Considering the life course more than implies engaging with wider evolving sociological thinking regarding the nature of contemporaneous social existence. At a broad macro-level fresh approaches have sought to account for, describe and consider the ramifications of the profound socio-cultural occurrences which have transpired over recent decades. While there remain contesting theories, they do however constitute points of departure which enhance sociological understanding of the essence of the contemporary life course and experiences throughout. What the competing theoretical frameworks tend to have in common is the conviction that Western societies (and not exclusively Western societies) can no longer be discussed in terms of the familiar and accepted characteristic of modernity. Rather, social transformations, including their impact on the life course, are best appreciated within fresh frames of reference. Thus the new terminology which began to arise towards the end of the twentieth century has come to enjoy widespread currency. Those of 'late' or 'high-modernity', 'post-industrial' or 'postmodernity' are not always precise but at least indicate that the present state of social 'development' (again an increasingly contentious term) is radically different from the initial emergence of modernity. There are important implications here for our understanding of the life course, not least of all in appreciating the social changes forging the culture and social institutions which broadly help broadly shape 'life events', life trajectories and core life transitions from birth to death.

THE ECLIPSE OF MODERNITY?

While conceptions of 'modernity' permeated sociological writings for generations as a clear and unchanging typology, it could not be sustained across the broad discipline by the close of the twentieth century. It became abundantly evident that Western society was undergoing rapid transformation in terms of the economy, technology and culture, and that there needed to be a re-appraisal of how the study of the life course was approached and theorised. The fresh perspectives recognised how profound changes – a number of which were as comparably far-reaching as the arrival of the industrial order of the nineteenth century – reshaped experiences of social life. This subsequently raised questions, or at least brought reconsiderations of rather taken-for granted assumptions about how the 'phases' of life and erstwhile institutions such as the family were understood. Put succinctly, the theoretical frameworks no longer adequately fitted and even the term 'modernity' seemed to be an antiquated one. This was not least of all in terms of the structure of the life course where discontinuities, reversibility, variations in the timing of important transitions, and complex life trajectories pointed towards radical social change.

As briefly explored in the opening chapter, the focus on modernity informed 'classical' sociological theorising, especially in establishing contrasts with so-called 'traditional societies'. Some early sociologists accounted for the rise of modernity; others were more concerned with its repercussions. While there was a measure of disagreement among the early commentators, some general themes emerged. Very often modernity was deemed to be practically synonymous with 'industrial civilisation', which was identified with several inter-related developments. First, a complex array of economic institutions that was associated with a 'free' market economy and industrial production. Second, that modernity stood for the emergence of particular political institutions, by which was largely meant the emergence of the nation state and mass democracy. Third, that modernity displayed a set of values and orientation towards the world, in particular the belief in 'progress' and social evolution which could be advanced by human effort: that human 'problems' could be overcome, especially through scientific advancements.

Clearly, early sociologists such as Emile Durkheim and Max Weber described a developing social order which provided the backdrop by which people led their lives. What remained unique about such accounts was that they tended not to foresee any different form of society arising out of the industrial capitalist order, with its pronounced division of labour and rationalising tendencies which tended to provide a greater organisation and predictability to life and more specialisation in age-related roles. It followed that sociological accounts of the life course were inclined to focus on a reasonably structured 'cycles of life' approach which identified fairly clear and structured 'stages' of life: in very simple terms, the formative childhood years of education and socialisation; adulthood marked by employment in the job marketplace and family responsibilities; and retirement from the workplace and decline into old age. However, as noted in the previous chapter, by the late twentieth century such models became less and less tenable. Many of their basic assumptions simply did not stand up to scrutiny. The principal questions were, given the profound socio-economic and cultural changes which were occurring, was it still meaningful speak of 'modernity' at all?; if not, what form of society and culture was replacing it?; what were the ramifications for the life course and experiences throughout?; and how could it be possible to theorise about these changes and experiences?

POSTMODERNITY

While 'modernity' was practically an uncontested concept – even though the causes of its onset and core dynamics were vehemently debated – this has not proved to be so with notions of 'postmodernity'. While it is possible to identify a number of important streams of sociological theory leading into the contemporary fascination with the postmodern as a viable paradigm, there is little agreement about the meaning of the related concepts involved in accounting for and explaining the emerging social order (the notion of 'order' being somewhat problematic). Thus, the implication for the life course is open to conjecture, and rather different approaches, or at least emphasis, may be observed in recent theorising. One such approach speculates on the arrival of a new form of society that is commonly referred to as 'postmodernity'. However, what the term actually implies is amenable to considerable conjecture.

Mike Featherstone has explored the principal sociological frameworks in the relevant writings accounting for and describing postmodernity, along with other related terms such as 'postmodernism' and 'postmodernization' (Featherstone 1991, 195–214). 'Postmodernization' in much of the sociological literature, he suggests, implies a process with degrees of implementation, rather than a fully-fledged social order. Thus, in one sense it is in the form of 'becoming'; a socio-cultural arrangement which has not yet been fully realised. Alternatively, in other usages postmodernity amounts to trends and identifiable processes, and does not (although he acknowledges that there is some disagreement) point to a new 'stage' in social development. Featherstone writes that if 'the modern' and 'the postmodern' are generic terms it is immediately apparent that the prefix 'post' signifies that which comes after, a break or rupture with the modern defined in counter-distinction to it (Featherstone 1991, 197). Yet, he argues, the term 'postmodernism' is more strongly based on a negation of the modern, a perceived abandonment of or swing away from the definitive features of modernity.

Featherstone recognises that in much of the sociological account there is the inherent assumption postmodernity constitutes an epochal transformation or break from modernity involving the emergence of a new social totality with its own distinct organising principles. For many commentators, however, the core debate is whether that new epoch has in fact arrived. Some writers, such as Jean Baudrillard and Jean-François Lyotard, are emphatic that modernity came to an end in the late twentieth century. Hence, they identify a period subsequent to modernity which can be described as postmodernity. At the same time, there are less radical interpretations. For instance, David Lyon states that the advent of postmodernity should not be understood to imply modernity has somehow ground to a halt. Rather, postmodernity is a kind of interim situation where some of the characteristics of modernity have been inflated to such an extent it becomes scarcely recognisable. Moreover, Lyon insists that what exactly the new situation amounts to, or even whether it can become 'settled', is as yet unclear (Lyon 2000, 7).

For Lyon, the 'inflated characteristics of modernity' which give rise to postmodern features relate above all to communication and information technologies (CITs) and the transference towards a consumerist society. Both are bound up with the restructuring of capitalism which had been underway by the last decades of the twentieth century. This gives a spur to core features of postmodernity which include the reorganisation of cities, the deregulation of financial markets and public utilities, the bypassing of nation state power by the dynamics of capitalism, global travel and tourism and, importantly, experimentation with conventional life courses. Thus, many current writings on the life course locate it within the postmodern condition, where economic and technological changes have profoundly impacted the cultural sphere.

Numerous commentators have stressed how the post-industrialised society has become transformed by the emergence of sophisticated technologies. These have impacted in different ways. The postmodern form of production would appear to be virtually synonymous with post-Fordism, the manufacturing of goods for niche-marketing rather than standardised production – a development only permitted by advanced technologies. Simultaneously, emerging new technologies have radically changed the nature of health care and brought controversies related to such areas as human reproduction. For the postmodernists, however, the greatest impact of new technology is frequently said to be in the sphere of culture, especially those related to mass communication. Here, postmodernity is associated with 'digitality', which enhances the power of personal means of communication exemplified by the high speed internet, e-mail and mobile phones. These permit individuals to engage with almost every dimension of the media environment. Such a development is explored by Marshall McLuhan (2003) who, while not a postmodernist theorist per se, considers the impact of living in a mass media world and suggests that it entails widespread global participation in a communicative culture which weakens the authority of local social traditions and pressures to conform to customary values – a subject matter explored by later analysts (e.g. Grosswiler 2010).

In his contribution to appraising the impact of technology Jean Baudrillard (1983) stresses how their new forms, especially in relation to information, mark a shift from a productive to reproductive social order in which simulations and models increasingly constitute 'the world', so that the cultural distinction between the real and appearance become erased. For Baudrillard, with the spread of a mass technology of communications, there is not only a great expansion of services and a leisure industry that is discernible, but a growing simulation of reality. In short, the implosion of 'signs' eventually undermines a sense of reality. The result is that, in the media-dominated world, the concept of 'meaning' itself (which depends on stable boundaries, fixed structures and shared consensus) dissolves. The media reconstructs an image of reality, which not only reacts with it, but attempts to re-establish an imaginary and nostalgic world. A further contribution is that provided by Manuel Castells (1989), who links technology more closely with economic developments. In essence, he sees the emerging postmodern order resting upon the dual pillars of consumerism and information technologies. For Castells, the proliferation of such technology and innovating forms of media in the 'information age' accentuates the power of the image which, in turn, enhances the cultural significance of consumption and lifestyles.

While such developments as the growth of the information media serve to connect technology and economics, Zygmunt Bauman (1992) focuses more on the latter and the tilt towards consumer capitalism and the service economy. The developing economic system is not just about consumption per se but a cultural transformation that emphasises choice. Consumer choice has, in turn, become the criterion for much more than shopping. The skills acquired for consumer choice are called upon in different spheres of life including education, health and the family. The slogan of 'free to choose' is relevant in so many areas and in this respect market culture displaces a sense of community belonging and citizenship with consumerism. There are many important implications here and, as identified in the chapters to come, the cultural notion of 'choice' has greatly impacted the life course in many important respects, as indeed have changes in technology.

Other commentators have taken a rather different slant in their consideration of the importance of consumer capitalism. Fredric Jameson (1991) refers to the superficiality or 'depthlessness' of postmodern culture which, more precisely, is the 'cultural logic' of late capitalism. Put concisely, there is little or no depth, emotion or meaning in culturally created 'signifiers'. What is seen is largely what is received and registered; there is no deeper cultural significance. Nothing stands behind the actual image of that viewed. What is portrayed is not positive or negative; it just is. Jameson identifies this tendency with the commercialisation of culture and the fetishism of commodities of late capitalism. Postmodernism, however, in Jameson's analysis, is not an all-encompassing trend but rather a cultural drift which nonetheless affects all cultural production. Michael Sandel (2012) picks up a related theme by exploring commercialisation and commodification in the way they have impacted the broad social sphere. His volume What *Money Can't Buy: The Moral Limits of Markets* describes a culture that has developed in the West that now puts market principles above all other considerations. It is a society where values like virtue, civility and democracy are undermined by the lust for money. The expansion of markets has meant that there not only exists a market economy but a market society where everything is up for sale and constitutes a way of being, a 'habitas' as it might be described, which impacts everything from family life, personal relations, to health, education and public life.

In considering the economic features of postmodernity Fredric Jameson and David Harvey have both viewed it as essentially related to what they describe as 'flexible accumulation', by which is meant an advanced phase of capitalism leading on from finance capitalism – a form of economy identified by investment speculations and pursuit of profit from the purchase and sale of bonds, stocks and 'futures' (commercial contracting based on the purchase or sale of specified quantities of a commodity at specified future dates), and the widespread lending of money with interest. Hence, the economic dimension of postmodernity is characterised by a highly mobile labour force and capital accumulation, and what Harvey calls 'time and space compression' brought about by satellite communication and declining transport costs. Put simply, this means greatly intensified rates of commercial, technological and organisational innovation marked by 'spatial' practices and rapid decision-making which impact at political and social levels and with profound implications for everyday life. This includes the increasing pace of life, the breaking down of the spatial and the reduction of social connectedness and sense of community (Harvey 1990, 147, 240).

In Harvey's analysis postmodernity clearly denotes cultural change. There are, however, further various directions in sociological thought in this respect. With a different emphasis, Lyotard (1984) argues that post-industrial society and postmodern culture began to develop in the mid-twentieth century, although the rate of development and the stage reached varies between and within countries. These transformations are essentially related to technology, science, and a number of distinct social developments which connect with changes in language and meta-narratives. In short, simple, and singular ways of seeing the world are eroded by contrasting understanding of its nature. Lyotard's specific interest is in the repercussions of the 'computerization of society' which has brought a restructuring of knowledge that erodes traditional social forms and brings the loss of meaning.

Theories of postmodernity, such as that of Lyotard, hold that today the decline in mega-narratives includes a universal disenchantment with the notion of 'progress' that informed modernity. There is less confidence about what the future holds and, in fact, that life chances are getting worse, not better. Second, there is the growing belief that science and technology no longer holds all the answers to human problems. It is at least implicit in a good number of postmodernist writings that contemporary society has created more problems than it has solved. Postmodernist writers thus observe a widespread cynicism regarding the very foundation of science and, above all, a questioning that objective reality and truth exist in any meaningful sense. In short, a culture has developed in which all 'truths' are relative, as are all values and systems of morality. It is not so much a matter of risk but the uncertainty and lack of guidelines which postmodernity brings in terms of once cherished moralities that informed the life course; for example, the notion that sex should be limited to marriage – a value construct enforced by the cultural and social power of the Christian Church – is increasingly hard to sustain in the relativistic post-Christian society. Anderson and O'Hara

(1991) make a not dissimilar point. Residents of the postmodern world are able to appreciate there are many beliefs, multiple realities and a daunting proliferation of worldviews in a social sphere which has lost its faith in absolute truth, meaning that people are now obliged to choose what to believe and, subsequently, employ choice in how to conduct their lives.

LATE INDUSTRIAL SOCIETY

It is undoubtedly indicative of contemporary Sociology that other commentators use a number of alternative terms to describe the current nature of Western society other than 'postmodernity'. Nonetheless, many of their views engage with several considerations raised by postmodernist analysts, as well as exploring a range of additional distinctive themes related to the life course. These collectively amount to a range of theories which attempt to detail the present in a way that also departs from 'classical' theorising but engages with significant social changes which are nonetheless still identified with modernity. Thus Anthony Giddens (1991a, 1991b) speaks of 'late', 'high' modernity or 'reflexive'; 'liquid' modernity is referred to by Zygmunt Bauman (1992); while Ulrick Beck (1992) alludes to the 'risk' society.

Giddens to some extent discusses phenomena which might equally well be considered as 'postmodern' but suggests they are best understood as the outgrowth of those features that forged modernity. It is the key characteristics of late-modernity which have shaped expectations and perceptions of life and the life course, Giddens suggests. While his writings may appear to be a less radical version of postmodernist theorising, there is a variance with postmodernist works in the discussion of the relevance of the advancement of science, rationalism, instrumentalism and, to some extent at least, the significance and trajectories of the ethos of individualism.

Many of the theories related to late-modernity seem to have notions of the life course as a central concern, and this is largely derived from a recognition that individualism as a cultural value and general orientation has come to the fore. Individualism, however, merges with other socio-cultural developments. Giddens provides a detailed account of what he calls the 'contours' of late- or high-modernity. He commences with 'the question of modernity' in which he concludes that developments at the turn of the twentieth century proved problematic to sociological enquiry and, moreover, that an analysis of observable transformations required a reworking of the major basic assumptions and premises regarding what precisely constituted modernity (Giddens 1991a, 1). A unique feature of contemporary institutions and processes, according to Giddens, is the way they undermine traditional habits and customs. In terms of globalising processes, there is erosion of taken-for-granted experiences of day-to-day life profoundly impacting the individual and his/her perceptions of self. Hence, the emergence of high modernity, with its identifying features including the reorganisation of time and space and the extension of the organisational characteristics of modernity, transforms the substance and nature of everyday social life (Giddens 1991a, 2).

Giddens also addresses the subject of 'ontological security', which late-modernity erodes. The term refers to secure mental states which are generated by a sense of continuity and stability in a person's life. Some life events can undermine this security. One obvious such event is death. Losing a loved one or close friend reminds individuals of how insecure and fleeting life actually is. When death occurs it may drive people to thoughtfully question the meaning and reality of the social frameworks in which they participate (Mellor and Shilling 1993). Giddens suggests that widespread ontological security largely emerges from incorporating a positive view of the self, social reality and the future. Nonetheless, Giddens conjectures that the general undermining of such security can be partly rescued by technical advances and professional expertise and, in economic terms, familiarity with the global spread of commercial brands and major chain stores. Another example is the capacity to use credit cards in a store on the other side of the world with the confidence that the transaction will safely take place.

There is a downside, however, which individuals attempt to address. Giddens points out that tradition and culture were once forged in a specific time and place in which life experience on the life course took place. Once this is eroded, generally as a consequence of social environments becoming increasingly altered as a result of purposeful human design, individuals are free to assign personal explanations for ways of life that were once simply to be assumed as part of a 'natural' social order. The result is that the world created in late-modernity adds to its insecure or changeable character. This brings a sense of uncertainty and anxiety, at the same time that individuals may attempt self-cultivation, self-actualisation, self-transformation and self-consciousness. Human beings nevertheless frequently alleviate such anxieties by seeking to build up their own knowledge systems of how the emerging social sphere operates.

This development Giddens incorporates into his notions of 'distanciation' and 'disembedding processes' which engender 'reflexivity' – a self-awareness of social processes and how they impact the self and identity. In his work *The Consequences of Modernity* (1991b) Giddens elucidates his concept of 'time-space distanciation', in which he explores how individuals partake of 'disembedded practices' or the means that continuity can be sustained across time and space rather than a particular place. In short, individuals are often 'lifted out' of their social relations in local environments of social interaction in which life was traditionally grounded. 'Distanciation' also suggests the tendency for self identities to be 'portable' rather than located in a town or neighbourhood; local traditions and routines become less essential.

A major feature of late-modernity, for Giddens, results from when what is familiar is not the local but simply the local reconfiguration of global phenomena frequently disembodied from its origins. Central to this tendency is consumerism, which offers little by way of a sense of the familiar and has at least the potential to embed itself in different global contexts. There are important implications here for a sense of community. Common experience is not a local phenomenon but is inclined to occur in 'virtual communities' connected by shared comprehension and knowledge of how life operates, shared tastes and associations engendered via personal choice rather than enforced by localised pressures. Thus the significance of community belonging is increasingly substituted by the 'virtual', which ensures that the self has little by way of an assured basis. Paradoxically, while identity may mean the reflexive cultivation of the ideal self, the desire for community belonging as a way to express it remains allusive. Importantly for Giddens, self identity also requires interpersonal trust, not just faith in impersonal systems and infrastructure. In particular, friendship becomes less a matter of local and family dependency and association, and more about treasured relationships based upon 'personal affection', albeit based on freely chosen affiliation and trust in the pursuit of a sense of security. Nonetheless, such associations may not necessarily counter a feeling of social isolation.

The search for fresh forms of personal association has also taken advantage of the new technologies. Much may be exemplified by the popularity of Facebook, which requires reciprocity, trust building and constructing virtual images of the self. They also constituent an essential part of what Castells (1996, 1997) refers to as the 'network society', which relates to the social, political, economic and cultural changes as a result of the proliferation of networked, digital information and communications technologies. These networks have become the foundations of contemporary society, advancing beyond the so-called 'information society'. Castells maintains that it is not merely the technology which defines this emerging world, but also cultural, economic and political factors which make up the network society. The impact of cultural socialisation, political organisations, religion and social status all aid in forging the network society. Similarly, van Dijk (2012) suggests that the 'network society' – as a form of society reconfiguring relationships in media networks – is gradually replacing or complementing the social networks of face-to-face communication, while personal communication is replaced by digital technology. As a result social and media networks are forging the principal form of organisational structures in the contemporary world.

The significance of location and the breakdown of conventional communities is also taken up by commentators concerned with exploring experiences of life outside of virtual social networks. A major spotlight is on how life is increasingly located in urban environments, especially the implications of the reorganisation of cities. This is not an insignificant consideration. Today, for the first time, more people in the world live out their existence in urban areas rather than rural ones. In the USA, for instance, 80.7 per cent of the population live in urban areas according to the 2010 national census. This development is comparable elsewhere in the Western world: in the UK and much of Western Europe the figure is almost 90 per cent. These developments are not new. In many countries from the eighteenth century people migrated from rural areas due to the mechanisation in farming to urban areas where there was employment in the factory system. In the late twentieth century the search for work has been joined by individual, commercial, social and governmental attempts to reduce the time and expense in commuting and transportation. This results from the endeavour to improve opportunities for employment, education, housing and access manufactured goods and specialised services.

The problems related to urban living are now well-documented and include transport congestion, lack of sufficient housing, over-rapid growth and environmental degradation. Many cities display particularly stark inequalities in housing provision, health and employment. Cities are growing larger, and some are dubbed as mega-cities (frequently defined as those with a population of at least 10 million people). It is also possible to speak of the 'postmodern city' identified by the transgression or 'freedom' from social codes, constantly shifting populations, and acute commercialisation and market-driven priorities of life (Watson and Gibson 1995).

The repercussions of urban living for life experiences have long attracted the writings of commentators. For instance, Richard Sennett (1970) scrutinised the development of cities in the twentieth century. Sennett explored urban life through his work *The Uses of Disorder*, an essay describing identity formation in cities and considering how individuals and groups make social and cultural sense of the material conditions in which they find themselves – negotiating between identity and community in physical spaces. People, he suggests, can become competent interpreters of their own urban experience, despite the obstacles cities may place in their way. Furthermore, the 'equilibrium of disorder' which generates a host of social problems can also bring cultural vibrancy and a constructive diversity to urban life.

GLOBALISATION AND ITS CONSEQUENCES

Globalisation constitutes a vast field of sociological study of which the growing interconnectedness between global cities is merely one element. Indeed, it provides an area which significantly concern theories of late/postmodernity and one where they frequently converge. Through the relevant literature, globalisation is perceived as displaying various consequences, not least of all for the life course and the wider cultural backdrop in which it is experienced. But what exactly does the term 'globalisation' mean?

Malcolm Waters (1995) has traced the interrelated developments of globalisation that inform sociological writings and offers a definition of what it amounts to. First, there is an emerging global culture or consciousness. This is arguably currently the most rapid phase of development. Second, globalisation impacts the systematic relationship of all individual social ties. In a fully globalised context, no given relationship or set of relationships can remain isolated or bounded. In this way globalisation increases the inclusiveness and unification of human societies. Third, the phenomenon of globalisation is reflexive. The inhabitants of a vast variety of societies orient themselves to the world market as a whole by way of economic consumption and counter-cultures. Globalisation, fourth, involves a collapse of universalism and particularism. This differentiation is registered in the distinction between life chances and lifestyles. Each person in any social relationship is simultaneously an individual and recognised as a member of the wider human community. Fifth, globalisation brings, paradoxically, elements of risk and trust. Concomitant with Giddens' work, Waters stresses how individuals trust unknown persons, impersonal forces and norms in technological communication and economic exchange – but each involves an element of risk, as in the case of disclosing personal banking details to commercial firms through the worldwide net (Waters 1995, 62–64).

Globalisation features in Giddens' account of high modernity which stretches out well beyond the milieu of individual activities and personal engagements: it is a world which brings its own risks and dangers and one which intrudes deeply into the core of self-identity and human emotions. For Giddens, globalising processes have accentuated aspects of risk, whether it is economic forces or political events in the world, and have brought far-reaching consequences for the lives of many by way of undercutting reflexive life projects. There may be considerable implications. For example, the global economy means that recession in one part of the world may have substantial impact on another. Thousands of people may be made redundant as a result of the collapse of an international company – their life prospects severely undermined and life opportunities placed outside of their control. Beck comes to similar conclusions by emphasising that contemporary society places a great deal of stress in organising a response to risk or a systematic way of dealing with hazards and insecurities induced and introduced by modernisation processes: pollution, newly discovered illnesses, terrorism and crime, problems which may be exacerbated by their global impact (Beck 1992, 21).

Globalisation, as already observed, has also been an integral part of post-modernists' theorising. From one perspective, globalisation can be seen as impacting localised culture in which life courses may be well established. Long before the twenty-first century, globalisation amounted to the beginning of a new epoch in human affairs. In recent decades even the furthest reaches of the earth have become more easily accessible through advances in technology and communication in a world that grows increasingly 'smaller'. Although the process of globalisation has a long history, it is today genuinely different in scale from what has gone before. The sheer impact, speed and intensity of global cultural communications are now unprecedented. The increasing diffusion of radio, television, the internet, satellite and digital technologies, and other forms of mass media, have made instant communication possible. Via such media people throughout the world are exposed to the dynamics of other cultures as never before. It follows that human life at a local level must now be studied within a global perspective. Communities and the individuals that comprise them have to be seen in the context of a shrinking international arena, or what is often referred to as the 'global village'. This is one where the societies of the world are increasingly interconnected.

Globalisation disturbs the way that 'culture' is conceptualised within a fixed locality. Indeed, 'culture' paralleled the notion of 'a society' as a bounded entity occupying a physical territory mapped by way of a political territory (the nation state wrought by *modernity*) and cementing individual meaning constructs into this circumscribed social and political space. There are various implications which globalisation brings. One such is that the collapse of a modernist way of seeing the world suggests that postmodernity also includes a desire to combine cultural symbols from very varied codes or frameworks of meaning, perhaps from different parts of the globe, even at the cost of disjunction and eclecticism. It follows that for postmodernist theorists, culture in contemporary societies has very many syncretic elements – a tendency brought about by the collapse of the boundaries between 'high' and 'popular' forms of culture. Especially through new technology and modes of communication, people all over the world now share many tastes in music, clothes and food, and often the same choices of lifestyles (Tomlinson 1999, 28).

THE CONTEMPORARY LIFE COURSE

From the discussion above it is evidently clear that profound changes in contemporary society, indeed the world order, forge a broad backdrop – a 'lifeworld' (Habermas 1984) or 'habitas' (Bourdieu 1977) – in which to live in late/postmodernity. But what does the postmodern or late-modern life course look like? Is it realistic even to speak of a 'course'? Given the diversity of social, cultural and economic transformations, and the range of sociological debates addressing them, is it possible to make any generalisations at all?

There are various direct or indirect ways by which late/postmodernist writers have approached the subject of the life course, and some of their speculations have been explicit or implicit in the above discussions. Perhaps most obviously, postmodernist theorists argue it is arduous to suggest that people pass through such clearly demarcated stages of life as in previous times and are now subject to complex life trajectories in which life transitions and 'life events' may occur at various times and even compounded by reversibility.

Writers such as Featherstone and Hepworth (1991) and Bauman (1992) see the postmodern life course as characterised by a number of overlapping, often disparate, conditions associated with the blurring of traditional chronological boundaries and the integration of formally segregated periods of life. Fixed definitions of childhood, middle age and old age are eroding under pressure from two cultural directions that have accompanied the profound movements in the political economy of labour, retirement and traditionally structured forms of inequality such as social class. There are various repercussions. One is that in late/postmodern culture, the prospect of an endless life has been revived through images of perpetual youth and a blurring of traditional life course boundaries. Now life in Western societies is reduced to a series of individual choices and projected plans for the future that have little community significance and give increasing credence to the importance of human agency in the life course.

To emphasis a point made in the introduction to this volume, it is advantageous to turn once again to Giddens, who points out that today living out a full life-span is practically guaranteed. This allows individuals to attempt to predict the future, calculate risks and plan ahead with a view to future possibilities and with alternatives in mind. Individuals can negotiate optional courses of action through making present decisions from a number of choices presented to them. They can potentially chart their way through the life course with a great deal of assurance that old age will be reached. In Western societies individuals are now inclined to anticipate risks and possibilities at least partly by choice. At the same time, late-modern society is void of communal obligations, and fixed social status and roles. Today, people frequently regard themselves as highly individualistic, given that individualism and individual choice are core values (Giddens 1991a, 5–6, 147–48). It follows that people may not necessarily pass through stringent and clearly marked out stages of the life course but make choices and negotiate risks surrounding such matters as whether to marry or have children, or at what age they wish to retire – a more or less previously assumed inevitable life event.

Postmodernist writers are less likely to talk in terms of life course 'risks' as emphasised by Giddens, and more in terms of the uncertainty and unpredictability. One of the key uncertainties comes from the fragmentation of 'self'. There is now a search for 'self', personal identity and meaning. Postmodernity confronts people with pluralism and choice in such areas as relationships, but also with an absence of tradition, which means that there is very little help provided by society in establishing identities and in selecting moral guides to living.

Postmodernity has also brought something different for the life-span. There is increasing demographic evidence that life-expectancy is drawing closer to life-span potential. Hence, Westerners ideally anticipate long, active and healthy lives. However, the features of postmodern ageing also derive from cultural industries that distribute pleasure and leisure across an unrestricted range of objects, identities, styles and expectations. In doing so, claims Katz (1995, 69), such industries recast the life-span in 'fantastic ways', in particular, 'the masking of ageing and the fantasy of timelessness'. Whether the contemporary approach to the lifespan is quite as radical as is suggested here is open to debate. What is clear, however, is that its restructuring does have weighty consequences for various aspects of experience of the life course.

SUMMARY

The implications of current changes accompanying late/postmodernity, as briefly overviewed so far, are indeed considerable. All phases of life, if it makes sense to speak of 'phases' in any meaningful sense, have been impacted by numerous transformations, whether structural changes related to family life or impacted by cultural and economic trends, including developments within what is conventionally conceptualised as childhood and youth. The chapters to come will explore some of these transformations, as well as the continuities, in more detail and consider how contemporary culture, economics and technology impact important trajectories of the life course dependent on which phase of life is encountered by generational cohorts and, moreover, how these factors impact 'linked lives' over time. One such continuity, as considered in the next chapter, are the important demographic variables which have long formulated aspects of the life course, namely age, class, gender and ethnicity. An analysis of these social categories will provide an appreciation that many of the current changes in Western societies which impact on the life course are supplemented by structures of social inequality which have by no means been eclipsed in the late/postmodern world or any other terminology that might likely be called upon.

FURTHER READING

Albrow, M. (1996) *The Global Age: State and Society Beyond Modernity,* Stanford, CA: Stanford University Press.

Albrow, M. and King, E. (eds.) (1990) *Globalization, Knowledge and Society,* London: Sage.

Beck, U. and Beck-Gernsheim, E. (2002) *Individualization,* London: Sage Publications.

Beck, U., Giddens, A. and Lash, S. (1994) *Reflexive Modernization: Politics, Tradition and Aesthetics in the Modern Social Order,* Oxford: Blackwell.

Castells, M. (1998) *End of Millennium. The Information Age: Economy, Society and Culture Vol. III,* Cambridge, MA and Oxford: Blackwell.

Docherty, T. (1993) (ed.) *Postmodernism: A Reader,* New York: Harvester Wheatsheat.

Docker, J. (1994) *Postmodernism and Popular Culture: A Cultural History,* Cambridge: Cambridge University Press.

Eagleton, T. (1986) *Capitalism, Modernism and Postmodernism,* London: Verso.

Elder, G. (1985) *Life Course Dynamics,* Ithaca, NY: Cornell University Press.

Falk, P. (1994) *The Consuming Body,* London: Sage.

Featherstone, M. and Hepworth, M. (1989) 'Ageing and Old Age: Reflections on the Postmodern Life Course', in B. Byetheway, T. Keil, P. Allat, and A. Bryman (eds.), *Becoming and Being Old,* London: Sage.

Grenz, S. (1996) *A Primer on Postmodernism,* Grand Rapids, MI: Eerdmans

Habermas, J. (1981) *Modernity versus Postmodernity,* in V. Taylor and C. Winquist (eds.), originally published in *New German Critique,* 22, Winter: 3–14, trans. by Seyla Ben-Habib.

Jencks, C. (1986) *What is Postmodernism?* New York: St. Martin's Press and London: Academy Editions.

Lash, S. (1990) *The Sociology of Postmodernism,* London: Routledge.

Lipovetsky, G. (2005) *Hypermodern Times,* Oxford: Polity Press.

Martell, L. (2010) *The Sociology of Globalization,* Oxford: Policy Press.

Robertson, R. (1992) *Globalization: Social Theory and Global Culture,* reprint edn., London: Sage.

Smart, B. (1990) *Postmodernity,* London: Routledge.

Chapter 3

Social differentiation and determinants of the life course

In accounting for those variables which may impact upon the life course – its experiences, opportunities and limitations – the dynamics of social differentiation and inequalities traditionally addressed in earlier sociological accounts by way of class, gender, ethnicity and age tend to be played down by late/postmodernity theorising. At the very least, they are interpreted more in terms of either largely social constructs or identified as structures that are rapidly disintegrating as sources of community belonging and identity.

This does not imply that in contemporary Western society individuals and social collectives fail to be impacted by processes that can have positive and negative repercussions for the life course. Nonetheless, late/postmodern theorists place less stress on 'determinants' such as 'class' in favour of the significance of self and identity and the related concerns of the impact of consumption and choice, and the opportunity or lack of opportunity to realise these in forging meaningful lifestyles. At the same time, in the relevant theorising, contemporary experiences of the life course are given greater emphasis by way of globalising forces which may undermine the sense of belonging to demographic categories. This chapter permits space in which to consider these themes. However, its core concern is to explore the extent to which more conventional forms of inequality – age, class, gender and ethnicity – still continue to shape experiences and enhance or limit opportunity on the life course and explore how these demographic features may have undergone change and what the implications may be.

LIFE CHANCES, LIFESTYLES AND THE CONSUMER SOCIETY

In many late/postmodernist accounts, the emerging social order confronts the individual with a complex diversity of choices, primarily in terms of lifestyle preferences. The world thus becomes full of potential ways of being and acting as part of a lifestyle, and thus, according to Giddens (1991a, 78–79), individuals see the life course as a series of 'passages' to be negotiated in terms of opportunities and risks. Life passages give particular cogency to the interaction of risk and opportunities especially when they are to a substantial degree initiated by the individual – perhaps by negotiating significant transitions of life and life events: leaving home, changing job, forming a new relationship, and confronting illness and a range of discontinuities including loss of employment.

An important dimension of choice, to situate theorising succinctly, is in constructing a meaningful lifestyle. The relationship of lifestyle to the self becomes prominent in forging more or less integrated life orientations that generate particular narratives of self-identity throughout the life course. This link connecting identity and lifestyle is put in broader perspective by Weeks (1990), who differentiates between social and personal identity. The former constitutes lived relationships with others; the 'personal' are reflections of experience which are highly complex and individualised in terms of their social significance, not least social networks. In late/postmodernity social identity is eroded, stripped from an anchorage in community belonging or at least subject to fleeting social interaction. The personal becomes more significant since identity is open to choice, transformation and negotiation. While identity is 'handed down' in pre-industrial societies, in the contemporary world, with its lack of tradition and generational roots, identity is subject to choice, agency and negotiation as an integral part of the construct of self.

From this perspective, people today are obliged to construct and maintain a coherent self-identity or face a 'crisis' of meaning or, to perhaps to put it rather misleadingly, may be subject to an 'identity crisis'. The process of late/postmodernity, its pluralism, fragmentation and rootlessness, is behind such a development. At the same time, however, contemporary society also provides the means for a purposeful construction of self, largely through lifestyle preferences. Moreover, the disintegration of traditional processes of socialisation means that the formation of self takes place in the context of the individual sense of self, rather than community contexts, and is void of references to well-established values, moralities and convention.

The consumer culture has observably become the principal site in which identity construction largely takes place. Now, 'we are what we consume': selfhood becomes a matter of lifestyle choice and the construction of an 'off-the-shelf' image which may change quite dramatically throughout life. It follows that there is a choice, or potential choice, of lifestyles associated with the different phases of life and life-planning as part of a reflexive process (Waters 1995, 140–41). This implies that both material and non-material items, including kinship, human affection and intellect, become commodified. That is, their value is assessed by the context of their exchange, rather than the context of their production or use. Commodification is intimately bound up with consumption in the sense that the extension and development of the consumer culture from the late twentieth century depended upon the creation of new markets, not least through the production of images and 'advice' on lifestyles (Featherstone 1991).

Consumerism

At this point, a little more needs to be said regarding the nature of the dynamics of the consumer economy and its accompanying culture. Perhaps the most important observation in respect of economic developments is that a late/postmodernised consumer culture may be said to experience hyper-commodification, in which minute differences between products or minute improvements in them can determine variations in demand, and in which consumption is differentiated on the basis of the signifiers recognised as 'brand names' (Crooks et al. 1992). Here consumption, or more precisely a capacity to consume, is itself a matter of reflexivity. This tendency is captured in such terms as 'taste', 'fashion' and 'lifestyle', which become key sources of social differentiation, displacing class and political affiliation, since they may say a great deal about income, status and the opportunity to realise choices. In addition, in the consumer culture of postmodernity the items consumed take on a symbolic and not merely a material value, or in the words of Baudrillard (1983) they become 'hypersimulated'. To this tendency may be added the significance of 'conspicuous consumption' – the idea that social status is at least partly achieved by flagrant and ostentatious public display of consumption of valued commodities.

It might be said that consumer culture is liberating in the sense that it is symbolically and globally mediated, freeing values and preferences from particular social and geographical locations. This it does by declassifying or dedifferentiating culture, by mixing high and low culture – important structures once found in modernity since they were closely associated with social class and class tastes. What is regarded as 'good' culture is now a matter of opinion and can be accepted or rejected at will under the relativising influences of postmodernity. In addition, globalising cultural flows enhance commodification and vice versa. In the globalised context there may be the influence of other cultures which can be pre-packaged for a new environment – whether African-style clothes or Peruvian music, or a whole variety of food genres from around the world. It may well be that interaction with these goods is a meaningful way by which identity is constructed and individuals make sense of their lives. Especially through new technology and modes of communication, people all over the world now share many tastes in music, clothes and food, and often the same choices of generalised lifestyles.

There is, however, an alternative, less affirmative interpretation which plays down matters of choice, one where the postmodern economy is best understood as transforming citizens into consumers by altering their self-images, their structure of wants, in directions that serve capitalist accumulation. This arises in societies where powerful groups, usually those seeking to accrue capital, encourage consumers to 'want' more than they 'need'. At the same time, for critics of the emerging economic order, commodification represents a distinct narrowing and convergence of cultural experience rather than an expanding experience of the world. This is succinctly put by Baudrillard (1983), who argues that in the postmodern society 'there is nowhere to go but to the shops'.

Problematising identity and the construction of self

Discussions related to late/postmodernity frequently focus on the theme of the self and identity as problematic, although the subject is often approached in contrasting ways. What is central to these perspectives, however, is a greater emphasis on the problem faced by individuals, rather than the group, in relation to identity. Hence, the disadvantages encountered on the life course are not so much derived from social structures such as class but rather the ability to deal with challenges to the self and identity – central concerns which are impacted by uncertainty, aspects of risk and restrictions in realising life potentials. These are a fresh and challenging range of problems which are understood to beset late/postmodernity.

Giddens talks about 'dilemmas of the self' (Giddens 1991a, 187–88). In conditions of late-modernity, in a way very different from that experienced in pre-modern and early modernity, globalising processes in particular bring the danger of the fragmentation of the self. The problem of uniting the self concerns protecting and reconstructing the self in the face of massive intentional and extensional changes. For Giddens, high modernity brings a new sense of identity which involves 'finding oneself' and this will inevitably entail biographical construction and reconstruction of the life course (Giddens 1991a, 12). While postmodernist commentators are preoccupied with the prevailing pessimism of postmodernity that comes through relativising impulses, Giddens is more concerned with the uncertainty brought by the breakdown of community and tradition on the one hand, and globalising forces on the other. At the same time, there has emerged the threat of personal meaninglessness – potentially disturbing existential questions that are not answered by the social order (Giddens 1991a, 121–22).

In Giddens' account, as explored in the previous chapter, late-modernity finds a way by which individuals can create an integrated sense of self. In the pre-modern context, the fragmentation of experience was not a prime source of anxiety. Trust relations were localised and focused through personal ties. Today, a range of possibilities present themselves, not just in terms of options of behaviour, but by way of 'openness of the world' to the individual. Quoting Erving Goffman (1967), Giddens argues (1991a, 191–92) that the individual can leave one social encounter and enter another and in doing so adjusts herself/himself to different contexts. Turning attention to the subject of the life course, Giddens stresses the contemporaneous reflexive project of self at its centre, one where individuals have become apt at adapting the self to different environments. Thus the late-modernity that fragments and creates problems in terms of identity also unites at different levels of social experience.

Giddens' overriding concern in his work *Modernity and Self-Identity* is to examine the emergence of new mechanisms of self-identity which are shaped by the institutions of late- modernity and a society where kinship and community structures continue to be eroded. While the problems that these generate may be addressed, globalising processes put much beyond the control of the individual – undermining coherent and structured aspects of the life course (Giddens 1991a, 2). This is a theme also taken up by Beck (1992). Global variables, as well as localised contexts, can profoundly impact on the individual's life experiences. While the cultural emphasis on the self and identity carries notions of individual responsibility, there are aspects of realisation which are out of the control of the individual. Nonetheless, for Beck, many of the hurdles that confront the individual from day to day are now culturally perceived as a consequence of individual actions rather than resulting from social background, such as class position or processes beyond his/her influence.

According to Beck, industrial society, based on the rational application of science, is being replaced by the risk society. Whereas industrial society was seen as an ordered and predictable social structure, late-modernity is perceived as a more perilous and unpredictable place, in which individuals are constantly confronted with risk. Such risks not only include the threat of nuclear war or environmental disasters but also a range of more localised risks which have to be negotiated throughout daily life. Importantly, with the decline of the social networks associated with older generations, people are now forced to negotiate these fresh dangers as individuals rather than as members of a community.

The body in late/postmodernity

The emphasis on the body in late/postmodernity constitutes a growing volume of sociological literature, including its significance for the life course, its connection with self and identity and how its social construction may generate forms of inequality. According to Giddens (1991a, 7), the reflexivity of the self extends to the body, where the body is part of the action system rather than merely a passive object and includes a constant observation of bodily processes often linked to levels of health, exercise and diet. Self-actualisation is understood in terms of a balance between opportunity and risk. Relinquishing the past, through the various techniques of becoming free from oppressive emotional habits, generates a multiplicity of opportunities for self-development. Via his own distinct approach Giddens suggests that the reflexivity of the self throughout life impacts the body as well as psychological processes. The body is decreasingly essentially a 'given', functioning outside the internally referential systems of modernity, but itself becomes reflexively mobilised.

A wealth of anthropological material reveals the body as being utilised in many societies to make statements about social status (e.g. Polhemus 1978). In Western culture, forms of body alteration are a significant part the medicalisation of life – from breast enlargement through to dieting, to spare-part surgery. The medicalisation of the body may also influence ageing throughout the life course through techniques applied to staying and looking young – techniques perhaps exemplified by 'face lifts' and other forms of cosmetic surgery. In this sense, the body marks the site of the quest, and perhaps success or failure, to obtain the status of youth and beauty.

As Featherstone (1982, 26) argues, the body is taking on increasing social significance in postmodernity. Bodily appearance has now come to signify the self and status, to the degree that 'the penalties of bodily neglect are a lowering of one's acceptability as a person'. An old, as well as the obese or disabled body, implies an undesirable self and a correspondingly reduced social status. As Featherstone and Wernick point out in their Introduction to *Images of Ageing* (1995, 3), the facility to give meaning to ageing, old age and death has changed, not only culturally, but also via biomedical and information technology, given their ability to alter the material structure of the body. While it is increasingly the site of self-improvement and status, the body is also the centre of discourse and controversy. Besides the issues related to such areas as the reproductive system, which are exposed to political and ethical debate, the body is also a contested area of medicalised interest – of medical control and the resistance to it throughout the various phases of the life course.

SOCIAL STRATIFICATION AND THE LIFE COURSE

It is through discussion of the themes of consumerism, lifestyles, risk, discontinuities and the body that late/postmodern theorists tend to approach the subject of inequalities rather than necessarily viewing them as a product of conventional social structures. Thus, to refer to social differentiation and determinants of inequality in respect of the life course may seem at odds with many of the principal themes developed in the previous chapter, which overviewed the key literature on late/postmodernity. Indeed, in this respect Harriet Bradley (1996, 1–3) speaks of 'a crisis of stratification theory': arguing that the approach of postmodernist writing would appear to undermine traditional sociological accounts of structured inequalities in various respects. First, that its emphasis on socio-cultural 'fragmentation' would appear to play down notions of coherent and structured formation of inequality such as social class. From this perspective, as noted above, the alleged demise of class in contemporary societies has largely been replaced by an emphasis on cross-cutting forms of social disadvantage and the degrees of opportunity open to make choices of lifestyle preference. Second, class, and gender for that matter, have been approached by postmodernists more in terms of social constructionist approaches, that is, how such social categories came to be classified as such in the first place. In short, the sociological task becomes one of deconstructing the building of social categories that force people, perhaps with negative consequences, into generalised identities. The latter approach, suggests Bradley (1996, 3), fits uneasily with material factors related to inequality and diverse forms of social deprivation.

The apparent disintegration of rigidly structured social divisions synonymous with modernity, perhaps most obviously class, would seem to render a discussion of 'determinants' of the life course somewhat redundant. Yet, the emphasis upon identity, consumption, globalisation and even reflexivity does not necessarily denote the complete demise of variables that influence the life course, its experiences and life chances. There remains, however, a certain ambiguity in how earlier sociological concerns, especially with the stringent inequalities derived from class, gender, age and ethnicity, are negotiated and utilised by postmodernist writers. In this sense, the uncertainty of Sociology in discussing such issues reflects a broader cultural uncertainty. This possibility is explored by Bauman (1992) in an article entitled *Is There a Postmodern Sociology?*, where he identifies an evolving new self-awareness in sociological discourse that seeks to account for the drastic changes observable in the contemporary world, including developing technology, the plurality of cultures, relativism, the proliferation of many 'lifeworlds', the apparent reversal of rationalism and the effects of consumerism. The result is the development of contrasting theories and complex debates, some of which relate to the interface between established and developing theories and their applicability to the emerging socio-cultural order.

One of the underlying concerns of current sociological debates, and this is not always evident in the relevant literature, is the recognition that society continues to shape and limit life experiences and life chances throughout the life course. The way in which this is manifest may not always be obvious or discerned by way of long-term trends; nonetheless, aspects of consumption and technological development, when fused with levels of status associated with class, gender, ethnicity, age, age cohorts and so on, indicate that society continues to impact throughout the life course. This is certainly observable through experiences of early life – childhood and youth – experiences which can have profound accumulated repercussions in later life, including levels of health (Holland et al. 2000). Moreover, the significance of age and ageing tentatively surveyed in this chapter (and considered in more detail in Chapter 11) continues to have profound significance in terms of status and intergenerational relationships.

THE PERSEVERANCE OF SOCIAL CATEGORIES AND INEQUALITIES: AGE

Age differences may be said to be a result of biological, social and psychological processes (Solomon et al. 2009). The former refers to biological development and personal physical health, while 'psychological age' typically refers to the capacities that individuals possess and the skills they may employ to adjust to changing biological and environmental challenges, including memory, learning, intelligence, motivation and emotion (Bjorklund and Bee 2008). This frequently includes how people perceive themselves: 'subjective age' or 'age identity' (Hubley and Russell 2009). Finally, 'social age' refers to age-graded societal expected roles and behaviours: the socially constructed meaning of various ages.

In elaborating on the latter dimension of ageing, Jane Pilcher (1995, 1) has noted that, like class, ethnicity and gender, age is a social category through which people define and identify individuals and groups as part of their social experience. In contemporary Western societies, age categories continue to create differential access to power, prestige, material resources and citizenship. The fact remains, however, that age differentiation may not now be so important largely because of the flexibility of the different phases of life and, perhaps, attendant discontinuities, as well as broader structural changes. At the very least, its relevance and meaning seem to have been revolutionalised.

The opening chapter of this volume explored how the significance of age categories is changing and declining in late/postmodernity. This is not to suggest that they fail to continue to inform aspects of social inequality. Western societies place a cultural emphasis on being young and the socially constructed advantages of 'youth' in terms of fitness and vitality, as well as adapting to the challenges of the workplace. At the same time, nonetheless, a lack of status is also marked in the years of youth and early adulthood, which are circumscribed by legal proscription outlining what young people can or cannot do and, in the current economic environment, the lack of opportunities open to them.

To be sure, individuals in Western societies continue to define themselves in terms of their membership of particular age categories or at least the perceived impact of norms associated with them. Self-perceptions, moreover, are closely bound up with how the young or the old see themselves, and this, in turn, is often dependent on how others see them. Identification with age, however, has been found to carry different weight throughout the life course. In the mid-twentieth century, Kuhn (1960), in a study of the USA, discovered that only 25 per cent of nine-year-olds identified themselves by age. Yet, 75 per cent of thirteen-year-olds identified themselves in this way. Thus, age awareness seemed to be of increasing significance in the teenage years, at a time that youth cultures were emerging as a new social phenomenon, and subsequently became associated with later age cohorts.

It is not just a matter of how those of a similar age see themselves but also how others see them. Clearly, what is regarded as 'old' in one community is not considered so in another. Much depends largely on the life-expectancy of any given society. In the West, for instance, old age is conventionally perceived as comprising the later years of adulthood and the final stage of life itself. This arguably begins from about the mid-60s. Moreover, age is given specific meaning in different contexts. In all different types of society individuals move through and participate in many varied social circles during their day-to-day lives. People respond to others in terms of different age categories. As they move from one context to another they are defined differently by those with whom they interact, depending on the nature of proscribed relationship norms and conventions surrounding age. This is certainly true in more 'traditional' societies, where this may be expressed in terms of status and authority. A rather exaggerated version of this authoritative association with the younger generation is to be found in Haiti, where parents are expected to strike their child if it is troublesome – even if s/he is 50 years old or more.

Modernity brought more highly structured norms to accompany clearly established stages of life, and, in some contexts, age required the adoption of a subordinate position, in others a dominant position. The way age was perceived carried different expectations concerning how individuals were meant to behave and respond to others. However, much of this may be changing in late/postmodernity, where there is a greater ambiguity related to the way people should behave according to their age and how they relate to other generations. To a great degree this is because clearly defined age categories are beginning to breakdown, along with strict norms as to how people of a certain age are expected to conduct themselves. Thus Bradley (1996, 7) prefers to speak in terms of social relationships and the way others categorise them rather than stringent age demarcations. Moreover, she argues that the relationships between different generations could be best understood in terms of 'dynamics' – various locations of age which may be impacted by aspects of gender and ethnic inequalities and occupational reward. Such distinctions are a social reality with very real consequences, but these distinctions are sometimes fixed and sometimes fluid. Furthermore, aspects of age status may not hold if chronological age is not in keeping with particular social responsibilities. For example, an unemployed and homeless young adult may not be afforded the same status as a peer who is more integrated into the adult world through the spheres of employment and family responsibilities.

Nor is the significance of age related to specific age categories. How the ageing process as a natural phenomenon is understood and perceived is also of consequence. Thus Featherstone and Wernick (1995) have drawn attention to the negative images portrayed in Western societies and their implications for self-image, including everyday interaction, experience and identity. Advertising and consumer culture, and government agencies in health education campaigns forge images of senility and 'second childhood', illness and inevitable death. Similarly, Hepworth (2000) has explored how perceptions of ageing involve a reciprocal process between stories of ageing involving an interplay between the external reality of everyday experience and internal subjective arenas of personal desires, anxieties, fears and fantasies. In essence, individuals contemplate the images and ideas regarding ageing disseminated by wider culture and this may impact the capacity to articulate self-expression and identity.

Demographic change and intergenerational discord

Discord between generations may constitute an important determinant in life experiences as much as generational continuities. 'Generational conflict' is an emotive term, and such conflict may have various origins. One important aspect of age stratification in modernity was the emergence of a distinct form of generational cultural divergence. Since the 1960s the notion of intergenerational conflict in Western societies largely centred on the opposed values of youth and adults and contrasting norms and values of age groups experiencing differing historical circumstances. As Attias-Donfurt and Arber (2000) note, however, the emerging conflict is not so much about politics and culture as economics derived from demographic changes. Thus, the issues may no longer be the refutation of generational, or for that matter gender, hierarchies inside the family or public sphere, but instead will increasingly focus upon the sharing of public resources between separate cohorts before, during and after working life. Therefore, the risk of conflict is now largely derived from generational inequality in welfare contributions, as well as in the distribution of benefits.

As already noted, the twentieth century witnessed a remarkable increase in life-expectancy. Improved standards of living over the decades promoted the health of people of all ages, while more recent medical advances have made some progress in fending off cancer and heart disease, afflictions common to older people. This increase in life-expectancy will prove to have significant consequences for the number of older people as a segment of the

Table 3.1 Life Expectancy (UK)

Date	1841	1881	1901	1920	1930	1950	1971	2001	2015	2030 (projected)
Average Life Expectancy	43	45	48	50	60	65	70	79	81	90

Sources: NHS, 'UK life expectancy expected to rise to late 80s by 2030'; Office of National Statistics; T. Lambert, 'A Brief History of Life Expectancy in Britain', nd.

population in many Western societies. By 2020, one in five people are likely to be over the age of 65 (Walker and Maltby 1997, 1). This considerable increase occurred as the 'Baby Boomers' born in the immediate post-war years reached their 60s before 2010. A similar pattern is emerging elsewhere in Europe, although there are differences across countries, with Ireland having the youngest population of the EU nations and Sweden the oldest.

There are several major implications of this projected rise of older people as a sizeable section of the population. Typically, industrialised nations have low birth-rates, and the long-term repercussion of this trend is frequently referred to as the 'demographic time bomb'. This highlights the dependency ratio – the number of dependent children and retired persons relative to productive age groups. Because of falling fertility and the decline in family size, the dependency ratio has been declining. The changes predicted for the twenty-first century suggest an underlying dilemma in the dependency ratio – there will be fewer and fewer people of working age, while more and more will be dependents. In the USA, by way of illustration, the age dependency ratio of dependents (people younger than 15 or older than 64 to the working-age) in 2013 was 50 per 100 working-age population (World Bank estimates). The implication of these shifting demographics clearly underlines actual or potential conflict between generations over resource allocation in what may be understood as a negative aspect of 'linked lives'.

Child poverty

In some respects, the economic position of older people has improved in Western societies, although high levels of poverty continue to exist among sizeable contingents (as will be explored in Chapter 11). Studies, however, conclude that a 'new poverty' has emerged and is to be found among younger age categories, especially children. This tendency is both a reminder of the continuing significance of economic deprivation and, in particular, how it impacts particular age categories, which may impact future life chances and accumulated disadvantages.

The numbers of children under 16 years old needing state assistance in the UK rose from 800,000 in 1974 to 2.3 million in 1991. In the mid-1990s, 10 per cent of children were designated as living below the poverty line (Funken and Cooper 1995, 12). According to one UK charity, the Child Action Poverty Group, in 2013, largely as a result of government cuts in social benefits in a time of severe economic global recession, there were some 3.5 million children living in poverty (27 per cent of all children). The charity estimated that this upward trend was expected to continue with 4.7 million children projected to be living below the poverty line by 2020.

Such trends more than hint at how disparities in wealth and income may be impacted by the vagaries of a global economy, thus indicating the significance of 'time and place' and the unique repercussions of individual's location in particularly historical periods for life course prospects. According to the US Census Bureau, 14.3 per cent of Americans were living in poverty in 2009. Building on these findings, analysis by US Congressional Budget Office (2009) projected the poverty rate in relation to unemployment during the global economic recession that began in 2008: suggesting that the overall poverty rate would increase from 12.5 per cent in 2007 to nearly 16 per cent by 2014 and that the child poverty rate would increase from 18 per cent in 2007 to nearly 26 per cent in 2014, adding about 10 million people and 6 million children to the ranks of the poor.

The fact that the economic downturn disproportionally impacts children is likely to be significant for their life chances – a tendency compounded by the cutback in benefits and social services in many Western countries as a result of deep-cutting austerity measures. A report by the charity UNICEF in 2014 noted that child poverty had increased in 23 countries in the developed world since the start of the global recession, potentially trapping a generation in a situation of material deprivation and reduced life prospects. The report stated that the number of children entering poverty during the recession was 2.6 million greater than the number who have been lifted out of it.

THE SIGNIFICANCE OF SOCIAL CLASS

Such evidence of levels of child poverty more than suggests that life chances continue to be laid down in the early years on the life course and are discernible even earlier. Certainly, it is clear that various factors can impact on human development before birth. This can include the mother's diet, her

---

Box 3.1 Levels of child poverty UK

- 3.7 million children are living in poverty
- 1.7 million of such children live in acute poverty
- 63% of children living in poverty are in a family where someone is employed
- 3-year-olds in households with incomes below about £10,000 are 2.5 times more likely to suffer chronic illness than children in households with incomes above £52,000.
- Infant mortality is 10% higher in the lower social group than the average
- Only 48 % of 5-year-olds entitled to free school meals have an adequate degree of development by the conclusion of their reception year, in contrast to 65% of all other pupils
- Less than half of pupils entitled to free school meals gain 5 GCSEs at C or above, including English and Maths, compared to 61% of those not eligible.

Source: Child poverty statistics and facts, Barnardos, nd

---

living environment, whether or not she smokes, her levels of alcohol consumption and quality of pre-natal care. Such environmental factors continue to be important throughout the life course: where people live, the kind of employment undertaken, and formal and informal relationships are all evident in positive or negative ways. Sociological theory and research continue to demonstrate that early life course experiences shape health outcomes well into adulthood, and social ties and health behaviour throughout the life course are significant at different life stages. These processes accumulate and reverberate throughout life (Umberson et al. 2010).

These factors are frequently linked to economic concerns and, in particular, conventional social class differences. In modernity, differences of class, alongside, age, gender and ethnicity, were the most important social divisions. In terms of class, the 'classical' Marxist analysis identified social inequalities as part of an enduring process. In Marx's defence, it may be acknowledged that, at the very least, economic well-being, or failure to realise it, is obviously a major determinant of experiences and chances throughout the life course. The reality, however, is that Marx's assessment of class is difficult to uphold today despite revisions of his theory. Works such as that of Erik Olin Wright (1979) retain notions of the polarisation of wealth and a monopoly of the ownership and control of economic production, while recognising that class structures have undoubtedly been transformed and fragmented.

The tendency over recent decades is to conceptualise class not so much in terms of the ownership of production but in terms of occupational reward by way of income and status, linking these to consumer power in relation to life-styles and opportunities. This approach recognised that the Western economy has moved from an emphasis on production to that of consumption. At the end of the twentieth century less than a third of the economically active population was engaged in industrial labour, marking the shrinking size of the working-class population. The middle-class, by which is generally meant the non-manual occupations that Marx had more or less ignored, now accounts for around 45–50 per cent of the workforce and has grown as traditional manual occupations have steadily declined (Eyde and Lintner 1996, 108).

Such class divisions seem to account for differences in life experiences and the degrees to which people can encounter negative events in their lives. Evidence in the 1990s, replicated continuingly since, pointed to the fact that infant mortality in the first year of life was three times higher in manual occupation families; manual workers were three times more likely to have a serious long-term illness; an unskilled manual worker would die around seven years earlier than a counterpart born to professional parents; divorce levels were four times higher among manual workers than professionals; and unemployment rates appeared to show more than 10 per cent difference between these occupational groupings (Macionis and Plummer 1997, 275).

This division of society into manual and non-manual occupations has, however, proved to be increasingly misleading. While it is convenient to call manual workers 'working-class' and non-manual workers 'middle-class', much disguises the vast differences *within* social classes. As far as the latter is concerned, there is a great deal of variation between well-paid professional people in stable careers and white-collar clerical workers with salaries and employment opportunities that do not compare favourably even with those of many skilled manual workers. There are other reasons too for paying less attention to 'classical' class differentiation. For Pahl (1984), social mobility in industrial class systems has been most pronounced near the middle, where people's social position is most likely to alter. This mobility has subsequently blurred the lines between classes, suggesting that they have all fragmented to the extent that class is no longer a meaningful concept. At the same time, according to Pahl, it appears that a general 'levelling up' has occurred, with traditional working-class communities largely vanishing and the lives of manual workers considerably forged by home ownership and a reasonable level of affluence and consumerism. Today, the overall standard of living in the societies of the West (along with Japan) is the highest in the world. Relative to most regions of the globe, fewer people face the most severe forms of life threatening inequalities that Marx once wrote about.

This does not mean, however, that there are not extremes of wealth and income in the Western world. Research has suggested that, although a larger middle-class may have gradually emerged, the gap between the wealthy and the poor in Europe and North America has been growing, and part of this development is that the number of poor in the population has increased in relative terms (Funken and Cooper 1995). In 2012, the US Congressional Budget Office (CBO) revealed how much of the income gains since the late 1970s had been appropriated by the richest 1 per cent of households. Over the 28 years covered by the CBO study, US incomes had increased overall by 62 per cent, allowing for tax and inflation. Middle income households were well below the overall average with gains of just 37 per cent, while the lowest paid fifth of Americans received only a small share, their incomes having grown by a modest 18 per cent.

There is more to the equation. From the 1980s there has also arisen what has come to be known as the 'underclass', comprising those people 'under' the class structure who are economically, politically and socially marginalised and excluded. This has been recognised in some works related to late/postmodernity. Giddens, for instance, identifies an underclass comprising a heterogeneous group of people including the unemployed, many members of ethnic communities, the disabled, the homeless, a sizeable section of older people, and one-parent families who appear to be outside of the increasing prosperity of contemporary society (Giddens 1991a, 85–86). This suggests that, while class structures have radically changed, the repercussions of a society in which there remains a considerable gulf between the 'haves' and 'have nots' continue to influence life chances.

Zygmunt Bauman (2011) takes a more global sweep. In referring to what he calls 'collateral damage', he describes one of the most outstanding dimensions of contemporary social inequality. For the political class, poverty is commonly seen as a problem of law and order – a matter of how to deal with individuals, such as unemployed youths, who are regarded as a social problem. Yet perceiving poverty as a 'problem' obscures the social roots of inequality, which lie in the combination of a consumerist life philosophy propagated and instilled by a consumer-oriented economy, on the one hand, and the rapid shrinking of life chances available to the poor, on the other. In the contemporary, liquid-modern world, the poor are the product of a profit-driven, consumer-oriented society – 'aliens inside' who are deprived of the rights enjoyed by others who are more affluent.

GENDER INEQUALITIES

Gender is an additional grounding of social stratification evident in the great majority of historical communities – those ranging from 'primitive' to complex industrialised societies – shaping life chances and opportunities through economics, family and work structures, and patriarchal ideologies. Until the 1970s, with the rise of a new wave of feminism, the sociological preoccupation with social class tended to obscure the significance of major gender divisions and inequalities in Western societies. Indeed, the conventional ways of defining class until relatively recently focused on male heads of households. Including women in the picture complicates the issue of social class and forges new controversies such as how child-bearing and child-raising fit into the labour structure.

While overt discrimination is illegal in most Western countries, women remain more likely to be concentrated into lower paid occupations such as social work, nursing, childcare, primary school teaching and secretarial roles. Many indeed are often dubbed 'female' occupations, as revealed in a selection of statistics offered by the United States Department of Labour (2013). Ninety-eight per cent of pre-school and kindergarten teachers were found to be female; 94 per cent of secretaries and administrator assistants; 72 per cent of cashiers; 92 per cent of receptionists and information clerks; 88 per cent of housekeeping cleaners; but only 34 per cent of managers. Across of all these occupational categories females earned markedly less than their male counterparts even if they could claim the same qualifications, expertise and experience. Although chances of promotion in various occupations were discernibly improving for women, the existence of what has come to be known as the 'glass ceiling' indicated that hidden aspects of discrimination in terms of career advancement exist despite legislation regarding equal opportunities. This appears to be most acute at the management level and Adebowale Akande (1994) has attributed much of this structural and systemic 'bottleneck' to factors which include 'old boys' networks. All these aspects of work may severely restrict life experiences and life chances of women in the employment sphere.

Women are also over-represented in the poverty statistics. In this regard, the term 'feminisation of poverty' describes the long-identified trend by which women represent an increasing proportion of the poor. Townsend (1987) has identified four groups of women that make up the 'female poor': single (including divorced) women with children, older women on state pensions, 'carers' who look after children or other dependants and women with low earnings. The feminisation of poverty is, in turn, part of a larger change: the rapidly increasing number of households – at all class levels – headed by single women. This trend, coupled with the fact that households run exclusively by women are at high risk of poverty, explains why women (and their children) represent an increasing share of the poor in Western societies. The problem with the feminisation of poverty thesis, however, as Fran Bennett (2014) points out, is that it tends to draw attention away from women workers with partners who are more prone to experience in-work poverty due to their own employment features and low earnings.

Dimensions of material deprivation are very general restrictions which women may face during the life course. In more specific terms there are particular junctures in the life course where women may face disadvantages. In this respect, Allat et al. (1987) provide insights into further difficulties faced by women through such areas as relationships in the teenage years, the restricted opportunities at school-leaving age, inequalities in late marital life, leisure opportunities, trade union activities and discontinuities throughout the life course. All these aspects compare poorly with the life experiences of many men, who either do not confront these difficulties or find themselves at a greater advantage.

Given the evidence of gender inequality considered above, one of the principal questions for feminists at the present time is in theorising the extent and nature of the ubiquity of patriarchy through which male domination and differentiated social roles are expressed in late/postmodernity. Almost certainly, many would take exception to Giddens' brief account, which strikes an over-positive and optimistic tone regarding women in the emerging socio-cultural order of late-modernity. Giddens sees women becoming the equal of men in many areas of public life given that there have also been major advances for women in the realm of self, the body, identity and contentious areas such as abortion. Giddens courts controversy, however, by claiming that women's attitudes to the world are radically different compared to men and that this is largely determined by their reproductive system (Giddens 1991a, 219–20).

Such a critique of Giddens engages with the concerns of what has come to be known as 'Third Wave Feminism' that is generally acknowledged as emerging in the early 1990s. This 'wave' includes several areas of concern. One such concern may be viewed as a response to the perceived failures of and backlash against initiatives and movements created by the 'Second Wave' emerging in the 1960s, centred on advancing women's rights (the 'First Wave' beginning largely associated with women's suffrage), and an analysis of the shortcomings of political policies and legislation enacted by governments related to these rights issues. Third Wave Feminism has also focused on additional issues. Among them has been the shift to recognising the complexities in women's lives and how gender is cut across by such factors as sexual orientation, ethnicities, nationalities, religions and cultural backgrounds. This interest dovetails with the writings of postmodernist feminists, who are more concerned with 'differentness' and the belief that women's subordination produces different life experiences and has no single cause or single solution.

For at least some feminists the postmodernist paradigm is more attractive, and this is so in relation to aspects of the life course. Traditional feminist Sociology and some aspects of postmodern theory overlap in their display of a critical content in the interpretation of contemporary society. The common ground is evident in social constructionist approaches. This is unmistakable, for example, in feminists' accounts of medicalisation. Much is exemplified by the notion of 'biology as ideology' – a term derived from R.C. Lewontin's work (1992). Lewontin argued that the biological determinism advanced by the medical profession is a philosophical, scientific and political theory which, from a feminist perspective, is set within the social and economic differences between the sexes – the goal being to legitimise inequality, to make it appear a natural and inevitable outcome. The discourse surrounding biological determinism would, from this perspective, seem to focus on information which supports the theory and ignores that which contradicts it (Albee 1982).

More recent feminist work continues to stress that women's biological, psychological and social development across the life course is compromised by cultural, political, and economic factors which forge lifestyles, habits, expectations and roles that place women at a disadvantage. Perceptions of the process of ageing may be cited as an example. Thus, Linda Gannon (1996) considers the social forces which shape such issues as psychological well-being, menopause and sexuality. Gannon suggests that these issues can only be addressed in a feminist context – one which challenges the traditional assumptions that ageing is necessarily associated with intellectual deterioration, depression, physical disability and social disengagement. Here, social skills and support, the woman's control over her life and body, and social and economic roles are advanced as major determinants of her well-being.

Gannon (1996, 1) argues that with age, biology becomes relatively less important, as the combined influences of trauma, sexism, ageism, poverty and access to quality care accumulate over a lifetime. She contends that such deconstruction is not incompatible with the postmodernist mode of thinking and its emphasis on the social deconstruction of discourse and categorisation. This view is shared by Yeatman (1994) who suggests that both feminist and postmodernist theorising contest the foundationist pre-suppositions of modernist discursive formations; in short, assumptions which ground the validity of knowledge claims with reference to taken-for-granted truths or meta-narratives. In this way, all knowledge becomes historically and culturally produced. Therefore, all discourse, common-sense assumptions about gender and medicalised concepts can be deconstructed to reveal patriarchal ideologies.

Not all feminist writers have been wholly content with the challenges of postmodernist theories. Alison Assiter (1996), for example, goes against the grain of current orthodoxies to challenge some of the postmodern assumptions and has defended many of the tenets of more traditional expressions of feminism. Assiter provides an argument for the continuing reality of gender inequality, the reality of the distinction between sex and gender, and insists that universal claims about the disadvantages experienced by women can be justified. This leads her to advocate a partial return to feminist modernist values. In doing so, she brings a defence of modernist realism and Enlightenment philosophy.

'RACE' AND ETHNICITY

Clearly Western societies are increasingly pluralistic in terms of 'race' or ethnic composition. Nevertheless, 'race' is a problematic concept in that it suggests the categorisation of individuals and entire groups of people on the grounds of their perceived physical attributes, and is often critiqued as a social construct and ideological attempt to justify so-called natural inequality. Frequently, the term 'ethnicity' is used as a substitute for that of 'race', as it appears to lack derogative connotations and merely designates people on the grounds of their cultural traits and geographical points of origins. Most sociologists would see ethnicity as a more valid way of classifying people than 'race', which may be interpreted as a social construct reflecting the dominant belief system of any given society, in particular, the attitude of acceptance or hostility of the 'other'. 'Ethnicity' however has proved to be conceptually problematic. Assigning individuals to a single ethnic grouping is growing in its complexity, especially at a time when the term 'ethnicity' is an increasingly evolving and contested social category, and there exists no commonly accepted definitions of the term (Phinney 1996). Also, in many surveys conducted in Western societies it is evident that more and more individuals described themselves as belonging to 'mixed' or 'other' ethnic groups than those listed by researchers. Given that the categories are expanded and there tend to be changes in self-identity between generations, it is arduous to make comparisons and generalisations.

A number of sociological approaches to 'race' and ethnicity have concentrated on their relationship with other forms of social stratification. Those who take this position have continuingly argued that class and status often coincide with racial and ethnic inequalities. 'Race' and skin colour simply make minorities more visible and more vulnerable to economic and class exploitation. On the other hand, sociologists such as John Rex (1970) have long maintained that this fails to give recognition to the unique problems raised by 'race' and ethnicity. In fact, both can dissect class lines, although certain perceptions related to distinct ethnic groups are built into Western culture and appear to have no connection to class. Often these connotations are used to justify discrimination directed towards a specific 'race', including its supposed biological inferiority, while unequal power balances are likely to have negative consequences for the self-image of designated racial groups. Being working-class and of low status as a minority can make them perhaps the most underprivileged groups in society and complicate simple assumptions concerning experiences and opportunities throughout the life course.

The postmodernist enterprise, however, is one which is more concerned with seeking to deconstruct categories of 'race' and 'ethnicity', even to the point of playing down the more obvious aspects of social and economic inequalities. One growing emphasis has tended to be on ethnicity and identity, especially in relation to culture in the global context. In this respect, some commentators recognise that the process of globalisation both negates and enhances ethnic identity. Once, in the pre-modern world, ethnicity was a taken-for-granted component of identity associated with tribalism and regionalism. The increasing integration of economic processes and the growing interconnectedness of political practices, along with the emergence of a common global lifestyle rapidly mediated by electronic communication and personal mobility, has established what has been referred to as 'Cosmopolitania'. In other words, it is increasingly difficult for ethnic communities to retain a distinct culture and sense of identity, a challenge to which they may respond in various ways (Smith 1991).

The important point in terms of the life course, from a postmodernist approach, is that global culture is created through the increasing interconnectedness of varied local cultures, which are becoming subcultures within the wider whole. But to this global interrelated diversity people can respond in different ways. There are, according to Smith (1991), 'cosmopolitans', and there are 'locals'. The former are a plurality of cultures and include a positive stance towards diversity itself – an openness and search for contrasts. Others try to localise themselves. For example, ethnic minorities, taken away from their territorial base of local culture, might encapsulate themselves within a reproduction of it. Hence, there may be a greater sense of cohesion brought by the very threats presented by these tendencies – relativism and a search for identities of the past in a postmodern world where identity is associated with lifestyle and taste, and is therefore constantly shifting and malleable. From one perspective this may lead to a revalorisation of the past and the construct of mythological values and narratives.

The relevant sociological writings tend to insist that in postmodern Western societies, which are practically synonymous with pluralism, relativism and multi-ethnic communities, a search for cultural and moral certainties through embracing traditional values and other attributes of ethnic identity, such as religion, is increasingly complex. At the same time, responses to racism and discrimination on the one hand, and the forces of cultural assimilation on the other, make identity formation particularly problematic. Moreover, while an ethnic cultural foundationism is perhaps evident in the postmodern world, some expressions of ethnicity may result in something more contrived, inconsequential and somewhat more superficial. In this way, Waters (1995, 137) suggests, the search for tradition can contribute to the postmodern ambiance by mixing the symbolic content of the past and the present to the extent that everyday life becomes an 'historical and ethnic Disneyland'.

It is clear that postmodernist commentators, as with so many other themes, have developed different approaches to ethnicity. This should not be too surprising given that they are describing the emergence of a radically new social order which has profound global dimensions. As with the approach to gender issues, the growing body of literature still has a long way to go in forging a distinct postmodern approach to ethnicity, especially one which can comprehensively account for the continuation of inequalities and discrimination throughout the life course.

The reality is that very profound inequalities do exist between ethnic groupings, although the picture is increasingly complicated. To be sure, over the generations growing numbers of members in most ethnic communities have begun to filter through to the better-paid professional occupations in

Western societies. However, since the 1970s the most important change in the overall position of ethnic and racial minorities of people is, in the case of the UK, very high unemployment rates among Asians and West Indians. The Joseph Rowntree Foundation's (1995) study of poverty in the UK continued to pay testimony to the problems facing ethnic groups since it was 'particularly concerned … at what is happening to the non-white population'. The charity found that one in three of the non-white population was in the poorest fifth of the overall population. Most significant here were significant rates of unemployment (worst of all among people of Pakistani origin) and, above all, the plight of Afro-Caribbean single-parent families. There is also seemingly a gender dimension in that black women appear in all categories related to the feminisation of poverty, especially where they were single and elderly (Glendinning and Millar 1987).

Bringing such matters more up to date, Kockhar and Fry (2014) consider what they refer to as 'The Great Recession' of 2008, which was fuelled by the crises in the housing and financial markets, and how it universally negatively impacted on the net worth of US families. Even as the economic recovery began to repair asset prices, not all households have benefited alike and wealth inequality particularly widened along racial and ethnic lines. The wealth of white households was thirteen times the median wealth of black households in 2013, compared with eight times the wealth in 2010, according to a new Pew Research Center analysis of data from the Federal Reserve's Survey of Consumer Finances. Likewise, the wealth of white households is now more than ten times the wealth of Hispanic households, compared with nine times the wealth in 2010. Lower levels of wealth, income and numerous other factors associated with social inequality may impact the life course with an accumulative effect. For instance, a breakdown by 'race' and ethnicity in the USA reveals a marked disparity in life-expectancy between black Americans and whites, both males and females, born in 2010 with the former anticipated to live on average 75.1 years and the latter 78.7 (Health United States, Centers for Disease Control and Prevention National Center Statistic 2013).

SUMMARY

The discussion above has been wide-ranging, but necessarily so. Late/postmodern theorising would seem to reconceptualise the matter of inequalities for life chances and experiences. This is because the late/postmodernist reduction of the life course is radically different from earlier sociological accounts locked within the framework of modernity, where many social structures and attendant inequalities were deemed to forge a more predictable life course. Rather, the fresh emphasis is on consumption and lifestyles which are understood as dissecting old class lines. Indeed, class is being replaced by 'lifestyle differences' and all sorts of complex inequalities related to such themes as the body. At the same time, postmodernist feminist approaches seek to move away from the stereotyping of women and have stressed diversity such as ethnicity, which may cut across class – marking the life chances of women in some ethnic communities as the poorest. For such women the postmodern world may be one of potential and possible self-actualisation, but their experience of it is one of risk, restriction and disadvantage.

The significance of late/postmodernity in forging inequalities, then, is that in a society of choice and lifestyles, economic factors and status may enhance and hinder the realisation of those things which are regarded as culturally desirable. This may not only be in terms of consumer durables by which to forge meaningful and healthy lifestyles but also by way of making significant choices and exercising agency in respect of the different phases of life. Within the consumer culture that is practically synonymous with late/postmodernity, one tendency is the fragmentation and differentiation of markets. In its most extreme formulation this is seen as entailing the end of the significance of social class and the increase in the consumption of an endless series of signs and images which do not cohere and cannot be used to formulate a structured lifestyle and set of tastes throughout the life course. In a more moderate view, however, patterns of consumption, largely influenced by inequality of income and wealth, set up a homologous relationship between the consumer's identity, notions of self, the body and the product (Sawchurch 1995, 174). These patterns of consumption can impact on life experiences, status and material qualities from infancy to later life.

Culturally speaking, there is a link between late/postmodern society and the power and symbols of consumption which directly influence the different 'phases' of life. Mass marketing has been replaced by ever-more sophisticated techniques of market segmentation, in which consumer markets are identified and targeted. Thus, the commodification of such phases begins with childhood – often linked not to the product but the brand identity. While this may help reflect age groupings, it plausibly reinforces it by creating age identities. But at the same time such markets may blur age categories, for example, make-up for female children or the discussion of sex in magazines for young teens.

Simultaneously, contemporary society is bounded by risks. This ensures that the life course is not only prejudiced by degrees of opportunities for realisation but also risks and discontinuities which continue to undermine life experiences and life chances. This is a point emphasised by Beck (1992) in his account of the 'risk society', where he stresses that inequalities continue to exert a powerful hold over people's lives, but they increasingly do so at the level of individual experiences rather than the social group or community. Yet, those inequalities are deemed to be related to individual actions and responsibility rather than to structural factors like social class, gender or ethnicity.

Whether the late- or postmodern paradigms constitute a viable proposition and forge a realistic basis for understanding experiences and opportunities throughout the life course remains highly contentious given the very real evidence of socio-cultural inequalities and their enduring structural underpinnings. It might be argued, however, that some form of synthesis of conventional emphasis on structured inequalities and the emphasis on the cultural and economic contours of late/postmodernity is possible. For one thing, the world of consumption is not available to all in the same measure and thus becomes itself a major marker of inequality. This consumption pattern may lead to various ways of excluding people and limiting choice. Many people simply do not have sufficient money to purchase all the latest foods or holidays on offer and suffer economic exclusion, and thereby social exclusion, as a result. The task of Sociology in analysing the social experiences and opportunities in terms of consumption, choice and indeed risk is to gauge the significance of such social categories of age, gender, ethnic background and more besides throughout the 'phases' of the life course.

FURTHER READING

Arber, S. and Ginn, J. (eds.) (1995) *Connecting Gender and Ageing: A Sociological Approach*, Buckingham: University Press.

Bauman, Z. (1992) 'Is There a Postmodern Sociology?', *Theory, Culture and Society*, 5(2): 217–37.

Bennett, F. (2014) *Gender and Poverty in the UK: Inside the Household and Across the Life Course*, 6 July 2014, https://www.opendemocracy.net/5050/fran-bennett/gender-and-poverty-in-uk-inside-household-and-across-life-course, accessed 15 November 2014.

Blakie, A. (1999) *Ageing and Popular Culture*, Cambridge: Cambridge University Press.

Butler, J. (1990) *Gender Trouble: Feminism and the Subversion of Identity. Thinking Gender,* New York & London: Routledge.

Cohen, L. (2003) *Consumer's Republic,* New York: Knopf.

Craig, G., Atkin, K. and Chattoo, S. (eds.) (2012) *Understanding 'Race' and Ethnicity: Theory, History, Policy, Practice,* Oxford: Policy Press.

Day, G. (2001) *Class,* London: Routledge.

Eriksen, H. (2001) 'Ethnic Identity, National Identity and Intergroup Conflict: The Significance of Personal Experiences', in R. Ashmore, L. Jussim and D. Wilder (eds.), *Social Identity, Intergroup Conflict, and Conflict Reduction,* Oxford: Oxford University Press.

Featherstone, M. and Hepworth, M. (1991) 'The Mask of Ageing and the Postmodern Life Course', in M. Featherstone, M. Hepworth, and B. Turner (eds.), *The Body Process and Cultural Theory,* London: Sage.

Fraser, N. and Nicolson, L. (1985) 'Social Criticism Without Philosophy: An Encounter Between Feminism and Post-Modernism', in A. Ross (ed.), *Universal Abandon? The Politics of Postmodernism,* Minneapolis, MN: University of Minneapolis Press.

Friedan, B. (1993) *The Foundation of Age,* New York: Simon & Schuster.

Healey, J. and E. O'Brien. (2014) *Race, Ethnicity, Gender, and Class: The Sociology of Group Conflict and Change,* London: Sage Publications.

Hockey J. and James, A. (1993) *Growing Up and Growing Old: Ageing and Dependency in the Life Course,* London: Sage.

Kellner, D. (1988) 'Postmodernism as Social Theory: Some Challenges and Problems', *Theory and Society,* 4(1): 239–69.

Mahony, P. and Zmroczek, C. (1997) *Class Matters: 'Working-Class' Women's Perspectives on Social Class,* London: Taylor & Francis.

Pilcher, J. (1995) *Age and Generation in Modern Britain,* Oxford: Oxford University Press.

Wood, J. (2005) *Gendered Lives,* Belmont, CA: Wadsworth/Thomson Learning.

Zmroczek, C. and Mahony, P. (eds.) (1999) *Women and Social Class: International Feminist Perspectives,* London: UCL Press.

Chapter 4

Reproduction, pregnancy and childbirth

This and the following two chapters will focus on the early phases of life: conception, infancy and childhood. In doing so, they will engage with a number of theoretical themes developed in earlier chapters. The next chapter will consider contemporary infanthood, excavating a number of topics related to what is often presumed to be an important marker of adulthood, namely parenthood – a topic followed through in Chapter 6, which takes childhood as its subject matter. In this chapter, the spotlight will be directed towards the very beginnings of life. The discussion below will detail various topics, including the complexities connected to reproduction and the medicalisation of conception, pregnancy and childbirth, and considers a number of crucial issues which currently surround them.

It is perhaps no exaggeration to suggest that core facets of early life have undergone considerable transmogrification in the contemporary Western setting. Such transformations have generated numerous political and public discourses which have problematised the first phase of the life course – partly as a result of medicalising influences and partly because of the way that economic and technological changes have impacted late/postmodernity and the transition to adulthood. Collectively, these dynamics seemingly undermine long accepted social norms and conventions around the beginning of life, while the growing cultural ethic of parental choice and lifestyle preferences have also complicated the picture.

Although this chapter is concerned primarily with recent developments in Western society, scope is also given to historical and cross-cultural perspectives, which will provide a comparative means of exploring the social construct of the commencement of the life course and their implications for early parenthood. The discussion below will also excavate the impact of social inequalities on the onset of life. In this respect, it will become evident that while many fresh changes are wrought in last/postmodernity, underpinning aspects of inequality remain, even if their expressions have in some instances undergone a reconfiguration.

REPRODUCTION: THE FEMALE BODY

The beginning of human life is frequently assumed to be conception, followed by maturity in the womb and finally birth into the physical world. In various ways human societies have dominion over these biological processes as they do with other phases of life, whether through the rites of passage associated with pregnancy more commonly identified with pre-industrial societies, or the near hegemony over the childbirth process exercised by the medical profession. Here is recognition that every society is concerned with the human reproductive capacity and, as seen again in a number of subsequent chapters, the related areas of sexuality, parenting and systems of morality associated with them.

Motherhood, commencing with pregnancy, is interpreted in feminist writings as a biological process that has been subject to social and ideological constructs, especially around the female body. Habitually identified are cultural notions of incapacitation which infer that biology limits women's social functions throughout pregnancy and care of the infant, whereas, in the words of Ann Oakley, 'reproduction is not a handicap, but an achievement of women' (Oakley 1980, 49). It is feminist approaches which most of all bring an appreciation that experience of being a mother is largely dictated by a variety of social institutions and pressures, and is often influenced by the parenting the woman herself received, whereby engendered perceptions of motherhood are passed down through the generations. This maternal (and indeed paternal) experience of parenting, however, as examined in the subsequent chapter, has observably become more complex and contested in the contemporary world. Even before conception, however, there is evidence of patriarchal control of the female reproductive system, and this is clear in taboos surrounding menstruation.

Historical examples abound in some number. For instance, among the Sioux indigenous tribe of North America a number of prohibitions surrounding female menstruation were once evident. At the time of her monthly period a woman was believed to be 'unclean' and in a state of taboo. She was thus expected to observe a number of ritual practices and be detached from contact with the wider community – dispatched to separate communal lodges where women were brought sustenance and were otherwise 'cared' for by female friends. There they remained until menstruation ceased. This segregation occurred because Sioux men believed that their food, sacred objects and war paraphernalia were subject to contamination if touched by a menstruating woman. Accompanying this set of superstitious taboos prevailed the belief that partaking of intercourse with a woman up to four days before a religious ceremony or conducting warfare could be detrimental to future outcomes.

Various explanations as to why women are regarded as being in a state of taboo at the time of menstruation have been advanced, the most celebrated perhaps being that forwarded by Mary Douglas (1966). Douglas interpreted the widespread regulations relating to menstruation and menstrual blood as often essentially manipulative devices by which men dominate and control women. By the use of religious taboos the former are able to assert an ideology of male superiority by contrasting females as unclean and polluting, as opposed to male purity. This entails the designation of separate male and female social spheres, which exclude women from male areas of life in order to control strategic resources such as food and tools, and to blame women for sickness and misfortune caused by breach of taboo regulations, possibly extracting compensation for them.

It might be suggested that the contemporary perception of female menstruation is liberated from aspects of wider social restraints and patriarchy. However, Chapter 10 will consider how the medical world has rendered problematic the end of menstruation (menopause) and perceived and treated it as part of the 'crisis' of a woman's mid-life experience and transition. There is more to consider, nonetheless, in that monthly periods can also be understood today to be problematic as a result of medical and commercial pressures. The Society for Menstrual Cycle Research (2012) (which includes academics, health practitioners and activists and policy makers) has shown how a woman's period has become medicalised and even commodified – what the research grouping refer to as 'selling sickness'. Here, bio-medical 'treatment' of menstruation becomes a form of social control and regulation of women's bodies, which has enhanced the stigma associated with a natural process. Pharmaceutical products concerned with female hygiene have proliferated and can be comprehended as part of a 'body-technology project'. This leads to menstruation being regarded as an 'inconvenience', 'disorder' and 'sickness' which undermines sex appeal, personal autonomy and lifestyle choices.

The emphasis on choice would seem to be more liberating in respect of the female's control of her own reproductive system. Nevertheless, a number of feminist commentaries stress that choice is not without its perils. A common-sense view is that medical and scientific advances have allowed women to limit their fertility and, by making childbirth safer, furnished them with more freedom in influencing their own natural processes and an important life event. Yet the shortcomings include, first, the contraceptive pill and the intra uterine device (IUD) – heralded in the 1960s as instruments of women's liberation – which have been found to carry significant health risks and a range of unwanted side-effects. Second, the technical possibility of fertility control coexists with cultural ideas – albeit now rigorously challenged – concerning motherhood: the belief that motherhood is the natural, desired and ultimate goal of all 'normal' women, and that there is something dysfunctional with women who deny their so-called maternal instincts.

PREGNANCY AND CHILDBIRTH

Whether or not maternal instincts are somehow 'natural', pregnancy and birth have historically proved to be precarious and uncertain life events. This is in stark contrast to expectations in Western society, where infant mortality during the early stages after birth is extremely low. Potential danger to mother and child in pre-industrial societies means that these natural processes are circumscribed forms of social control and are structured by religious beliefs and rites of passage which are assumed to provide supernatural help for both mother and child. Fruzzetti's account (1982) of Islamic rituals in Bengali culture provides a suitable example of how particular rites seek supernatural assistance but at the same time display patriarchal overtones. Following birth, the mother and child are secluded for a period from family and friends – a time related to beliefs bound up with impurity and where boundaries become paramount. Although such social exclusion for the mother may seem curious to Westerners, it is not dissimilar from the now largely superfluous tradition known as 'Churching', whereby the new mother was not permitted to rejoin her church congregation for a month after giving birth on the grounds that she was in a defiled state.

Social control of the female reproductive system is by no means limited to pre-industrial societies. In 1975, Ivan Illich published his influential critique of modern medicine and the medical profession. Illich attempted to show how the profession had increasingly come to control many areas of life, including its natural processes such as birth and death. Historical evidence suggests that, in the Western world at least, pregnancy and child-birth, except in some larger cities where very basic and unhealthy hospitals existed, was largely a female preserve, limited to the domestic field, up until the seventeenth century. Increasingly, the hospital became part of a male-dominated medical field. Over time the medical profession extended its hegemony to manage the process of childbirth and, in doing so, eclipsed the traditional and largely exclusive role of female midwives (Johanson et al. 2002). This medicalisation of childbirth is evident in the dramatic increase in the proportion of babies born in hospital (in 1900, almost all births in the USA occurred outside of the hospital setting; the proportion of out-of-hospital births fell to 44 per cent by 1940 and to 1 per cent by 1969, where it remained through the 1980s), alongside the proliferation of medical techniques for monitoring pregnancy, intervening in childbirth and for the care of new-born infants.

Many of the themes developed by Illich have subsequently been extended by other commentators. Control by the medical profession over mother-hood is now identified as so extensive that it has become a major feminist issue. Despite the increasing presence of women, the profession remains dominated by men, who have come to oversee the female natural process of childbirth as part of the wider cultural control of the female body. All this involves the use of a medical frame of reference to make sense of and shape expectations, experiences and aspects of risk during pregnancy and childbirth. A different approach is to consider male dominance through the professional–patient relationship, one which is essentially a power relation-ship hedged around by a dominant patriarchal discourse (Tew 1990). Other commentators, such as Duelli-Klein (1989), have considered the harmful effects on the self brought about by medical insemination, while Stanworth (1987) and Rowland (1993) have detailed the negative implications of emer-ging reproductive technologies.

One of the core issues which emerges for feminists is how women experi-encing a major life event and natural process of childbirth are reduced to 'patients' who are subject to routine medical intervention through labour-inducing drugs, spinal epidurals, foetal monitoring, episiotomies and surgical delivery in the case of approximately one-third of births (Finn 1998). The medicalisation of pregnancy is not limited to the birth process itself. Medical intervention in most cases occurs early through genetic testing, ultrasound screening, which attempt to negotiate symptoms and negate risks. The area of 'monitoring' has grown in significance and it is now routine to test a foetus for a range of genetic and other abnormalities. Ultrasound screening is a standard procedure for seeking out various morphological anomalies, while the Maternal Serum Alpha-Fetoprotein Test (MSAFP), which screens for trisomy chromosomal disorders such as Down Syndrome, does not even require formal informed consent from patients (Chervenak and McCullough 2006). The increasing control of the birth process has become so hegemonic that alternative options when considered, such as so-called natural childbirth, become regarded as unsuitable and even dangerous. This arguably negates the woman's autonomy, including choices when complications in pregnancy occur (Crossley 2007).

Healthism and pregnancy

Medicalisation intervention may be frequently less direct. Some aspects of pregnancy do not directly involve clinical interventions but entail self-monitoring by the pregnant woman, who is recommended to regulate eating and drinking patterns, avoid smoking and alcohol, avoid weight gain, follow exercise routines, adopt a suitable sleeping position, express emotions, avoid exposure to some basic household products, adopt certain sexual activities and bring many other aspects of their lives into harmony with the standards instituted by medical professionals (Kukla 2005). All of these recommendations and proscriptions may be understood as part of the growing cultural tendency towards 'healthism' – a negative neologism that expresses a range of ideological constructs related to health and medicine which cast problems of health and disease at the level of the individual, individual liability and the implications of choice in indulging in perceived unhealthy lifestyles (Crawford 1980).

The tendency to put increasing emphasis on women for responsibility for their own health and that of the foetus they carry during pregnancy, according to Armstrong (2003) and Golden (2006), has become the source of widespread social anxiety over such 'disorders' as Foetal Alcohol Syndrome. In such accounts these concerns are viewed as frequently deteriorating into a 'moral panic' over mothers engaging in what wider society imagines as self-indulgent or decadent lifestyles, rather than an evidence-based response to risk. Focusing on the consumption of alcohol or drugs as a particularly pernicious form of risk-taking, then, seems to have more to do with images and ideologies of maternal responsibilities and censuring deprived social groups than with reasoned concern for foetal well-being. Neither does this self-monitoring focus exclusively on expectant mothers. Health policies now consider the responsibilities of the expectant father. In the UK, for example, a National Health Service website, headed 'Pregnancy, Birth and Beyond for

Dads and Partners', suggests that 'basic health advice is just as important for you (the father) as it is for her'. This includes both prospecting parents embracing healthy eating habits and stopping smoking, and it recommends seeking support of ultrasound scans and additional tests.

The result of this self-monitoring is that women are expected to perceive their pregnancy as a high risk 'natural' occurrence which has nonetheless become pathologised on the one hand and, on the other, includes a reliance on medical 'expert' advice and self-responsibility in aiding the 'perfect birth' as part of a health trajectory. To this, as previously argued, has been added a commodification of the pregnancy process: the utilisation of technological interventions by the non-medical sphere, which includes the current expansion of 'boutique' foetal ultrasound centres that offer expectant parents 'pictures of the baby' (Chervenak and McCullough 2005). Consumption of such provisions has led to a vibrant competitive market, as exemplified by the website which allows the browsing of 'America's 100 Best Hospitals for Patient Experience' in satisfying the pregnant woman's choice of the best institutional setting for her perceived needs in terms of care and the application of medical technologies.

A number of critics point to standardised routines of technocratic childbirth as not only insensitive and unnecessary, but even counter to the woman's well-being. Anthropologist Robbie Davis-Floyd (2004) has suggested that the process is now practically void of meaning for the mother and the wider community. In the preface to her book, *Birth as an American Rite of Passage*, she stresses the positive dimensions of rites of passage – evident across cultures and throughout history – where humankind has transmitted cultural beliefs and values to the individuals participating in those rites. In non-Western cultures, specific rituals, often involving the entire community, accompany such life-changing events as birth, puberty and death. These rituals generally served to provide individuals in transition with a sense of the immense importance of birth for the group and of the place of the individual within that group. Although pregnancy and childbirth are life-changing events, in the technologically oriented society there appear to be few widespread humanistic rites of passage to initiate the new mother.

In considering the medicalisation of pregnancy and childbirth some commentators have also pulled attention to the profound ethical issues involved in respect of the foetus. A prevailing concern in obstetrical ethics relates to at what stage of development the foetus should be viewed as a patient in its own right. The area is crucial for the medical profession with their obligation to patients, not least of all in respect of legal consequences.

Chervenak and McCullough (1996) have drawn attention to how this also becomes a critical decision for the pregnant woman as well: whether or not to attach the status of patient to her unborn child and at which stage. The ethical dilemma does not stop there, however, since Chervenak and McCullough point out that once the foetus has the status of a patient, the medical doctor has an obligation to safeguard its well-being and balance its care with the health requirements of the pregnant woman.

When considering the evidence above, as the management of pregnancy and childbirth has passed into the control of the medical domain, many women may be left with a sense of being mere onlookers in the essential process of giving birth – reducing another sphere of power over their own lives. The need felt by some women to circumvent the medicalisation of motherhood has led some to opt for one variety or another of the 'natural' childbirth techniques that the medical profession is so sceptical of. This includes the Alexander Technique (releasing muscular tension to increase breathing capacity and restore the body's original poise and proper posture); the Bradley Method (which emphasises nutrition and exercise rather than medical drugs); hypnosis (conducive for a state of total relaxation and awareness); the Lamaze method (which uses distraction during contractions, such as deep breathing to decrease perceptions of pain and discomfort); and water delivery (for buoyancy to alleviate pain and pressure).

Each of these techniques is a burgeoning element of a commercialised market for 'alternative' childbirth and seemingly enhances the opening up of choices for mothers weighing up various risks involved in either the medicalisation of childbirth or the various 'alternatives' now on offer. The reality, however, is that out-of-hospital births are still fairly rare in the Western world, even though the percentage of such births increased from 1.26 per cent of births in 2011 to 1.36 per cent in 2012 in the USA, continuing an increase that began in 2004. While such a tendency will be likely to impact clinician training, resource allocation and health care costs, the risk profile of out-of-hospital births is measurably lower than for hospital births (MacDorman et al. 2014).

AGE OF CONCEPTION, BIRTH RATES AND MORTALITY AND CHILDLESSNESS

The cultural element of choice has seemingly liberated women in one respect: the decision *when* to have children or whether to have them at all. Nonetheless, of the nearly 16.5 million births to women who have married that occurred from 1983 through 1988 in the USA, approximately 5.8 million, or 35 per cent, were unintended. Of these, about 70 per cent were mistimed (ideally wanted at a later time). More recently, statistics from the 2015 National Survey of Family Growth in the USA reveal an apparent increase in unwanted births for the first time since the widespread acceptance of the most effective methods of contraception available in the mid-twentieth century.

Despite these perhaps unanticipated trends, the timing of first births has notably changed in the developed world. In the USA, for example, the average age of first-time mothers increased by 3.6 years, from 21.5 years in 1970 to 25.0 in 2006 (Ventura and Hamilton 2009). During the same period the proportion of first-time births to women aged 35 years and over increased nearly eight-fold. This trend is likely to impact the size, composition and future growth of the US population, as will similar trends elsewhere in the Western world on their own populations. At the same time, the conventional 'marker' of parenthood being linked to transition to an adult status is significantly delayed, with a higher proportion of people postponing parenthood to a later age.

One of the important elements of the broad 'nature versus nurture' debate of human behaviour is whether there exists anything which can be truly called the 'mothering instinct'. In short, whether nature tells a woman that it is time for her to reproduce and bring a child into the world and mother it or whether socialisation, in very subtle ways, puts pressures on her to contribute to the next generation upon which society relies for its survival. Whatever the answer to this debate, it is evident that in contemporary societies having children, and when to have them, is now more a matter of choice, and even lifestyle preference, than ever before. Couples are tending to postpone marriage (if they indeed decide to marry) and first births, and have sharply reduced the number of third and fourth births. There are some notable considerations here for fertility rates – or the natural capacity to produce children – in respect of family life and the wider population. These rates can impact on family dynamics by way of how many children there are per household or cohort size, as evident with the post-Second World War Baby Boom generation. As already noted in the previous chapter, how varying rates will impact generational relations and how significant this may prove to be with the current largely static birth rate at a time when the older population (60+) is increasing raises crucial issues of social policy.

Another observable trend is the increase in intentional childlessness. Between 2007 and 2011 the fertility rate in the USA declined some

9 per cent, with the Pew Research Centre reporting in 2010 that the birth rate was the lowest in US history, and childlessness rose across all racial and ethnic groups to about 1 in 5 compared to 1 in 10 in the 1970s (Sandler 2013). In the past, for both sexes, childlessness was viewed as a notable personal tragedy, involving much emotional pain and grief, especially when it resulted from a failure to conceive. Before conception was scientifically understood, childlessness frequently generated a woman's feelings of guilt and inadequacy in not performing what was understood as a social duty. In short, childlessness was stigmatised.

Evidence seems to imply that to a degree this traditional idea remains in North America, and giving birth signifies an important rite of passage into adulthood (Davis-Floyd 2004). Paradoxically, however, research suggests that marital happiness significantly declines after the first child is born and does not improve until after the last child has left the family home. In particular, employment outside the home and receiving less support from extended family, among other considerations, generate the degree of stress associated with raising children and decrease overall marital satisfaction as a consequence. Childless couples are more likely to take holiday leave, exercise and live a healthier life style in general than those that have children (Gilbert 2007).

The stigma of childlessness is apparently countered by the increasing tendency for many women to consider that children may not be their foremost life concern and are to be weighed up against career considerations. This means that the conventional mandate of motherhood, where it was essential and central to a woman's identity and adult status, has been challenged in recent decades. Now it is not a question of when to have children but whether to opt to have them at all. The number of women who have decided to remain childless has been growing, so that it is presently around 20 per cent of those born in the mid-twentieth century in the USA. The decision to refrain from having children is intrinsically tied to the freedom of women to control their reproductive system through contraception, with the pill remaining the most popular form – a quarter of all women aged between 16 and 49 take advantage of it.

The capability to produce children is at least partially connected with age and related biological factors. Fertility rates are impacted by couples in relationships deciding what years in the life course they wish to have children. While there may be various considerations, one factor is invariably a matter of lifestyle choice. A calculation by Henri Leridon (2004) suggests that by the age of 30 the percentage of women who will have a live birth without fertility drugs or in vitro fertilisation will be about 75 per cent; 66 per cent will have a conception ending in a live birth within one year at age 35; 44 per cent at age 40. Evidence more than suggests that for a woman the risks involved in having children at a later stage of life increases. About 9 per cent of pregnancies for women aged 20 to 24 end in miscarriage. The risk rises to about 20 per cent at age 35 to 39, and more than 50 per cent by age 42. At age 25, a woman has approximately a 1-in-1250 chance of delivering a baby with Down Syndrome; at age 30, a 1-in-1000 chance; at age 35, a 1-in-400 chance; at age 40, a 1-in-100 chance; and at 45, a 1-in-30 chance.

Age is also a consideration in the fertility rate of men. In studies that control for female age, comparisons between men under 30 and men over 50 found relative decreases in pregnancy rates between 23 per cent and 38 per cent (Kidd et al. 2001). One explanation is that the sperm count declines with age – men aged 50–80 years produce sperm at an average rate of 75 per cent compared with men aged 20–50 years (Silber 1991). Research also indicates an increased risk of health problems for children of older fathers. For instance, children of men 40 or older are 5.75 times more likely than children of men under 30 to have an Autism Spectrum Disorder (Reichenberg et al. 2012). For both men and women aware of these dangers, calculating when to have children thus becomes an important element of risk in choosing to defer starting a family in favour of career, financial advantages and other lifestyle considerations.

Also informing the picture of birth rates is the matter of infant mortality, which is widely recognised as a measure of the health of any given society. In England the mortality rate of infants under one year old has fallen by three-quarters since 1960 and is now at its lowest ever level. However, according to a report by the UK Office of National Statistics (2013) infant mortality rates remain worse among disadvantaged groups and poor areas of the country, and they are intrinsically linked to levels of education, work, income and living environment. The report concluded that around one quarter of all deaths under the age of one would potentially be avoided if all births had the same level of risk as those women with the lowest level of deprivation.

ETHICAL ISSUES AND NEW REPRODUCTIVE TECHNOLOGY

Medical developments, especially in the context of the so-called new reproductive technologies, may arguably advance the safety and choice of pregnant women and partners, but they are often perceived as offset by their perils. Certainly, in late/postmodernity many such emergent technologies have brought with them far-reaching ethical debates. Embryo research, sperm banks, ovary and egg donation, genetic selection, cloning, surrogacy and 'artificial wombs' are all issues which are now well established and will continue to generate controversy into the future. The key theme related to many of these issues is that, when it comes to manipulating life, what is technically possible may not always be ethically desirable.

A measure of concern has been raised in regard to the increasing routin-isation of prenatal testing, in that it may be tantamount to eugenics. As the term is paradigmatically used, eugenics involves an intentional, top-down planned social programme for engineering an entire population so as to eliminate perceived 'undesirable' traits. Some commentators have argued that as today's culture increasingly values and takes for granted the med-ical authority to control whether offspring have particular 'undesirable' traits, a form of 'hidden' eugenics is emerging and becoming normalised. Nonetheless, John Robertson (1996) typifies the defence of the right to pro-creative liberty inherent in prenatal testing against charges that it should be understood as ethically equivalent to eugenics by emphasising autonomous parental choices in controlling this technology.

Genetic selection procedures conducted either on foetuses, through pre-natal screening, or on embryos that are outside a woman's body, through Preimplantation Genetic Diagnosis (PGD), seek to discover the presence of genetic sequences linked to a variety of conditions and characteristics. A cell is extracted from an embryo at its eight-cell stage and analysed. Embryos with the selected characteristics can be implanted in a woman's uterus to develop. PGD was initially developed to allow couples at risk of passing on a serious genetic disease to have children not affected by it. Since its intro-duction in 1990, PGD has been most widely used to prevent the birth of children with conditions such as Down Syndrome, Tay-Sachs disease, cystic fibrosis, sickle cell condition, Huntington's chorea and Cooley's anaemia.

PGD is, however, increasingly being used for other reasons. These include sex selection, creating 'saviour siblings' who can provide bone marrow or other transplant tissues to sick older siblings, and selecting against embryos with genes correlated with late-onset and non-fatal condi-tions. Some clinics have even offered the technique for purely cosmetic traits including eye colour, hair colour and skin complexion. A newer variation of PGD, called Preimplantation Genetic Haplotyping, allows for numerous more genes to be tested, and for greater accuracy. Many disability rights advocates, in particular, have been critical of PGD and prenatal screening, arguing that the definition of 'disease' or 'disability' is to some extent subjective. Most such advocates support a women's right to decide whether or not to have a child at a given time, but are critical of basing this decision on the traits of the particular embryo or foetus.

A variety of ethical concerns have also been raised with respect to how prenatal testing may impact future children. Some commentators are concerned that prenatal testing helps to inculcate an inappropriate stance towards parenting: perhaps encouraging parents who wish for 'designer children' built to their 'specifications'; this may translate into an overly controlling attitude towards their children later in their lives or that children will match an advance set of idealised expectations as to how they will develop (Rothschild 2005).

Also attracting ethical concerns is the process of assisted conception, a method for couples who cannot conceive naturally, which entails one of two procedures: the utilisation of drugs to induce ovulation in women by intra-uterine insemination (IUI), as well as the attempt to stimulate female egg production; or in vitro fertilisation (IF); and other treatments such as intra cytoplasmic sperm injection (ICSI) and egg donation. These procedures are not without their risks. This includes those associated with drugs used to stimulate egg production; surgical risks associated with egg removal during IVF, ICSI and egg donation; and those linked to producing an abnormal foetus following several of these treatments. There is also the possibility that an undesired multiple pregnancy may result from the use of drugs, IVF/ICSI or egg donation.

For those couples who experience problems in conceiving there is the opportunity in many countries for them to opt for fertility treatment, with artificial insemination as a common option. This choice, in a globalised world, has led to the development which has come to be known as 'fertility tourism' in the case of legal prohibitions or regulation in the prospecting parents' country of origin. Sperm may also be exported as part of a commercial concern, leading to a further commodification of the reproductive system and opening debates about what could be understood as another form of eugenics. For example, Denmark has a well-developed system of sperm export, where the father might be either anonymous or non-anonymous to the receiving couple. This success mainly derives from the reputation of Danish sperm donors for being of 'high quality' and, in line with 'baby design' preferences, Nordic sperm donors tend to be tall, with rarer features like blond hair or different colour eyes and a light complexion. Debatably, this amounts merely to a form of eugenics generated by the choice of prospecting parents.

Coping with childlessness has led to emerging controversy in regard to anonymous sperm donors. Hitherto, men who have donated sperm for childless couples have enjoyed the legal right to be anonymous. However, a generation of children is growing up who wish to know who their biological fathers are. In Holland and Sweden they now have that opportunity. Other Western countries are debating the issue. The discourse related to this particular debate is surrounded by the issue of 'rights'. Children demanding information as to who their fathers are may speak of the 'right to know'. The fathers who donated their sperm have frequently argued for the 'right to privacy'. The biological mother and her infertile husband may have different thoughts on the issue.

Adoption and surrogacy

Adoption is a process whereby a person or couple (sexual minority adoption is considered in the following chapter) take responsibility for the parenting role of a child from its biological or natural parents. It generally entails the permanent transfer of all rights and responsibilities for the child. In most cases this involves a legal arrangement. One reason for adoption is to satisfy the requirements of childless parents (estimated at between 11–24 per cent in the USA). Childlessness is at least partially an explanation for the recent development of 'international adoption', which involves the placing of a child for adoption outside that child's country of birth. The laws of different countries vary in their willingness to allow adoptions by parents residing in other countries. Recognition of the difficulties and challenges associated with international adoption, in an effort to protect those involved from the corruption and exploitation which sometimes accompanies it, led to the rulings of the 1995 international Hague Adoption Convention.

Box 4.1 Adoption in the UK

- There were 69,540 'looked after' children in the UK in 2015
- The majority of 'looked after' children (61%) are looked after by the state due to abuse or neglect.
- The majority of children (73%) are from a White British background.
- 52,050 (75%) were in a foster placement.
- 5% of the children looked after were under the age of 1.
- 53% (2800) of children adopted during the year ending 31 March 2015 were boys and 47% (2530) were girls.

Source: adapted from 'Adoption Facts and Figures', AdoptionUK, 2015

Another controversial issue is that surrounding 'surrogacy'. Surrogacy refers to artificial insemination with sperm donation via IUI or IVF for the purpose of carrying a pregnancy for intentional parents who are genetically unrelated to the foetus. It may be carried out for heterosexual couples who cannot have a child of their own or gay couples who wish to take advantage of the procedure. Various ethical issues have been raised with regard to this process, which include matters of financial abuse and questions including: to what extent is it right for a woman to make contracts regarding the use of their bodies? What is the relationship between surrogate and genetic motherhood? Should a child born via surrogacy have the right to know the identity of any/all of the people involved in that child's conception and delivery?

Different countries have contrasting policies regarding surrogacy and they are often very complex and frequently related to issues of 'rights'. In the UK, for instance, surrogates are the legal mother of any child they carry even if not genetically related, unless they sign a parental order after they give birth transferring their rights to the intended parents. Informal surrogacy contracts are not enforced by law, even if a contract has been signed with the intended parents and a payment exchanged. The child's legal father or 'second parent' is the surrogate's husband or civil partner unless legal rights are given to someone else through a parental order or adoption, or the surrogate's husband or civil partner did not give their permission to their wife or partner. If a surrogate has no partner, or they are unmarried and not in a civil partnership, the child will have no legal father or second parent unless the partner actively consents. By contrast, although under review in respect of commercial exploitation, law in Russia permits the issuing of birth certificates in the baby's intended parent's names.

Laboratory fertilisation to surrogate motherhood seemingly creates, in some instances, problems with traditional definitions of the family. In this instance, the question might be asked: who is the real mother? In 1991, Arlette Schweitzer, a 42-year-old woman in the USA, became the first woman on record to give birth to her own grandchildren (in this case, twins). Because her daughter was unable to see a pregnancy to full term, Schweitzer agreed to have her daughter's fertilised embryos surgically implanted in her own womb. While this case illustrates how new reproductive technologies have created fresh choices for women, in the eyes of critics it further provides evidence of the undermining of the conventional family as a core social institution.

Contraception and abortion

Contraception has also brought profound social consequences and raised ethical issues other than those already considered. The family has, in various respects, been radically re-shaped by the choices offered by contraception. One repercussion is that the average number of children per family is declining and now stands at 1.8 in the UK and is falling. This includes those children adopted – the rate of which has also fallen sharply, for example, 6000 adoptions in England and Wales in 1994 compared with 21,000 in 1971. The rapid decline in the birth rate, as noted above in the case of the USA, and consequently a trend towards smaller families, was a pattern initially chosen by professional and middle-class couples, but followed later by manual occupational groups.

Rising consumerist and career aspirations, declining infant mortality and, more recently, the widespread use of contraceptives, encourage and enable parents to opt for a smaller number of children by means of fewer pregnancies. The proportion of couples having seven or more children during the second half of the nineteenth century was 43 per cent for marriages contracted in 1925. This proportion has now fallen to some 2 per cent. In terms of broader demographic trends there will be significant implications. In 1901 34.6 percent of the population in the UK was under 16; in 1981 22.3 percent was under this age.

Abortion refers to the voluntary termination of a pregnancy, resulting in the loss of life of the foetus or embryo. The legalisation of abortion on request is endorsed in legislation in the great majority of developed societies but with certain restrictions. For example, in the UK the Abortion Act 1967 covers England, Scotland and Wales (but not Northern Ireland, a more religious society by various indexes, where performing an abortion is an offence except in specific cases such as for the purpose of preserving the life of the mother). Under UK law outside of Northern Ireland, an abortion can usually only be carried out during the first 24 weeks of pregnancy (with the recommendation that it is performed as early in the pregnancy as possible, usually before 12 weeks and ideally before 9 weeks, where credible) as long as certain criteria are met: abortions must be carried out in a hospital or a specialist licensed clinic; and two doctors must agree that an abortion would cause less damage to a woman's physical or mental health than continuing with the pregnancy. There are also a number of rarer situations when the law states an abortion may be carried out after 24 weeks. These include: to prevent grave permanent injury to the physical or mental health of the pregnant woman, and if there is substantial risk that the child would be born with serious physical or mental disabilities.

Statistics in the USA (by Alan Guttmacher Institute 2012) reveal that about four in ten of unintended pregnancies end in abortion. Nearly three in ten women will opt for an abortion by the age of 45 (the overall US unintended pregnancy rate increased slightly between 1994 and 2008, but unintended pregnancy increased 55 per cent among poor women, while decreasing 24 per cent among higher-income women). Overall, however, the abortion rate decreased by 8 per cent between 2000 and 2008. Some 1.06 million abortions were performed in 2011, down from 1.21 million abortions in 2008, a decline of 13 per cent. Nine in ten abortions occur in the first 12 weeks of pregnancy. A broad cross section of US women undertakes abortions: 58 per cent are in their 20s; 61 per cent have one or more children; 56 per cent are unmarried and not cohabiting; and 69 per cent are economically disadvantaged.

Controversies relate to lower age categories. In 2010, the abortion rate of teenage women in the USA was 14.7 per 1000 women. This was 44 per cent lower than the peak rate of 61.8 in 1988 when abortion was legalised, thus registering a long term decline. From 1986 to 2010 the proportion of teenage pregnancies ending in abortion dropped from 46 per cent to 30 per cent. However, marked differences in rates between ethnic groups remain. The abortion rate for women per 1000 was 8.5 among whites, Hispanics registered 15.3 and blacks 35.3. All of these statistics, nonetheless, indicate a decline among the major ethnic constituencies.

Abortion is clearly a controversial and emotionally charged issue and perhaps *the* quintessential bioethics topic, with 'pro-life' and 'pro-choice' abortion camps, the former stressing the value of an unborn human being and the latter emphasising the choice of the mother in making choices in respect to her own body. Conflict between 'pro-life' and 'pro-choice' factions remains emotionally charged and often highly contentious, involving political, medical and financial interests, religious and philosophical beliefs. They have in this way contributed to what has come to be dubbed in the USA as the 'culture wars' – a conflict between those values considered traditional or conservative and those understood to be progressive or liberal over a number of concerns, particularly so-called family issues, which also include divorce, sex before marriage and homosexuality. These issues, as David Lyon suggests (2000, 47), can also be understood as elements of 'body politics' – generated by postmodernity with its technological advances in intervening and altering the body and attempts to perfect it in terms of identity and lifestyle preferences.

Arguments on both sides, perhaps predictably, tend to be couched in terms of 'rights', although the issues are far more complex. Those who believe abortion is morally wrong use arguments focusing on the destruction of 'innocent' human beings and the rights of the unborn; that the foetus is a unique potential person with a distinctive genetic code and with all of the life opportunities enjoyed by others (hence the appeal to the rights of the 'unborn baby'); that abortion entails pain and suffering; that it leads generally to a lack of respect for life; and that it contravenes divine moral principles.

Those arguing for abortion tend to stress that the foetus is not yet a human being and only when it has reached a particular stage of development is it possible to describe it as a moral 'person' with inherent rights. Moreover, that it is not always wrong to end the life of an innocent person – there are always good moral reasons for doing so (for example, in the case of conjoined twins, where the operation to separate them may cause one twin to die). Furthermore, it is contended that under some circumstances these moral considerations override the foetus' right to live, including the right to ownership of the woman's own body, which may become acute in cases of rape; and the right to decide her own future, particularly at a time of economic hardship, where a child might be subject to a life of poverty and disability. Among pro-choice advocates, sexual-equality discourses often involve the additional debate regarding to what degree the potential father should have a choice in deciding whether or not to abort the developing foetus.

Births outside of marriage and teenage pregnancies

After steadily rising for five decades in many Western countries, the share of children born to unmarried women, despite common assumptions, has in fact declined. Once largely associated with stigmatised poorer women and some ethnic minorities, motherhood without marriage is now more socially acceptable. The fastest growth in the last two decades in the USA has occurred among white women in their 20s who have some college education, according to government data. Among mothers of all ages, a majority – 59 per cent in 2009 – are married when they have children. But the surge of births outside marriage among younger women – nearly two-thirds of children in the USA are born to mothers under 30 – is symbolic of both the transforming nature of the family and emerging generational change.

When these trends are considered, alongside those that indicate that some women are having children later in life, it is clear that the years of mother-hood are extending and becoming more flexible. Identifying such trends, however, is not without its difficulties. The problem of presenting data related to what was once dubbed 'illegitimacy' in this way is that it tends to be rather misleading given that high rates of births out of wedlock are not new. Historical evidence shows that in a not untypical village in England between 1870 and 1880 some 80 per cent of all the children dwelling there were illegitimate. It was not until the first half of the twentieth century that the rate of illegitimacy declined considerably.

Despite such apparent historical fluctuations, it has become one of Western governments' major concerns to find a way to reduce the number of teenage pregnancies (defined as occurring between 13 and 19 years of age; hence the term 'adolescent pregnancy', which describes the emotional and biological developmental stage often referred to as adolescence), given that it is perceived as personally and socially undesirable (Holgate et al. 2006). Much government emphasis is currently placed on encouraging this age group to learn and understand aspects of sexual relationships, espe-cially through sex education in schools. Yet, it is feared by critics that such a strategy merely encourages young people to indulge in sex by portraying it as the norm for teenagers. The other side of the debate is the belief that young people will already be aware of sex, and this is a principal way to help them participate safely in matters of choice as future consenting adults, as well as encouraging sexual activity to become less of a taboo subject for discussion. Moreover, critics suggest that the core issue is not about sexual activity per se, but more about the consequences in terms of the cost to the welfare state, alongside the alleged problems facing immature teenage single mothers in bringing up children.

The reality is that while such pregnancies generate concern, only about 5 per cent of single mothers are teenagers. Furthermore, the general impres-sion is that teenage pregnancies are a relatively new development and are products of an increasingly 'permissive' society. However, the evidence suggests otherwise. Childbirth to teenage mothers in the USA peaked in the mid-1950s at approximately 100 births per 1000 teenage girls. In 2010, the rate of live births to teenage mothers in the USA dropped to a low of 34 births per 1000. This was the lowest rate of teenage births in the country since 1946. Among girls of 14 and younger, the rate of pregnancy is about 7 per 1000. Some 85 per cent of these pregnancies are unintended. Evidence points to a link with social class, poverty and variations between ethnic groups, with Hispanic and black women having higher (but declining) rates than whites. At the same time, teenage pregnancies were more common in the upper age group, with nearly 70 per cent found among 18–19-year-olds (Alan Guttmacher Institute 2010). Globally, the evidence implies that the more educational, occupational and economic opportunity available to teenage girls, the more likely they are to postpone pregnancy and childbirth (Cherry and Dillon 2009).

The link between deprivation and teenage pregnancies is, however, a complex one. For example, Harden et al. (2009) found that teenage pregnancies are not always unintended but are subject to reflexive choice based on three main reasons disclosed during interviews: dislike of school (where having babies was reported by young girls interviewed to be an alternative); poor material circumstances and unhappy childhood (including family conflict and breakdown – a factors also associated with young fathers, who additionally stated lack of suitable role models); and low expectations for the future (evidence by both young mothers and young fathers who believed that few opportunities were open to them apart from poorly paid, temporary work in jobs that they disliked). Harden et al. note that while programmes aim to promote engagement with school through learning support, ameliorating unhappy childhood through guidance and social support, and raise aspirations through career development and work experience, none of these approaches directly tackles all the societal, community and family level factors that influence young people's routes into early parenthood.

The stigma associated with teenage pregnancy seemingly remains, and this is additionally extended to teenage fathers. Jennifer Weber (2012) has shown how, in addition to negotiating the stigma often associated with teen pregnancy, teenage fathers also confront stereotypes that label them as self-indulgent and uncaring. In telling their stories, these fathers utilised various gendered discourses to deny responsibility for the pregnancy: the feminisation of birth control; a discourse of uncontrollable male sexual desire; and love. Aligning themselves with certain notions of masculinity seemingly serves as a resource for denying responsibility for the pregnancy while also signifying their manhood, but these same discourses are also constraining in that they reinforce stereotypes of teenage fathers as selfish, even predatory. While these approaches may allow such fathers to claim masculine identities, they also stigmatise them as the 'wrong kind' of men. In short, teenage fathers are not only negotiating the potential stigma of teen pregnancy, they are also negotiating their identities as men.

SUMMARY

This chapter has attempted to explore the earliest phase of life through a discussion of a multiplicity of recent trends – technological, cultural and economic – around the complexities connected to reproduction and the medicalisation of a significant life event: pregnancy and childbirth, and the ethical issues which have arisen from them that have engendered politicised and public debates and discourses. Clearly, there are various often contra-dictory but co-joining trajectories to be observed – medical hegemony, matters of choice and commodification and aspects of risk management. This chapter has also noted how structured inequalities and demographics work their way into the picture, including age, gender and ethnicity. There are clear overlaps in matters of human reproduction with those of contem-porary parenting and childhood. These themes are revisited in the next two chapters – themes which generate their own public discourses and contentions that arise essentially from profound socio-cultural changes.

FURTHER READING

Bonell, C. (2004) 'Why is Teenage Pregnancy Conceptualised as a Social problem? A Review of Quantitative Research from the USA and UK', *Culture, Health & Sexuality,* 6 (3):1–18.

Davis, D. (2001) *Genetic Dilemmas: Reproductive Technologies, Parental Choices, and Children's Futures,* New York: Oxford University Press.

DeVille, K. and Kopelman, L. (1998) 'Moral and Social Issues Regarding Pregnant Women Who Use and Abuse Drugs', *Obstetrics and Gynaecology Clinics of North America,* 25(1): 237–54.

Duden, B. (1993) *Disembodying Women: Perspectives on Pregnancy and the Unborn,* Cambridge, MA: Harvard University Press.

Ermisch, J. (2003) *'Does a 'Teen-birth' Have Longer-term Impacts on the Mother? Suggestive Evidence from the British Household Panel Survey,'* Institute for Social and Economic Research.

Jennings, P, and Kramer, W. (2013) 'A New Path to Grandparenthood: Parents of Sperm and Egg Donors', *Journal of Family Issues,* 34(10): 1295–1316.

Jones, G. and Bell, R. (2000) *Balancing Acts: Youth, Parenting and Public Policy,* York: York Publishing Services for Joseph Rowntree Foundation.

Lamb, M. (ed.) (1987) *The Father's Role: Cross-Cultural Perspectives,* Hillsdale, NJ: Erlbaum.

Leishman, J. and James M. (2007) *Pre-Teen and Teenage Pregnancy: A Twenty-First Century Reality,* Keswick, UK: M&K Update.

Morgan, K. (1998) 'Contested Bodies, Contested Knowledges', in S. Sherwin (ed.), *The Politics of Women's Health*, Philadelphia: Temple University Press.

Mullin, A. (2005) *Reconceiving Pregnancy and Childcare: Ethics, Experience, and Reproductive Labor*, New York: Cambridge University Press.

Office for National Statistics (2014) 'Teenage Conception Rates Highest in the Most Deprived Areas. Link between deprivation and teenage conception rates in England, www.ons.gov.uk/ons/rel/regional-trends/area-based-analysis/conceptions-deprivation-analysis-toolkit/conceptions-deprivation-measures--2009-11.html, accessed 12 August 2015.

Richardson, D. (1993) *Women, Mothering and Childrearing*, Basingstoke: Palgrave Macmillan.

Chapter 5

Infancy and parenting

This chapter focuses on the interrelated topics of parenting and infancy. It is probably true to say that few other aspects of the life course remain under such public scrutiny as parenting and concerns around the 'risks' that are understood to be entailed. A good number of the discourses around risk in this respect are connected with changes in the role of parenthood, which can be accounted for by many of the dynamics of choice and cultural change in adult relationships and the multitude of family structures associated with late/postmodernity. Some of the major observable changes that will be engaged with here include trends in parenting in developed societies, motherhood and fatherhood, child socialisation, single parent families and same-sex parenting. As in earlier chapters, there will be an element of historical and cross-cultural comparison in order to place the discernible transformations for parenting in perspective and to explore the extent to which parenting and infanthood are influenced by social constructs of what constitutes 'good parenting' and the conditions which problematise early phases of life.

INFANCY

The terms 'infant' and 'infancy' have no precise definitions, although national laws of many countries frequently stipulate a period often related to a state of 'being a minor' – typically from birth to one or two years old. The original word 'infant', however, is derived from the Latin word *infans* or 'unable to speak', suggesting that infancy is a formative period which lasts until the young child displays the rudimentary ability to communicate a language. Another definition of infancy is bound up with theoretical debates concerning human attachment and its vulnerability. In essence, this amounts to contentions around evolutionary theory stipulating that from an early age the child will go through a primal phase in which it seeks attachment to others or a particular person as part of a natural survival mechanism. This approach conjectures that the infant has an innate ability to make attachments, which develops approximately between the ages of six months to three years. In many of the relevant theories there is frequently the assertion that attachment has a wider social implication in that it develops over the time of the life course from a crucial relationship with one individual to an extending number of people and in such a way as to provide a marker of transition of personal maturity and stability.

The most well-known and contended version of this premise is that elucidated by John Bowlby (1969), whose 'attachment theory' focused on the implications of the failure of what he saw as a pre-programmed biological drive for attachment, especially at times when the infant experiences fear and insecurity – most importantly the presence of strangers. In Bowlby's human evolutionary theory, the infant is believed most likely to become attached to its mother, who is well placed to respond to its biological needs and provide care, thus establishing the grounding for exploring the world. It follows that lack of attachment is likely to result in negative consequences displayed through psychopathic tendencies and lack of affection and affinity with others. Bowlby argued that mothering should ideally not be delayed until the second year of the infant's life, with the risks related to lack of attachment extending to the age of five (Bowlby 1944). Moreover, he attempted to prove that interruption in this relationship over the first two years was likely to have dire long-term consequences and generate 'maternal deprivation'.

Bowlby's work formed the basis of additional studies, sometimes in the form of critiques. Michael Rutter (1972) suggested that there is a pool of individuals who infants might become attached to, including fathers, siblings and peers. Rutter saw these alternative relationships as having differing consequences, including dysfunctional psychological deficiencies for the infant, particularly the lack of intellectual stimulation and social interactions from which attachments are formed. Nevertheless, these consequences could be countered if adequate care was administered. Bowlby believed that 'children thrive better in bad homes than in good institutions'. Nonetheless, there proved to be little satisfactory evidence in support of this. Rutter (1979) points out, that many institutions in fact provide adequate and satisfactory care. Although deviant behaviour displayed by children in institutional care is above average for the population, it is demonstrably less than the deviancy of children from family homes in which they experience disturbances and distress.

Bowlby's work attracted further criticisms. If, as he conjectured, the mother was the most important care giver and figure of infant attachment, the infant required her constant attention, implying that her life should centre on the domestic sphere rather than the workplace. However, as explored in this chapter, historical and cultural studies point to a number of significant individuals who might be engaged with care giving. Thus, some commentators maintain that a constant association of adults can bestow satisfactory care and, in fact, provide a broader range of care provisions than the mother may be able to meet (van Ijzendoorn and Tavecchio 1987). Bowlby's work also seemed to have little scope for the nurturing and socialising role of the father – that an absent or emotionally detached father figure has detrimental effects on the male child in particular, with consequences for deviant behaviour in later life.

Finally, the picture of infant development painted by Bowlby is far broader, his critics have suggested, in that he adequately failed to raise questions related to aspects of infant socialisation, not least into socially proscribed gender roles from an early age. Moreover, Bowlby neglected to largely recognise that motherhood, and indeed parenting, child-raising practices and infant socialisation are social constructs, influenced by numerous factors – cultural, economic and political – that also inform the structure of the family in which the processes of attachment and infant development are largely located. It is these considerations with which the discussion will further engage.

PARENTING: ANTHROPOLOGICAL AND HISTORICAL APPROACHES

Early socialisation, as an integral part of child-raising, varies considerably historically and cross-culturally; the evidence from across the world clearly shows an infinite variety of possibilities. For instance, the anthropological studies by Bronislaw Malinowski (1954) at the beginning of the twentieth century provided comparative evidence which demonstrated that much of what was taken for granted in the West concerning specific age groups need not occur universally. Writing in the inter-war period, Malinowski described the life of Trobriand islanders (islands located off the eastern coast of New Guinea) – children and adolescents – as considerably less restrained than that of similarly aged Western contemporaries in terms of taking responsibility for their own activities and in sexual exploration. Furthermore, parental roles were considerably limited, while children were raised from the onset as part of a well-knitted community.

Even today childhood in many cultures is experienced in a very different way from that of Western society. In Haiti, for instance, children live in one of the poorest societies known. When they reach the age of about four years old they begin a life of hard labour, and unappreciated and unrelieved work. The parents' attitude towards their offspring is often severe or at the very least ambivalent. Contemporary childhood in rural Haiti is one where children may be fortunate enough to attend school; yet their way of life is much more akin to Medieval Europe than anything approaching contemporary Western culture.

Several authors have also enriched the appreciation of cultural variations in child-raising in Western societies of the past. Some social historians identify the changes occurring with the onset of modernity and changing cultural conditions. This is evident in the writings of De Mauss (1976), who identified transformations in parent–child relationships as part of the progress of industrialisation in Europe. In particular, De Mauss believed that changing concepts of childhood were linked to the evolution of the family. Six prevalent social attitudes were evident in Europe. First, up until the fourth century children were expendable, since families were large and infant mortality high. Second, until the thirteenth century abandonment was common and amounted to the handing over of the child to be raised by others. Here, children had no specific social status; they were 'unseen' and childhood constituted what was perceived as an irrational period of life. Third, until the eighteenth century there was an attitude of ambivalence, where the child began to enter the parent's emotional life.

The fourth stage, from the early eighteenth to the early nineteenth century there prevailed an 'intrusive' orientation when parents attempted to conquer the child's mind and will by shaping 'little adults' at a time that life-expectancy increased. Commencing with the middle-classes, children began to slowly enter social life, and the period of childhood became more clearly defined. Fifth, there emerged the period from the nineteenth to the early twentieth century, during which an increasing emphasis on socialisation was observable that constituted the attempt to raise socially acceptable human beings and foster infant obedience. The child was seen as a miniature and potential adult, although there was a greater separation of childhood and adulthood by the emergence of the 'adolescent stage', which indicated the growing establishment of a fairly demarcated life-cycle. Finally, from the early twentieth century there evolved, as noted above, the 'helping mode' that included awareness of the child's needs and a move towards 'permissive rearing', at least partly shaped by popular psychoanalytical literature.

Edward Shorter (1985) adds to this historical picture by considering parenting in the context of changing relationships in terms of the privacy of the nuclear family, the idealisation of romantic love between spouses, the priority of nurturance given by the mother and the more stringent boundary line between the family and the wider community as the family increasingly looked inwards. All these developments were products of modernity, as was a further development – the growth of the state and its proliferating concern with child welfare. Child welfare became a social issue from the late nineteenth century, with the initial concern mostly focused on physical welfare, commencing with legislation limiting child labour in factories which eventually transformed childhood from being a time of initiation in the workforce to a time of schooling.

In the early twentieth century there occurred considerable changes in beliefs about motherhood and the family, where women were judged on their child-raising competence through medical and psychological discourses. These changes helped forge a new ideology of childhood as a distinct period in its own right. Certainly, the mid-nineteenth century saw the evolution of a more romantic view of childhood, where the working child was seen as 'unnatural'. The state acknowledged the child as unique, helpless and vulnerable, rather than as a small adult or chattel of adults. Much was typified by the proliferation of state-run orphanages and legislation aim at protecting the child. In the UK, the first country to industrialise, the Factory Act of 1806 applied to orphaned apprenticeships and recognised the well-being of a class of young citizens and the state's responsibility towards them. This was accompanied by the growth of private charity organisations to facilitate the well-being of children and advance their education. In 1889, legislation was enacted in England and Wales protecting children against mistreatment, while in 1895 the Society for Prevention of Cruelty Against Children received its Royal Charter.

Parenthood and child socialisation

Prior to the end of the nineteenth century parenthood was scarcely recognised as a precise 'stage' on the life course, given that it largely constituted a lifelong 'career' compared to contemporary parenthood, where parents not unusually complete their child-raising functions with some one-third of their lives to go. The combination of relatively late marriage, short life expectancy and high fertility as a result of ineffective contraception rates before the twentieth century rarely permitted an 'empty nest' stage. In addition, marriage was frequently broken by the death of a spouse before the end of the child-raising period. Despite this stark comparison with contemporary parenting today, as seen in the previous chapter, there is now a growing diversity of the onset and ending of parenting ranging from a relatively high number of teenage parents to the postponement of parenting chosen by couples opting to commence a family in their 30s, 40s or even later. While a good number of teenage pregnancies may not be 'planned' in many instances, for many parents the operative word is 'choice' in the decision when to commence a family.

At least until relatively recently parenting has been culturally regarded as a marker of transition to adulthood maturity and a meaningful aspect of life. Equally, a division of labour between men and women conventionally ascribed the major responsibility for parenting to the latter. What may be understood as an engendered ideology has not always been aided in the past by the sociological enterprise. In this respect, much was exemplified by the work of Talcott Parsons (1959), who offered his theoretical contribution to understanding parenting and family responsibility in modernity. It was crucial, maintained Parsons, that the child's intrinsic 'natural' and frequently disruptive qualities should be quelled by effective socialisation. While, according to Parsons, socialisation into core cultural values of modernity could be inculcated on a daily basis as a 'normal' round of social life, the family was best suited to this role with its close and emotional environment, and this predominantly meant the nuclear family and the mature female role within it – an assumption which more than hinted at the biological bonding between mother and infant.

Parsons theoretical framework came to be heavily contested, not least of all by feminists, who regarded it as so much ideology and the family itself as a corrupting mechanism by which the patriarchal society was reproduced. In short, the family, through socialisation, subscribed childhood roles and gender structures that are far from 'natural'. Indeed, since the 1970s significant research indicated the preconceptions held by parents concerning their new-born children. An early study by Goldberg and Lewis (1972), for example, even examined parents' expectations of social roles before the child was born. Findings indicated that daughters were anticipated to be rated as 'softer' than sons, having finer features, expected to be physically smaller and to be more inattentive.

Other studies denoted that expectations around gender behaviour and roles were very likely to generate a self-fulfilling prophecy, whereby the socialisation of infants resulted in gender behaviour that is perceived as 'natural' (Rubin et al. 1974). Even in the contemporary Western setting the information that encircles the infant and which s/he internalises is initially derived from within the family arena through parent–child interactions, role modelling and everyday interaction via parental approval or disapproval of what is understood as suitable socially required behaviour (Santrock 1994). Evidence suggests that from infancy into early childhood, playing with dolls and engaging in domestic activities for girls, and playing with toy cars and participating in sports activities for boys, are all are deemed by parents to anticipate future gender roles (Etaugh and Liss 1992), with a consciousness of adult gender role divergence identified even in two-year-old infants (Cowan and Hoffman 1986). Such socialisation into gender roles appears to have long-lasting impact on the development of the child which endures into adulthood. A child's growing sense of self and identity results from the multitude of ideas, attitudes, behaviours and beliefs that s/he is continually exposed to. As children develop, these gender stereotypes become firmly entrenched and the stereotypes they observe in the domestic unit are reinforced by other elements in their environment – peer groups, kindergarten and schools – which are then continued throughout childhood and on into adolescence (Martin et al. 1990).

This may have detrimental consequences. For example, Gail Wyatt (1997) has shown how the sexual identity of black women, set down from the earliest stage of the life course, has forged negative self-images largely as a result of dominant ideologies of masculinities present to some measure in black culture. The consequences are manifested in later life with the women's sceptical attitudes towards relationships, marriage and sexuality. This type of evidence, however, is countered by additional research indicating that, in an era of choice of 'alternative' forms of child-raising, there is the scope for parents to choose to inculcate more egalitarian values regarding gender roles in their children. There is at least some verification that this stance has beneficial effects. Children socialised in this way have been found to display appreciable levels of self-esteem (Lundy and Rosenberg 1987), a coherent sense of identity (Orlofsky 1977), and are likely to be more understanding of partners in adult relationships (DeLucia 1987) in later years.

PARENTING IN CONTEMPORARY SETTINGS

The historical and cross-cultural evidence presented earlier indicates no single and universal pattern attached to any particular set of socially prescribed parental roles. Nonetheless, in the Western world today such

roles are seemingly negotiated and subject to numerous possible variations, to such an extent as not previously observed before. Partly this results
from the cultural motif of choice, but also marks a response to contrasting and sometimes the contradictory so-called expert advice on offer for
parents or prospective parents. Much of such advice involves a therapeutic-
psychological discourse that is the hallmark of contemporary society and
which plausibly constrains aspects of choice of parenting modes identified
with late/postmodernity.

Undoubtedly, the mixed response of women to motherhood is at least
partly impacted by the confusion surrounding 'expert' recommendation on
child welfare and the status of the child. In this context Wyness (2000)
examined a number of policy reforms and professional initiatives within
educational childcare and legal environments and noted profoundly competing viewpoints. Moral ambiguities now exist, along with debates around
child protection and the individualisation of schooling, childhood and citizenship. Wyness concludes that despite the impetus on protecting children
they are increasingly encouraged to be competitive and perceived as having
the capacity to take on social roles and responsibilities which suggest not so
much the terminal decline of childhood but its contested nature.

Selwyn (2000) similarly notes that there is no agreement on what constitutes 'expert advice', since one orthodoxy is quickly replaced by another.
Moreover, advice has impacted differentially throughout the population.
There exist various levels of acceptance, with ethnic and cultural differences
remaining in an increasingly pluralist environment. Within minority ethnic
communities significant alternatives exist to what may be perceived as white
middle-class forms of child-raising. For example, Jackson and Nesbitt's
(1993) survey of the Hindu population in the UK showed childhood experiences changing, but still informed by the distinctiveness of gender roles,
diet, religious ritual and other essential elements of cultural transmission of
a well-integrated community.

There is more to consider. Despite the volume of professional advice which
exists, the younger generation is frequently perceived as one that is over-
indulged, with negative consequences: that infants and children are spoilt
through mass consumerism and have little sense of social responsibility
instilled from an early age. This indulgence would seem to mark the impact
of the new-found affluence for many families by the beginning of the twenty-
first century. This is the theme developed by Dan Kindlon in *Too Much of
a Good Thing* (2001), which explores how many American parents tend to
indulge their children, especially in their demand for material satisfaction,

in a way that is in stark contrast to the discipline of previous generations. Kindlon found that half of American parents he surveyed stated they are less strict and more spoilt than they were as children.

The fact that many children are being socialised in a growing sense of affluence arguably prepares them to become consumers from an early age has been viewed as a major culprit responsible for over-indulgence. This is enforced, as David Marshall (2010) explores, by commercial advertising campaigns and branding which profoundly impact children and young people. Whether fashion, toys, food, branding or money – from TV adverts and the supermarket aisle to the internet and peer pressure –the growing presence of marketing forces directed at and influencing children as active consumers is evident.

These observable trends may create dilemmas for parents. In the UK, research by the Industrial Society (2001) indicated that parents increasingly displayed feelings of guilt about spoiling their children, and the lack of discipline was ultimately responsible for negative developments discernible among the younger generation, from lethargy to drug abuse. Yet, in turn, children may not see being lavished with material goods as wholly beneficial, since the survey found that 77 per cent of 11–16-year-olds believed that a 'good' parent is someone who gives love and affection rather than satisfying endless material needs. That acknowledged, in a web posting for *Psychology Today* Ann Smith (2011) lists a number of sources of guilt that parents reflect upon in hindsight, which, in turn, induce feelings of shame, worthlessness and a negative sense of self as a parent. These sources include not spending adequate time with the child; not being sufficiently affectionate; being too critical; striking the child; providing a poor role model; placing too much pressure on the child to succeed; not protecting the child; and the repercussions of opting for a divorce.

Clearly, the current debate around parenting is one which is informed by notions of choice, but restricted by feelings of inadequacy in bringing up a child, and at the same time circumscribed by the rhetoric of children's 'rights' and parental 'responsibility', as well as discourses related to the repercussions of discontinuity and risk throughout the life course. This generates a key question: is it parents who are best placed to decide how to bring up their children? For Zoe Williams (2014), this dilemma commences even before the baby is born and impacts on the life regimes of expectant parents. Williams suggests that parents have managed perfectly well for centuries before the advent of competing and often contradictory 'expert' advice and should ideally raise their children according to their own judgement.

Supplementing this debate is the conjecture that the nuclear family context is far from conducive for constructive child-raising. One argument is that the contemporary nuclear family is essentially dysfunctional, and this has resulted in its breakdown: it is claustrophobic, emotionally over-charged, and generates stress and conflict – problems exacerbated by the isolation of the family unit. From this perspective the family may be seen as limiting freedom, preventing self-actualisation and narrowly defining intimacy. This theme was explored in R.D. Laing's renowned work (1976), which epitomised influential critiques of the family in the mid-twentieth century. Laing believed that many of the problems of family life were linked to the tension of a child's early dependence on its parents and its eventual strivings towards independence. Parents were depicted by Laing as being highly ambivalent in encouraging the child's independence and the development of its individual identity.

In the early twenty-first century, debates began to rage over what came to be known as 'Paranoid Parenting', a term attributable to Frank Furedi (2001), who explored how parental fears have been stoked and families harmed as a consequence of a number of acute social concerns. This is evidenced by constant warnings that children are under threat and that it is the responsibility of parents to be constantly on their guard, where babysitters, schools, supermarkets, public parks and much else are perceived as posing a peril. Partially, this paranoia results from the ever-increasing insular and inward-looking nature of the nuclear family, which fears the 'other' and imagines dangers of the outside world. A culture of fear has thus led parents to restrict their children's independent outdoor activities. At the same time parents are continually informed by governments, charitable agencies, the media and so-called experts of the threats to children's health, safety, welfare and constant risk potentials. Furedi opines that the clearest symptoms of paranoid parenting are public concerns over child safety, which are frequently so highly charged that a single incident can generate a major public debate and demands for new regulations. For example, while the development of the internet has a remarkable potential to enhance children's lives by providing educational opportunities, it is widely seen as a pernicious danger which generates public discussion on how to protect young people from stumbling across 'adult' sites or fall foul of the machinations of paedophiles.

The actual or perceived threats to which Furedi alludes have become public and political issues that governments are expected to address as part of a wider agenda of child welfare and parental rights. Some policies would seem to be beneficial. This includes the instigation of statutory parental leave for a stipulated period after the birth of the child or adoption, which allows for maternity pay. More recently, in many Western nations these rights now extend to paternity leave and/or an arrangement in which parents' leave can be shared. However, there is a tendency for problems in society such as low achievement at schools, low self-esteem, drug-taking, obesity, crime and mental health difficulties to be viewed as crucial issues in which the state should intervene if parental deficiencies are perceived to be their underlying causes. The question which subsequently arises is essentially that of how much the state should be involved.

Critics of state initiatives around childcare frequently suggest that they negate parental responsibilities and generate an extension of the 'nanny state', and such measures are little more than a further attempt to usher in the social control of children in the endeavour to counter what are perceived as deficiencies in parenting, deemed responsible for a range of social ills. What remains true, however, is that governments in the Western world often endeavour to balance state intervention and parental rights with parental responsibilities. In the UK, for example, successive governments have stipulated that parents have the role to provide a home for the child; protect and maintain the child; discipline the child; choose and provide for the child's education; agree to the child's medical treatment; and look after the child's property (Gov.uk nd).

In many Western European countries such as the UK, government policy is often couched with reference to providing good-quality education and care in their earliest years for success at school and later in life in contributing to a society where opportunities are equal regardless of social background. This includes the aim to create affordable and easily accessible childcare for 'working families' and thus create more opportunities for parents who wish, or need, to work and raise children at the same time. In the UK, policies have been aimed at extending early learning places to two-year-olds through childminders helping schools in order to offer affordable after-school and holiday care. Such policies are clearly geared to the expectation that both parents are likely to be out to work.

The assumption is apparently well-founded. In the UK in 2008, according to a survey commissioned by uSwitch.com, merely 2.2 million parents were based at home, down on 2.8 million on 1993, with the remainder in some form of employment – the rising cost of living cited as the main reason for returning to work. There was indication also that the decision for both parents to work was driven by the desire for a greater level of consumer affluence. Nonetheless, the survey found that one-third of working parents thought their children would have a better quality of life if one stayed at home, and 7 in 10 parents would do this if money was no object.

MOTHERHOOD

As already noted, child-raising practices have long been impacted by so-called expert advice, and such advice has frequently been engendered with a particular focus on motherhood. The advice presented by the special-ised literature regarding child-raising practices has clearly changed consid-erably over the years, and sometimes what they have on offer has proved blatantly contradictory. This plausibly generates questions, especially for first-time mothers, of whether or not women are conforming to what experts believe are good mothering techniques. If women believe that motherhood is essentially biologically driven, they may do whatever they discern is best for their child and rely on what they possibly perceive as their 'material instinct'. However, over the decades there have been many competing ideas of motherhood supporting the evidence that it is, to some degree at least, socially constructed.

Cultural, medical, political and psychological factors all play a part in the analysis of motherhood, depending on which discourse is most favoured at any given time. For instance, John Watson's behaviourist psychology proved to be extremely influential in the first half of the twentieth century, advo-cating that children required strict discipline: rigid sleeping patterns, feed-ing and toilet schedules, which he maintained would build up the character of a child (Richardson 1993). Watson also suggested that women should become emotionally detached from their infants. For behaviourist theorists such as Watson the child would inevitably respond in a positive way, and, as a consequence, the 'balanced', mature adult would develop. This stringent regulation of the behaviour and natural drives of the young infant appeared to be very much in line with the virtues of self-discipline that were practic-ally synonymous with early twentieth-century modernity.

From the mid-twentieth century, there was a discernible move towards 'permissive' child-raising practices, and much of this reflected the work of psychoanalyst Benjamin Spock, who pioneered this approach. Spock suggested that mothers should indulge their children: feed them on demand and provide them with affection and attention whenever required. Above all, mothers were urged to follow their natural instincts, since they were the real experts regarding their own children. This liberal stance, in turn, reflected the emergence of the so-called permissive society, in which a range of traditional and cherished social and political institutions were challenged in favour of 'alternatives' and experimentation. Spock expressed concern about the use of nurseries by working mothers, stating that the environment produced within them was insufficient and superficial, and failed to be as caring as the infant's family. This idea was circulated at a time when women had gained some independence in their work outside of the home, and Spock had undoubtedly more sympathy for working mothers than John Bowlby later expressed.

Experiences of motherhood

For many women, motherhood has become a flexible phase in the life course, rather than a 'career' or fixed transition, and seemingly there is an increasing sense that women's identity is derived from employment outside of the home as much as motherhood. Arguably, this brings challenges to patriarchal control over fertility and sexuality, and marks an advance in overcoming an oppressed gender identity. The emphasis on a career outside of the family was initially most likely to be found among middle-class rather than working-class women. In more traditional working-class communities raising children and organising the home once provided the woman with the basis of her status, although, from the 1960s there were strong indications that this was slowly changing in line with the aspirations of middle-class women, especially when the former began to rejoin the employment sphere (Willmott and Young 1973). Thus working- and middle-class norms associated with mothering seemingly began to converge, reflecting changing experiences for both. As a result, by the end of the twentieth century more generalised sociological appraisals could be directed towards the 'average' mother, although important class differences remained.

Several sociological studies have examined experiences of contemporary motherhood, suggesting that different attitudes can still be discerned and at least partly attributed to the enduring significance of class. In her work *On Being a Mother* (1983), Boulton found that mothers display four basic contrasting experiences of parenting. First, there is the 'fulfilled' mother, where the woman expresses a strong sense of meaning and purpose, and enjoys the immediate situation of childcare. Second, 'alienation', where the experiences are reversed and there is a prevailing weak sense of meaning and purpose. Here, the woman is irritated by the immediate situation of childcare. Third, some mothers describe themselves as 'satisfied' – an intermediate category between these two poles. Here, the response is one of enjoyment, but the sense of meaning and purpose is weak. Finally, there was an alternative intermediate category, 'in conflict' – where the immediate reaction is one of irritation with the motherhood role but the sense of meaning and purpose remains strong.

Boulton discovered that roughly half the mothers in her survey enjoyed their new-adopted role of childcare; half were frustrated with it and found it difficult and stressful to resolve conflict between housework and childcare responsibilities. In contrast, a greater number of middle-class women felt that childcare monopolised their lives and made them feel a loss of individuality. In addition, Boulton considered the impact of the father's support and help on the mother's experience. In her sample only nine of the husbands gave 'extensive help', 18 'moderate help' and 23 (about half) 'minimal help'. Social class differences were discernible in that middle-class, rather than working-class, husbands were more likely to provide 'extensive help' and display more nurturing tendencies.

Today, the role of motherhood is often viewed as a source of personal fulfilment, identity and a principal dimension of the psychological development of a 'normal' woman. However, normative social constructions tend to be implied, rather than clearly defining what constitutes a 'good mother', and many assumptions are made that it is still the mother's responsibility to ensure her children 'turn out correct' (Phoenix et al. 1991). What remains true, however, is that giving birth to her first child is a significant 'life event' and may radically alter the woman's self-image and identity in what amounts to an important 'transition' of the life course.

Weaver and Usher (2008) found that in interviewing a small number of first-time mothers there are several main themes involved in this transition. The women felt that they had lost some control over their lives in the early stages of pregnancy and after the birth. The early changes in their self-image and the shift in focus from themselves to the needs of the foetus indicate that the transition may begin at a very early stage. The unfamiliar territory of pregnancy and early motherhood creates a need for many mothers to find a mentor or mentors to aid in guiding them through the transition and to 'normalise' their feelings and experiences. Finally, the women recognised that the act of child-bearing fundamentally transformed them and their partners from individuals or a couple into founding members of a new family. This transition nonetheless left the women with a sense of unmet needs for support at this critical time.

It might be concluded that there is little doubt that motherhood is now far more complicated a social role and life trajectory than ever before. Even though there is an increasing choice afforded in late/postmodernity as to whether a woman becomes a mother or not, for some becoming a mother continues to be regarded as a significant achievement and raising the child is the most important activity they can be involved with in terms of its development and socialisation. However, the departure away from the standard nuclear family, and the emergence of single and same-sex mothers, further substantiates that there is no one model of what good mothering amounts to.

Single-mothers

There were nearly 2 million lone parents with dependent children in the UK in 2011 (representing 26 per cent of all families with dependent children), compared with 1.7 million in 2001. Women accounted for 92 per cent of lone parents with dependent children according to YouGov research (2011). In 2011, 45 per cent of lone parents were aged 40 or over; and only 2 per cent of lone parents were aged under 20: the same percentage as ten years earlier. Fifty-one per cent of lone parents with dependent children had never been married: an increase from 42 per cent in 2001. One contributory factor to this, advanced by the report, was the increase in cohabiting couples, whose relationships are believed to be less stable than married couples – in 2001, 25 per cent of live births in England and Wales were to cohabiting women, which increased to 31 per cent by 2010. There are also differences in the marital status of male and female lone parents with dependent children; 35 per cent of male lone parents have never been married, compared with 52 per cent of female lone parents. Further, 7 per cent of male lone parents with dependent children are widowers, more than double the percentage of female lone parents.

There are a number of reasons advanced as to why the number of single-mothers is growing. Today, there is obviously less social pressure to embrace marriage, but possibly more so to become sexually active. Entering the job market has additionally bolstered women's income capacity to be single-mothers and due to state benefits this is becoming at least partially financially viable. Child benefit in many Western nations is payable to all mothers on behalf of children, which guarantees a mother's income, and means that they do not necessarily have to depend on the father of the child for financial assistance.

Noting such changes as early as the 1970s, Rapoport and Rapoport (1975) also saw the rise of single-parenthood as a symptom of increased choice and tolerance of diverse family forms in contemporary society. In this respect, single-parent families may be regarded as an important and now fairly well-established variant and are thus becoming accepted as a legitimate alternative to traditional family structures: a large number of single parents interpret their situation as ideal and actively choose it as an option rivalling dual parenthood. In contrast, Morgan (1986) conjectured that the proliferation in lone parenthood could partly be due to changing relations between men and women. Here, the important factors causing the rise include the expectations that both sexes have of marriage and the growing choice of women to develop a life for themselves outside of marriage and long-term relationships.

Despite the fact that there are an increasing number of women opting for single parenthood, there are clearly profound social anxieties which exist in regard to state benefits payment, child personal development and wider social consequences (Cherry and Dillon 2009; Evans and Thane 2012). A measure of contemporary research points to the conclusion that growing up in a lone-parent family may disadvantage children. Some studies, often informed by distinct ideological agendas, indicate a father and mother each make a distinctive contribution to a child's social development, suggesting that it is unrealistic to expect one parent alone to perform as constructive a role as two working together. For instance, evidence implies that children of lone-parent families fare worse in finding employment and are more criminally inclined than children from two-parent families (in the USA, they are also twice as likely to be imprisoned for a variety of crimes).

There would seem to be some evidence that the consequence of single parenthood is also reflected in terms of the educational performance of the child. In 2001, according to a study by the Institute for Social and Economic Research in the UK of more than 1000 children, those with two parents perform better at school than those from single-parent families. The gap between the exam achievements of children with single-parents and those from traditional family backgrounds is as wide as that between children from the poorest and wealthiest families. The report concluded that these differences ultimately translate into differences in earnings throughout the life course.

The 'problem' with single-parent families has particularly focused on the absence of the father. Sociologists such as Dennis and Erdos (1993) have even argued that in some geographical areas single-parent families are so widespread that a male generation has grown up without the discipline of a father figure. This they claimed amounted to a form of paternal deprivation which was largely responsible, besides a number of other forms of deviant behaviour, for urban riots in England during 1991. Similar conclusions were reached by the UK government after the widespread urban riots of 2011, which were blamed on the dysfunctional aspects of what is increasingly termed 'complicated families' that became almost synonymous with single parent families and the dysfunctional attributes frequently associated with them.

Whatever the merits of this conjecture, the greatest perceived 'problem' is seemingly a financial one. A UK government published paper (1993) indicated there did not appear to be a link between single-parent families and criminality; however, it is poverty, rather than the absence of a second parent, which is associated with young offenders. On average, according to some findings, children growing up in such families start out with disadvantages and end up with a lower educational achievement and lower incomes and face a greater chance of forming lone-parent families themselves (Popenoe 1988). Despite growing economic independence, lone parenthood apparently greatly increases the risk of poverty for some mothers, as it can limit the woman's ability to work and to further her education. Hence, lone-parents form a core of a perceived rising problem of child poverty in Europe.

By comparison, Cashmore (1985) has questioned the assumption that children brought up by one-parent families are significantly disadvantaged compared to those brought up by two parents by way of emotional and psychological support and in terms of overall levels of care. Researchers from NatCen Social Research (2014) enforced this view when they concluded that family composition has 'no significant effect' on the happiness of children. Rather, it is the quality of relationships at home which are most strongly linked to a child's well-being. Children raised by a single parent are no less happy than those living with two biological parents, one study has found. The results challenge the popular conception that children in two-parent families are more likely to be stable and content than those raised in 'broken' homes. Researchers compiling the report analysed data from the Millennium Cohort Study and examined children from three family types: those living with two biological parents; those living with a step-parent and a biological parent; and those with a single parent (Holmes and Kierman 2010). Of the children living with a lone parent, 36 per cent claimed they were happy 'all the time', while the remaining 64 per cent reported being happy 'sometimes or never'. Exactly the same percentages were recorded when the question was put to children from the other family types. The results were largely unchanged when other factors which could influence

---

Box 5.1 Single mothers USA

- There are 13.7 million single parents in the USA, and those parents are responsible for raising 22 million children.
- This number represents approximately 26% of children under 21 in the USA.
- Approximately 82.2% of custodial parents are mothers and 17.8% fathers
- Of the mothers who are custodial parents:
    - 44.2% are currently divorced or separated
    - 36.8% have never been married
    - 18% are married (in most cases, these numbers represent women who have remarried)
    - 1.1% were widowed
- Of the fathers who are custodial parents:
    - 53.5% are divorced or separated
    - 24.7% have never married
- 76% of custodial single mothers are employed (53.2% work full time, year round and 22.8% work part-time or part-year)
- 85.1% of custodial single fathers are employed
- In 2009, 14.3% of the total US population lived in poverty
- 30.4% of custodial single mothers and their children lived in poverty
- 18.8% of custodial single fathers and their children lived in poverty

Source: adapted from 'Custodial Mothers and Fathers and Their Child Support, 2009, U.S. Census Bureau

---

a child's well-being – such as their parents' social class or the affluence of the area in which they live – were taken into account. The question then is fundamentally about the quality of parenting, whether undertaken by one or two parents.

FATHERHOOD

It is more than significant that the topic of fatherhood had for so long escaped the sociological radar. Only relatively recently has it been established as a mainstream concern, unlike motherhood studies which are wide-ranging in their surveys. Fatherhood, then, was once perceived as more marginalised, reinforcing the idea that men's identity came largely from the public sphere of paid work. A number of issues brought the subject of fatherhood to the fore, not least public controversies over 'absent fathers', the related issue of single parent mothers and the implications for what came to be perceived as a range of social ills.

In sociological circles, works on the subject of fatherhood tended to be advanced by feminist perspectives. One focus was how the family and conventional fatherhood gave expression to dominance for heterosexual masculinities. Thus Dobash and Dobash (1980) highlighted the male expectation to be revered by their partners and children, especially in terms of the traditional roles they perform. Moreover, it was the link between masculinities and male aggression that could lay behind domestic violence.

More recently, the specialism of Fatherhood Studies has attracted a number of disciplines and approaches which include psychoanalysis of fatherhood as a 'normal' phase in male individual development and the question of how fathers draw on cultural patterns in their everyday fatherhood activities. According to Lewis and Lamb (2007) these approaches often converge on a number of key concerns: fatherhood and employment, relationships with their partners and the wider impact of social policy among them. In overviewing recent research, Lewis and Lamb found that surveys pointed to the growing diversity in fatherhood experiences, which may be impacted by such factors as age, contact with children, tensions between 'social' and 'biological' fatherhood, ethnicity and disability and other hindrances in performing the fatherhood role.

A good number of research surveys on fatherhood clearly point to historical change (La Rossa 1988). The traditional definition of fatherhood conformed to the social ideas and realities of the mid-twentieth century, with the exception of during the Second World War, when men were drafted into the armed forces and women temporarily assumed traditional masculine occupations in civil and defence undertakings. The time from the late 1930s up to the 1970s has sometimes been referred to as the period of the 'absent father', but in a difference sense from the way it was used by the end of the century, at least regarding his role in the conventional home environment during this period. The major image of the father in the typical appraisal was of the aloof, emotionally distant breadwinner, who within the domestic unit was thought of as reserved and firm, yet benevolent. Typically, a father was respected but emotionally remote. His interaction with his children was characterised as restricted to a brief interaction at bedtime, typically masculine work activities in the home at the weekend, Sunday outings and an annual summer two-week vacation, in a way that appeared to epitomise, and constituted, a period that is still nostalgically recalled as the 'golden age' of family life. Busfield and Paddon (1977) note the symbolic limited role of the father at the birth of a child at this time, while the extent to which fathers continued to remain peripheral within the household depended upon the way mothers coped with child-raising problems, especially in the early stages of childhood.

From the 1980s onwards, a father's role in the home was perceived to be undergoing change due to the economics of social mobility and equality of opportunity. There thus developed a culturally venerated egalitarian approach to parenting, with the father taking his fair share of domestic responsibilities. There also emerged the increasing influence of single fathers and househusbands, and an awareness and acceptance of men in nurturing roles. Some fathers, particularly middle-class men with established careers, were expected to relish the prospect of being more actively involved in parenting. This fresh perspective in fathering is frequently said to reflect the emergence of the 'New Man' – the sensitive, caring male who sought to escape the restrictive and dominating traditional masculine roles – and that this transformation was evident in more involvement in child-raising. This innovative orientation would seem to challenge the traditionally perceived function of fathers – one where the adult male presented a role model, especially for the young son. Here, the father's task was believed to be to prepare the child for the challenges presented by life and in facing up to responsibilities. The 'New Man', by contrast, seemed to be more about the self-exploration and realisation that constitute the new-found attributes which are more in line with postmodern culture.

The fact remains, however, that in terms of moving towards a more egalitarian approach to parenting, the New Man may be more myth than reality given the evidence related to nurturing the child. Boulton (1983), as part of her research, considered the impact of the father's support and help on the mother's experience and similarly found social class differences. Middle-class, rather than working-class, husbands were more likely to give extensive help and display more nurturing tendencies. The more recent study in the USA by Miller and Sassler (2012) also identified social class differences in domestic duties (based on interviews with 30 working-class cohabiting couples between ages 19 and 35). The study indicated that men did not see domestic labour as a means of contributing, as it challenges their masculinity. Most men preferred to have a partner who also worked for pay. About one-third of the couples were actively attempting to share equally the burden of making money.

It is tempting to predict that in the future men are likely to play changing roles in regard to child-raising. This might be evident with the impact of social policy, including growing opportunities for fathers to take paternity leave, as it is understood by Western governments as important for them to be present for the early days of a child's life. In turn, this can be seen as an important step for the father–child relationship in starting and aiding the father to establish a caring role and a greater responsibility in child-raising. Paradoxically, participation might in fact be declining. Over 25 per cent of children in the UK, for example, are growing up without fathers in the home and this statistic is rising. The divorce rate and a surge in single motherhood point to more children passing through their formative years with weaker ties to their father than before. This has certainly proved to be the case in Sweden, where 28 per cent of children living with only one parent never see the other parent, and this parent is primarily the father. By comparison, when the father has custody the child tends to have more contact with the 'other parent': nine out of ten children living with their father had contact with their mothers. One explanation given for this is that women, who have greater involvement with their children prior to divorce, are more attached to their children and are thus more anxious to continue meaningful relationships (Hwang 1989, 133).

Fathers in the post-divorce situation face other challenges too. From the early nineteenth century men had almost complete rights over their children. Today, with the rise of women's rights and increasing divorce rates, it is the mother who is generally favoured with custody after a relationship break-up. The statistics for fathers in winning custody of their children is, however, increasing, depending on the circumstances. During the year 2000, in the UK the percentage of children that lived with their fathers in the post-divorce situation doubled from one to two per cent. Nonetheless, this was generally in cases where mothers were not considered as reliable due to drug addiction, alcoholism, depressive illness or health problems of comparable gravity. In a number of recent cases it has also been seen that an expectant father has been awarded control over his partner's decision to abort the foetus.

Debate rages regarding the father's access to and responsibility towards children after divorce or separation. In 1991, the Conservative government in the UK set up the Child Support Agency (CSA), which aimed to force absent parents (mainly fathers) to contribute towards their children's upbringing. A bureau was established to administer it and collect money from absent fathers – focusing especially in the first instance on low-income fathers who were easier to locate (through social security offices). This led to considerable controversy and a highly organised campaign against the CSA (called APART, Absent Parents Asking for Reasonable Treatment). To some extent this was because the bureau did not take into account the obligations a parent might have towards a second family, and that if the parent with the child was already on income support, finances collected were recouped by the Benefits Agency.

Enforcing public and political concern over fatherhood has been a measure of sociological research. One view suggests that contemporary fatherhood is in 'crisis' or at the very least is fraught with a certain amount of ambiguity. Marsiglio (1995), for instance, argues that after the birth of a child fathers often feel 'mixed up' or 'scared', as their feelings do not fit neatly with gender role perceptions, while there exists little by way of education as to what constitutes a 'good father' any more than a model exists for the 'good mother'. So, for the father the egocentric stage of life which may have typified youth has come to an end, and he thus enters the unknown new state or transition relatively unprepared. Clearly, the transition to parenthood for fathers, much like mothers, is a major life event and time of change and inconsistency.

What may be concluded, nonetheless, is that the evidence suggests that definitions of fatherhood have evolved to one in which the importance of the fathering role is recognised as central to the child's well-being. Indeed, Lamb (1987, 7–8) argues that fathers now constitute part of the fourth of a series of changes in popular conceptions of the father's roles and responsibilities: those of the moral teacher, the breadwinner and the sex-role model are subsequently replaced by that of the 'new nurturant father'. The emergence of the latter is not to suggest, however, that the earlier roles have disappeared entirely. Indeed, in late/postmodernity the emergence of the pluralist society means that various conceptions coexist and may be shaped by lifestyle constraints and sub-cultural differences forged perhaps above all by ethnic cultural traditions. In regard of the latter, Delcroix (2000) provides the example of Muslim Asian parents, particularly the role of the father, which continues to be influenced not only by religious values but also the instilling of a strong motivational element among their children against a background of social disadvantage and prejudice – intimating the perseverance of the moral instructive, economic and gender role-model of the male.

GAY AND LESBIAN PARENTING

Cutting across notions of what constitutes the 'good parent' is the emergence of same-sex parenting and the debates which accompany this new development. While its greater legitimacy may be linked to increasingly liberal attitudes towards sexuality, the adoption, surrogacy, co-parenting or foster care of children by gay and lesbian couples constitutes, for the most part, a lifestyle choice. The complexities do not stop there, however. A gay man, a lesbian or a transgender person who undertakes gender transition later in life may have children within an opposite-sex relationship in a so-called mixed-orientation marriage. According to the 2000 US Census 33 per cent of female same-sex couple households and 22 per cent of male same-sex couple households reported at least one child under the age of 18 living in the home. In the USA in 2005, an estimated 270,313 children lived in households headed by same-sex couples, which nevertheless renders same-sex parents very much a minority.

These statistics, however, challenge many traditional notions about the 'normal' family, even if evidence indicates that many gay and lesbian couples perceive the same satisfaction in child-raising as 'straight' couples do. This has not prevented surrogacy and custody of children enduring as a vehemently debated issue despite the normalisation of same-sex marriage. In 1989, Denmark became the first country to formally recognise gay marriages, as well as conferring legal advantages for inheritance, taxation and joint property ownership. Many European countries followed suit and have also come to allow gay couples to adopt children, while, in the USA, same-sex marriage was recognised in 2014 by the Federal government and has been legalised in at least 36 states.

Despite more accepting attitudes towards sexual minorities in the Western world, debates still endure regarding their suitability as parents. One of the prevailing arguments is that children with gay parents do not constitute a 'natural state' of affairs. In short, children need a stable family with a father and mother providing suitable gender role models. There is a set of responses to these issues which would support adoption/surrogacy by gay couples. First, gay women with partners bringing up children claim that they have grown up to be mature, stable and usually heterosexual. Second, and this is perhaps the key argument in favour of gay adoption, even if there are problems, gay adoption must be better for the child than being passed from one foster home to another. Third, that sexual orientation is irrelevant: the important consideration is parental love and commitment. Indeed, Perrin et al. (2013) found the quality of parenting, much like single-parenting and families' economic well-being, was more important than sexual orientation. It is clear from this that the points of view advanced by both sides of the debate are couched not so much in terms of moral criteria as utilitarian arguments related to apparent 'harmful' consequences and the language of the 'rights' of the adopted child not to be ridiculed or the 'rights' of gay couples in seeking surrogacy and subscribing to an 'alternative' lifestyle choice.

Initial studies addressing the effects of LGBT parenting on children tended to be rather small samples and lacked total validity, but nonetheless provided good evidence that there were no notable differences in children reared by lesbian mothers versus heterosexual mothers. However, a major study by Simon Crouch and fellow researchers (2012) in Australia (MMC Public Health) found that same-sex couples' children fare better when it comes to physical health and social well-being than children in the general population. The research surveyed 315 same-sex parents with a total of 500 children across Australia. About 80 per cent of the children had female parents and about 18 per cent male parents. Children from same-sex families scored about 6 per cent higher on general health and family cohesion, irrespective of the parent's education and household income. However, on most health measures, including emotional behaviour and physical functioning, there was no difference compared with children from the general population. Moreover, Crouch et al. suggested that the greater stability among same-sex families was derived from an equal distribution of work: same-sex couples are likely to share responsibilities more equally than heterosexual ones. The study also pointed out a major problem facing same-sex families: stigmatisation. According to the study, about two-thirds of children with same-sex parents experienced some form of stigma because of their parents' sexual orientation, but nonetheless these children showed considerable resistance in regard to their psychological and sexual health despite economic and legal problems and social stigma.

SUMMARY

This chapter has analysed a range of topics related to infanthood and parenting. What co-joins many of these topics around infanthood and parenting is the tendency for them to be subject to various forms of social constructionism through shifting cultural perceptions and identified problems couched in medicalised and psychoanalytical discourses. Social constructions and societal perceptions clearly point to observable change and continuity. Changes point to the cultural choice generated by late/postmodernity with its emphasis on the value of choice, which lead to a number of variations observable in parental roles and practices that nonetheless are apparently infused with contradictions and are subject to increasing political and public debates surrounding a major life trajectory. A number of transformations also relate to wider changes in the structure of the family and its dynamics, and further explorations of these will inform the subject matter of Chapter 9. Continuity is also to be found, especially around aspects of motherhood, fatherhood and parenting in general, which nonetheless tend to remain highly engendered and will seemingly impact on infanthood and the early stage of the life course with implications for experiences throughout life. Collectively, many of the themes developed in this chapter overlap with that of childhood, and it is childhood which will form the discussion in the next chapter.

FURTHER READING

Berryman-Fink, C., Ballard-Reisch, D. and Newman, L. (1993) *Communication and Sex Role Socialization*, New York: Garland Publishing, Inc.

Blankenhorn, K. (1995) *Fatherless America*, Seattle, WA: University of Washington Press.

Bretherton, I. and Munholland, K. (1999) 'Internal Working Models Revisited', in J. Cassidy and P. Shaver (eds.), *Handbook of Attachment: Theory, Research, and Clinical Applications*, New York: Guilford Press.

Davies, B. and Banks, C. (1992) 'The Gender Trap: A Feminist Poststructuralist Analysis of Primary School Children's Talk About Gender', *Journal of Curriculum Studies*, 24(1): 1–25.

Denick, L. (1989) 'Growing Up in the Post-Modern Age: On the Child's Situation in the Modern Family, and on the Position of the Family in the Modern Welfare State', *Acta Sociologica*, 32(2): 155–80.

Fagot, B., Leinbach, M. and O'Boyle, C. (1992) 'Gender Labeling, Gender Stereotyping, and Parenting Behaviours', *Developmental Psychology*, 28(2): 225–30.

Guzzo, K. (2011) 'New Father's Experiences With Their Own Fathers and Attitudes Towards Fathering', *Fathering: A Journal of Theory, Research, and Practice about Men as Fathers*, 9(3): 268–90.

Kaufman, G. (2000) 'Do Gender Role Attitudes Matter?: Family Formation and Dissolution Among Traditional and Egalitarian Men and Women', *Journal of Family Issues*, 21(1): 128–44.

Layne, L. (2015) '"I Have a Fear of Really Screwing It Up": The Fears, Doubts, Anxieties, and Judgments of One American Single Mother by Choice', *Journal of Family Issues*, 36(9): 1154–70.

Marsiglio, W., Lohan, M. and Culley, L. (2013) 'Framing Men's Experience in the Procreative Realm', *Journal of Family Issues*, 34(8): 1011–36.

Nixon, E., Greene, S. and Hogan, D. (2015) '"It's What's Normal for Me": Children's Experiences of Growing Up in a Continuously Single-Parent Household', *Journal of Family Issues*, 36(8): 1043–61.

Phoenix, A. (1991) *Motherhood: Meanings, Practices and Ideologies*, London: Sage.

Rossi, A. and Rossi, P (1990) *Of Human Bonding: Parent-Child Relationships Across the Life Course,* New York: Aldine de Gruyter.

Rutter, M. (1979) 'Maternal Deprivation, 1972-1978: New Findings, New Concepts, New Approaches', *Child Development,* 283–305.

Valencia, L. (2015) 'Being a Mother, Practicing Motherhood, Mothering Someone: The Impact of Psy-Knowledge and Processes of Subjectification', *Journal of Family Issues,* 36(9): 1233–52.

Weisner, T. and Wilson-Mitchell, J. (1990) 'Nonconventional Family Lifestyles and Sex Typing in Six-Year-Olds', *Child Development,* 61(1): 1915–33.

Chapter 6

Childhood: issues and perspectives

Until relatively recently, the scope of the social sciences in respect of childhood had been rather restricted to the interrelated topics of developmental psychology and child socialisation. Both of these approaches tended to provide a rather limited focus – one that largely followed a cultural assumption which viewed childhood as a natural 'stage' on the life course rather than as a social phenomenon established within the structural confines of modernity. Such a restricted orientation has subsequently been addressed by the emergence of what is frequently referred to as the 'Sociology of Childhood'. This specialism has attracted considerable interest, mostly from the social constructionist approach, which sets out to prove that 'childhood' constitutes an impressive example of an 'invention' of stages of life and, as tentatively explored in the previous chapter, one that is not infrequently accompanied by a number of public anxieties.

   This chapter will consider some of the key issues related to childhood through the lens of a cultural and historical analysis which allows the exploration of the social construct of this early phase of life. Much of the discussion in this chapter relates to the context of the family, engaging with conventional themes of 'child-raising' and socialisation from a sociological perspective, although scope will be given to aspects of discontinuity in the contemporary context. The chapter will also explore crucial structural elements impacting childhood, including ethnic pluralism and the implications of a range of social disadvantages. It will conclude by connecting with the significance of formal education in forging experiences of the formative years and future life chances, in that it provides a fine example of how childhood events may shape people's lives 40 or 50 years later as well as bringing cumulative advantages and disadvantages (Ferraro and Shippee 2009).

CHILDHOOD: FROM MODERNITY TO POSTMODERNITY

The previous chapter mapped the evolution of parenthood in the Western world – a development that went hand in hand with the emergence of a distinct stage of life which came to be known as childhood. To put things succinctly, childhood initially emerged as a unique phenomenon from the late seventeenth century among middle-class urban families in Europe and North America. A fresh definition of the meaning of childhood was patently related to the retreat of the family into domesticity, the separation of the workplace from the domestic sphere, the redefinition of the mother's role as the principal custodian of the household and the emphasis on emotional attachment rather than the instrumental relations as the foundation of family life.

The emergence of modernity brought a new order which shaped the perceptions and experiences of early life, with childhood regarded roughly as the age span ranging from birth to adolescence and incorporating infancy as its earliest 'stage'. By contrast, as noted in the opening chapter, demographic, social and cultural factors combined to produce only a minimum differentiation in the stages of life in pre-industrial societies. The decisive point is that what has come to be understood as 'modern' childhood was not regarded as a well-defined juncture of life in most historical cultures. In the greater number of such communities the young were considered miniature adults, gradually assuming adult roles in their early years and slowly socially maturing into adulthood. Today, in many Majority World countries these experiences remain much the same: children are engaged in work, often in demanding circumstances and in such a way that the Westerner would find morally repugnant (Lancy 2014).

Pre-modern Europe displayed the same ambiguous attitudes towards childhood as are observable in many parts of the Majority World today. This is cogently described by Aries, in his classical work *Centuries of Childhood* (1965), which provides evidence that in Medieval society the notion of childhood did not exist: children were, for the most part, 'invisible'. The child was absorbed into the adult world soon after infancy and its status was not established in terms of age or physical maturity. The involvement in the adult world continued practically up to the beginning of the twentieth century, where, in most Western nations, children were expected to work at a very early age and for long hours; in many other respects they were not regarded as significantly different from adults. While an impressive example of historical Sociology, Aries' work has not been beyond criticism. In particular, his claim that childhood did not slowly emerge until the seventeenth century has been rigorously questioned by some commentators (Cunningham 1995; Pollock 1983), who provide historical evidence to the contrary and that the earlier integration of children into the adult world was not as complete as Aries insists.

Whatever the merits of the historical evidence presented, more recent works such as that of Chris Jenks (1996) have endeavoured to show how in Western societies concepts of childhood are culture-specific and continue to change over time; from the pre-modern period, through modernity and into postmodernity. Jenks notes that perceptions of childhood in modernity, as compared to pre-modernity, have in Western societies included philosophical underpinnings. This was exemplified, Jenks suggests, by Jean-Jacques Rousseau's work *Emile*, which asked and attempted to answer the question, 'what is a child?' For Rousseau, writing in the early nineteenth century, childhood constituted a particular orientation to the world which amounted to a time of innocence – an innocence corrupted by the adult sphere. Even earlier the English philosopher John Locke pioneered ideas which encapsulated many of the emerging ideas about childhood when he postulated that the mind of the infant at birth was akin to a 'blank slate', and it was the duty of parents to inculcate the child with socially acceptable attitudes.

In many respects, these philosophical speculations ran counter to prevailing Christian ideas of the sinfulness of fallen man and the inherent evil to be found even in the newly born babe. The Christian perception was nonetheless supplemented in the nineteenth century by the idea of the child as 'a savage'. Later influenced by modernist anthropological 'evolutionist' writings, colonialist discourses insisted that the child was to the adult as the savage was to the civilised man. The child would grow, indeed 'evolve', into a civilised human being as long as it was taught and disciplined as part of a socialising process.

Attitudes towards childhood were to change as modernity progressed. The new child-centredness of urban domestic families in Western Europe in the late eighteenth, nineteenth and early twentieth centuries were characterised by the increasing focus on the parents and their children, rather than on a kinship group or lineage. For Aries, this development was largely a response to two major demographic changes: the decline in infant and child mortality and the increase in the conscious performance of family life. Thus commenced the transformation of modern attitudes towards children, one later forged in the second half of the twentieth century by the growth in leisure as clearly demarcated from work, alongside the emergence in state welfare that was ever more concerned with the physical, social and educational needs of the young. This endeavour helped shape the legal systems of many countries that now designate an 'age of majority', stipulating when childhood officially ends and a person legally becomes an adult. This currently varies from the ages of 15 to 21 years old, with 18 being the most common.

Long before these developments, factory legislation and laws concerning the child's welfare and education proved important factors in constructing a distinct period that is now designated 'childhood' between infanthood and adolescence. From the mid-twentieth century, however, legislation went radically further. In the case of the UK, the introduction of the National Health Service as part of the construction of the post–Second World War comprehensive welfare state included wide-ranging child benefit provisions, while the development of a universally applied educational system reflected a prevailing cultural concern for the child. This concern was seen to take on board fresh criteria in the 1989 Children Act, which provided the child with a number of fundamental rights. This arguably also eroded the notion that children are exclusively the property of their parents and gave children the liberty to have their views taken into account, particularly in divorce custody cases.

By the mid-twentieth century, childhood had become the subject of a growing body of child-raising and family advice literature. Advice books and magazine articles popularised the concept of childhood and the so-called needs of children, prescribing the means to allow them to socially, psychologically and emotionally grow as children. It was clear that such accounts re-enforced generalised conceptions of a 'natural' life-cycle. Many of the most popular accounts were rooted in developmental psychology which involved a study of the development of the mental functions of the child, particularly in relation to psychological deficiencies and hence their potential social dysfunction. Much was typified by the work of Jean Piaget (1964) who maintained that all children acquire cognitive competencies according to a traceable sequence up to the state of adulthood. Put succinctly, within Piaget's model each stage of intellectual growth of the child was characterised by a specific 'schema' or clearly delineated sequence of physical and mental behaviour in his/her orientation to the world.

Despite criticisms of Piaget's work, it did engender some sociological interest, especially his insistence that there was a gradual progression from intuitive to socially acceptable behaviour via social interaction and the challenge to younger children's thought processes by the ideas of those children who were more advanced in their development. Piaget's theory also enhanced the legitimacy of developmental psychology, which suggested that childhood could be sub-divided into a number of 'sub-stages': infancy, early childhood (play age), middle childhood (school age) and adolescence (puberty through to post-puberty). For Jenks, this psychoanalytical approach to childhood epitomised the spirit of modernity, not least of all because it increasingly called upon cognitive and affective adult labour or in his words '... established (the) patterning of acquisitions as a "natural" right policed by an ideology of care, grounded unassailably in emotions' (Jenks 1996, 100).

Modernity also came to generate a culture in which adults (especially women) were expected to 'sacrifice everything' for the child. It was a strictly moral dimension of dependency, one produced within the nuclear family which, in turn, was a creation of advanced modernity, though loving and supportive in its self-image. The ideology of care legitimised and aided the investment of economic and cultural capital in the 'promise' of childhood. It was also founded upon what Jenks calls 'futurity', in short, a preoccupation with 'caring', 'enabling', 'facilitating', as part of the nurturing process (Jenks 1996, 100).

Jenks maintains that postmodernity brings a fresh version and vision of childhood. Partly this was due to novel patterns of consumption and to some extent because there were fresh modes of relationships which have outgrown the mid-twentieth-century nuclear family. The family has changed and so too the character of relationships within them. Previously assumed points of attachment of the individual with the collective life, notably social class, work group, local community, as well as the family, are losing their influence and this is concomitant with the demands of the post-Fordist mode of production, global economies, networks of communication and the new techno-science, all of which occupy previously located spheres of knowledge and authority. This consequently forges the dynamics of discontinuity rather than continuity, which, in turn, impacts perceptions and experiences of childhood.

In postmodernity, mass education and consumption have shortened and undermined a certain unique quality associated with childhood. It is increasingly difficult, argues Jenks, for the child to forge a sense of identity as part of the reflexive project of self. This is also observable in how adults now understand and relate to children. The fixed identities of adults, children and families have become transmogrified. The previous normative markers of social experience, especially in the form of status are now relativised, while an erosion of the view of childhood generated by a culture of 'progress' once synonymous with modernity has taken place. There are also many 'alternative lifestyles' challenging the 'correct' way of bringing up the child – to the extent that parents are unsure what they are supposed to be 'alternative' to. Now, postmodernity has re-adopted the child, while childhood has become a site for the re-location of discourses concerning stability, integration and social bonds.

Jenks sees parent–child relationships in postmodernity as unchosen, unnegotiated forms of association and sites of ambiguous emotions. The trust which was previously anticipated as underpinning marriage, partnership and friendship, which have proved uncertain and transient, is now invested more generally in the child. Much is evident in the effectual prolongation of adolescence, the disputed terrain that childhood constitutes during parental divorce, the uprating of children's status through advances in children's rights, and campaigns against addiction and criminality. Thus, the child has become *the* last remaining primary and trusting relationship (Jenks 1996, 107).

Edward Shorter (1985), in anticipating postmodern analysis, also placed emphasis on childhood as part of the changing context of the family. While he identified a 'hysterical proposition' that the family is breaking up, he points to two variables that have a direct or indirect impact on childhood in relation to the family. The first is the sexual revolution which has undermined marriage as a permanent union, exposing children to the discontinuities that come with dissolved marriages. The second is the economic independence of women. While this alters relationships with their partners, it also tends to undermine the mother–child relationship in that woman's employment takes her out of the domestic sphere. These developments have led to what Shorter refers to as 'the destruction of the (family) nest' (Shorter 1975, 279).

While such works as that of Jenks and Shorter have considered childhood in terms of social change, other commentators have brought into focus the significance of the child as an active agent. In particular, the postmodern condition has arguably created a space where the child can negotiate what childhood identity and parent–child relationships actually means as part of the 'rethinking of childhood'. This is Berry Mayall's approach, which discusses the child's personal agency – the capacity to make sense of the social world around them. For Mayall, there are now greater opportunities for the child to act as an independent reflexive agent at home rather than school, since in the former there is greater scope for interpretation and negotiation of core culturally channelled aspects of childhood (Mayall 2002, 109–10). The emphasis on the importance of interpretation and reflexivity has also been extended to consider how children today react to gender role socialisation as part of a dynamic negotiation and reflective process which includes what they perceive as the discrepancy between their own gender identity and culturally prescribed gender role stereotypes (Brinkman et al. 2012).

The end of childhood?

Through the discussion above it becomes evident that contemporary Western societies bring contradictory images of childhood. In particular, Jenks' assertion that postmodernity has re-adopted the child and childhood as the only remaining principal location of trusting relationship would seem to be at odds with rhetoric around the claimed demise of childhood as a distinct phase of life. These apparent contradictory viewpoints are not, however, totally irreconcilable, as the following discussion may confirm.

Childhood might be thought of as the formative years of life, free from the burdens of the adult world, where the separate haven of childhood still retains its predominant cultural representation. Indeed, in postmodernity there has emerged what Baos (1996) regards as a kind of nostalgic 'time warp' – a form of 'cultural primitivism', in which childhood is still idealised as some kind of golden age. The media, in particular, reconstructs a view of the world that attempts to establish an imaginary and longing celebration of childhood. Yet, this image is in stark contrast to the reality of an age of high divorce rates, where there is an increasing level of exposure to 'adult' programming on television – all providing evidence that children are no longer protected from the grown-up domain and encapsulated within their own culture. Today, we are seeing, according to Winn (1983), the development of a 'hurried child' syndrome, meaning children have to grapple with images of sex and violence as well as fending for themselves as a result of a conjugal arrangement where both parents are working and perhaps neglectful of childcare.

This kind of reasoning points to the conjecture that childhood is now in 'crisis'. Niel Postman, in *The Disappearance of Childhood* (1996), argues that there is little by way of special children's food, games and clothes, little respect for elders, where children's crimes now feature in crime statistics and children are exposed to sexual imagery. Critics of this view, nonetheless, counter there is no convincing evidence of any dramatic shift in society's conception of childhood. Further, they note that the 'hurried child' thesis overlooks the fact that children in the lower classes have long assumed adult responsibilities in comparison to their more indulged middle- and upper-class counterparts. The former have long been compelled to deal with many of the practical difficulties of the real world and have rarely been protected from life's hardships (Lynott and Logue 1993).

Another aspect of a supposed looming 'crisis' would appear to be the increase in violent acts against children, as well as the emergence of something amounting to a moral panic regarding paedophilia, with paedophiles becoming the latest 'folk devils'. Indeed, Kieran McCartan (2010) has drawn attention to how the current public concern surrounding paedophilia, which has developed since the late twentieth century, has come to have an increasing profile, one that has been partly created by the proliferating media interest in sex offences, particularly in regard to high profile cases often expressed through media campaigns of the lower quality press.

This observation does not detract from the fact that there is plentiful evidence of violence and abuse within the family itself. It is perhaps curious, then, that at a time when parents are believed to increasingly spoil their children, a counter-trend is observed in the proliferating cases of reported cruelty by parents against their offspring. In the USA, for instance, roughly 4 per cent of all children are believed to suffer abuse each year. Edleson (1999), among others, reports behavioural, emotional, cognitive and long-term problems that are statistically associated with a child's witnessing of domestic violence. Child abuse is seemingly most common among the youngest and most vulnerable children, while the vast majority of child abusers are parents, step-parents or trusted kin (Strauss and Gelles 1986). Although the effects of witnessing domestic violence appear to diminish with time, they can continue through adulthood. Around 90 per cent of child abusers are men, but they do not conform to simple stereotypes. Most, however, share one trait: they have been abused themselves as children (Gwartney-Gibbs et al. 1987).

Although the statistics are rising, this does not necessarily mean an increase in incidence, perhaps only that more cases of violence and sexual abuse are being discovered. Jenks notes that in this respect the politicisation of the 'discovery' of child abuse as if it was something that had not previously existed has occurred (Jenks 1996, 97). Jenks argues that such social problems do not just 'appear'. Deconstructing this 'trend', Jenks suggests that the pre-occupation with abuse enforces the conventional view of child-hood because it assumes a betrayal of dependency, which side-steps cultur-ally sensitive issues such as child sexuality. Abuse has always been present, it has now become unthinkable. The apparent contradiction between child centredness and child abuse is thus solved; the 'discovery' of abuse high-lights the cultural concern with the welfare of the child and a prevailing myth of the 'golden age' of childhood.

DISCONTINUITIES IN CHILDHOOD: THE CONSEQUENCES OF DIVORCE

Child abuse may be viewed as part of the 'crisis' of childhood. Divorce and parental separation are arguably others. The latter will be discussed here largely as examples of one of the principal discontinuities of the early life course and other inherent contradictions of a culture which is supposedly child-centred. However, divorce and separation are only two forms of dis-ruption to the family and discontinuity in an early stage of the life course. In most Western societies only about one-third of family disruptions are caused by divorce. Nonetheless, over half of couples divorcing in the UK in 2007 had at least one child aged under 16 (amounting to over 110,000 children), and 20 per cent of these children were under 5 years old. In add-ition, many more children experience parental separation annually that is not included in such statistics, as their parents are not married.

Some commentators have interpreted divorce mostly in terms of its social consequences. Among those explored by Thompson and Amato (1999) are the parents' responsibilities after divorce, how the prevalence of divorce has changed the family form, structural factors that have contributed to various social problems and the implications of these developments for public policy. Perhaps most of all such assumed 'problems' hinge on the supposition that divorce generally adds to the increasing proportion of fatherless families (since in most cases children come under the custody of their mothers) and is said to be at the heart of a whole diversity of maladies, from rising crime to mushrooming welfare costs for child-support, all of which has reinforced social anxieties around childhood (Laumann-Billings and Emery 2000). Taking this stance, Blankenhorn, in his book *Fatherless America* (1995), argues that societies with high divorce rates are not just facing the loss of fathers, but also the very erosion of the idea of fatherhood with negative social consequences, since many children are now growing up without an authority figure to turn to in times of need. This speculation regarding the repercussions of divorce for the child in terms of delinquency is by no means settled. Undoubtedly, there is some link, yet there is also a correlation between the death of a parent and anti-social behaviour. Because divorce and delinquency both tend to occur in lower-income families, it is quite possible that consequences of poverty other than the specific psychological effects implicated with divorce impact significantly on the child.

Despite such findings, considerable debate rages amongst the 'experts' as to whether the estranged couple should remain married despite hostilities and unhappiness, since this still provides their children with a level of stability. Some experts regard divorce as a disaster, given that it takes many children from their familiar surroundings, entangles them in bitter family feuds and frequently distances them from a parent they love. There is also evidence that children often blame themselves for their parents' break-up. For these reasons some commentators have suggested divorce can radically change the trajectory of their entire lives in a negative way (Goetting 1981). Much, however, may depend on the age of the child in the divorce situation, and this is plausibly linked to the developmental stages of childhood. For instance, research suggests that among the effects of divorce on children under nine years is the tendency to blame themselves for their parents' separation, alongside the hope that their parents might be reconciled at some later stage. As a result of the divorce, they might become even more dependent on their parents. Adolescents (children between 9 and 13 years) seemingly react in a polar direction, tending to behave more independently while carrying a sense of betrayal (Claessens 2013).

La Follette (1996) believes that a child's response to divorce is always linked to its understanding of parental relations and the reasons for the separation. If a child does not see any reason why his or her parents are opting for a divorce, if there are few outward signs of discord, then the child's response may be to blame her/himself. La Follette maintains that, better than divorce, staying together will benefit the child under almost any circumstance. Divorce rarely brings the benefits that adults seek, and the losses can be catastrophic since estranged spouses are often stripped of financial resources, friendships are affected and the relationship with the family declines, all as a result of the search for what is perceived to be a happier and more rewarding life.

Added to such findings was an influential study into the consequences of divorce conducted by the Pennsylvania State University, USA, in 2001. Based on the research of 2000 couples and 700 of their children who had reached the age of 19, the study found that children may suffer significant emotional damage if one unfulfilled parent leaves the marriage early to seek happiness elsewhere. However, the study conjectured that the only consideration more damaging for children was for them to remain in a family in which there was constant and violent conflict between parents who did not separate (some 40 per cent of divorces in the Pennsylvania study involved marriages in which there had been high levels of conflict beforehand).

Such conflict was hitherto believed to impact the health and emotional development of children: it interfered with their schoolwork and made them more aggressive towards their peers. This was not, however, wholly substantiated by the Pennsylvania study for the 60 per cent of the marriages which ended in divorce. Where it proved to be the case, however, was with couples who often went along 'moderately happy' for many years but in which one or both partners felt unfulfilled. In these instances divorce seemed to bring turmoil to the children because it was not anticipated and deemed inexplicable. The children in the latter group showed signs of poor mental health by the time they reached adulthood. They found it harder to make a commitment because they failed to trust relationships and tended to delay marriage, preferring cohabitation instead. Once they did marry, they were quicker to think about divorce if the relationship went wrong.

Additional research does not support the view that problems in adulthood are necessarily prevalent. Rather, most children of divorced parents become well-adjusted adults. For example, Hetherington and Kelly (2002) outline a 25-year study in which Hetherington followed children of divorce and children of parents who remained together, finding that 25 per cent of the adults whose parents had divorced experienced serious social, emotional or psychological troubles compared with 10 per cent of those whose parents remained together. These findings suggest that only 15 per cent of adult children of divorce experience problems over and above those from non-divorced families. Moreover, while many children experience short-term negative effects from divorce, especially anxiety, anger, shock and disbelief, they tend to decline or disappear by the end of the second year after divorce.

Further evidence suggests that children benefit from their estranged parents going their separate ways: they might better endure a parental divorce than remain in a family torn by tension or even violence. Hayman (2001) has argued that marriages in which a couple displays conflict are extremely damaging for children. Estranged parents make children unhappy, especially as they know their parents are unhappy themselves. In these cases, the child may feel a sense of relief when the parents eventually divorce. Hayman argues that it is counter-productive to hide marriage problems from children: they need to be told there are difficulties.

Children and the post-divorce family

Increasing academic interest has focused on children in 'reordered' families after divorce has taken place and at least one of the estranged parents has entered a new relationship. In 1994, Exeter University's Department of Child Health published the results of research on 152 children in the UK aged between 9 and 10, and 13 and 14. These children consisted of 76 who lived with both parents and 76 whose parents had split up. The research also highlighted the importance of step-families. The children from the two groups were paired on factors such as age and social class. In the second group, 31 were in lone-parent households, 26 had become part of a step-family and 19 had experienced multiple disruptions through at least three different homes.

Of the 76 children in 'reordered' families, only a third had frequent, regular contact with the parent who had left the family home. In terms of problems of health, behaviour and school work, those with parents whose relationship was cordial had the least problems. Those with both parents, where the relationship was problematic, had more difficulties. In addition, those in reordered families had twice as many problems. The 21 who had experienced multiple family disruption were ten times more likely than those in intact families to have a low opinion of themselves and eight times more likely to need remedial support with school work and to have health complications. Of the children whose parents had separated, scarcely any had been given the chance to discuss preparations for the change and 21 per cent had received no explanation from either parent as to why they had broken up. Children from post-divorced homes seemed to fare best if they had a chance to discuss their distress, if mediation services minimalised post-separation conflict between parents and where regular contact was maintained with the absent parent.

Insights provided by the work of Bretherton (1997) identified significant discrepancy between mothers' and children's views on the post-divorce situation. Whereas a minority of the mothers had a fairly positive co-parental relationship with the fathers of their children and were able to communicate about co-parental issues, negative views prevailed, with the mothers who reported their ex-husbands' serious alcohol or drug problems feeling particularly negative. The mothers' negative feelings regarding the father as a co-parent and his involvement in child-raising seemed problematic because fathers remained important to the children. Although boys and girls differed in the frequency with which they enacted particular story themes, both chose to frequently incorporate the father into their personal narratives.

At the same time, there is also the issue of whether individual mothers and fathers have very different ideas on how children should be raised in the post-divorce situation. Children may be faced with situations in which they have to accommodate to a new step-parent who may be living with them and who brings their own standards and expectations of parenting. The child may also receive care from another step-parent who lives with the non-residential parent and who may have different standards and expectations (Smart and Neale 2001). Because of such complications some Western governments, frequently as a result of 'expert' advice, are seemingly keen on encouraging the involvement of biological fathers in the care of their children after divorce.

In a further study, Dunn (2002) interviewed 29 people aged 18 to 32 with former step-parents and found that relationships fell into three categories: those who never embraced their step-parent as a family member; those who considered the step-parent to be a parent figure during the marriage, but not afterward; and those who continued to consider their ex-step-parent as a family member after the divorce. Taking a different tack, other studies have found children in step-families to be susceptible to peer pressure and deviant peer relationships, which may lead to later delinquent behaviour such as an increased risk for drug/alcohol use (e.g. Steinberg 1987). Because children in step-families and single-parent families report more negative stress in their lives, behaviour problems and adjustment difficulties are understood to be a reaction to stress. Importantly, when these difficulties are reported for step-children behaviours typically appear within the normal range for such behaviours. Moreover, compared to children in intact, unhappy first-marriage families, step-children are better adjusted.

The gender of the child is another factor affecting outcome. Some evidence suggests that girls have more adjustment problems in step-families than do boys (Steinberg 1987). Higher stress may lead to adjustment difficulties such as poor academic performance and problem behaviours. Parents tend to report an increase in negative behaviours in daughters following remarriage and a decrease of such behaviours in sons. This is often explained by the close mother–daughter relationships formed prior to the remarriage and the perceived threat to that relationship by the addition of a step-father. Such tendencies may be cut across by the age of the child. Adolescents, in particular, have been found to display difficulties in adjusting and may show a reluctance to establish ties as they strive for autonomy and turn toward peers for support. Whereas younger children may show some reaction and behavioural changes with a remarriage, once a consistent routine is established adjustment problems typically reduce (Kalter 1990).

CHILDREN OF ETHNIC MINORITIES

Despite numerous factors identified with changing perceptions of childhood and its discontinuities regularly discerned as cultural products of late/postmodernity, there are considerable structural considerations which continue to impact childhood experiences. As Mills (2000, 9) opines, childhood is not just about historical periods of time. Rather, the shaping of childhood and childhood experiences are still inextricably linked to demographic and structural variants. Mills argues that the deconstructionism offered by the postmodernist approach should not be at the expense of considering economic factors related to class, gender constraints and ethnic variations which continue to impact childhood, not least in terms of childhood identities. Aspects of social class and gender in regard to childhood have been partly addressed in this and earlier chapters. However, a measure of analysis needs to be brought to bear on the significance of ethnicity and how this relates to broader social inequalities including levels of poverty, health and discrimination and the significance of family structure, all of which aid in the identity formation of children of ethnic minorities.

Poverty is seemingly one factor which may shape experiences of ethnic groups in childhood. Calling on statistics largely assembled by Her Majesty's Stationery Office, the 'Poverty Site' (2010), geared to measuring aspects of poverty and social exclusion, points out that approximately two-fifths of people from ethnic minorities in the UK live in low-income households, twice the rate for white people. Within this, there are major variations by ethnic group: compared to 20 per cent of white people in such households, 30 per cent of Indians and black Caribbeans, 50 per cent of black Africans, 60 per cent of Pakistanis and 70 per cent of Bangladeshis were derived from this social background. For all ages, people from ethnic minorities were found to be, on average, much more likely to live in low-income households than white families were. This included almost half of all children from ethnic minorities who live in low-income households compared to a quarter of white UK children.

Various explanations have been advanced for such disparities. In the UK, Palmer and associates (2007) present a number of complex findings, of which a few may be mentioned in simplified form. What stands out for black Africans and Caribbean households is, among other factors, the high percentage of lone parents. A major factor for Pakistanis and Bangladeshis was that households with working-age groups with children have low incomes or registered high rates of unemployment. Other studies have considered the effects of poverty for various ethnic groups. For example, Acheson (1998, 92–94) points out that children who come from families of ethnic minority groups are more likely to describe their health as poor compared to the majority of the population and that ill-health is related primary to poverty and social class position.

Ethnic identity, and wider societal reaction to it, remains an important element of childhood experiences for children from ethnic minorities. It is clear that initially such children learn about their cultural identity and sense of history and community belonging through early socialisation in the family and via parents in similar ways to ethnic majorities. It is in this context where children learn their 'differentness' and sense of belonging to a group that is designated by wider society as constituting the 'other'. However, as the child grows older and is influenced by peers and ever-increasing encounters with other social networks, other factors, including discrimination, begin to have an influence.

While there are different ways of approaching how a sense of ethnic identity is established, Stephen Quintana (1998) provides some detailed insights based on a development model which calls on a variety of relevant literature with references to minority ethnicity and 'race' in the USA. Between approximately the ages of 3 and 6 children of minorities are able to classify attitudes (including prejudice) towards ethnic groups without understanding their origins. Here, parents are most influential. Between the ages of 6 and 10 peers become increasingly important, and definitions correspond more closely with those of adults. Between 10 and 14 there is a growing recognition of the differences of social class and status between ethnic groups. Finally, in adolescence there is the ability to integrate their own and other's experiences as part of self-identity and as part of a group with strong in-group/out-group demarcations.

Clearly discrimination on the grounds of ethnicity and 'race' is an encumbrance experienced by many children. Numerous studies have explored the repercussions. Coker et al. (2009) analysed data from a study of fifth-grade students and their parents from public schools in the USA. A high percentage of children reported perceived racial/ethnic discrimination, with 80 per cent recording that discrimination occurred in the school setting. A greater percentage of black (20 per cent), Hispanic (15 per cent) and other non-white (16 per cent) children gave testimony to perceived racial/ethnic discrimination compared with white (7 per cent) children. Children who reported perceived racial/ethnic discrimination were more likely to have symptoms of mental health conditions: depression, attention deficit hyperactivity disorder, oppositional defiant disorder and conduct disorder.

CHILDHOOD AND FORMAL EDUCATION

So far, in this and the previous chapter, childhood has been discussed largely within the context of the family. There is more to consider, however, since a good part of the experience of childhood, as the child extends his/her social interaction, is within the remit of formal education. Indeed, the link between education and the emergence of modern childhood is indisputable. Historically speaking, childhood was only slowly to evolve in its idealised cultural form from the nineteenth century as part of the modern preoccupation with the family and the development of schooling, which provided children with their own age-specific experience, with school classes graduated into what might be regarded as age-sets. Formal education has long been regarded as central to the socialising process and provides a cultural link between the generations, supposedly imparting core values for a younger generation even in rapidly changing contemporary societies.

Moreover, education generates culture in as much as it is not only concerned with the acquisition of particular skills, but is also frequently held to be a liberating experience in which individuals explore, create, use their initiative and judgement, and freely develop their potential, faculties and talents to the full, including in the employment sphere. There is, in fact, a historical link between education and employment that can be seen in the light of economic development in Western societies. As the industrial revolution created a need for an educated and skilled labour force, schooling became no longer merely the prerogative of the middle-classes and was slowly provided for the mass of ordinary people and undertaken in specialised institutions from kindergarten through to schools, colleges and universities.

Over recent decades the time which is spent in what might broadly be termed 'the educational system' has expanded considerably. This means that the social role of education and how it shapes life experiences from childhood onwards, for better or for worse, is of increasing significance: thus setting the stage for establishing social relationship and networks, and contributing significantly to future life-chances and the possibility of overcoming actual or potential risks.

The contemporary educational system also increasingly reflects the culture of the consumer society, so that matters of parental choice or, at the very least, matters demarcated by the discourse of 'choice', have recently come to the fore. Education, then, is in step with the major attributes of late/postmodernity. This would seem to be evident in legislative enactments. In the UK, for instance, the 1988 Education Act brought in a number of sweeping changes. This included the right for schools to 'opt out' of the Local Educational Authority system if a majority of parents in a secret ballot elected to do so and become 'grant maintained'. The main thrust of these changes was to introduce the market forces of supply, demand, competition and parental choice into all levels of education. By more closely assessing the performance of schools and publishing the results of assessments in 'league tables' the Conservative government of the time, enthused by a neoliberal ideology, maintained that it would generate competition between schools, as well as enabling parents to make practical preferences regarding where to send their children.

At the same time, economic restraints generated by post-2008 austerity measures have resulted in the reduction of government spending on education. For example, the Conservative/Liberal Democrats coalition government in 2010 raised tuition fees for university students in England from £3000 to a maximum of £9000 a year for the annual tuition costs. This rise in fees effectively runs counter to the rhetoric of equality of opportunity for younger people from poorer backgrounds entering higher education, thus highlighting the clear relationship between structured inequalities, demographic variables and opportunities to fulfil educational potential. In reality, a complex range of inequalities forged by social class, gender and ethnicity impact educational performance long before, indeed throughout, the various phases of childhood.

In line with Beck's notion of 'individualization' (Beck 1992), educational experiences are becoming individualised and packaged as consumer products. Performance 'league tables' encourage parents to 'shop around' for the best school for their children, and a growing range of educational credentials and courses may lead young people to regard educational services as 'products'. As a consequence, changes in the delivery of education and the increased use of certification mean that they and their parents are obliged to take personal responsibility for educational achievement. Consequently, failure is equated with poor choices or a lack of effort or talent rather than being influenced by social class. Yet, despite the far-reaching nature of changing educational experiences, there is little evidence that the relationship between social class and educational attainment has substantially weakened.

While UK governments have been keen on promoting a philosophy of freedom of choice in the educational system, central state intervention in matters linked to the syllabus and assessment has grown. The 1992 Education Act introduced new centralised arrangements for school inspection through OFSTED (the Office for Standards in Education). This was meant to enhance the shift towards a meritocracy and a new development that is frequently labelled a 'parentocracy'. The latter amounts to a system where a child's education is increasingly dependent upon the financial capabilities and wishes of parents, rather than the ability and efforts of pupils.

There is a further dimension to consider. Evidence suggests that the emphasis on educational 'performance' has impacted children in negative ways, where the stress on 'competition' seemingly marks another indicator of how children are being 'hurried' into the adult world with an ethos of 'achievement'. According to findings released by the UK-based charity MindFull, stress at school is the biggest contributor to depression, self-harm and attempted suicide among young people (54 per cent of those surveyed), as well as worrying about the future and low self-esteem. Participants in the MindFull survey, aged 16–25, were asked to reflect on their earlier experiences of school. More than 12 per cent of participants said that when they were under the age of 16 they felt as if they were a failure on a daily basis.

THE PERSISTENCE OF EDUCATIONAL INEQUALITIES

Structural restraints linked to social inequalities would seem to negate notions of 'choice' in the realm of education and government commitment to the equality of opportunity and the development of a meritocracy as the foundation to the modern democratic way of life. Obviously, poorer parents find it difficult to send their children for nursery pre-school training, to hire private tutors or to purchase items like books or personal computers which give children from more affluent backgrounds an advantage. At the same time, the less affluent tend to experience greater environmental and health problems that, in turn, have repercussions on their performance at school. For example, of fourth grade (9–10-year-olds) students in the USA from low-income backgrounds, 80 per cent have been found to score below grade level in reading (National Assessment of Educational Progress 2013). There are direct repercussions here of various indexes linked to rates of poverty.

Numerous studies have shown that children from an unskilled or semi-skilled occupational background have a poorer diet and worse attendance at clinics to receive immunisation. They also suffer to a greater extent from chronic illness which may disrupt progress at school. A study by Washbrook and Waldfogel (2008) showed that in the UK and the USA children born into low-income families are at a disadvantage even when they start school. The study analyses data on around 19,000 children born in the UK in 2000 (the Millennium Cohort Study) and parallel data on around 10,000 children born in the USA in 2001 (the Early Childhood Longitudinal Study Birth Cohort). The children in both studies were followed from the age of nine months onwards and completed tests in language, literacy and mathematics skills at ages three, four or five. Although the UK appears to be relatively successful in promoting equality among children in families with incomes above a moderate level, the poorest 20 per cent are equally disadvantaged as the equivalent American children. According to the study, children from low-income backgrounds are raised in environments that fail to promote their cognitive, social and health development adequately, and, as a result, they are more likely to begin school with deficits in their learning ability and social behaviour.

Parental attitude towards education has also long been seen as an important factor by sociologists in accounting for the under-achievement of working-class children (Douglas 1964; Willis 1977), although it is far from substantiated that working-class parents are any less interested in their children's education than their middle-class counterparts (Ball et al. 1994). What they tended to lack, however, were the material resources and knowledge of the educational system which made it possible for many middle-class parents to be constructively informed about the secondary school their children attended and make 'choice' a reality. Many working-class parents preferred to send their children to the nearest school because of family demands and other factors, which included limited transport facilities.

Research evidence continues to throw light on pre-school parenting. Washbrook and Waldfogel's (2008) research indicated that low-quality parenting could determine the 'school readiness' of children from low-income backgrounds in the UK and USA, which significantly impacts the poorest fifth of children in both countries. Among the key explanatory variables was the inclination for higher-income mothers to interact more positively with their children when they were as young as nine months old, display superior sensitivity to their needs and provide more cognitive stimulation. These types of parental behaviours are then strongly related to children's performance at the time of entry to school and in particular to language development.

Finally, influential studies applying the theories of symbolic interactions have documented the perspectives of teachers and students, the processes through which school classes are constructed and negotiated, the different student roles and cultures that emerge within classes, and the impact of social stratification, whether gender, class or ethnicity, on these interactions. What has been referred to as an 'invisible pedagogy' (Bernstein 1975), or hidden ranking system, in school culture can significantly influence academic performance and, in turn, the long-term life chances of students through a self-fulfilling prophecy.

Ethnic variations in achievement are evident in many Western educational systems. Early research and reports in the UK, as elsewhere, showed that these variations often coincide with social status differences between ethnic groups and are frequently linked to the variables of social class and gender (Rampton Committee 1979; Swann Committee 1985), where in general Afro-Caribbean children perform to a lower level than Asian children at school, and in both cases boys did less well than girls. Asian girls may often perform better than white boys, but black males regularly appeared to be the poorest achievers. Such reports noted the lack of suitable pre-school provisions, a good degree of irrelevance of the curriculum to the needs of ethnic groups and poor communication between the school and the parents.

More recent research has added to the complexity of the picture. In the UK context, Tackey et al. (2011) overviewed the most important findings in pre-school education, noting that non-white children are under-represented but those who are able to obtain it perform better than white children. At primary school, children of white background display greater achievement levels, while those of mixed white and black Caribbean background do less well than average. The research conjectures that at secondary school poverty was the primary driver of differential performance, while there was a sustained decline in the performance of black Caribbean boys – especially those from deprived households. In respect of post-16 education, Pakistani and Bangladeshi young people achieved fewest qualifications. However, non-white students are over-represented in Further Education colleges. Nonetheless, there is a limited take-up of apprenticeships and vocational qualifications by many minority ethnic groups thereafter. In higher education, ethnic groups are generally over-represented, apart from black Afro-Caribbean males and white males from lower socio-economic backgrounds. Yet, with some exceptions, students from minority ethnic groups are less likely to achieve a higher class degree.

Such findings would seem to be at variance with the values of many ethnic minorities. Research by Connor et al. (2004) in the context of higher education emphasised the influence of parents and families in providing a 'stronger push' by ethnic minority groups to succeed through gaining higher qualifications, especially professional/vocational subjects. Prospective university students themselves also held more positive attitudes towards the benefits of a higher education than their white counterparts. Integral to such attitudes was the effect of family and parental status and their own experiences of higher education.

Previous studies in the USA demonstrate the positive effects of parental involvement on student grade point averages, standardised tests scores and other academic outcomes. Nonetheless, obstacles often arise prohibiting such positive involvement between the family and the school, especially for inner-city African American parents. Williams and Sánchez' study (2013) based on parents and school personnel at a predominantly African American inner-city high school completed in-depth interviews regarding the barriers to involving parents in their children's education. The barriers identified were: time factors, lack of access, lack of financial resources and lack of awareness of opportunities.

Education and gender

Beginning in the 1970s, several sociological studies revealed how and why girls were usually disadvantaged at school. Stanworth (1983) researched a mixed group of students, and found that teachers gave more attention to boys than girls even up to the standard of A-level teaching. Rosemary Deem (1980) demonstrated that education for girls in the past largely centred upon how it would prepare them for their roles with the family rather than the world of employment, while Dale Spender (1982) found curricula saturated with 'sexism' and schools steered girls towards 'feminine' subjects. As a result of such experiences, girls learned to lack faith in their abilities, and some studies emphasised how this might impact income from those of economically poorer backgrounds in particular (Kuh et al. 1997).

Nevertheless, there has been evidence which indicates that gender performance in education is changing: boys appear to be doing less well and

girls performing better. Statistics in the UK in 1998 showed girls outperforming boys in national curriculum tests at 7, 11 and 14 years, a trend
which has largely continued since. In terms of the proportion of pupils gaining five A to C grades, the gap between boys and girls had widened nation-
ally to 9 per cent in just ten years. In some subjects, 15 per cent more girls
were achieving this academic benchmark. The gap was widest in English,
where 59 per cent of girls achieve grade C or above compared to 41 per cent
of boys. Yet, boys were also behind in traditionally 'boys' subjects' such as
maths, science and technology. Girls are evidently less likely to fail. In 1998,
only 21,500 girls left school without any exam passes, compared to 28,500
boys. Into the twenty-first century the difference seemed to be widening.
According to figures, some 24.8 per cent of exams sat by girls were graded
A* or A, compared with just 17.6 per cent of those taken by boys. The gulf –
7.2 percentage points – was larger than at any other time since the introduction of GCSEs in the late 1980s.

Partly, the increasing success of girls is a consequence of a shift in educational policies. The national curriculum in the UK, for instance, insists that
all boys are compelled to take a language and all girls must choose a science
subject; while most schools and universities now have equal opportunities
policies. Furthermore, since the 1990s girls have increasingly become less
family-focused, giving more weight to education and work (Sharpe 1994).
No longer are they attaching primary importance to marriage and having
children and now endorse the imperative of finding a job or career and
emphasise self-sufficiency.

At the same time, there appears to be the continuing development of
what is commonly called 'lad culture' (frequently discerned as responsible
for under-achievement) amongst boys. Over three decades ago, Paul Willis'
(1977) influential study found that working-class boys generated an anti-
school culture and 'deviant' attitudes largely centred on their masculinity.
They had little respect for the middle-class school values and official qualifications, which they frequently regarded as boring, effeminate and superfluous to their immediate needs. These boys related good pupil performance
with femininity and embraced deviant forms of behaviour that made them
popular with their peers such as handing in work that was late and of poor
quality. Now the stereotypical image of the average boy appears to be one
who dislikes being labelled 'a swot' and is more likely to be involved in
non-educational pursuits at home such as watching television and playing
computer games (Ghail 1995). By contrast, recent cohorts of girls have a
new-found assertiveness grounded in feminism, 'girl power' and expanding

economic opportunities. The emergence of fresh identities among females, then, in contrast to enduring aspects of masculinity by way of negative consequences, is impacting in terms of educational performance. The general trend is, however, rather complex. In 2014 boys were found to be catching up with girls at A-level – and even moving ahead in terms of elite A* grades. Moreover, what is clear is that some continuities were observable – that boys were twice as likely to study maths, three times as likely to study further maths and more than four times as likely to take A-levels in physics. By contrast, twice as many girls than boys studied English.

SUMMARY

The above discussion of childhood has ranged widely, perhaps necessarily so given the rapidly changing perceptions in late/postmodernity of childhood and the experiences of children themselves within family life, formal education and the wider cultural sphere. Indeed, the evidence implies that the early stages of life, from birth to childhood, are undergoing considerable transformations in the Western world. For instance, while stereotypical roles regarding young males and females have concerned sociologists for several generations, the improving educational standards of females indicates that attitudes have changed over time, while inequalities related to occupational background and ethnicity continue to inform life chances and opportunities (discussed in Chapter 7). Simultaneously, significant alterations in the family structure and the breakdown of the family have transformed, for many children, the experience within childhood to one of major discontinuities.

These transformations have been accompanied by different perceptions of childhood and practices of parenting, with possible positive and negative aspects, alongside a great deal of cultural uncertainty as to what constitutes childhood and how children should be raised and socialised. There are, moreover, contradictory trends which make predictions regarding the future uncertain. However, it is likely that many of the developments in the decades to come will be tied to the fortunes of the family, and it is this institution which will be discussed from various further perspectives in Chapter 9.

At the same time, there has been a restructuring of childhood, suggesting that its span is shortening; this is fundamentally related to early transition into the adult world, at least in some respects. This 'hurried childhood' is not just in terms of adults that the child is exposed to, but also the commodification of various aspects of childhood. To some extent, this results from manufacturing nostalgic images, alongside the commodification of the early teenage years or the emergence of the 'teenie' market typified by girl magazines which deal with themes of an 'adult nature' and the preoccupation with heterosexual relationships. In the educational field, the earlier assessment of the child in many Western nations, often by way of formal examinations, would appear to bring the competitiveness associated with the adult world to the heart of the school experience. As a result of these developments, childhood might be shortened at the same time that the next phase of life – that of adolescence and youth – is extended.

More broadly, over recent decades there have been far-reaching changes in the ways in which sociologists think about children, and a growing cross-fertilisation of ideas between researchers in a variety of social science disciplines is discernible. This is marked fairly recently by attempts to integrate the significance of the confluence of local and global influences on the child in Western societies. For instance, Holloway and Valentine (2000) have explored how children's identities are constituted in and through particular 'spaces'. Local cultures plausibly include notions of masculinity and these may be played out through the home and the school, while there is the globalising impact of economic trends and information technologies which bring change to key areas such as vocational training even from a very early age – an element that would seem to add to the processes which speed up the child's entry into the world of the adult, resulting from a number of the major characteristics of late/postmodernity.

FURTHER READING

Alanen, L. (1988) 'Rethinking Childhood', *Acta Sociologica*, 31(1): 53–67.

Amato, P. (1994) 'Life-span Adjustment of Children to Their Parents' Divorce', *Future of Children*, 4(1): 143–16.

Amato, P. and Keith, B. (1991) 'Parental Divorce and Adult Well-being: A Meta-analysis', *Journal of Marriage and the Family*, 53(1): 43–58.

Appel, A. and Holden, G. (1998) 'The Co-occurrence of Spouse and Physical Child Abuse: A review and Appraisal', *Journal of Family Psychology*, 12(4): 578–99.

Ayoub, C., Deutsch, R. and Maraganorr, A. (1999) 'Emotional Distress in Children of High-conflict Divorce: The Impact of Marital Conflict and Violence', *Family Conciliation Courts Review*, 37(3): 297–314.

Belsky, J., Youngblade, L., Rovine, M. and Volling, B. (1991) 'Patterns of Marital Change and Parent-Child Interaction', *Journal of Marriage and the Family*, 53(2): 487–98.

Chishom, L. (ed.) (1990.) *Childhood, Youth and Social Change: A Comparative Perspective*, London: Falmer.

Corsaro, W. (1997) *The Sociology of Childhood*, Thousand Oaks, CA: Pine Forge Press.

Cummings, E. and Davies, P. (1994) *Children and Marital Conflict*, New York: Guilford.

Elkind, D. (1981) *The Hurried Child,* Reading, MA: Addison-Wesley.

Emery, R. (1999) *Marriage, Divorce, and Children's Adjustment*, 2nd edn., Thousand Oaks, CA: Sage.

Hetherington, E. (1991) 'Coping with Family Transitions: Winners, Losers and Survivors', in M. Woodhead, P. Light and R. Carr, (eds.), *Growing Up in a Changing Society*, London: Routledge.

Hetherington, E. (ed.) (1999) *Coping With Divorce, Single Parenting, and Remarriage: A Risk and Resiliency Perspective*, Mahway, NJ: Erlbaum.

Kelly, J. (2000) 'Children's Adjustment in Conflicted Marriages and Divorce: A Decade Review of Research', *Journal of the American Academy of Child and Adolescent Psychiatry,* 39(8): 963–73.

Lieberman, A., and Van Horn, P. (1998) 'Attachment, Trauma, and Domestic Violence: Implications for Child Custody', *Child Adolescent Psychiatric Clinics of North America*, 7(2): 423–43.

McLanahan, S. (1999) 'Father Absence and Children's Welfare', in E. Hetherington (ed.), *Coping With Divorce, Single Parenting, and Remarriage: A Risk and Resiliency Perspective,* Mahway, NJ: Erlbaum.

McNeal, C., and Amato, P. (1998) 'Parents' Marital Violence: Long-Term Consequences for Children,' *Journal of Family Issues*, 19(2): 123–39.

Meyrowitz, M. (1984) *The Adult Child and the Childhood Adult*, London: Routledge.

Montgomery, H. (2008) *An Introduction to Childhood: Anthropological Perspectives on Children's Lives*, Oxford: Wiley-Blackwell.

Nairn, A., Griffin, C. and Wicks, P. (2008) 'Children's Use of Brand Symbolism: A Consumer Culture Theory Approach', *European Journal of Marketing*, 42(5–6): 627–40.

Neighbors, B., Forehand, R. and McVicar, D. (1993) 'Resilient Adolescents and Interparental Conflict', *American Journal of Orthopsychiatry*, 63(3): 462–71.

Owen, M. and Cox, M, (1997) 'Marital Conflict and the Development of Infant-Parent Attachment Relationships', *Journal of Family Psychology*, 11(2): 152–64.

Pilcher, J., Delamont, S., Powell, G. and Rees, T. (1988) 'Women's Training Roadshows and the "Manipulation" of Schoolgirls' Career Choices', *British Journal of Education and Work*, 2(2): 61–66.

Pilcher, J. and Wagg, S. (eds.) (1996) *Thatcher's Children? Politics, Childhood and Society in the 1980s and 1990s,* London: Falmer Press.

Rosenbloom, S. and Way, N. (2004) 'Experiences of Discrimination Among African American, Asian American, and Latino Adolescents in an Urban High School', *Youth & Society*, 35(4): 420–51.

Sorbring, E. (2014) 'Parents' Concerns About Their Teenage Children's Internet Use', *Journal of Family Issues*, 35(1): 75–96. Vandewater, E. and Lansford, J. (1998) 'Influences of Family Structure and Parental Conflict on Children's Well-being', *Family Relations*, 47(4): 323–30.

Wagg, S. and Pilcher, J. (eds.) (2014) *Thatcher's Grandchildren? Politics and Childhood in the Twenty-First Century*, Basingstoke: Palgrave.

Zill, N., Morrison, D. and Coiro, M. (1993) 'Long Term Effects of Parental Divorce on Parent-Child Relationships, Adjustment, and Achievement in Young Adulthood', *Journal Family Psychology*, 7(1): 91–103.

Chapter 7

Youth and emerging adulthood

There is much in respect of the broad subject of 'youth' which exemplifies the social construct of the life course and, indeed, shifting cultural perceptions of various phases of life. Sociological evidence also points towards the significance of youth in terms of age cohorts, alongside aspects of age stratification, differentiation and associated social status. Perhaps above all, an analysis of current youth as a social category reflects many of the changes and continuities discernible in late/postmodernity. In that respect, contemporary youth may be said to constitute a 'social generation' which has lost much by way of community belonging and is subject to trends towards 'individualisation' and cultural fragmentation (Woodman and Wyn 2014). Youth is also now identified by economic insecurities and the vagaries of the employment market in a globalised world, consumerism and commodification and the impact of profound technological change, in which the current generation has become submerged like none previously. Continuity is nonetheless evident in that youth remains a significant and relatively 'separate' phase of life, to some degree or another informed by youth cultures, and one continuingly surrounded by the discourse of deviance and rendered problematic by older generations. Moreover, continuity remains evident in that social demographics and inequalities – class, gender and ethnicity continue to shape young lives and influence future life chances. All of these themes will be considered in this chapter.

'YOUTH' AS A MODERN INVENTION

Generally recognised as a transitional period between the stages of childhood and adulthood, 'youth' is commonly perceived as a troubled time – a biological period accompanied by emotional upheavals caused in part by abundant hormones present around puberty. It follows that the young body will mature and progress towards the 'calmer' stage of adulthood. In addition, the period of youth is viewed to be significant as a stage of development associated with the search for a sense of identity – adjusting and recognising the personal self, and forging attitudes regarding many areas of life, especially in relation to 'linked lives' – with peer groups aiding in furnishing a solution for some of the problems generated by a sense of anomie. In many ways, this popular assumption was evident in early academic theorising: the period of youth was necessary in order to socialise young people into value orientations and skills required for modern life and to negotiate future adult relationships and responsibilities (Eisenstadt 1956).

The increasing number of years that constitute the period of youth, however, now make these popularised assertions regarding biological processes and social relationships somewhat simplified. Developments in contemporary society undermine notions of 'youth' as a clearly defined stage of life. For one thing, precisely what years constitute youth at the beginning of the twenty-first century is difficult to ascertain. In the UK, in a designation which is not dissimilar elsewhere, youth is defined by the influential charity the British Youth Council as constituting any individual who falls within the 16 to 25 age group. Among other considerations, the extension 'upwards' beyond the teenage years, once almost synonymous with 'youth', denotes the proliferation of higher education opportunities which, for many young people, postpone entrance into the adult sphere of employment. For such reasons, the term 'Emergent Adulthood' (one often attributed to Jeffrey Arnett [2000]) constitutes a phase of the life-span between adolescence and mature adulthood which has gained growing currency. At the same time, this is supplemented by developments that would also seem to take the years of youth back into what was previously understood to be childhood. The earlier onset of puberty, alongside the increasing tendency of children to adopt teenage styles in terms of fashion and attitude, arguably pushes the period in a downward trajectory.

Official classifications of what constitutes youth would seem to point to the imperative of approaching youth as a social construction, as does further evidence which might be considered. Historically, the 'discovery' of the stages of 'adolescence' (usually deemed to equate with the commencement of puberty) and 'youth' occurred in the latter part of the nineteenth century and followed a similar pattern to the emergence of childhood. While puberty is a universal biological process, the alleged psychological dimension associated with adolescence was only gradually drawn attention to by the medical profession during that century. Moreover, educators and urban reformers began to observe the tendency of young people to affiliate strongly with peer groups and recognise their modes of behaviour associated with distinct cultural attributes. Hence, there emerged a 'new' stage of life which, from the beginning of the twentieth century, became the focus of literature and popular media, where the boundaries between childhood and adolescence and between adolescence and adulthood became more demarcated. By the mid-twentieth century, the sociological interest in youth began to grow as unique youth cultures came under scrutiny, with a primary theme focusing on relationships with older generations and the wider social environment, not to mention what was perceived as the dysfunctional elements such cultures displayed.

Academic research also began to explore cross-cultural appraisals of young people, throwing additional light on the social construction of a specific age category and thus providing insights into broader social change. One primary observation was that in many pre-modern societies the concept of youth, as with childhood, had no meaningful connotation in their cultural environments. Anthropology, in particular, embraced studies of different formations of youth in numerous national contexts, including those in the Majority World, and later in the context of globalisation – exploring experiences in a variety of urban settings in particular. Such research thus highlighted the virtue of a comparative dimension, putting Western youth in clear context (e.g. Amit-Talai and Wulff 1995; Brake 1985).

YOUTH SUBCULTURES

Early sociological research on the topic of youth initially centred on post-war youth subcultures – a term referring to a semi-autonomous culture, in some ways similar to and in other ways different from mainstream society. Thereafter, youth tended to be seen as constituting a social collective which widened the breach between young and older people, or the so-called 'generation gap', identified by symbolic expressions of distinct age cohorts (Spates 1983). From the mid-twentieth century – if not before (Fowler 1995) – an entire new range of marginal cultural expressions, all in one way or another initiated by young people, began with a more or less homogeneous subculture identified largely by rock 'n' roll – a music style that originated in the USA and which impacted lifestyles, fashion and attitudes of youth across the Western world.

While commodification, as discussed in this chapter, might be the distinguishing marker of contemporary youth, its relevance was evident in Mark Abram's early study *The Teenage Consumer* (1959), where he recognised youth as an emerging consumer group with market choices. In the relative affluence of the 1950s, young working-class males in particular, at a time when their traditional communities were in decline, found themselves with fewer obligations towards parents than earlier generations and with more disposable income, enabling the purchase of such items as music records, motorcycles, cosmetics, stylish clothes and other recreational goods. Hence, Abrams saw youth culture as the distinct orientation of a specific leisure group whose spending preferences reflected a tendency towards hedonism.

The development of youth cultures since the 1950s also pointed to matters of cohort differences of the experience of youth according to historical circumstances. It became evident that each separate generation claimed an exclusive identity, one defined by different characteristics which proved that the category of youth was a fluid rather than a fixed age group. Recent examples of different generational cohorts include, first, Generation X (usually designated as those born in the early 1970s to the early 1980s and the generation following the post-war Baby Boomers), which had experienced the problems related to economic uncertainty. Second, the Millennial Generation (with birth years ranging from the early 1980s to the early 2000s) – that found itself subject to many social changes, in particular the conditions of a revitalised economy but with few opportunities in the job market. Finally, Generation Z or 'post-millennials' are usually identified with those born around the year 2000 and beyond. Because each of these generations grew up under contrasting circumstances and social influences, they share a similar sense of identity but one radically different from earlier cohorts.

In considering youth cultures, many sociologists initially took the tone of Cohen, who stated that they 'express and resolve, albeit magically, the contradictions which remain hidden or unresolved in the parent culture' (Cohen 1985, 82–83). In other words, youth is a stressful period forged by social circumstances to which young people are obliged to negotiate their own responses. In doing so, youth styles may come to be viewed as a form of resistance in which the young consciously and purposefully use their own agency to work out their culture and image as a way of handling a string of diverse problems. Whether, for example, drain-pipe trousers as the style of dress for the teddy boys, the 'bother' boots of the skinheads, or the provocative attire of the punks, all say something about the felt need to establish a distinct identity in reaction to the wider social environment. Of a different ilk, the so-called primitives that emerged in the 1980s attempted to oppose the de-humanising consequences of mass consumption and sought to retreat into an independent ('indie') lifestyle. This enduring movement attempted a symbolic bodily use of resistance associated with tattoos, piercing and hair sculpting as an expression of the search for a different, authentic and autonomous way of life (Ferreira 2011).

There has always been more to the picture, however. Cohen (1971) was also perhaps the first to consider moral panics regarding youth cultures through the conflict between Mods and Rockers in the early 1960s, where the media amplified gang violence and vandalism. Here, the term 'moral panic' was given to mean an exaggerated fear that cherished social values were under threat by 'outsiders' or 'folk devils'. From this approach, youth are generally viewed as a 'problem': they are either seen as trouble or in trouble. The young, then, were beset by predominantly negative images and stereotypes: media talk of rising juvenile crime and various other woes which serve to increase the likelihood of them 'acting the part', reinforcing such disapproving evaluations through self-fulfilling prophecies.

The theme of moral panics has also been explored in regard to the acid house movement of the late 1980s. The movement was largely centred on a distinctive form of music (a fusion of 'Chicago house' dance styles and the 'Balearic beat' of the Ibizan jet-set associated with a particularly raucous lifestyle and frequently with the 'designer drug' ecstasy). According to Redhead (1993), one of the reasons why the movement was so negatively perceived was because it threatened the peace and quiet of respectable suburbia, where dance events were regularly described as 'rural riots'. Media reports presented their news to the adult public in such a way that young girls were seen as losing their innocence to drugs, and 'schoolchildren' were induced into a promiscuous lifestyle. Similarly, Welch et al. (2002) point out how the term 'wilding' or uncontrollable youth in the USA has become particularly significant due to its racial connotation, perpetuating a stereotype of young black and Latino males belonging to a 'dangerous class', attended by media perceptions of the fear of crime – a form of moral panic symbolising not only a threat to society at large, but also to a political economy that reproduces racial and social disparities.

YOUTH CULTURES AS 'PROTEST'

Moral panics apart, it is evident that at least some youth subcultures possess their own unique cultural orientations and are inclined to be counter-cultural in the sense they can be opposition or political, explicitly challenging the conventional values of adult mainstream society and the status quo. Much was exemplified by the hippie movement in the USA, which campaigned for peace during the Vietnam War in the 1960s, and the punks of the 1970s, whose overtly nihilistic inclinations brought direct opposition to traditional moralities and law and order. In these examples is to be found a defence of the idea that the primary meaning of youth culture is protest, even if merely symbolic in nature, which, despite different cultural styles, seems to register resistance against the alienation of the modern world.

Having acknowledged that some youth subcultures are culturally resistant, the relationship between them and the political world may be expressed differently according to historical circumstances. This is the theme of Hall and Jefferson's *Resistance Through Rituals* (2006). Here the authors state a case for seeing 'rave' youth cultural resistance as a 'symbolic' solution to the problems and contradictions facing youth in late-capitalism. Resistance is 'magical' in the sense that its counter-culture did not address the real material basis of subordination and failed to subsequently develop organised radical political action. Instead, the rave culture opted for resistance through rituals operating via the sphere of leisure – 'political' but in a very misguided way. Hall and Jefferson explain how 'rave' culture, with its excess of alcohol and 'designer drugs', turned its back on the problems of mature adulthood in order to live entirely in the present. This was at a time of economic uncertainty, too much pressure to succeed and too few real opportunities for having a real influence on one's life and on political processes. To put it simply, protest and the call for change was recognised by the young as not even worth attempting. Redhead (1993) comes to similar conclusions, explaining that a kind of 'cultural contradiction' emerged for young people who adhered to the rave movement. They were faced in the late twentieth century with a context in which a gap opened up between the ethic of hard work and thrift on the one hand and the economic reality of youth unemployment, under-employment and poverty on the other. Faced with this, young people, middle-class and working-class alike, resorted to the realm of pleasure – a form of hedonism in hard times – that lacked anything as antiquated as 'class consciousness' and was void of specific reference to a head-on assault on industrial-capitalist society.

YOUTH IN POSTMODERNITY

A scrutiny of the relevant literature indicates that postmodernist commentators have developed contrasting but sometimes overlapping themes in their discussion of contemporary youth trends. A prominent concern has been in exploring how youth cultures are largely redundant or are at least perceived as increasingly a product of consumption. That, in short, they have undergone a process of ever-increasing commodification which erodes any expression of political radicalism and generates more mainstream attitudes. What many sociological reports also have in common, however, is reference to 'alienated youth', where young people struggle to find a sense of meaning and a coherent self-identity in a society in a state of flux. This seems to be particularly the case for Generation Z – a generation brought up with more affluence than previous age cohorts but which has lost association with former generations. They have never known a world without mobile phones and the internet, and have grown up with images of violence and pornography easily accessible. It is, however, in some accounts, a generation subject to widening social inequality, political apathy and economic uncertainty, while displaying ever more hedonism and narcissism (Combi 2015).

It may be argued from a postmodernist perspective that young people join subcultures after a period of 'surfing' the youth culture market, and then only on a temporary basis before opting for another. Certainly, at the present time youth cultural styles are extremely eclectic. Partly because of a widely expressed common youth language of popular music, cable and satellite TV, and film, many aspects of youth culture depend on borrowing from several sources in an increasingly globalised world. Individuals are seemingly free to actively experiment with cultural motifs, constructing a 'bricolage' of diverse cultural strands in their own lives, mixing styles of fashion and music. This, in turn, marks a reflection of wider social and cultural diversification. Thus today there is a range of youth subcultures including cyber-punks, ravers, rastas, grunge, primitives and so on. Certainly, by the mid-1990s the situation was largely one of plurality and styles mixing and matching different genres that even adopted and adapted previous youth cultures, derived from a particular place and time, in a kind of nostalgic time-warp which, nonetheless, frequently became the subject of commodification.

If current modes of expressing youth represent a response to the growing complexity of options, choices and lifestyles in wider society, this raises important questions. First, are youth cultures now merely 'fashions'? Does their significance begin and end with trends in consumption and the expansion of markets amongst young people? A related question is whether youths are now merely 'slaves' to consumerism as a result of youth markets being manipulated by the corporate world, where 'street' styles are appropriated, commercialised and diluted by large business concerns.

Some commentators, then, have portrayed youth cultures as completely channelled by music and clothing industries that have sought to exploit a specific market segment and rendered youth highly vulnerable to global capitalism interests selling what Furlong and Cartmel (1997) refer to as 'identity scripts'. From this standpoint what increasingly matters today are the brands and emotional attachment to them by young people who are exceptionally brand conscious and vulnerable to the dictates of the large corporates. Companies such as Nike, Apple, Disney, Calvin Klein, Gap, Microsoft, Starbucks, McDonalds, Virgin and Intel represent not so much their 'products' as their brand name and image – many attractive to a younger generation. Such developments may, however, produce new forms of inequality. Thus Croghan and associates (2006) argue that the link between styles and branded designer goods makes the maintenance of a style identity economically costly. Yet there are also social costs associated with falling short of maintaining such an identity: the consequences of a 'style failure' for young people in relation to issues of peer group social exclusion and status loss.

Furthermore, consumer dimensions of youth culture now seem to be increasingly moved down to the younger teenager age range. Identification of the so-called tweenies market is a case in point. Niche publications such as *CosmoGirl, ElleGirl* and *Teen Vogue,* aimed at 12- to 16-year-old girls (now increasingly moving on-line), appear to take for granted their hyper-awareness of brands, while the teen market in the UK alone is estimated to be worth some £8.4 billion annually. The problem with this top-down, corporate-consumer emphasis, however, is that it tends to make young people 'cultural dupes' without any real sense of agency and creative capacity. At the very least, it fails to differentiate between an 'authentic' youth culture as opposed to mainstream culture on the one hand and the youth culture industry which creates fashions and market products on the other.

What does seem the case, however, is that, even with more radical groups, consumerism quickly appears to take up, popularise and effectively weaken stylistic and creative subcultural expressions. For instance, while punk music and style of dress was originally the product of unemployed working-class youth, within a very short space of time the movement was commercially exploited in the youth marketplace by commercial interests. Thus, when a subcultural symbol like punk music is commercialised, instead of providing a long-term focus with which the movement can coalesce and identify, the symbols are rendered harmless by the popular music industry, reprocessed and repackaged to a wider audience which does not associate in any meaningful way with its original context of protest and rebellion. Michael Jeffries (2011) comes to comparable conclusions concerning hip-hop culture, which has come a long way from its origins in the Bronx in the 1970s when rapping and DJing were merely part of an energetic local scene. Now hip-hop is a global phenomenon and, in the USA, a hugely successful corporate enterprise predominantly controlled and consumed by whites, even though black music artists remain its most prominent performers.

YOUTH CULTURES – VARIATIONS ON A THEME

The stress on the commodification of youth and 'individualization', which devoid the young of a sense of identity and even radical edge, has, however, been criticised. In this respect David Muggleton (2005) has drawn attention to how subcultural theory, through the application of symbolic interactionism and the problem-solving of Marxism to youth, especially its deviant expressions, has tended to be replaced by 'post-subcultural studies'. However, Muggleton warns of the danger of abandoning the subculture concept altogether, arguing that coherent youth cultures remain in addition to the postmodern traits of flux, fluidity and hybridisation in the early twenty-first century. Hence it is important to retain the significance of youth cultures, discussed here in terms of the way they give expression to significant gender, ethnicity and, more recently, sexual diversity.

Female subcultures

One of the most significant limitations of many early studies of youth subcultures was the conspicuous near-absence of any meaningful analyses of females within them. In the vast majority of studies girls scarcely received a mention and were largely referred to only within the context of their dependent relationship with young males, and even then primarily as sex objects. In fact, in sociological works (largely written by male academics) girls were usually merely portrayed through the eyes of the 'lads' (Heidensohn 1985) and occupied subordinate positions, reflecting their lower position in wider patriarchal society (McRobbie and Garber 1976).

At the same time, distinctively female youth subcultures have tended to be less public, less street-based and therefore less observable forms as a result of the greater social restrictions placed upon girls, while also displaying significant aspects of culturally informed femininity (Nayak and Kehily 2013) that contrast starkly with youth masculinities (Richardson 2010).

Despite these observations, it is clear that female peer groups have a distinct and significant existence within the larger youth group. Evidence suggests that girls share much activity in common. They are more likely than boys to know details of the top popular music recordings, to read teenage magazines and to be familiar with the latest dance routines, which they perform, usually in a kind of 'protective togetherness', at dance clubs and other venues. This togetherness has been highlighted by a number of feminist sociologists who have provided insights into a rich female subculture which has underlined the close relationships of girls within the peer group (Greenfield 2002; McRobbie 1978; Ward 1976). Here they offer each other intense and long-lasting friendship, contributing emotional and practical support, trust and loyalty over a protracted period of time. Leonard's study (1980) of young girls found that when 'going steady' with a boyfriend there remained clearly allocated 'girls times', with a tendency to retain strong friendship contacts when entering employment, job training or college. Moreover, Griffin (1985a) suggests that young girls' relationships are divided into clear stages, according to their age. From 'going round with a boy', usually in a mixed sex group at the age of about 13 or 14, the girls 'progressed' to the more coherently delineated 'going out with a boy' from about 14 or 15, and from there to more regular boyfriends and 'courting', which might lead to further commitment. 'Going out with' often involved undertaking social activities in foursomes as a kind of chaperoning.

Sue Lees (1993, 16) takes a different approach, however, and observes that much theorising about identity and relationships has overlooked the contradictions inherent in female identity. Forming an identity as a young girl involves establishing a firm sense of self – in opposition to the popularised depiction of girls as sex objects. The dilemma for young girls in particular is that they tread a very narrow line: they must avoid being regarded as promiscuous, but equally they do not wish to be thought unapproachable or sexually cold. McRobbie has also emphasised romantic love as a cultural value more readily enculturated for females: meeting the 'right man' and falling in love – a norm projected through the media, which 'elevate to dizzy heights the supremacy of the heterosexual romantic partnership' (McRobbie 1978, 17, 20).

Earlier studies also tended to play down the more deviant aspects of female youth culture. However, a developing range of literature began to consider the phenomenon of girl gangs. For example, Esbensen et al. (1999) explored the extent to which gang girls are similar to or different from gang boys in terms of their attitudes, perceptions of their gangs and their involvement in gang-like illegal activities. Findings indicate that gang girls are involved in a full array of deviant gang activities, although not as frequently as the gang boys. Whereas similarities exist in behavioural activities and in reasons for joining gangs, girls report greater social isolation from family and friends and lower levels of self-esteem than boys.

More recently, sociological studies have focused on female youth culture as it connects with late/postmodernity, suggesting a high level of conformity to mainstream culture through commodification. For example, Deutsch and Theodorou (2010) focus on how consumerism, as a social ideology, and consumption, as an individual activity, are used by adolescents to mark and mask differences in the process of identity construction. The act of consuming for the adolescents forms an integral part of their identity performance irrespective of race and class. For females, consumption is seemingly linked to gender performances based on the maintenance of an attractive and fashionable appearance as dictated by social perceptions of femininity and ambitions for the freedom that money is believed to bring.

Ethnic subcultures

While all young people plausibly display the difficulty of forging a workable identity, for ethnic minority youth this may be particularly acute. Many are frequently presented with two potentially conflicting adult models. That of a citizen in a Western society, sharing equal rights and duties with whites; and the matter of identity of black, Asian or some other ethnic minority group, visibly distinct and with a unique cultural heritage. The problem may be compounded by the experience of prejudice and rejection, since self-identity partly depends on how others appraise the individual and collective to which s/he belongs. Hence, the cultural life of ethnic minorities – especially if constituting recently immigrant groups and particularly of the young – cannot be divorced from dimensions of discrimination and stereotyping.

Commonly, largely negative characterisations of Afro-Caribbean culture, even by sociological accounts, tend to present two polarised male stereotypes. First, the 'hustler', who copes with the difficulties of the employment market by 'hustling' a living out of dealing in drugs, gambling, pimping or stealing. He is characterised as existing in some style, sporting smart cars and well-cut clothes, and displaying a 'laid back' attitude to life. This popularised image tends to focus on the lack of patriarchal responsibilities as providers and heads of households and the retreat to a compensatory hyper-masculinity centred on sexuality and violence of 'black macho' fantasies, which, for the black women, generate negative self-perceptions, that are passed down to younger generations.

That stereotypical views of ethnic youth subcultures are so widespread, may partly be attributed to the mass media. Henry Giroux (1997), in his account of the ways that black youths are perceived, puts particular emphasis on the role of the visual media, which saturates contemporary cultural life. Such media brings negative portrayals through a complex deconstruction of black youth image when associated with film characters, tarnished real-life idols such as O.J. Simpson, alongside sexualised presentations of black youth as permissive, and this may lead to a self-fulfilling prophecy in that some young blacks may act out these negative role models. This can be contrasted with perceptions of Afro-Caribbean youth dominated by the 'Rasta' movement that is defensive and an inevitable part of the cultural tradition of a group actually or potentially subjugated. Hence, the retreat into Rastafarianism, which traces its spiritual roots back to Africa as exemplified by plaited hair and some aspects of dress which imitate African origins. These two stereotypical views of Caribbean youth cultures, however, tend to draw attention away from the degree that most Caribbean young people are assimilated into a wide variety of mainstream values and other youth subcultures.

Assimilation, whatever its merits, clearly has its difficulties for the young of various ethnic groups, who might find themselves being caught between the pressures of two different cultures, thus emphasising the importance of generational differences. Asian youths, for example, may be pressurised by dominant Western culture, including youth culture, on the one hand, and the values of their parents and grandparents on the other. Asian culture, typified by the religious values of Islam or Hinduism and more patriarchal family structures, may run counter to more liberal and 'permissive' attitudes of Western culture. Young people can thus find themselves obliged to choose between these contradictory cultural values, making 'growing up' an especially difficult process (Singh 1993). Subsequently, the forging of distinct youth cultures were once thought relatively unlikely.

Despite the difficulties that some ethnic youths may have in embracing distinctive youth subcultures, the frequent social construction of such subcultures as a social problem is a subject highlighted by research of what appear to be growing anxieties towards ethnic 'gangs'. Alexander (2000), for instance, has shown how the Asian gang has been 'discovered' as a 'new' and urgent social concern. The image portrayed in the media has proved to be one which sees their emergence against the backdrop of urban deprivation and an underclass, combined with fears of growing youth militancy and masculinity in 'crisis'. The result has been to position Asian and especially Muslim young men as the latest 'folk devils'. The 're-imagination' of Asian male youth has focused on violence, drug abuse and crime set against a backdrop of cultural conflict, generational confusion and religious fundamentalism. Alexander, however, does not interpret the Asian gang as deviant or constituting 'resistance'. Rather, it is much more mundane and ordinary, a source of peer group identification, but where the broader family is still very much a central life focus and where a response to a multi-ethnic society, via non-deviant activities, is at the centre of youth identification. This is a source of belonging which carries a great sense of loyalty and community but where religion is not a particularly important element. The gang thus gives expression to Asian youth cultural ambivalences and contradictions of identity and marks a way of dealing with broader social exclusion.

Post-9/11 a fresh 'urgent social problem' has been aggravated by fears over the radicalisation of Islamic youth in the West. There can be little doubt of the increasing multiple and contested roles of religion and personal faith in the fashioning of contemporary youthful Muslim identities. Such insights thereby often challenge secular Western master narratives. Young Muslims have been thrust into the global spotlight in relation to questions about security and extremism, work and migration, and rights and citizenship. Herrera and Bayer (2010) show that while the majority of young Muslims share many common social, political and economic challenges, they exhibit remarkably diverse responses to them. As they migrate, forge networks and assert themselves in the public sphere Muslim youth has emerged as an important a cultural and political actor. One challenge has come to be known as Islamophobia, which clearly plays a role in shaping the attitudes of young Muslims. For instance, according to a Zogby (2009) poll in the USA, 75 per cent of young Muslims said they or someone they know has been discriminated against on the grounds of their religious faith.

Sexual minority subcultures

Recent research has also extended to the subject of LGBTQ (lesbian, gay, bisexual, transgender, queer/questioning) youth and have taken various trajectories related to subcultures. One focus has been on a sense of well-being and the importance of affiliation with those who face similar challenges in being part of a sexual minority. Higa et al. (2012) found that challenging negative factors were associated with families, schools, religious institutions and community or neighbourhood; positive factors were associated with supportive peer networks and involvement in the wider LGBTQ community which emphasise the importance of fostering a positive LGBTQ identity. Walls and colleagues (2009) come to similar conclusions by stressing the importance of sexual minority support groups in schools and how they positively impact experiences, whether or not the sexual minority youth is an actual member of the group.

Susan Driver (2008) points out the complexities of queer youth subcultures in their cultural practices, given that they are not classifiable as either mainstream or marginal but rather are criss-crossed by the commercial mass media and grassroots subcultural and activist spheres. These spheres permit person agency concerned with 'meaning making' in the attempt to be empowering as tools of self-expression and social communication and symbolic creativities. The complexities of social life for queer youth are enhanced by matters of class, 'race', ethnicity, geographics and even relationship with older LGBT age categories. This ensures different levels of social acceptance, but also informs discrimination, pathologising 'expert' discourse, and educational neglect – making queer youth unintelligible to mainstream society and often creating cultural marginalisation and stereotyping. Moreover, negative reactions are exacerbated by the time of youth, which is still viewed as a period of transition between adulthood and childhood – rendering the status of queer as particularly problematic in a context when young people are coerced by normative developmental ideals of self and maturation.

YOUTH AND DEVIANCE

An all-pervasive theme focusing on youth as a problematic period is the emphasis on deviance which the discussion above more than suggests. There is further evidence to support this assertion. While the years 2011/12, according to the Youth Justice Statistics for England and Wales, showed a continued decrease in youth crime, those committed by those aged between 10–17 years old still registered fairly high rates:

- Of all crime recorded, 13.6 per cent was committed by this age group (or 10.8 per cent of all those of offending).
- In the same period there were 273 Anti-Social Behaviour Orders and 2807 assaults committed in custody.
- The number of young people re-offending also seemed to be increasing with more than 47,000 criminals (or 32 per cent) aged between 16 and 21 committing new crimes within 12 months of being cautioned, convicted or released from prison.

Although young people are often over-represented in crime and delinquency statistics, only a minority appear to be habitual re-offenders over a protracted period of time. Indeed it has long been recognised that for the majority deviance is not a dedicated way of life. Rather, it is something which young people 'drift' in and out of during the youth phase of the life course. Delinquent youth subcultures may maintain an independent set of values and beliefs differing from the majority culture, but nonetheless most of those involved will eventually grow out of deviant activities (Matza 1964).

If this assertion is correct, then the stress on deviance and non-conformity are part of a much larger concern of sociological enquiry that also encompasses aspects of parenting, alongside matters of peer pressure at the youth stage, which stresses the continued importance of those of the same age group. Brauer and De Coster (2015), for instance, argue that it is important to assess the behavioural orientations of 'significant others' and find that 'social learning theory' (focusing on cognitive processes taking place in a social context through observation or direct instruction) is best equipped to explain peer influence; however, the developmental perspective (how individuals change or stay the same over the course of their life) appears more applicable to parental influence. These two influences may interact. Chan and Chan (2011) have shown how adolescents' susceptibility to peer pressure is related to their relationships with mothers and emotional autonomy from parents. In short, mothers' behavioural and psychological control can enhance adolescents' susceptibility to peer pressure.

The impact of peer group pressure in respect of 'learning' deviant behaviour has been explored in various ways. Kosten et al. (2012) considered peer conformity in a sample of USA middle-school students from a developmental perspective and found that those most prone to youth peer pressure were more likely to be male, white and have low self-esteem. Social learning theory has been applied to a further variety of criminal, delinquent and deviant behaviour. Winfree et al. (1994) excavate the utility of the theory to the examination of youth gangs. Group-context offending seems closely connected to both social learning and gang membership. Other forms of self-reported delinquency, however, while linked to social learning, were unrelated to gang membership. In a further study, the opposite seems to be possible. Higgins et al. (2010) thus show how peer rejection can relate to delinquency/crime especially among young males. Finally, it has long been assumed that disadvantaged urban neighbourhoods may be another feature which must be considered in understanding delinquent behaviour – that there is a close relationship between neighbourhood social structure, social processes, delinquent opportunities for delinquency and rates of adolescent delinquency. However, research by Kingston et al. (2009) indicates that while locality may have some impact, the major causes of youth delinquency/crime in such neighbourhoods were perceptions of limited opportunities for the future.

Deviance: some current concerns

Although negative aspects of parenting and peer group pressure may impact aspects of deviance, there are matters of youth deviance that are of habitual concern. Others, which have arisen more recently, seem to have been generated by a range of cultural, economic and technological developments. One perennial anxiety is the matter of sexuality and sexual activity of young people. By the late twentieth century these anxieties appeared to have been amplified by risks associated with the rise in teenage pregnancies, debates over the age of consent for heterosexuals and gays, fears of sexually transmitted diseases (STDs) and the increase of sexual relationships commencing at an earlier age.

It is probably true to say that sexual activity among adolescents is a matter of concern for adults, who feel it is their responsibility to regulate and protect teenagers from many perceived tribulations, and marks a source of anxiety in generational relations. In turn, the increase in sexual activity at a younger age could at least partly be due to the compulsion to rebel, knowing that adults would disapprove in a similar way to drinking, smoking, drugs and so on, many of which activities may be sources of moral panics, resulting, in the case of sexual activity, from the contested area of the 'young' body.

Box 7.1 Sexually Transmitted Diseases UK

- In 2009 there were 482,696 new STI diagnoses in the UK, 3 per cent more than in 2008.
- Those aged 15–24 years are habitually the group most affected by STIs in the UK. In 2009, around two-thirds of new STI diagnoses in women were in those aged under 25, and over half of new diagnoses in men were in under 25s.
- Rates of acute STIs were highest in residents of urban areas, reflecting higher incidence of socio-economic deprivation and higher concentrations of groups of the population who are at most risk of infection, such as young people and men who have sex with men.

Source: adapted from 'Sexually Transmitted Infections Factsheet', fpa.

One of the main reasons for increased activity may simply be that puberty is emerging earlier, and hence young people reach sexual maturity earlier (today, in the UK one in four girls and one in five boys have partaken of sex by the time they are 16 years old.). It might also be argued that the general trend towards sex at an early age is inevitable in a society which is increasingly sexualised. Sex itself has become commodified, the subject of much advertising and it is, in particular, the way that women are portrayed in the dominant culture (Attwood 2006). The pressure of the young to be sexually active therefore becomes more acute. Moreover, the increasing availability of contraception and access to advice from doctors and family planning clinics possibly encourages the ease with which teenagers can lead an active sex life.

There is more to consider. Attitudes towards sex have been found to be largely engendered. Jones et al. (2012) engage with Erikson's (1950) lifespan theory and speculate that the physical changes associated with puberty serve as a catalyst for adolescents to question childhood identifications. For males, pubertal changes have implications for sexual identity development and self-perceptions of masculinity during adolescence. While young males are often regarded as sexual predators, girls by contrast associate having a boyfriend as part of being 'grown-up', and therefore a direct way for them to feel mature (Griffin 1985b).

A further current anxiety has arisen around risk-related behaviour and consumerism. For example, Hayward and Hobbs (2007) consider how the contemporary commercialised night-time economy has transformed UK town centres into liminal spaces, especially for the young, where social transgression is encouraged by alcohol-related excitement and excess on the one hand and social agencies which seek to exert a measure of rational control over the drink 'problem' on the other. Hayward and Hobbs argue that it is the logic of the market which informs governmental policy on alcohol, where the binge drinker is central to the spectacle of the night-time economy as a form of self-gratification which also embodies forms of repressive control.

Finally, amplifying the negative impact of social media technology, there is the matter of so-called cyberbullying that is identified with a variety of effects on the mental health of younger people. Cyberbullying occurs when youth use technology as an instrument to harass their peers via email, in chat rooms, on social networking or mobile phones. Patchin and Hinduja's study (2010) sheds light on the potential causes of adolescent aggression in this form, suggesting that those who experience problems in their own lives are more likely to participate in both traditional and non-traditional forms of bullying. Peguero and Williams (2011) extend research on this topic by considering how youth who violate racial and ethnicity stereotypes may experience particularly derogatory treatment. The study indicates that family socio-economic status and sports participation nonetheless moderate the relationship between bullying victimisation and race and ethnicity. Research by Parris et al. (2011) also revealed three primary coping themes among those surveyed: 'reactive coping' included avoiding the cyberbullying situation by deleting or ignoring messages; 'preventive coping' strategies included increased security and awareness; while some reported that there was no realistic way to reduce cyberbullying.

A further growing concern which such bullying draws attention to is youth mental health. Research, including that constructed by the World Health Organization, highlights the fact that a comparatively high number of young people suffer from a range of social and psychological maladies which stress the 'risk' of being young, particularly in the developed world. Research in the UK by Collishaw and colleagues (2004) found that the rate of emotional problems such as anxiety and depression had increased by 70 per cent among adolescents over a 25-year period. Boys were more likely to exhibit behavioural problems and girls (one in five of 15-year-olds) to suffer emotional difficulties. Negative behaviour, such as lying, stealing and being disobedient, more than doubled during this time. The report suggested that these increases could not be explained by the rise in divorce and single parenthood because comparable increases were found in all types of families, ethnic groups and social classes, although there was a higher rate of adolescent mental health problems in single-parent families. Rather, increase was linked to chances of experiencing a range of poor outcomes as adults such as homelessness and dependency on benefits and poor physical health. This was understood as related to the transition route youth take to adulthood, which has become more arduous with the constant pressure to obtain qualifications and succeed.

THE 'BURDEN' OF YOUTH

Consumerism as a cultural motif implies that late/postmodernity appears to impact the period of youth in terms of choice. Yet, choice may be constrained by economic fluctuations, unemployment and dimensions of opportunity and risk that restrain, or at least complicate, the experience of certain categories of youth in the transition to adulthood and enhance some of the 'problems' discussed above (Rohrbach et al. 2005; Settersten and Ray 2010). Since the early 1990s in many Western countries governments have continued the process of marketisation in higher education: introducing student loans and fees, ideally to make students responsible and enthusiastic consumers while simultaneously saving public money. In sum, the education policies in recent years have supposedly further tied the aims of the educational system to the needs of a competitive economy, especially since the economic crisis of 2008.

Expansion in higher education took off in the late 1980s to the extent that the term 'mass' higher education has enjoyed common currency. Peter Scott (1996) gives various reasons for this expansion. Perhaps most obviously, there is the need for acquiring personal transferable skills in the ever-changing post-Fordist economy. In addition, Scott argues, participation in higher education is now a key component in the manufacturing of social and personal identities. In particular, attending university is presently not so much about being middle-class, but related to occupational and cultural credentialism. In short, as Western societies have become more technologically based, culturally diverse and socially mobile, diplomas and degrees supposedly say a great deal about 'who you are'. Moreover, qualifications such as advanced degrees serve as a shorthand way to differentiate between those who have or do not have the 'correct' manners and attitudes sought by many employers. Finally, higher education has become part of what Scott calls the 'entertainment-learning-leisure-heritage complex'. This means that education has now emerged as a powerful cultural commodity which is produced and consumed as a segment of a developing educational marketplace. Lengthening the period of education, and hence the stage of youth, means that the young can find it arduous to forge adult identities, maintain coherent biographies and develop strategies to overcome obstacles. Much is linked to the fact young people now negotiate a set of risks which were largely unknown to their parents: this is so, irrespective of the individual's social background or gender.

From the 1990s, even those with relatively few qualifications at the age of 16 years frequently opted to stay in full-time education, although in many depressed geographical areas this was partly because there are so few credible alternatives in the labour market (Furlong and Cartmel 1997). Yet, those who venture into higher education often find themselves entering employment with crippling student debts that may take years to pay off. Neither does higher education avoid the consequences of social inequalities. Ricardo Stanton-Salazar (2011) considers those younger people in the context of social capital – defined in terms of key resources and support provided by institutional agents. High-status, non-kin agents who occupy relatively high positions in the stratification system are well positioned to provide key forms of social and institutional support, often through network-related capacities and skills. Put succinctly, occupation advancement becomes a matter of 'who you know' and displaying the 'correct' cultural nuances.

Since the 1990s the well-established relationship between the family, school and work seems to have weakened and young people embark on their journeys into adulthood along a wide variety of trajectories, many of which appear to have unpredictable outcomes. These changes in the experiences of the young are clearly discernible in the world of work. The youth labour market has changed so drastically that it would be almost unrecognisable to those of previous generations. The course of the last quarter of the twentieth century onwards has thus witnessed a dramatic reversal in the fortunes of young people. From being a key beneficiary of the post-war political commitment to inclusion and concession, youth became re-constituted as a much more costly 'state' to be in. Thus, at present young people may have to rely financially on their parents for longer and in general are living at home until a later age, which causes the period of adulthood, and all that entails in terms of adult responsibilities, to be suspended, generating a new form of youth alienation (Mizen 2003).

Cote and Allahar (1996) highlight the dilemmas facing marginalised and alienated youth. In North America, Western Europe and Japan, many youths can expect to have a lower standard of living than their parents. They are conditioned to stay younger longer in education and have, as a result, become socially and economically ostracised, finding it difficult to establish adult identities. With fewer employment opportunities available, the young are paradoxically targeted by businesses, but increasingly as consumers rather than producers. As new technologies continually reduce the workforce and transform the social fabric, an entire generation of young now find it difficult to keep up with developments. Many young workers are forced to accept low pay and are poorly placed to begin to accumulate resources necessary for a good standard of living throughout the life course.

Increasingly, employment instability would seem to complicate this transition and the move from youth to responsible roles, and the self-sufficiency associated with maturity and adulthood. Plainly, youth today spend years moving in and out of different education and work statuses until they settle into stable employment. Krahn et al.'s (2012) longitudinal study reveals how month-to-month fluctuations in employment and educational statuses from age 19 to 25 predict employment success at age 32. Early employment instability was linked to lower income at age 32 and, among men, to lower occupational status and career satisfaction. In general, the study suggests that labour market stability in the early 20s might best be described as 'floundering'.

There is more to consider in explaining why the young are disproportionally disadvantaged. Youth unemployment is more often than not higher than adults partly because younger people are entering the labour market for the first time and are consequently more at risk from unemployment. Second, many jobs entered on when first starting work are unskilled and semi-skilled, in the manufacturing and service sectors – those traditionally associated with high rates of labour turnover. In addition, in times of relatively full employment some young people may change jobs either to find variety in work or until they settle down, again placing themselves at risk of unemployment.

The economic problems are undoubtedly enhanced by the so-called Great Recession since 2008. According to Bell and Blanchflower (2010), the resultant sharp increase in unemployment and decrease in employment is mostly concentrated on the young. This has occurred at a time when the size of the youth cohort is relatively large. There is evidence that much like all unemployed groups the young have particularly low levels of well-being, experience depression, display low levels of life satisfaction and are especially likely to be in financial difficulties. That acknowledged, unemployment impacts on different social groups in diverse ways depending on their previous experiences and expectations. Roberts et al. (1989) suggest that while young people do not enjoy unemployment, they are in many respects better equipped to deal with it than older workers. For immediate school-leavers there is no work identity to be undermined and fewer financial obligations. Many of their peers may often be in the same situation, while some can rely on the support of their families. Moreover, it has been found that the majority of young people manage to keep a level of self-respect and do not suffer extensively from the range of social and psychological maladies often associated with unemployment (Willis 1977).

Yet this is not to say that there are not repercussions, with Willis (1977) suggesting that youth unemployment has profound effects on family life and relationships. Willis (1977) uncovered evidence among males of creating mythical 'macho' exploits such as marathon drinking sessions. Factors like these may account for the increase in substance abuse and crime, and they provide a convincing argument as to why the period of youth may be particularly difficult. Without work, leisure activities have less meaning and increasing amounts of time are spent in the home. Perhaps the most important consideration, however, is that young people are left in limbo, unable to look forward to or make the transition to adult status, and are subject to boredom, frustration and demoralisation, which may lead to stress and conflict within the family.

EMERGING ADULTHOOD

The transitional period from youth to adulthood – extending into the 20s – is a rapidly growing area of research which has come to recognise that it is now so complex that it has been dubbed 'Emerging Adulthood'. This is acknowledged as a recent and developmentally distinct phase in the life-course characterised as a period of identity exploration, informed by the context social and economic instability considered above, being self-focused, feeling 'in-between', and a period of possibilities. However, within this period important cultural and national differences in how emerging adulthood is experienced is increasingly the subject of research (e.g. Arnett et al. 2011; Jeffrey and Mcdowell 2004; Negru 2012).

Within the 'emergent adulthood' classification of the young, important age differences have been identified. Banks et al. (1992) found that this was so with a sample of 16- to 20-year-olds regarding attitudes and experiences. The average 16-year-old experienced far less social and emotional development than those in their early 20s: few experiences of longer-term close relationships outside of the family, and displayed little sense of the moral responsibilities often associated with adulthood. Managing their own money, their time and their lives generally were not revealed to be problems that many faced. A good number of 20-year-olds, by contrast, had moved closer to adult identity. Yet, within this age group there was found to be a wide variation in the rate of transition from full-time schooling to employment. Here there were various routes to transition, at least some of which had long-term repercussions in terms of life opportunities. On the other hand, there are choices which are, in the short term, less consequential. These choices include political party allegiances, leisure activities, patterns of spending and personal relationships. Such choices constitute part of a whole range of life options which are unstable and frequently reversed when adult identity is achieved. However, in terms of aspects of social identity it is clear that some attitudes were already forged by the age of 16 and therefore only reinforced afterwards. These attitudes include orientations towards authority, gender, commitment to employment and views towards fatalism. The picture drawn by Banks and associates suggests continuities of values and opinions, but at the same time differences in experiences of major transformations result largely through various routes to the workplace.

Other sociological studies have researched the significance of risk and choice and found that social variables may influence how they are negotiated by young adults. Longitudinal research by Thompson and associates (2002) indicated that across a number of different backgrounds there are 'critical moments' in young persons' biographies which have implications in processes of social inclusion and exclusion. Yet, there is a relationship between social and geographical location and the life events that they report as having particular biographical significance. The character of these 'critical moments' is essentially part of a reflexive project of self, as are young people's response to them. The study showed an interaction of choice, chance and opportunity. The notion of 'critical moments' forges a middle path between the way young people talk about their lives and what actually happens to them. Whilst most young people make references to individual choice, the required resources and opportunities are not necessarily available, and this is recognised by young people as they anticipate the future.

A study by Du Bois-Reymond (1998) also indicated that young people vary in the way that they think about time – in particular in relation to their present condition of being young and the way they envisage their future adulthood. In the case of less economically privileged young women, attitudes were found to be very present-day orientated and perceptions of their future lives were taken by an unquestioning acceptance of how they saw their parents' situation. They did not think in terms of choices and opportunities or of seeing the future as being something of their own making. Rather, the future was perceived as a fairly scheduled, standardised life course. Du Bois-Reymond concludes that for many of the young people the navigation of the transition to adulthood is influenced by their perception and experience of time and involves aspects of personal agency, including planning and making choices, but that this incorporates the very real restrictions that may be present.

Such studies clearly throw doubt upon simplistic notions of agency and the reflexive self in late-modernity – an observation also made in a comparative study by Branem and Nilsen (2002) of young people in the UK and Norway. Among their conclusions is that for less privileged young females, notions of a negotiated future involving opportunities and risks were almost entirely absent. Such young girls tended to envisage their future in terms of their parents' circumstances, while, far from considering future prospects, the emphasis was very much present-orientated. Additional studies have also suggested that as active agents those situated in emergent adulthood may be influenced by how they perceive what mature adulthood identity actually amounts to rather than a realistic understanding of what this entails (Schwartz et al. 2012).

SUMMARY

'Youth' is not the only stage of life where individuals experience major physical and psychological changes and are obliged to make readjustments to social roles and expectations. Parenthood, mid-life and the transition to later life are all accompanied by such readjustments, although it may be conjectured that the adults involved in these changes will adapt to social norms more easily and retain a strong sense of self, having experienced more life experience. Under such conditions, then, it is perhaps not too surprising that, historically speaking, youth subcultures develop as a response to unique challenges to a specific time and place – all of which may be impacted by periodic moral panics and negative appraisals, which nonetheless can cut across the positive image of looking and 'being' young. Moreover, where everyday life experience is one of subordination and low status, it is evident that subcultures emerge to deal with or even exacerbate inter-generation tension.

The situation in late/postmodernity is now more complex. If youth has conventionally been interpreted as a developmental 'crisis', then the nature of that crisis is observably undergoing change. It is one informed by complex choices, individualisation and opportunities, discontinuities and problems of identity generated by risk and uncertainty. Nearly a century ago Margaret Mead (1928) was able to contrast developments in the West with pre-industrial societies. Those older children who had not reached adult maturity lived in a kind of 'temporal no-man's land' which had an ambiguity of status that involved a significant rite of passage into adulthood. It may be that many young people in the West now feel that they are in a kind of liminality in their transition to adulthood, as a result of discontinuity and disruption, without even the psychological support of such rites.

There are good grounds for asserting that more recently, as Sukarieh and Tannock (2014) explore, 'youth' and youth identity has come increasingly into focus as an age category across the world as a societal concern. Government policy, media attention and public debates have proliferated internationally against a backdrop of contemporary political economy. The rise and spread of global capitalism and its attendant neoliberal philosophy has meant an attempt to extend social control of the young. There are growing fears of the repercussions of mass youth unemployment and a 'lost generation' in the wake of the global financial crisis of 2008 in numerous national environments.

This might suggest that youth are becoming more 'passive', a passivity enhanced by a culture of consumerism. However, the period of youth is now one of multiple transitions – personal, social, legal and political. During these transitions, opportunities may arise for young people to become actively involved in shaping the decisions that will influence their future and possibly empower them (Roche et al. 2004). One aspect of this is that in recent decades, a series of transformations have occurred which changed young people's relationships with the political sphere. In most Western countries, they vote less and protest more. Thus interest directly oriented to political issues and causes, particularly those relevant in young people's everyday lives, can be identified and is plausibly associated with a form of resistance (Soler-i-Marti 2015), but in such a way as to render it profoundly different from that which forged early youth subcultures.

FURTHER READING

Acevedo-Polakovich, I., Bell, B., Gamache, P. and Christian, A. (2011) 'Service Accessibility for Lesbian, Gay, Bisexual, Transgender, and Questioning Youth', *Youth & Society*, 45(1): 75–97.

Agnew, R., Matthews, S., Bucher, J., Welcher, A. and Keyes, C. (2008) 'Socioeconomic Status, Economic Problems, and Delinquency', *Youth & Society*, 40(2): 159–81.

Arnett, J. (2002) 'Adolescents in Western countries on the Threshold of the 21st Century', in B. Brown, R. Larson and T. Saraswathi (eds.), *The World's Youth: Adolescence in Eight Regions of the Globe*, New York: Cambridge University Press.

———. (2004) *Adolescence and Emerging Adulthood: A Cultural Approach*, 2nd edn, Upper Saddle River, NJ: Pearson.

Bently, T. and Gurumurthy, Y. (1999) *Destination Unknown: Engaging with the Problems of Marginalised Youth*, London: Demo.

Cohen, P. (1997) *Rethinking the Youth Question, Education, Labour and Cultural Studies*, Basingstoke: Palgrave Macmillan.

Connor, H., Tyers, C., Modood, T. and Hillage, J. (2004) 'Why the Difference? A Closer Look at Higher Education Ethnic Students and Graduates', Institute for Employment Studies, Research Report RR552.

Cotterell, J. (1996) *Social Networks and Social Influences in Adolescence*, London: Routledge.

Danesi, M. (2003) *Forever Young: The 'Teen-Aging' of Modern Culture*, London: Hutchinson.

Davis, J. (1990) *Youth and the Condition of Britain: Images of Adolescence*, London: Sage.

Facio, A., Resett S., Micocci, F. and Mistrorigo, C. (2007) 'Emerging Adulthood in Argentina: An Age of Diversity and Possibilities', *Child Development Perspectives*, 1(2): 115–18.

Griffin C. (1993) *Representations of Youth: The Study of Youth and Adolescence in Britain and America*, Cambridge: Polity Press.

———. (2001) '"The Young Women Are Having a Great Time": Representations of Young Women and Feminism', *Feminism & Psychology*, 11(2): 181–85.

———. (2004) 'Good Girls, Bad Girls: Anglo-Centralism and Diversity in the Constitution of Contemporary Girlhood', in M. Fine and A. Harris (eds.), *All About the Girl*, Abingdon, UK: Routledge.

Griffiths, C. (2002) 'Girls' Friendships and the Formation of Sexual Identities', *Lesbian and Gay Psychology: Fresh Perspectives*, Malden, MA: BPS Blackwell.

Irwin, S. (1995) *Rights of Passage: Social Change and Transition from Youth to Adulthood*, London: UCL Press.

Jones, G. and Wallace, C. (1992) *Youth, Family and Citizenship*, Milton Keynes: Open University Press.

Jones, R., Dick, A., Coyl-Shepherd, D. and Ogletree, M. (2012) 'Antecedents of the Male Adolescent Identity Crisis: Age, Grade, and Physical Development', *Youth & Society*, 46(4): 443–59.

McRobbie A. (1991) *Feminism and Youth Culture: from "Jackie" to "Just Seventeen"'*, Basingstoke: Palgrave Macmillan.

Mizen, P. (2003) *The Changing State of Youth*, Basingstoke: Palgrave Macmillan.

Muggleton, D. (2005) 'From Classlessness to Clubculture: A Genealogy of Post-War British Youth Cultural Analysis', *Nordic Journal of Youth Research,* 13(2): 205–19.

Musante, D. (2010) *Family Predictors of Negative Instability in Adopted Emerging Adults*, Amherst, MA: University of Massachusetts.

Owens, R. (1998) *Queer Kids: The Challenge and Promise for Lesbian, Gay and Bisexual Youth*, Toronto: Harworth Press.

Parris, L., Varjas, K., Meyers, J. and Cutts, H. (2011) 'High School Students' Perceptions of Coping With Cyberbullying', *Youth & Society*, 44(2): 284–306.

Pilcher, J. and Williamson, H. (1988) *An Uphill Struggle: A Guide to Young People's Experiences in a Changing Labour Market*, London: Youthaid.

Pole, C., Pilcher, J. and Williams, J. (eds.) (2005) *Young People In Transition: Becoming Citizens,* Basingstoke: Palgrave Macmillan.

Roberts, K. (2015) 'Youth Mobilisations and Political Generations: Young Activists in Political Change Movements During and Since the Twentieth Century', *Journal of Youth Studies*, 18(8): 950–66.

Schwartz, S., Côté, J. and Arnett, J. (2005) 'Identity and Agency in Emerging Adulthood: Two Developmental Routes in the Individualization Process', *Youth & Society*, 37(2): 201–29.

Shulman, S., and Ben-Artzi, E. (2003) 'Age-related Differences in the Transition From Adolescence to Adulthood and Links with Family Relationships', *Journal of Adult Development*, 10(4): 217–26.

Stearns, E. and Glennie, E (2006) 'When and Why Dropouts Leave High School', *Youth & Society*, 38(1): 29–57.

Straw, W. (1991) 'Systems of Articulation, Logics of Change: Communities and Scenes in Popular Music', *Cultural Studies*, 5(3): 273, 368–88.

Sussman S. (2010) 'Emerging Adulthood and Substance Abuse', in L. Berhardt (ed.), *Advances in Medicine and Biology*, vol. 6, Hauppauge, NY: Nova Science Publishers.

Talburt, S. (2004) 'Intelligibility and Narrating Queer Youth', in M. Rasmussen and M. Rofes (eds.), *Youth and Sexualities*, New York: Palgrave.

Williams, T. and Sánchez, B. (2013) 'Identifying and Decreasing Barriers to Parent Involvement for Inner-City Parents', *Youth & Society,* 45(1): 54–74.

Woodman, D. and Wyn, J. (2014) *Youth and Generation: Rethinking Change and Inequality in the Lives of Young People*, London: Sage.

Chapter 8

Adulthood: work, leisure and consumption

Adulthood is popularly envisaged as a major age division not only in the Western world but also as a significant partition in the life course identified by numerous non-Western cultures and throughout historical periods. Frequently, adulthood is associated with concepts of 'generation' – that belonging to a unique 'adult' generation forges identity and 'mature' relationships related to notions of 'responsibility'. However, as Blatterer (2007) points out, there scarcely exists a coherent 'Sociology of Adulthood' and certainly not one which can be seen as comparable to the established study areas of childhood, youth and old age. Blatterer observes that each of these stages of the life course is defined in relation to adulthood: childhood is typically seen in contrast to adulthood; youth is regarded as the transition to adulthood; and old age is perceived as a decline from adulthood into dependency and the relinquishing of responsibilities. Moreover, sociological works, reflecting common cultural perceptions, have tended to conceptualise adulthood by way of a range of criteria and signifiers that converge to fashion adulthood, including legal markers, 'practical accomplishments' and 'a repertoire of appropriate behaviour'. All such criteria point to the social construction of adulthood, which calls upon notions of biological and psychological developments and how they relate to societal roles and status. In this sense, it is possible to speak of 'social adulthood' marked out by the process of transition from pre-adulthood.

'Coming of age' in many pre-industrial societies often involves a rite of passage marking the onset of adulthood and may involve a series of 'tests' by which a young person is expected to demonstrate that they are sufficiently primed for adult life. In modern societies, typically void of such rites, the assumptions regarding adult roles and responsibilities nonetheless remain. In legal terms, this frequently connects with the concept of 'the age of majority', which designates independence and self-sufficiency. However, it is increasingly clear that in the Western world the two may not necessarily coincide. Although an individual may have progressed biologically as an adult and reached the age of majority, they may lack the capacities to fulfil social expectations. Because of such ambiguities, markers of adulthood such as 'mature' relationships and employment are undergoing considerable transformations in that they are impacted by insecurities, discontinuities, aspects of risk and prolonged youth, all of which undermine the straightforward transition to adulthood.

Such transformations more than hint at some of the core motifs of late/postmodernity. Thus, the conceptualisation of adulthood now provides the unarticulated background of social enquiry, consequently spawning the challenge to provide a measure of structure to an analysis of the major determinants of what is in reality a lengthy 'phase' of the life course. This chapter and the next will consider work (and non-work) experience and the family and 'adult' relationships. Given that adulthood constitutes a broad period beyond pre-adulthood, its further sub-divisions such as 'mid-life' or 'old age', which form 'later adulthood', will provide the focus of Chapters 10 and 11 of this volume.

EMPLOYMENT

Focusing on employment in the context of adulthood requires some justification. Employment is clearly an economic activity connecting with life course chances via income reward and status. Employment shapes life opportunities and experiences in positive and negative ways, with implications for perceptions of self. It also entails the acquisition of financial resources for the individual, which permits the capacity to share those resources with others in networks of linked lives and those are responsible for including family members. This chapter considers employment via a number of themes, including the changing nature of work in a globalised world, work and identity, work satisfaction, unemployment and its consequences, and how many of these considerations relate to structural inequalities.

This chapter, however, ranges wider in examining 'non-work' via the topics of leisure and consumption. A unique feature of contemporary Western societies is the shift from production to consumption. Thus adult life is not entirely informed by work experiences for those employed. Consumption and leisure patterns have become increasingly significant in shaping focal points of adult life. Consequently, in late/postmodernity the stress on adult identity is not restricted to the workplace. The rise of the consumer society and its accompanying culture means that consumption and lifestyle rival work experiences as the major factors behind identity construction in adult life. Indeed, it may be said that conforming to consumption patterns has generated a number of new 'markers' of adulthood. 'We are what we do' is therefore supplemented by 'we are what we consume'. In turn, consumption, to one degree or another, impacts upon leisure pursuits as an important variable shaping non-work experiences. Hence, this chapter gives scope to the significance of leisure in adulthood.

The changing world of employment

Understanding work experiences and how employment shapes life chances must invariably now be approached in globalised terms. As Richard Sennett (2005) identifies, a global flexible version of capitalism has emerged and is underscored by the ideology of neoliberalism. These changes, which radically depart from the older industrialised nature of work, impact everyday life and generate a fresh work ethic transmitting beliefs about merit and talent. While tranformations may include high levels of social mobility, alongside the discourse of meritocracy and the 'open' society, they invariably also generate insecurities and what Sennett calls 'the specter of uselessness' felt by professionals as well as manual workers in an ever-changing economy.

Companies now relentlessly compete, and the dynamics of the global economy mean that larger enterprises have to 'down-size', de-centralise and call upon innovating technologies in order to gain the necessary flexibility to compete. These trends invariably lead not only to replacing the number of people on the payroll, from managers to shop floor workers, but also replacing long-term employees with temporary workers. By hiring 'temps', companies are able to 'cut corners' by not having to provide insurance, paid vacations or pensions, and offer zero hour contracts (whereby no particular number of hours or times of work are specified). Moreover, the flexibility related to post-Fordist production and work insecurities ensures that there is no longer a guaranteed 'job for life'. Rather, 'multiple careers' (either changing careers or holding more than one job simultaneously) has become a growing trend. Arguably, this is a propensity which impacts younger generations in particular. For instance, of skilled young adults sampled in

Germany, only one-third could claim continuous careers in the first eight years after graduation and over half were employed in other occupations at least once (Heinz 2002), thus complicating transitions into adulthood as discussed in the previous chapter.

The nature of work undertaken remains significant. Throughout recent years, a wealth of sociological literature has grown up around the theme of the relationship between work and identity, including how the nature of employment has changed over time and impacted identity formations (Kirk and Wall 2011). Another emphasis has been on the link between identity and status, the sense of self-esteem and personal well-being. Conventionally, it is the status of a person's work that frequently determines how individuals perceive themselves and the means by which others appraise them, while also forging life opportunities, income and lifestyles. Although the time spent at work has greatly diminished over the last century or so, for many people it still occupies over half their waking hours. It is not surprising, then, that work overspills into other areas of life with profound consequences.

Such considerations are accompanied by recognition of changes in the nature of work. The arrival of the post-industrial economy meant that by the 1970s in numerous Western societies over half the workforce was involved in the service sector rather than the industrial and agricultural spheres. The expansion of service occupations is one reason for the growth of the middle-classes. Many of the jobs associated with these social constituencies can be described as 'white-collar', including sales positions, clerical and secretarial employment with incomes and status closer to that of most manual work-ers than that of the professional. Put otherwise, an increasing number of occupations in these post-industrial times provide only a modest economic reward that constrains life course opportunities, levels of consumption, meaningful leisure activities and lifestyle preferences, all of which are said to be core values of the Western world. More widely, the infinite fragmen-tation of the workforce in terms of income has undermined coherent class structures, which were a major interest of 'classical' sociological accounts of, for example, the coherence of working-class communities.

Particularly in more prestigious white-collar occupations associated with the middle-classes, career aspirations remain an important frame of reference frequently exercised by individuals to interpret at what point they are in the life course and what they anticipate to be, in a reflexive way, their personal development and direction in the future. Here, there is a discernible link between career structures, the negotiation of risks and choice, and the construction of personal identities. Of all occupational categories, it is professional people who may most of all attempt to make sense of who they are in terms of their location along a career trajectory and possibly draw comparisons with others in the workplace. However, a rapidly changing economy and job structure ensures that this sense of future certainties has, for most professions, been undermined, and the prospect of discontinuity and career change are the experiences of even higher paid professionals.

In comparison, there is the secondary labour market that is comprised of jobs frequently providing the minimal benefit to employees. This segment of the labour force is employed in the low-skilled, blue-collar type work found in routine assembly line operations. It is a sector which tends to offer little by way of income, demands a longer working week and affords less job security and less opportunity for personal advancement. Furthermore, it is in this sector that workers are most likely to experience alienation and job dissatisfaction; research has long found evidence that such negative experiences at work most commonly beset women and ethnic minorities, who are overly represented in this quarter of the labour force (e.g. Kohn and Schooler 1982). There may be important implications here for generating low self-esteem and a meaningful sense of identity.

Some commentators such as Beck et al. (1980) have suggested that the link between work and identity is generally undergoing a significant decline – not least because of employment insecurity. However, others have attempted to confirm that work remains an important source of identity, as well as a fount of meaning and social affiliation, across a range of workplaces (Doherty 2009). One source of such identity may indeed be the modern work processes in manufacturing and service organisations in a globalised world. In particular, companies are obliged to increasingly rely upon responsible and competent employees who are willing and able to engage in tasks which require the continuous learning needed for flexible specialisation, and these processes enhance the importance of work as a site of meaning and identity (Brown et al. 2005).

Work satisfaction

Sociological debates concerning identity at work clearly connect with the matter of work satisfaction and how this overlaps with non-work experiences. It still remains probable that those in high-status jobs with successful careers are likely to be at their peak employment period at a mid-life stage and will maintain a high level of engagement with their work. Others disappointed in their career ambitions or involved in non-professional occupations plausibly turn to other sources such as family, leisure or community to find fulfilment in their lives. In the workplace, this lack of advancement may lead to what Robert Merton called 'ritualism', whereby individuals merely go 'through the motions' – lacking intrinsic work interest and ambitions (Merton 1969).

It might be argued that unfulfilling, mundane work is part of the payment which people living in advanced industrialised societies are prepared to endure for their good material standard of living – allowing opportunities for leisure and high levels of mass consumption – and these standards can only be achieved by the systematic utilisation of technology that, in turn, has its negative repercussions.

'Alienation' is the term usually associated with low degrees of work dissatisfaction, especially employment which does not call upon a high level of skills and creative and social capacities. The increase in processes of de-skilling is evident in George Ritzer's (1983) exploration of 'McDonaldization'. Large-scale commerce and manufacturing now penetrate almost every region of the world in a globalised economy. Typified by McDonald's, the US fast-food chain, what is produced is a fairly standard package. It is the same all over the world – the same image and the same product. The advantage of such strict control for the corporation is that variation is reduced to a minimum, costs are kept down and efficiency increased. One of the principles of the standardising impulses of McDonalization is 'control'. This suggests that the operation of employees is reduced to a series of machine-like actions. The implication here is not just in terms of de-skilling, but the de-humanisation of workers: in other words, alienation.

Such alienation is not confined to manual work and may impact the white collar sector – a theme developed by C. Wright Mills (1951), who maintained that the expansion of the service sector of the economy in advanced capitalist societies generated its own alienating tendencies. Just as manual workers become akin to commodities by selling their 'skills with things', a similar process develops with non-manual workers who sell their 'skills with persons' on the open market. According to Mills, a market price is adjoined to personality characteristics, and as a consequence people sell small fragments of themselves. However, since aspects of personality are bought and sold like any other commodity, individuals are alienated from their true selves. Their expression of personality in the workplace is insincere and manufactured. Mills thus draws a picture of individuals prostituting their personalities at work in search of individual gain.

Fairly recently, there has been considerable debate as to the ramifications of the emerging technology upon work satisfaction. Some commentators question whether these technologies bring the much-heralded flexibility and requirement of new and innovating skills. It may well be that many jobs have not been re-skilled with the arrival of these technologies but have simply been expanded to include a greater range of tasks that require little skill (Pollert 1988). At the same time, flexibility may mean more job security for some but not others, depending on their specialised work (Atkinson 1985). Managers, designers and technical sale staff, technicians and craftsmen are likely to be multi-skilled employees who are capable of working in different areas within a firm. In contrast, clerical, supervisory and component assembly workers are less secure in their work. They are easier to recruit, are more likely to be offered short-term contracts and can readily be laid-off in times of recession, since their skills are in plentiful supply.

Dissatisfaction is more often voiced in relation to specific aspects of a job, such as pay, promotion prospects or conveniently flexible hours of work, but it is the nature of the work itself which remains significant. Employees who work in repetitive and tedious jobs are faced with the daily need of coping, and there are various ways by which people do so. The concept of 'managing the self' and 'others' provides some insights into how people survive the monotony of work: daydreaming, absenteeism and the frequent changing of jobs are all ways in which people cope. Then there is the matter of job insecurity in times of recession. In 2012 in the UK 5.6 per cent of those who were employed in 2011 had lost their employment. While losing one's job clearly has its psychological consequences, it has been found that the fear of unemployment is as detrimental to a sense of well-being as losing the job itself (Chirumbolo and Hellgren 2003).

An emerging broader concern has arisen from the distortion of work/non-work balance. Research has indicated that the demands of contemporary work culture are perhaps the most pressing challenges regarding lifestyle and subsequently the mental health of the general population. According to the Mental Health Foundation (nd), a UK charity, 40 per cent of employees are neglecting other aspects of their life due to work obligations, which may increase their vulnerability to mental health problems when working long hours. More than a quarter of employees surveyed felt depressed (one-third felt anxious and more than half felt irritable). Regarding levels of 'unhappiness' many more women (42 per cent) reported unhappiness than men (29 per cent), which the charity suggests is probably a consequence of competing life roles and more pressure to 'juggle' work and domestic roles. Neither is it just a matter of increasing working hours. Work processes and obligations may interrupt non-work life. One of the major culprits is technological innovation, typified by e-mail communication. Company culture, where a quick reply or action is expected by management, colleagues and customers, may be such as to demand that employees feel obliged to spend time addressing e-mails outside of working hours, neglecting their non-work time as a result (Waller and Ragsdell 2012).

GENDER AND EMPLOYMENT

Since the industrial revolution the positions of men and women in employment, and the benefits that they have derived from it, have differed considerably. During the war years of the twentieth century women carried out numerous jobs which were previously the exclusive province of men. On returning from war, men again took over most of these occupations, but the earlier established pattern had been broken. In the UK, the working population grew from 23.8 to 25.6 million between 1961 and 1975. Practically the whole of this expansion was accounted for by the increase in the number of working women. In 1931, 10 per cent of married women were active in employment. By 1951, this had risen to 30 per cent, and in 1987 it stood at 60 per cent. The occupations entered into followed the general changes in the occupational structure but may be said to have varying benefits for women.

Estimates by the Equality and Human Rights Commission (EHRC) suggest there are 5400 women 'missing' from top jobs in the UK. According to the EHRC report *Sex and Power 2011* since 2003 women held just 10.2 per cent of all senior posts in business, 15.1 per cent in media and culture and 26.2 per cent in politics. The report also reported that a persistent wage gap remains for such occupations as health and legal professionals. Until age 34, the difference in average pay between men and women remained below 10 per cent. It then increased to 30 per cent by age 40, peaked at 45 per cent at age 49, and narrowed again to 28 per cent by age 59.

While at least some professions could be said to allow women more freedom in negotiating their careers throughout the life course, it has brought restrictions in other respects. Martens (2000, 215–16), in her comparative study of Holland and the UK, discovered that in some professions notions of work commitment favoured masculine concepts of a career and what it stood for by way of work continuities. By contrast, women's discontinuities, due to childcare responsibilities, enhanced the idea that women are less committed workers and are more suitable for part-time employment.

Arguably, some trends towards female employment are breaking down the conventional view of the woman being the home-maker and man the breadwinner. Like their male colleagues, female career-orientated women are increasingly expected to be rational, non-emotive and competitive. As women enter the workplace in greater numbers the cultural norms that traditionally informed their behaviour and orientation, ones of nurturance and submissiveness, may be reversed, creating its own 'crisis' of identity in the competitive world of work. The working wife and mother, therefore, may find herself having to display different sides of the 'self' in working and domestic life. This provides an observable counterpoint to the inherent contradiction of the so-called 'New Man' in the domestic sphere and the competitive careerist male in the workplace.

The significance of women in the workforce in Western societies has been recognised through legislation enforcing equal pay legislation for males and females. Nonetheless, as we have seen (Chapter 3) women are still to be found in typically 'female' occupations – especially supportive and caring roles. These jobs tend to be at the lower level of the pay-scale, offer restricted opportunities for advancement and are subject to greater supervision. Second, there is insecurity of employment which may bring disruptions and discontinuities throughout the life course, since they constitute a 'reserve army of labour'. Put succinctly, women are a spare pool of potential recruits which can be brought in or released into the economy through the periodic cycles of booms and recession (Beechy 1983). Moreover, women are more likely to work part-time. The UK office of National Statistics found that in the period 2011–12 the vast majority of men were in full-time employment (87 per cent) compared to just over half of all women. Significantly more employed women worked part-time (43 per cent) compared to men (13 per cent).

Changes to the labour market since the financial crisis of 2008 have also proved detrimental: substantial job cuts in the public sector, where women have been prevalent, mean many women have moved to private sector jobs where the pay gap is significant, according to ONS statistics. Many of the new jobs created as the economy comes out of recession are zero–hour contracts, part-time or temporary. In 2012 the official UK unemployment figures, according to the Institute for Public Policy Research, suggested the major cause was job losses in the public sector, where women disproportionately work (65 per cent). Older women (50 to 64) have been particularly affected – years when it is crucial in building up their pension contribution – and in some instances are obliged to undertake lower status, lower paid work out of necessity.

Studies have also indicated the continuing connectiveness between female employment and traditional domestic roles. Rosemary Crompton (1999, 209–11) maintains that throughout Europe the fact women are moving in increasing numbers into managerial and professional occupations is both cause and consequence of wider developments in the family, the relations between the sexes and social attitudes more generally. Yet, certain cultural distinctions seem to be fairly universal even among professional women, especially those in a caring capacity, such as doctors, when compared to the business world of female bankers. Variations in the demands and ethos surrounding these jobs impact differentially, with those women involved in the former seemingly having a greater responsibility for domestic tasks. Domestic conjugal roles are also a consequence of life course planning offered by the two forms of occupations. Women who go into medicine make a career decision at a fairly early stage – allowing a combination of employment with family life – especially by choosing particular medical specialties that do not make excessive time demands. Under the pressures of the financial world, however, females in the banking sector are 'forced' to involve their partners in childcare.

Adding to the picture of employed women and family life, Innes and Scott (2003) draw attention to working-class women with dependent children as part of a life course transition, from full-time caring to education and eventual labour market participation in a low-income area of the UK. The issues involved in managing paid work and unpaid care are particularly sharply focused for young mothers from low-income households, because they have few material resources with which to compensate for any resulting tensions or discontinuities. Without educational qualifications, and with only limited work experience in some cases, they are in a poor position to compete for income.

UNEMPLOYMENT

The dynamics of the global economy in the late/post-modern world indicate that every industrialised society has some degree of unemployment, which, in turn, marks one of the major sources of life discontinuity. Much of it is temporary; jobs disappear because occupations become obsolete, as businesses close in the face of domestic and foreign competition, and as recessions force lay-offs and bankruptcy. Mass unemployment, which has been evident from the 1970s, is now a fact of economic life. The 'Great Recession' of 2008, the worst since the end of World War II, was a result of the general economic decline observed in world markets around the end of the first decade of the twenty-first century. In the UK, when the global financial crisis impacted, the unemployment rate was a little over 5 per cent (1.6 million). Towards the end of 2009, it was almost a million higher at 2.5 million (8 per cent). Unemployment peaked at almost 2.7 million at the end of 2011, its highest level for 17 years.

Commenting on the consequences of the onset of mass unemployment in Western societies in the 1970s, Adrian Sinfield (1981) suggested that there were five major groups who are more likely to become unemployed in Western industrial societies: those who experience redundancies due to economic change, older workers who face enforced retirement, unemployed women, those who have experienced irregular employment over a long period of time and unskilled youth attempting to make the transition from school to work. Many of these observations still hold, but another social constituency has increasingly become more vulnerable to unemployment, namely ethnic groupings.

In the UK, ethnic minorities are facing significant barriers, according to a report published by the Centre on Dynamics of Ethnicity (Li 2014), despite levels of educational attainment improving significantly for ethnic minorities, this has not translated into improved outcomes in the labour market. Chinese, Indian, Irish, Bangladeshi and black African students are outperforming their white peers in the highest school grades, while all black and ethnic minority groups have seen significant improvement in access to degree-level qualifications. The report found that although ethnic minorities have experienced growth in clerical, professional and managerial employment, they are still facing significant barriers to enjoying the levels of social mobility of their white UK peers. The report's survey of the 2011 Census for England and Wales black African noted black Caribbean women have experienced a 15–20 per cent fall in full-time employment rates since the beginning of the twenty-first century, while those for white women have remained stable. Thirty-nine per cent of Bangladeshi women and 35 per cent of men worked part-time, double the levels of two decades previously.

The situation of many ethnic groups was made worse by the economic crisis of 2008. Between 2012 and 2013, unemployment levels for the UK as a whole and for white ethnic groups remained constant, but unemployment among ethnic minority groups rose from 13 per cent to 14 per cent. The rise was particularly noticeable among black ethnic minorities (up from 16 per cent to 17 per cent) and Pakistani/Bangladeshi communities (from 17 per cent to 19 per cent). The report by the Centre on Dynamics of Ethnicity found that ethnic demographics were cut across by the variables of age and gender. Younger groups were particularly affected by unemployment: 16–24 year olds from ethnic minorities displayed an unemployment rate of 37 per cent compared to the UK as a whole (21 per cent). The rate of one in seven adults aged 25 to retirement from ethnic minorities not working but wishing to was much higher than that for white people.

The repercussions of unemployment

When unemployment occurs it will inevitably bring negative implications for the lives of individuals and their families and represents a major source of life discontinuity. In terms of economic resources there may be repercussions throughout the future life course for individuals. Moreover, there may be cumulative effects financially even for future generations of the family, including chances of social mobility of those who find themselves unemployed for a significant length of time. The implications of unemployment are not, however, solely financial.

Many studies suggest those unemployed will suffer an experience akin to that on hearing of a serious illness; an initial shock, followed for a short while by denial and optimism. There may even be a sense of being on vacation for a period and a feeling of freedom. Nonetheless, this is soon followed by distress and anxiety. If the unemployment continues for a long time, it may lead to resignation and the need to adjust in practically every area of life.

Unemployment has been linked to ill-health, psychological problems, premature death, attempted and actual suicide, marital breakdown, child abuse and racial conflicts. In terms of ill-health, Laurance (1986) found that unemployed school leavers in the UK experienced higher levels of poor mental health and a higher mortality rate compared to the employed, irrespective of social class. From a study of the impact of stress on health in 300 men, Linn et al. (1985) assessed every six months men who became unemployed after entering the study and compared them with an equal number, matched for age and ethnicity, who continued to work. Psychological and health data after unemployment were found to be symptoms of depression and anxiety which were significantly greater in the unemployed than employed. Analysis showed those with higher esteem had more support from family and friends than did those with low self-esteem. Furthermore, unemployed men made significantly more visits to their doctors, took more medications and spent more days in bed sick than did employed individuals.

Perhaps the most obvious effects of unemployment are financial. The UK Office of Population, Census and Surveys (1990) found that over two-thirds of families with parents under 35 were in debt after three months of unemployment. Yet there are many other social consequences as well, and these are less easy to measure than financial ones. They include a loss of sense of identity, since work provides a social role and source of social relationships outside of the family. Unemployment tends to reduce social contacts and activity. According to Fagin and Little (1984), in their study of unemployed men, most of those surveyed discovered it immensely difficult to create a framework which would impose a regular, purposeful activity and found it hard to occupy themselves. A subculture of despair may thus emerge among those who feel that they are excluded from wider society and fail to enjoy all the things that other people expect, while unemployment tends to particularly impact those who already have fewer resources to cope. The men Fagin and Little surveyed lacked the opportunities to develop skills and creativity and displayed little sense of purpose. This was reflected in some men making statements such as 'I'm surplus to requirements'. Moreover, according to this particular research, the great virtues of income from employment were freedom and control outside of the workplace. In particular, it created the possibility of engaging in leisure activities, many of which incur financial expenditure. Unemployment negates these opportunities.

Finally, studies have found that only certain types of activity increase with unemployment (e.g. Hill 1977). The unemployed spend more time watching television, conducting housework, reading or engaged in hobbies. Social life decreases, as do participation in sport and spectator sports. Overall, it appears that leisure is not an adequate substitute for work because most of what it entails is solitary and passive and fails to compensate for the loss of contacts at work.

Economic recessions since the 1980s spurred research into areas that were understudied, particularly the implications of unemployment for women. Partly, as Sinfield (1981) suggests, this is because female employment rather than male unemployment was less often seen as a problem. Fresh research started to challenge such assumptions. Using data from questionnaires and interviews, Henwood and Miles (1987) compared the situation of unemployed men and women. For women who seek work as a means of escape from the home, unemployment could be especially harsh. Women, like men, respond by trying to meet a broad range of people, attempt to keep occupied most of the day, lack a sense of contributing to society, feel that they are not respected by others and suffer from not having regular activities to undertake during the day. Indicative of changing attitudes by younger women, Warr et al. (1985) also found that unemployed 17-year-old females reported more distress, depression and anxiety, and were considerably more concerned than their male counterparts about the stigma of being unemployed.

Also providing insights is Pauline Anderson's study (1993) investigating women's experiences of unemployment in one UK city. Contrary to the dominant sociological paradigm which marginalises the importance of women's unemployment, the evidence presented in her research demonstrates that waged work is a central and valued part of women's social identity. The data shows that as a result of unemployment women lose their economic identity and this has a detrimental impact upon their social and domestic identities. Women's domestic role did not compensate for the loss of their paid employment. Rather, the experience of unemployment made women value waged work more. Finally, around one-third of unemployment was borne by parents with dependent children. The impacts of unemployment on families included poverty and hardship, strained relationships, poorer health and housing stress, and could also harm children's development and employment futures (McClelland 2000)

LEISURE

Perhaps the most popular form of escape from alienating aspects of work is to retreat into leisure time activities. It is in leisure, as a result of work void of meaning and expression, that people can indulge in what they wish and involve themselves in more agreeable pastimes. C. Wright Mills' work (1951) explored this theme and provided the image of people selling little pieces of themselves for financial remuneration during week days and attempting to re-claim themselves in the evenings and at weekends. Mills described this differential attitude to work and leisure as 'the great split'. It might be argued that today the pursuit of leisure, as some kind of meaningful substitute or otherwise for work satisfaction, appears to have greater significance on the late/postmodern life course in terms of identity and experience of adult life than ever before.

In recent years a growing body of literature has been concerned with the link between leisure and identity. Shanir (1992), developing Stryker's earlier work (1987) on the connection between identity, roles and relationships, proposes that 'leisure identities' can become highly salient to the self-concept for three reasons. First, leisure identities express and affirm individual talents and capacities. Second, they provide some degree of social recognition. Third, they affirm the individual's central values and interests. Additional writings in the area suggest that people are motivated to develop and maintain a consistent and positive self-concept or identity, and, consequently, they engage in a form of leisure behaviour allowing them to affirm or validate their own 'desired identity image'. Indeed, it has been shown that participation in certain types of leisure activities allows this through physical appearance, personality, skills and abilities, while some individuals may wish to prove something to themselves by 'sign value' (Haggard and Williams 1991).

Life-cycle and the adult life course

Speculation as to which social variables inform, enhance or prohibit the realisation of the advantages of leisure has long informed the relevant sociological literature. There was a tendency in the early sociological work, perhaps exemplified by the research of Parker (1973), to relate adult leisure patterns to experiences and satisfaction in the workplace, with manual and non-manual occupations constituting the major divergences. Alternatively, a life-cycle approach seemed to be an attractive framework by which to understand leisure patterns. Such a perspective was offered by Rapoport and Rapoport (1975), who argued that the life-cycle, along with family life, was largely responsible for shaping leisure, although other factors such as class and gender might be significant. At different stages of the life-cycle, individuals exhibit varying attitudes to work, family and leisure. The Rapoports identified four main stages in the life-cycle, with each having implications for leisure pursuits: 'Adolescence', where the major preoccupation was a quest for personal identity; 'Young Adulthood', where the principal interest is with creating a social identity that reflects the concerns with occupation, relationships and friendship; the 'Establishment Phase', between roughly the ages of 25 and 55, during which time people attempt to establish satisfying adult lifestyles where home-centred leisure activities are more central; and the 'Later Years', the final phase, commences roughly at the age of 55 or with retirement and includes a sense of social and personal integration. Patterns of leisure nonetheless varied, according to the Rapoports, and depend on such variables as health and income, which may restrict some people in their activities.

Ken Roberts (1978) took a wider view of leisure than Parker and the Rapoports and seemed in many respects to anticipate late/postmodernist approaches. While not denying that work and the life-cycle were important, he also stressed the variety of leisure patterns which were available and that leisure was progressively open to matters of choice. Individuals were increasingly engaging in leisure when they felt they were choosing a meaningful activity in their free time. Roberts therefore attempted to allow for the significance that people gave to leisure. Thus, activities such as gardening and home decorating should not be seen as leisure activities unless an individual defines them as such. Moreover, there are many different social factors which display an enormous variety of leisure interests. Leisure activity is, for example, influenced by variables such as class, gender, age, education and marital status.

GENDER AND LEISURE

Until the 1980s, women were for the most part conspicuously absent from sociological studies of leisure activities. Early feminist contributions critiqued the work of Parker, especially his distinctions between work and leisure (Green et al. 1990). Rather, the inequality brought about by the sexual division of labour was best understood with the difference of leisure activities for men and for women. There were various observations to be made concerning women's experiences. First, women's work is often not involved in earning a living, thus women in full-time housework are automatically excluded from Parker's framework. Domestic activities associated with the 'housewife' tend to overlap with and undermine the quality of a woman's leisure. Second, the distinction Parker makes in his categories of work and work obligations was found to be fairly meaningless for women in partnerships. The domestic part of work obligations is a large part of the woman's total work at home. Third, the central feature of the life of women is that of domestic activity, which allows few escapes into leisure since there is little real free time.

While both men and women have very high rates of participation in watching television, visiting or entertaining friends or relatives, and listening to the radio or music, there are important differences in regard to the leisure activities of males and females. Not only do men and women tend to take part in different types of leisure, but women also have less access to leisure opportunities than men do. The General Household Survey (1993) of the UK indicated that the sport and physical activities which women took more part in than men were indoor swimming, keep fit/yoga and similar pursuits. Some 59 per cent of men, but only 38 per cent of women participated in one activity other than walking pursuits. At the same time, there was less variation in home-based leisure patterns between men and women: marked differences exemplified by participation in DIY (Do It Yourself) activities predominantly preferred by men; and dress-making, needlework or knitting, overwhelmingly undertaken by women which undoubtedly reflect conventional conjugal roles. A more recent example is research finding that women are less likely to use computer-based technologies – reflecting the gendered nature of the employment sphere – for leisure activity than men (Martinson et al. 2002).

Green et al. (1990) claimed that it is much harder for women to psychologically disengage from work and put aside specific time periods for leisure. For them, leisure time has a greater possibility of being interrupted because they are constantly at the demands of the family. Women also have less financial resources to spend on activities, and many remain financially dependent on their partners, which obviously limits the forms of leisure they could engage in. Other crucial factors affecting women's leisure include: having access to private transport; the degree of confidence in themselves and determination to do what they want; a sense of a legitimate right to leisure; and a network of support which may range from a friend or partner to an entire household or group of people (Deem 1986).

Furthermore, several studies have indicated that the attitudes of men restrict the options open to women (e.g. Crawford et al. 1991). Many women are expected to choose their leisure time pursuits largely from a limited range of home and family-orientated activities that are culturally defined as 'proper' family pursuits. The social control of a male-dominated society thus extends to leisure. Nonetheless, women are slightly more active than men in voluntary organisations and are more likely to attend evening educational or physical development classes, all of which include social interaction, plausibly freeing women from dependence on men in the sphere of leisure.

Finally, Green et al. also indicate that gender and leisure may be cut across by the significance of ethnicity. Although women of Asian and Afro-Caribbean minorities share common cultural attributes, traditions suggest that their leisure patterns are frequently very different. In some Asian families cultural and religious factors may mean less autonomy and equality. Asian men are often reluctant to encourage women to be mobile and may restrict what they can and cannot do. In contrast, Afro-Caribbean women are rather less limited in their leisure; they have more power in their families than Asian women and encourage this independence. Leisure is less home-based than for Asian women but is still restricted. Although patterns of recreation and leisure pursuits are changing among ethnic groups, continued research points out that it remains difficult to draw generalisations (Stodolska 2000).

THE CONSUMER SOCIETY AND THE COMMODIFICATION OF LEISURE

Earlier chapters have included brief references to the emergence of the consumer society and its relevance to late/postmodernity, including how consumerism has impacted the spheres of childhood, youth and even earlier phases of life. At this juncture it is conducive to explore the significance of consumerism for the sphere of leisure in generalised terms and how it impacts adult life in particular (consumerism in mid- and later life will be discussed in subsequent chapters).

Until very recently, the traditional approach to the modern economy by sociologists centred on the production of goods, with a focus on either particular industries or employers and work experience. More recently, they have increasingly come to recognise the importance of not just what the economy produces and how it produces it but also what is now consumed and how. Western societies, both economically and culturally, are increasingly 'consumer societies', and consumption and shopping have become the most popular leisure activities. Part and parcel of all this is the growth of the shopping mall with megastores such as Virgin Records, hypermarkets like Tesco, chain stores including Argos, retail parks and DIY centres. To this can be added the growing popularity of on-line shopping and such facilities as Amazon. There is a proliferating market for an array of 'armchair services' – from shopping and banking to travel and public services – which are now on offer. Hundreds of channels with interactive shopping services come 'on line' through the television and the Internet, and all are available through credit card purchases.

These services are accompanied by the vast expansion of all kinds of commodities; sports clothes geared to sports of every type, new technology including computers and ever more sophisticated technology aimed at home amusement. Moreover, new forms of entertainment and leisure complexes are emerging as a common feature of the urban landscape. There are now new modes of eating out, from fast foods to upmarket dining, in addition to centres geared towards pure escapism, as typified by theme parks and Disneyland holidays. Today, the tendency is to use credit cards to pay for many of these commodities and services. This has huge economic repercussions. In the UK, at least a third of all consumption is based on credit and there are over 56 million credit cards currently in circulation. Such tendencies serve to emphasis the cultural importance of consumerism as a motivation for employment and the focus of leisure.

For Clark and Critcher (1985), leisure, in much the same way as work, is largely forged by the capitalist economy. It is now big business and an important source of profit. The commercial provision of leisure is dominated by large companies which have a wide variety of leisure activities to offer. These enterprises enjoy the potential power to persuade consumers of their leisure needs. The leisure industry creates new products and services and then endeavours, through widespread advertising, to convince consumers that they should purchase them. In some areas of leisure provision, such as entertainment, a few large companies dominate the market and, therefore, according to Clark and Critcher, actually restrict consumer choice.

More recent critiques of the consumer society may not be so far-reaching, but nonetheless raise pertinent questions as to whether it has really brought positive change and improvement in life experiences. It is evident that the extension and development of the consumer culture from the late twentieth century onwards has depended upon the creation of fresh markets, not least through the production of images and advice on lifestyle preferences. However, the emergence of so much consumption has given rise to a great deal of speculation as to whether it has added to the quality of adult life.

It might be conjectured that commodification enhances choice in a more genuine way. In short, that choice, a core motif of late/postmodernity, is extended. Consumption has become the means for a higher standard of living, as well as a chance not to stifle culture but to enhance it. Goods and brands spread through the world, liberating the consumer through choice. With the packaging of CDs in megastores or purchased on-line, for instance, global music has developed and, consequently, the sheer range of music presently available has dramatically increased. The same is true of food, with supermarkets now making available ingredients and recipes once unknown. Thus contemporary culture can be seen to be enriched – giving the great majority of adults a greater choice and more control over their lives than ever before.

One growing dimension of the consumer culture, which arguably has proved a mixed blessing, is personalised technology. It is partly linked to lifestyle preferences, although it has influenced contemporary life in other respects too. The scope of technology in opening up new markets has also added to the 'modelling' and remaking of the body beyond what medical science now has to offer. In this sense technology can bring a certain 'personalisation' for the individual and this is typified in the realm of entertainment. Hitherto, entertainment has been almost exclusively social: the music venue or cinema, or family TV, whereas there is now the 'personal computer' or iPad, even the facilities of the cell phone. All are significant through the media of personalised consumption.

There is a counter view to that which argues the consumer society generally enriches human existence. It is one which states that consumerism is enacting a detrimental effect; destroying traditional culture, human relationships and civic responsibilities (Bryman 1995). Some critics maintain that the unfolding culture is one of instant gratification and, with the market dominating, leads to a general 'levelling down' of life – destroying social interaction and communities. In short, it is the 'Coca-Colarisation' of the world, where children mass consume McDonald's fast-foods and learn to become unquestioning consumers in adulthood. Much can be seen to lead to the weakening of shared and moral values and the rise of a crass materialism. Arai and Pedlar (2003) maintain this is part of the 'crisis' of postmodernity and, in particular, that leisure has lost its community edge. In fact, from the latter years of the twentieth century, the social relevance of leisure has diminished as consumption and individualism came to dominate leisure and recreation. The change from work to leisure, where individuals invest their life activity and meaning, would therefore seem to be linked to levels of alienation and accompany the shift in the economy from production to consumption.

Certainly, some commentators have stressed aspects of alienation in the consumption of leisure. This is fairly implicit in Featherstone's account of the various forms of escapism into fantasy and dreamworlds (Featherstone 1982, 28–29), while for Baudrillard (1983) commodification undoubtedly represents a distinct narrowing and convergence of cultural experience, rather than its widening, given the emphasis on the shopping experience. So many mass leisure activities are orientated towards astonishing, exciting and titillating in a spontaneous way – creating a kind of fantasy world into which even adults can escape. Within consumer culture one tendency is the fragmentation and differentiation of markets. In its most extreme formulation this is seen as entailing the end of the social connections and the emergence of consumption as an endless series of signs and images which do not cohere and cannot be used to formulate a structured lifeworld and set of tastes that, in turn, undermine coherent and stable concepts of self.

Another more negative view is not to see variety in consumption, one enhanced by globalising processes, but the dominance of a particularly Western and rather standardised lifestyle. Thus, far from globalisation impacting the West through consumption, Latouche (1996) views it as an integral part of the growing hegemony of Western culture. In short, the spread of Western influence is not just in economic terms but is also a sameness of styles of dress, eating habits, architecture, music, urban lifestyles, mass media, philosophical ideas, a range of cultural values and attitudes about liberty, gender and sexuality, science and rationality, which have all impacted global cultures.

While the discussion in this chapter has focused upon the generalised significance of consumption on adulthood, one under-research area is the question as to whether patterns of consumption change over the life course and whether particular generations display different patterns (mid-life and later life consumption patterns will be discussed in Chapters 10 and 11). Among the few studies in the area is that of Leach et al. (2013) who have studied the post-war Baby Boomers (born 1945–54) in the UK. This was the generation which carried and reflected profound social changes in the latter half of the twentieth century onwards. The researchers note how this generation has come under particular scrutiny because it is perceived by the public as a liberal-thinking and radical age cohort constituted by the first teenagers of the affluent consumer society. Findings suggest that the Baby Boomers display a wide variety of consumption patterns, ageing identities and experiences of work and retirement which dictate these patterns, as do wealth, class, education, health and marital status. This is a generation readily prepared to spend acquired wealth rather than passing it on to successive generations. Leach and associates also found evidence for a 'bridging' identity maintained by Baby Boomers in relation to consumption practices; an age cohort prepared to consume goods they identify with their youth, such as music and fashion.

SUMMARY

This chapter has been concerned with a number of broad overlapping themes which nonetheless converge on crucial aspects of late/postmodernity that help construction experiences of 'mature' adulthood. It has attempted to show how employment, as an essential 'marker' of adulthood, shapes life and gives expression to structured inequalities in discernible and less obvious ways throughout adult life. Work can also provide the foundation of subcultures, social relationships and perhaps above all help forge notions of self and identity, especially given the time spent at work.

As much can be said about leisure. The experience of leisure, especially where it connects with consumption, has changed as rapidly as the world of work and is likely to continue to do so for the foreseeable future. Leisure, especially through consumption, increasingly dominates adult life as well, arguably offering new opportunities of choice. It is now possible to suggest that leisure is replacing work to a greater extent as a central life interest in late/postmodern society as individuals strive to enjoy the time and financial resources to at least seek greater fulfilment throughout adult life. Not all social groups, however, are able to escape into more and more leisure, while it is clear that work continues to shape leisure activities. A number of professional jobs have become more demanding, while many people find themselves having to work longer to afford what the consumer society has to offer, including its alluring leisure pursuits. Moreover, as leisure becomes increasingly dominated by market forces some may enjoy better provision and opportunities; others, however, frequently find themselves at a profound disadvantage which continues into later life.

FURTHER READING

Bradford, L. and Raines, C. (1992) *Twentysomething: Managing and Motivating Today's New Workforce*, New York: Master Media.

Ferri, E. (ed.) (1993) *Life at 33. The Fifth Follow-up of the National Child Development Study*, London: National Children's Bureau.

Greve, H. and Seidel, M.-D. (2014) 'Adolescent Experiences and Adult Work Outcomes: Connections and Causes', in H. Greve and M.-D. Seidel (eds.), *Research in the Sociology of Work*, vol. 25, Bingly: Emerald.

Hakim, C. (2006) 'Women, Careers, and Work-Life Preferences', *British Journal of Guidance and Counselling*, special issue edited by A. Al-Sawad and L. Cohen, 34(3): 279–94.

———. (1993) 'The Myth of Rising Female Employment', *Work, Employment and Society*, 7(1): 97–120.

Haller, M. (1994) 'Female Employment and the Change of Gender Roles: The Conflictual Relationship Between Participation and Attitudes in International Comparison', *International Sociology*, 9(1): 87–112.

Haslett, B., Geis, F. and Carter, M. (1992) *The Organizational Woman: Power and Paradox*, Norwood, NJ: Ablex.

Haywood, L., Kew, F., Bramham, P., Spink, J., Capenerhurst, J. and Henry, I. (1995) *Understanding Leisure*, Cheltenham: Stanley Thornes Ltd.

Hutson, S. and Jenkins, R. (1989) *Taking the Strain. Families, Unemployment and the Transition to Adulthood,* Milton Keynes: Open University Press.

Jordan, W. (1978) 'Searching for Adulthood in America', in E. Erickson (ed.), *Adulthood,* New York: W.W. Norton.

Kelly, J. (1972) 'Work and Leisure: A Simplified Paradigm', *Journal of Leisure Research,* 23(4): 301–13.

Krahn, H., Howard, A. and Galambos, N. (2015) 'Exploring or Floundering? The Meaning of Employment and Educational Fluctuations in Emerging Adulthood', *Youth & Society,* 47(2): 245–66.

Long B. (1998) 'Coping With Workplace Stress: A Multiple-Group Comparison of Female Managers and Clerical Workers', *Journal of Counseling Psychology,* 45(4): 65–78.

Mayseless O. and Scharf, M. (2003) 'What Does It Mean To Be an Adult? The Israeli Experience', *New Directions for Child and Adolescent Development,* issue 100: 5–20.

Mcdonald, S. (2013), 'Networks, Work and Inequality', in S. Mcdonald (ed.), *Research in the Sociology of Work,* vol. 24, Bingly: Emerald.

Sennett, R. (2006) *The Culture of the New Capitalism,* New Haven, CT: Yale University Press.

Shaw, S. (1994) 'Gender, Leisure, and Constraints: Towards a Framework for the Analysis of Women's Leisure', *Journal of Leisure Research,* 26(1): 8–22.

Talbot, M. (1987) 'Women and Leisure', in A. Graefe and S. Parker (eds.), *Recreation and Leisure: An introductory Handbook,* State College, PA: Venture Publishing.

Tomlinson, M. (2013) *Education, Work and Identity: Themes and Perspectives,* London: Bloomsbury Academic.

Tweedie, D. (2013), 'Making Sense of Insecurity: A Defence of Richard Sennett's Sociology of Work', *Employment & Society,* 27(1): 94–104.

Wimbush, E. and Talbot, M. (1988) *Relative Freedoms: Women and Leisure,* Milton Keynes and Philadelphia: Open University Press.

Chapter 9

Adulthood: relationships, intimacy and family life

As observed in the previous chapter, adulthood is often associated with the development of a 'mature' self emerging from biological change and growth. Yet adulthood is also subject to social pressures, whereby the individual comes to appreciate and adopt a number of responsibilities and roles as an integral part of identity transformation. One dimension of this maturity is perceived to be seeking and sustaining a range of adult relationships which come in various forms: from friendship, intimacy and various associations within the family context. These relationships and others associated with adulthood are the subject matter of this chapter.

A person's life is synchronised with those of others – family relatives, friends and partners – across a period of time as a crucial example of 'linked lives'. It is clear that in the late/postmodern context, relationships of various forms are undergoing profound transformations related to life discontinuity. Because of social and geographical mobility, individuals are not always able to sustain a close connection with distinct communities, while family networks continue to break down and life-long friendships prove difficult to uphold. At the same time, late/postmodernity generates a culture of choice not just by way of consumer durables, but also from choices of lifestyles and morality which may have profound consequences on relationships across the life course. This is enforced by the ethic of individualism as an integral motivation for establishing and sustaining relationships. Continuity is evident, however, in the way that demographics structured by class, gender, sexuality, age and ethnicity continue to inform different modes of relationships.

FRIENDSHIP

Human relationships clearly come in various expressions of which friendships are merely one formulation. 'Friendship' can be defined as a nonsexual relationship freely entered into and founded upon common interest, familiarity and closeness. In a context characterised by loss of community, of increasing social mobility, geographical distance in the pursuit of educational or occupational qualifications and of choice, friendships have become a major life focus for individuals to develop a sense of belonging and identity throughout life. In short, they are a significant means by which a concept of self is forged. In an ever-changing world, however, it is increasingly difficult to sustain friendship at a time when social isolation has become a problem for a growing number of people. Nonetheless, these developments have led to various personal innovations to enhance freely entered into connectiveness. A Pew Internet (2004) survey indicated nearly 80 per cent of adult respondents from the USA stated that they use the internet to retain communication and 9 per cent reported using an online social network such as Facebook or Twitter (a Pew Internet survey [2002] also reported that because of new technologies, college students are likely to have greater social ties with their friends than their family members).

Providing a theoretical basis to developments in the essence of friendship, Anthony Giddens maintains that the pursuit of personal happiness and stability through one-to-one 'pure relationships' is of increasing importance in late-modernity with the decline of a cohesive moral and social world. Social relationships, such as friendships and partnerships, are now freely entered into for their own sake, largely for what can be derived by each person from an enduring affinity with another; one which is continued only in so far as it is thought by both parties to deliver sufficient satisfaction for each individual to remain within them (Giddens 1992, 58). Giddens' notion of the 'pure relationship' is not, however, beyond criticism. It is an approach that views relationships as largely culturally unmediated constructs (apart from being largely individualistic and instrumental in orientation), saying little of gender differences and non-heterosexual relationships.

Taking a rather different tack to Giddens' theorising, Zygmunt Bauman's (2001) exploration of relationships is framed within his notion of 'liquid modernity', where the individual – male or female – lacks fixed or enduring bonds. In Bauman's account, people attempt to tie whatever bonds they can muster with others, using their own ingenuity, skills and dedication. Yet there is no guarantee these bonds will endure, suggesting that they tend to be superficial in nature. They must be tied loosely so they can be easily untied again when circumstances inevitably change in a fast moving world. This frailty of human bonds invariably generates feelings of insecurity on the one hand and conflicting desires to tighten the bonds yet keep them at distance on the other.

A range of sociological literature has also focused on how males and females feel different obligations towards friends and associates which also inform wider social relationships. The research suggests that men's cultural upbringing and experiences of the workplace encourage the formation of social relationships with others, yet limit the number of close friends and the depth of relationships, as well as restricting what they disclose about their personal life and how much emotion they are prepared to display. In comparison, women appear to 'really know each other', and are ready to genuinely provide a greater self-revelation and empathy for others (Hey 1997).

How males relate to people generally is seemingly related to forging aspects of culturally defined masculinity. Thus Seider (1989) argues that males constantly fear that they are not 'man enough' and are relentlessly under pressure to affirm their male identities. This has an impact upon their relationships in the wider social world and is fundamentally a consequence of men being the dominant inheritors of the foremost value of modernity – rationalism. Mastery of the self and the body has perennially been constructed as an ideal to which all individuals should aspire but which men, rather than women, are more likely to achieve. Within the rationalist convention, men treat emotions as 'distractions' which depart from the path of reason. For men it is always 'others' who have emotional needs, but they also often have to learn to deal, frequently inadequately, with emotions and feelings of their own. Aggressive emotions nonetheless are given a greater scope in the world of the male, with an emphasis of being 'out of control' – sometimes purposely amplified by alcohol consumption or indulging in risky activities and competitive sports to enforce the 'hardness' expected of them.

Adding to this picture, feminists' accounts stress how, in a patriarchal society, it is acceptable for women to display emotions; for this only confirms their weakness and prescribes a culture where men are expected to be independent, self-sufficient and relied upon. Those emotions which are acceptable in man, such as anger, aggressiveness or triumph, are frequently regarded as 'unattractive' in women. Thus, there is a strong link between perceived femininity and emotionality. Women are regarded as being 'naturally' good at dealing with other people's emotions because they are themselves understood to be inherently emotional and that this is most discernible in the supposed natural mother–infant bond (Nauright and Chandler 1997). While such analysis provides insight into generalised gender differences in social interaction and bonding – based along the lines of an emotion/non-emotion dichotomy – they also inform dynamics of friendship and also relate to relationships of an intimate nature, which will now be addressed.

INTIMATE RELATIONSHIPS

Intimate relationships may be referred to as a form of human association which entails physical and/or emotional intimacy often entailing romantic and/or sexual closeness. In the contemporary cultural environment such relationships increasingly display wide diversity and complex dimensions. Thus Sharon Sassler (2010) stresses how marital delay, relationship dissolution and high divorce rates extend the amount of time individuals spend in search of tender and intimate relationships outside of marital unions: 'hooking up', internet dating, 'visiting' relationships, cohabitation, marriage following childbirth and serial partnering over different stages over the life course. These developments have spawned a growing range of sociological literature exploring the complex nature of intimacy and indeed how intimacy might itself be defined (Jamieson 2011). Nonetheless, familiar themes such as the gendering of heterosexual relationships remain core to the relevant research.

According to Seider (1989), as far as heterosexual relationships are concerned, it is women who are, more often than not, relied upon to undertake much of the emotional work. Men are dependent on partners to interpret how a relationship is developing and to sustain it, while they often feel that it is self-indulgent to attempt to fulfil their own emotional requirements. This can create problems within relationships; for example, it may leave women feeling guilty about satisfying their own needs. While men very often subscribe to notions of romantic love it is, more often than not, associated with sexual conquest.

This gendering of intimate relationships has also been translated into new forms of partnership-selection. Elizabeth Jagger (2001), in her deconstruction of heterosexual dating advertisements, maintains that in the postmodern consumer culture men are furnished with a wide range of resources in which to create 'desirable' identities, but for women reflexive self-fashioning is more problematic. Men stress financial and occupational resources, alongside more conventional masculine images. In contrast, female self-images, in the attempt to 'sell themselves', are quite restrictive and more closely associated with sex role stereotypes based on physical attractiveness, desirability, and body shape.

Nonetheless, changing gender norms may well be impacting heterosexual relationships. Certainly, Sue Lees (1993, 1–2) speaks of a 'crisis' in the relationship between adult men and women. In particular, men's attitudes to women have not kept up with the dramatic changes altering women's lives. Explanations of such changes include rapid transformations in the economy, the breakdown of traditional morality and the growing confidence of women to contest their subordination. Moreover, Lees sees this 'crisis' as in part derived from the transforming nature of male identities, especially in the restructuring of working-class families and the proportion of women entering the job market, which derives from a new-found economic power.

Adding to a complex picture is the use of new technologies, which have clearly added a fresh dimension to initiating intimate relationships through contemporary 'dating'. Wysocki (1998), for instance, has considered how people participate in sexually explicit bulletin boards on websites or 'sex on-line'. She concludes that they subscribe for various reasons. The most common is to fulfil particular fantasies which were not being fulfilled in their relationships offline, and to share their fantasies with the like-minded. Thus the relevant websites have become consumerised 'fantasy lands' for people to talk about sexual activities which they could not live out in real life. However, once contact is made, face-to-face meetings might prove to be an unrealistic illusion.

A further sociological emphasis is on exploring the basis of establishing intimate relationships as a form of 'exchange', which includes personal 'benefits' and 'costs' – a conceptualisation which also addresses the question as to why relationships dissolve. It is an account which seemingly endorses accounts of the character of a range of contemporary personal associations based upon instrumentality and individual agency. Sprecher (2001), by way of illustration, reports the findings of a longitudinal study with romantic couples to examine the importance of equity relative to other social exchange variables, such as 'rewards', 'investments' and 'alternatives', in predicting relationship satisfaction, commitment and stability. A felt lack of benefits in a relationship was found to be associated with a lower level of satisfaction and commitment and thus conducive to a greater likelihood of breakup. Among other findings, it was evident that women's commitment was the strongest predictor of relationship stability. In addition, women's 'rewards' and satisfaction and men's satisfaction were very often associated with relationship stability.

Studies have also been conducted into how and why relationships progress should they endure over a reasonable length of time. For instance, a study by Sassler et al. (2010) examined the factors associated with relationship progression into sexual involvement and co-residence derived from the Marital and Relationship Survey that obtained information from low- to moderate-income married and cohabiting couples. Over one-fifth of male and female respondents reported becoming sexually involved with their current partner within the first week of dating. Entrance into shared living was also quite rapid; about one-third of respondents began to cohabit with their partner within six months, while approximately two-thirds of married respondents initially cohabited with their partners. Sassler et al. conclude that indicators of disadvantaged family backgrounds were likely to accelerated entrance into sexual involvement and co-residence – a factor more pronounced for women than men.

Romantic love

While relationships today may increasingly be dictated to by instrumentally orientated 'rewards' and 'costs', Western society continues to place considerable premium on love as a source of meaning, purpose, fulfilment, partnership selection and long-term commitment. However, the concept of romantic love, and indeed the general notion of love, is especially difficult to quantify. Nevertheless, in the West there remains a cultural code of romantic love continuingly reaffirmed by the media and popular discourse.

The widespread notion of being romantically attached through pre-marriage courtship is generally believed to have grown to prominence in early modernity. Goode (1982) asserts that the main connection between the element of romantic love and developments associated with modernity is historically associated with the family unit and its growth as relatively independent of the larger kinship group, so husband and wife were free to love each other without serious competition from kin members and their attempt to influence partnership selection. Second, given that the parent–child tie is strong in Western societies, falling in love permits the young person to free her/himself from this attachment in order to enter the independent status as a spouse and mature adult. Young people, who in other marriage systems would be directed into marriage by their elders, are motivated to marry because of love.

The link between romantic love and partner selection has, however, been supplemented by more recent trends. Dating in the 1970s and 1980s changed in three ways. First, there were greater opportunities for informal opposite sex interaction, such as in the workplace. Second, it was more and more acceptable for women to initiate dating activities and share responsibility for the economics of the date and, arguably, a greater equity within developing relationships. Third, dating behaviour became less formal than in previous generations and was no longer a set progression of stages from first meeting to falling in love to greater commitment until the time of marriage.

The future, however, looks quite different altogether. Relationships are increasingly exposed to information technology, lifestyle preferences and perhaps the growing commercialisation of romantic love which culturally contradicts the sexual permissiveness and choices open to sexual lifestyles. This leads Beck and Beck-Gernsheim (1996) to claim how the nature of love is being transformed, creating opportunities for equality or chaos in personal life as men and women are increasingly becoming the authors of their own styles of life. The nature of love is changing fundamentally in conjunction with revolution in sexual life and family forms. Love, as Beck and Beck-Gernsheim argue, is becoming an empty notion, which partners themselves are obliged to attempt to fulfil in relation to their own biographies and emotional lives. The consequence of this situation is the possibility of creating forms of equality in personal life, while there is the potentiality for 'chaos' in the wider struggle to harmonise family and career, and 'new' motherhood and fatherhood, which engender their own numerous anxieties.

Sexualities

Today sex and sexuality have become a major cultural focus of Western societies as conventional norms and prohibitions are increasingly challenged (Jackson and Scott 2004). Giddens (1992) suggests that the radical 'permissive' changes related to sexuality are intrinsic to the development of modern societies as a whole and to the broad characteristics of that development. Emancipation, opportunity and risk are now crucial ties in life which have transformed intimacy. For the first time in history, women are becoming equal to men – allowing an exploration of the potentialities of the 'pure relationship' in intimate terms – in relationships that presume sexual and emotional equality. Giddens thus discusses the emergence of what he calls 'plastic sexuality' – sexuality freed from its intrinsic relation to reproduction – in terms of the emotional liberation implicit in the pure relationship, as well as women's demand for sexual pleasure. Plastic sexuality can be moulded as a trait of personality and identity, and thus becomes bound up with the reflexivity of the self.

Mary Evans (2003) comes to a similar conclusion in identifying what she sees as a 'crisis' in heterosexual relationships. Evans argues that the cultural practices underlying love have shifted. Contemporary culture has personalised and sexualised love, and unhitched it from marriage – the coupling of which began in early modernity. At the same time society has de-eroticised sex and in doing so undermined emotive bonds. The result is that people now have impossible expectations which may ultimately be emotionally damaging. It is now a matter of romanticised and commercialised love often void of care and commitment. Evans concludes that, in terms of relationships, Western society has produced a confused culture which, through love and sexual relationships, has brought emotional insecurities that do not bode well for future generations.

The liberalising scope of Western views of sexuality has also shifted sociological attention to sexual variations and LGBT relationships, yet their significance across the life course remains under-researched (Yip 1999). The scientifically imposed designation 'homosexual' has observably swung to the preferred self-designated term 'gay' at a time when gay men and lesbians have opted to 'come out' and have subsequently been increasingly accepted in mainstream society. Nonetheless, problems of identity remain for adults associating themselves with sexual minorities. Heaphy and Yip (2006) have explored the implications that processes of de-traditionalisation and individualisation are said to have for some core aspects of social life, generating the common assumption that non-heterosexual ways of living are primarily 'prime' experiments which have wider relevance for understanding late-modern ways of living. Heaphy and Yip thus point to the notion of 'do-it-yourself' biographies that are said to be emerging in the contemporary era and are characteristic of sexual minority identities. There are the 'uneven possibilities' which exist for the development of these kinds of biographies. While the data indicates the possibilities that such biographies are open for negotiation and chosen with reference to gay and lesbian relationships in late-modern societies, Heaphy and Yip point to the factors – felt discrimination and earlier life experiences – that clearly limit negotiation and choice for sexual minority adults in their relational lives, thus indicating that these relationships may differ considerably in comparison with those of 'straight' people.

If gay equality has been achieved in law, including same-sex marriage and gay adoption, there are other indications that parity with heterosexuals has not yet been achieved. Waites (2003) contends that in late-modernity so-called expert discourse circumventing the subject of gay sexuality is less likely to confirm that a 'fixed' gay, and for that matter bi-sexual, identity has been established by the age of 16 in a way it is assumed for heterosexuals. Hence, legal equity does not imply recognition of homosexuality and hetero-sexuality on all fronts. Moreover, it also suggests an increasing medicalisa-tion of gay sexuality. As Epstein (2003) notes, in the USA the development of health policy for 'special populations' has led to the medicalisation of the identities of LGBT people. While the rights of sexual minorities can be traced to gay and feminist movements since the 1970s, they are now subject to medical scrutiny. The consequence of medicalisation is to encourage the public to see sexual and gender identities as fixed biological or cultural types and, crucially, as an illness category. Far from becoming 'sexual citizens', the medicalisation of the sexual alternatives may merely be yet another form of social exclusion.

Despite the evidence of continued discrimination, sexual variants are gaining legitimacy in Western culture and may, arguably, be a product of it. Indeed, Storr (1999) goes so far as to see variants in sexuality, exempli-fied by bisexuality, as essentially a postmodern phenomenon. Storr explains that the existence of a self-conscious bisexual identity by way of community association, organisation and politics came with the advent of postmod-ernity of the 1970s. Indeterminacy, instability, fragmentation and flux are all part of the postmodern condition. If modernity had structured hetero-sexuality, postmodernity brings its own form of sexuality that is increasingly varied and challenges the ideal heterosexual relationship. LGBT relation-ships, however, are merely one form of relationship which is cut across by a number of variations in how they might be organised and structured.

RELATIONSHIP VARIANTS

Marriage

Historically, in industrialised societies, laws enforcing universally prescribed monogamy through state recognised marriages uniquely brought an insti-tutionalised form of relationship joining two heterosexual partners for life. This development built upon Christian religious proscriptions, economic factors, and idealised views of heterosexual romantic love. The high level of divorce and remarriage, however, suggests that 'serial monogamy' may be a more accurate description of Western marital practices today, signifying the ease by which annulment can be attained and perhaps the consequences of an increasing life-span (Cherlin 2004).

The historical evidence nonetheless paints a complex picture of the popularity of marriage and the age in which it has been embarked upon (Smock 2004). During the twentieth century there occurred a remarkable increase in the marriage rate. Between 1911 and 1954 in the UK, the portion of women aged between 20 and 40 who were married grew by nearly one-third. In 1931, the figure was 572 per thousand, in 1951 it grew to 731, and in 1961 it had reached 808. In 1996, the number of marriages in the UK was, however, at a 70-year low. There were 201,000 first marriages in 1994, half that of 1970. There is also evidence that couples are marrying at an older age: a late twentieth-century development was the average age of marriage in the European Union: in 1993 it was 28.5 for men and 26.1 for women. Such statistics render the lower age of marriage in the early and mid-twentieth century as something of a historical curiosity. The current later age chosen for marriage brings wedlock back to the patterns observable in the seventeenth and eighteenth centuries. That said, because of other major life events, the decision to marry frequently results in marriage today occurring at a variety of stages on the life course (Guzzo 2006; Pittman and Blanchard 1996).

Generally speaking, people will marry someone of similar age, education, social class background and lifestyle. Goode argues that since the marriageable population of the Western countries is segregated into pools of people with comparable class origins, even a 'free' dating pattern with some encouragement to fall in love does not threaten the stratification system; generally people fall in love with 'the right kind of people' (Goode 1982, 80–90). In fact, there never is a completely free-market in courtship or mate-selection. Rather, as in some economic exchanges, there are many smaller markets in which only certain people are eligible to participate and tend to be dictated by preferences which are racially and class homogeneous and dictated by such factors as religious background (Blackwell and Lichter 2004). However, into the twenty-first century there is evidence that the situation is beginning to change, with the most significant indicator of demographic limitation of eligibility – namely 'race' – seemingly breached, particularly by younger generations. For example, in the USA the number of inter-racial marriages increased by 9 million in 2010, or 2.9 per cent of the total population, of which 5.6 per cent were under age 18 (2010 National Census).

Cohabitation

Even if marriage has enjoyed a continuing popularity in Western societies, various alternatives have also emerged. One is cohabitation – defined as the sharing of a household by an unmarried couple, although it would seem to neither significantly challenge nor replace the institution of marriage. This arrangement has nonetheless become more popular, with the proportion of all non-married women in the USA aged 18 to 40 cohabiting doubling since 1981 to 25 per cent of all couplings, although it is most frequent among young women in their twenties and divorced people.

Initially, evidence suggested that cohabitation rarely lasted more than two years, and usually ended in marriage. In Europe, almost half of those between 25 and 44 years of age have cohabited at some point. This provided confirmation that social attitudes towards this arrangement had changed considerably and that ideas of 'living in sin', which indicated the widespread disapproval of sex outside of marriage, now have little credence. With cohabitation carrying far less stigma, especially with younger generations (Brown et al. 2008), it was initially interpreted as constituting a 'trial marriage', whilst simultaneously providing a marker of cynicism around the institution of marriage. More recently, 'serial cohabitation' – over a period of time – has become more increasingly observable (Lichter and Qian 2008). It might be argued that fair few individuals may opt for cohabitation as a result of high levels of divorce and a belief that should they wish to end their relationship sometime in the future, then it would be less traumatic than if there were a formal union. In the UK 70 per cent of first partnerships were cohabitations, while 60 per cent of all cohabitations moved into marriage in 1980 (2 per cent of women had children while cohabiting). In 1997, the numbers of cohabitations had risen to 22 per cent (Ermisch and Francesconi [2002] and the Institute of Social and Economic Research [2002]).

By the age of 30, three-quarters of women in the USA have been married and about half have cohabited outside of marriage, according to a report on cohabitation, marriage, divorce and remarriage by the Centers for Disease Control and Prevention (2010). Using the data from the US National Survey of Family Growth (NSFG), Karen Guzzo (2006) documents the extent to which cohabiters begin their union with intentions to marry (indicated by either being engaged or having definite plans to marry) and how this is related to subsequent cohabitation transitions. Almost half of all first cohabitations began with intentions to marry, and having marital intentions increased the likelihood of marriage and decreased the odds of dissolution.

However, the National Center for Health Statistics (2002) found that in the USA unmarried cohabitations overall are less stable than marriages. The probability of a first marriage ending in separation or divorce within five years was 20 per cent, but the probability of a premarital cohabitation breaking up within the same year was nearly 50 per cent. After 10 years, the probability of a first marriage ending was 33 per cent, compared with 62 per cent for cohabitations. The study suggests that both cohabitations and marriages tend to last longer under certain conditions, such as a woman's age at the time cohabitation or marriage began; whether she was raised throughout childhood in an intact two-parent family; and whether she had a higher family income or lived in a community with high median family income, low male unemployment and low levels of poverty.

Long distance relationships

A fairly recent form of relationships are so-called long distant relationships (LDR). A long-distance relationship or 'blue sky relationship' (a term often used specifically for relationships across international borders) is an intimate relationship established and sustained between partners who are geographically isolated from one another and lack regular face-to-face contact, but nonetheless seek to meet up on a regular basis. Such contacts are frequently supplemented by interacting through new technologies, including Skype and the internet, which were not previously available (Haque 2013).

Ulrich Beck and Elisabeth Beck-Gernsheim (2013) investigate many types of LDRs, including marriages and families stretching across countries, continents and cultures. These LDRs comprise so many different forms that they refer to them as 'world families', by which they mean love and intimate relationships between individuals living in, or coming from, different countries or continents. In all their various forms these world families share one feature in common: they are the focal point in which different aspects of the globalised world become embodied in the personal lives of individuals.

LDRs remain an under-researched and little-understood form of relationship, although financial gain, career advancement and family obligations are seen as key reasons why people undertake such arrangements (Green et al. 1990; Guldner 2003). While it is difficult to gauge the number of LDRs, in 2005, according to The Center for the Study of Long Distance Relationships, an estimated 2.9 per cent of marriages in the USA were long-distance, with one in ten marriages reported to have included a period at long distance within the first three years. This means that in 2005 approximately 3.5 million people in the USA alone were or are involved in long-distance marriages (and an estimated 4 to 4.5 million college couples in the USA who were in non-marital LDRs (Rohlfing 1995)).

By their very nature LDRs are qualitatively different from geographically close relationships, and those who partake of them confront a number of difficulties, including lack of face-to-face and physical contact; high expectations by partners for the quality of limited face-to-face meetings when they do occur; increased financial burdens to maintain relationships largely through travel costs; and judging the state of a relationship from a distance (Rohlfing 1995). Maintenance behaviours have been separated into different categories: assurances in relation to love and commitment in the relationship, openness in sharing mutual feelings, conflict management, positive interactions, sharing tasks, giving advice to the partner and using social networks for support (Dainton 2000; Stafford et al. 2004).

The single alternative

As an alternative to sustaining relationships, a greater number of people are living apparently alone as a single person in Western Europe now than ever before, in a context where a certain stigmatisation of singlehood remains (Byrne and Carr 2005). By 1995–96, a quarter of all households in the UK housed just one person living in residence. To be sure, many of those living alone (about half) are older people who are retired, with older widows representing the large share of single people. Yet a new group of divorced men under the age of 65 has become the second largest contingent to live alone: there were two and half-times the number of men living a single life in 1996 than in 1971, and this figure continues to rise. According to one body of research, it seems to be men in particular who choose not to commit to a partner, especially through marriage. Included among the main reasons are that sex is available without marriage; that they wish to avoid the risk of divorce and its costs; that men want to wait before having children; that marriage requires change and compromise; and that men wish to own their own house before finding a wife (National Marriage Project, Rutgers University 2002).

A rather different picture is also emerging for those singles who have few family contacts during mid-life. For many reaching mid-life, marriage and family life do not come into the equation in embracing a personal lifestyle.

Table 9.1 Percentage of Usually Resident Household Population (age 16 and over) Living Alone By Age Group

16–24	25–34	35–49	50–64	65–74	75–84	85 and over
4%	10%	12%	17%	23%	38%	59%

Source: National Census 2011, licensed under the Open Government License v.3.0

A report by Emma Besbrode (2001) found that an increasing number of single people were living a 'monastic' life which leaves them less happy than married couples. In contrast to the popular view that most unattached adults enjoy a carefree way of life dominated by socialising and romance, most singles lead mundane lives in which drinking alcohol, dating and recreation play only a small part. This is particularly the case as they become older, with one in four 'mid-life singles', those aged 35 and above, admitting they had not had a relationship in five years. That the tendency for singlehood was not a lifestyle choice is suggested by the fact that only 5 per cent of this age group claimed they were able to meet a wide range of potential partners.

RELATIONSHIP BREAKDOWN

Breakdown of long-term relationships of various forms may be regarded as a major form of life discontinuity and the evidence suggests that the causes of breakdown are complex and diverse. A study conducted by Campbell et al. (2010) addressed the question as to why some individuals experience greater fluctuations in relationship over short periods of time and the processes which destabilise relationships and may lead to their dissolution. The research found that individuals who trusted their partners less reported greater variability in perceptions of relationship quality. Second, they also perceived daily relationship-based conflict as a relatively more negative experience. Third, greater variability in relationship perceptions predicted greater self-reported distress, more negative behaviour and less positive behaviour during conflict resolution. Individuals tend to compartmentalise positive and negative features of their partners if they experienced greater variability in relationship and were involved in higher quality relationships.

In a further study, Knopp and associates (2014) found that greater fluctuations in dedication were correlated with poorer relationship adjustment and more dissolution consideration. Detrimental effects of fluctuations in dedication were strongest for individuals who reported higher levels of initial dedication but were disappointed with the progression of the relationship. Arriaga et al. (2006) in their study discovered that individuals whose perceptions of partner commitment fluctuate over time were more likely to be in a relationship which eventually ended than were individuals whose perceptions remained relatively steady. Moreover, Arriaga (2001) found that individuals who exhibited greater fluctuation in their repeated satisfaction ratings were more likely to be in relationships which eventually ended, even after controlling for overall level of satisfaction. Individuals with fluctuating levels of satisfaction also reported relatively lower levels of commitment.

While relationship breakdowns can come in various modes, it is the increasing divorce rate in Western societies which has drawn the most attention. Statistical rates cannot of course measure the incidence of spouses who stay together in the same household even though their marriage is 'dead', for practical and financial reasons or for the 'sake of the children'. Divorce rates, nevertheless, can be monitored and they are undoubtedly proliferating in most Western societies. The USA displays the highest rate at around 50 per cent of marriages. In 2011 the marriage rate was 6.8 per 1000 total population and the divorce rate 3.6 per 1000. Sixty-seven per cent of second marriages end in divorce, along with 73 per cent of third marriages (National Marriage and Divorce Rate Trends 2002). There is also a strong probability that second marriages will end in separation or divorce (23 per cent after 5 years and 39 per cent after 10 years).

There is a tendency for rising divorce rates to be seen as an essentially Western phenomenon and a cause for concern. In reality, many pre-industrial societies have been known to have substantially higher divorce rates than any measurable in the West (Goode 1982, 404). Neither is there anything particularly new in increasing rates in Western societies. There had been a long-term upward trend in the number of civil divorces in the nineteenth century. However, prior to 1914, the annual number of divorces never exceeded 10,000 in England and Wales, and 1000 in Scotland. There were substantial increases in the wake of both World Wars, but the numbers fell back during the 1950s. From the early 1960s the trend has been upward, with the 1970 figure more than doubling that of 1960. The peak period for divorce in the UK was the 1970s, although the rapid rise has stabilised since the mid-1980s (at around 160,000 per year). It is now expected that 40 per cent of recent UK marriages will end in divorce. It might be suggested on such evidence that several generations of high divorce rates have seriously weakened the idea that marriage is a life-time commitment. Looking back over history, however, marital relationships are about as durable today as they were a century ago, when many marriages were cut short by death.

In the USA the National Center for Health Statistics (2002) reported that marriages ending do not always result in divorce but often terminate in separation (the statistics of which are impossible to calculate) and do not proceed through the divorce process. Separated white women are much more likely (91 per cent) to divorce after three years, compared with separated

---

Box 9.1 Divorce UK

- Between 2011 and 2012, the number of divorces in England and Wales increased by 0.5% (117,558 to 118,140).
- In 2012, 10.8 people divorced per thousand married population. This was a decrease of 19% compared with 13.3 in 2002.
- The number of divorces was highest among men and women aged 40 to 44 in 2012.
- In 1997, almost a third of marriages had ended within fifteen years. This was in contrast to 22% of those marriages in 1972 ending within the same time period.

Source: Office of National Statistics, licensed under the Open Government License v.3.0

Hispanic women (77 per cent) and separated black women (67 per cent). The probability of remarriage among divorced women was 54 per cent in five years – 58 per cent for white women, 44 per cent for Hispanic women, and 32 per cent for black women. The likelihood that divorced women will remarry has, however, been declining since the 1950s, when women who divorced displayed a 65 per cent chance of remarrying. Data for 1995 show that women who divorced in the 1980s only had a 50 per cent chance of remarrying.

Roughly a quarter of children can now expect to find their original parents divorced by the time they are 16; although the trend of ending marriage may have slowed down at the beginning of the twenty-first century, it does nonetheless seem a stable Western cultural pattern. More general explanations for divorce include the following. First, divorce is legally easier to accomplish and is cheaper than before. In the UK the Divorce Law Act of 1969 (which gave a sharp upward shift to the total number of divorces since 1971) established that it was sufficient to claim an 'irretrievable breakdown of marriage' to obtain a divorce. It is a phrase general enough to be interpreted to include virtually all conceivable reasons for divorce (the most common reason for women to be granted divorce is the 'unreasonable behaviour' of the man; for men, it is the adultery of the wife [Social Trends 1997, 48]). Second, the long-term background to the erosion of marriage as a permanent and binding commitment is the decline in formal religious belief. Marriage is less often seen as a sacred, lifelong spiritual union but more as a personal and practical commitment which can be abandoned if it fails.

Third, the value placed on individualism. Beechy (1983) points to the rise of a culture where people expect choice and control over their lives, where beliefs in equality are important factors in explaining rising divorce rates. A cultural drift has moved towards an ethos of individualism which spurs a search for personal happiness and success rather than with the well-being of families and children. Fourth, there may be the factor of diminishing romantic love. Since Western culture has long emphasised romantic love as a basis for marriage, relationships are more vulnerable to collapse as sexual passion subsides. There is now, arguably, widespread support for the notion that one may end a marriage in favour of a fresh relationship simply to renew excitement and romance.

A fifth explanation for the rising divorce rate, according to Beechy (1983), connects with the discussion earlier in this chapter: women are now less dependent on men and display changing expectations. Increasing female participation in the labour force has reduced a wife's financial dependence on her husband. In addition, women have largely come to expect more from life than being merely the homemaker. They are more likely to demand freedom from the dominance of the husband, making it easier to walk away from unhappy marriages. Up to the time of the change in divorce legislation in the UK in 1969 twice as many men filed for divorce as women. This figure was reversed after the change in law. Finally, there is the 'stress factor'. With both spouses working outside the home, employment consumes time and energy. Raising children can be difficult in this context. Thus, divorce is most common during the early years of marriage when working couples have young children.

Divorce has various consequences, and in Chapter 6 there was a consideration of the implications of the end of marriage for children. Another obvious repercussion is for the estranged spouses themselves. Hetherington (1991) found that most divorcees report divorce as an extremely painful experience, but that the most traumatic period is when spouses separate for the last time. After divorce, it is men who generally feel more detrimental effects. Both the estranged may experience emotional distress, psychological issues and health problems as integral to the process of adapting to new roles and perhaps new relationships as part of a settling down period which may average some two years. After divorce, however, females seem to adapt more readily than males. Married men, compared to married women, live longer than single men, have better mental health and report being happier. Yet, this is reversed after divorce, with men finding it more difficult to cope on their own and displaying deteriorating levels of physical and mental health.

THE FAMILY AND FAMILY LIFE

Various previous chapters of this volume have engaged with diverse aspects of family life. Clearly, it is a significant social institution which conjoins individuals into different forms of relationships over the life course, at least conventionally. However, the nature of this institution and relationships within it are clearly undergoing profound changes.

Throughout the world, families have historically formed around the institution of marriage – a legally sanctioned and, ideally, enduring heterosexual relationship involving economic co-operation, as well as normative sexual activity and child-bearing. On a universal basis individuals are, typically, initially born into a family composed of parents and siblings – an arrangement generally referred to as the 'nuclear family' or 'family of orientation' given that it is usually perceived as central to the socialisation process. In adulthood, if not opting to remain childless, couples forge a 'family of procreation' in order to produce or adopt children of their own. Today, the 'extended family', which conventionally numbered relatives beyond the nuclear family, is growing in its variation and structure and takes in the so-called beanpole family, which is multi-generation, a pattern which is 'long' and 'thin', with the decline in attachment with more distant relatives (aunts, uncles etc.) reflecting fewer children being born in each generation, but with family members living longer.

Changes in the extended family exemplify the fact that the family is one key social institution which has been undergoing something of a structural and cultural revolution for some time (Burgess and Locke 1953). Nonetheless, in the 1980s Robert Chester (1985) argued that there were signs of a reversal of some of the trends in what he called the 'new conventional family' which emerged in the mid-twentieth century. Furthermore, Chester suggested that the complexities of the contemporary life course make it inevitable that at any one time some people will not be members of a nuclear family household. Yet, he maintained there was little evidence that people were choosing to live on a long-term basis in alternatives to the nuclear family. In the USA, researchers attribute the possible re-emergence or at least consolidation of the nuclear family to many factors, including that the divorce rate has fallen from its peak in 1980 when there were over five divorces for every 1000 people; by 1999 the rate had dropped to four in 1000. Also, out of wedlock births have been levelling off. In 1970, roughly one in ten births pertained to unmarried mothers. Although the rate surged to one out of three in 1994, it has since virtually stayed at the same level.

The apparent 'return' of the nuclear family should, however, be put in perspective. The economy, for example, may have played a significant role. Between 1991 and 1996, the average financial situation of many families improved considerably. These improvements reduced the number of divorces, since spouses invariably felt more economically secure. The reality, however, was that in the 1990s in the USA less than one in four households approximated the traditional image of a married or cohabiting couple with children. Stacey (1996) estimated that in the USA less than ten per cent of households conformed to the modern patterns of bread-winning father, home-making mother and one to four children under the age of 18.

The extent of change and variation in family life was clearly evident by the late twentieth century. Thus, for example, cohabitation may lead to a family with children, while after divorce a lone-parent family frequently forms or amounts to a chosen lifestyle without marriage, or, on re-marriage, a step-family or re-constituted family may possibly result. As more and more people forge non-traditional family ties and replace them with 'families of choice', with or without legal or blood ties, the family is increasingly defined on the basis of how individuals develop a sense of belonging together in a unit (Weston 1991). Moreover, such variations of family life may be viewed as a form of social experimentation which might be reduced to a cultural motif of late/postmodernity. For example, Burgoyne and Clark's (1984) study of stepfamilies in one UK town found that at least some relationship couples regarded themselves as 'pioneers of an alternative lifestyle'.

Despite mixed evidence about the endurance of the nuclear family, it is clear that considerable diversity has long been forged by a number of demographic factors. Earlier studies suggested that social class was a major determining element. Rubin (1976), for example, identified not only a difference in financial security and range of opportunities but also that class could affect family size, structure and values embraced. In turn, these variables forged attitudes towards family and married life, reflecting differential levels of education and work satisfaction, and they accompanied, for the middle-classes at least, a greater emphasis on verbal skills, flexibility and initiative. In addition, middle-class couples shared a wider range of activities, while traditionally working-class domestic life was more sharply divided along gender lines. In such homes, Rubin explains, conventional masculine ideas of self-control stifled emotional expressiveness on the part of working-class men, prompting women to turn to each other as confidants and develop strong bonds between them. The privatisation of middle-class family life, by comparison, was highly compatible with extended friendship networks and was displayed in the relative lack of involvement in the social life of the immediate neighbourhood, suggesting that friendships were more organised and less spontaneous. Over recent decades, however, the predictions of Willmott and Young (1973) have undoubtedly been fulfilled in the shifting of working-class families to conform closer to the middle-class stereotype, although outcrops of traditional working-class family structures and norms may be observable among semi- and unskilled workers.

As with social class, there are dangers in generalising about ethnic minorities and their family structures and relationships. Just as there is enormous diversity behind the so-called white nuclear family, so there is great variety among the families of the major ethnic groups. At the same time, ethnic family forms in the UK, for instance, have been subject to change over the past half a century. In the early days of mass migration (1950–70) there was a severe disruption of family life, as patterns found in the former homes began to disintegrate. Nonetheless, subsequent new forms of stable family types have emerged. Having recognised this, there remain differences that are quite striking compared to the standardised Anglo-Saxon family (Hernandez 2004).

The Asian population across the world generally displays a very strong extended family system, which is to one degree or another replicated in the Western setting. There are, however, distinctive cultural variations between Bangladeshis, Pakistanis, Punjabis, Tamils and other ethnic groups and nationalities regarding family structures, values and norms which are as great as their similarities. Irrespective of structure or tradition, Westwood and Bhachu (1988) have nonetheless identified a number of transformations, including the tendency for some Asian families to have become more nuclear in structure and to display a greater diversity of family life and a more open attitude to women working outside the home.

Afro-Caribbean families account for less than one per cent of all families in the UK, but do provide a stark contrast to other ethnic groups (Skellington and Morris 1996, 20). Today, around 37 per cent are headed by a female (compared with 9 per cent of white families). In such families, marriage is often weaker, female-headed households are more common, and the husband/father role is likely to be less pronounced than Asian families. There is also a parallel in the USA, where Afro-American families are of a similar structure. This is often seen as linked to the historical cultural legacy of Caribbean society. Originally, whilst marriage was much valued in the Caribbean, other patterns of sexual union were always possible: common-law family households with unmarried cohabitation, as well as women-headed households.

Given the evidence, Hanson and Lynch (2013) point out that families today are multi-dimensional and differ in almost every way: size; membership; socio-cultural and socio-economic status; language, cultural, racial and ethnic identification; beliefs; values and traditions. This variation would seem to be confirmed by popular definitions of the family which mark a radical change in cultural attitudes. In the USA a variety of definitions have emerged among people surveyed, whereby the family is defined as constituted by a heterosexual couple with children (99.8 per cent); husband and wife with no children (92 per cent); an unmarried couple living together with children (83 per cent); same sex couples with children (64 per cent); same sex couples with no children (33 per cent); cohabitating unmarried couples with no children (39.6 per cent).

These definitions provide recognition of the vast variety of family structures which now exist. In 2010 there were 74.2 million children (0–17yrs) in the USA: 66–77 per cent lived with two married parents; 4 per cent with unmarried but cohabiting parents; only their mothers (23 per cent); only their fathers (3 per cent); neither parent (4 per cent): 3 million children: 54 per cent with grandparents; 21 per cent with other relatives and 24 per cent with non-relatives (Federal Interagency Forum on Child and Family Statistics 2007). Moreover, in the USA 60 per cent of people have stated that if a social unit labels themselves as a family then they are indeed a family (Allan and Crow 2001).

Such findings have led to sociologists attempting to define the family with broader criteria. For example, David Morgan (2011) approaches the nature of the family in terms of a sense of belonging, particularly through the routine actions of family life: feeding children, doing DIY, washing up, laundry, washing, etc. are influenced by beliefs about rights and obligations within the family. Morgan prefers the concept of 'family practice' to that of 'family structure' as a way of describing how people construct their understanding of it throughout the life course and in terms of relationships. Thus, families are not concrete 'things' or structures but are what people actually *do* and the meaning they give to activities. Morgan concludes that family practice allows an appreciation of the 'realities of everyday experience' of family life because of the greater freedom to choose how families organise relationships. Yet he concedes that social change has an impact in that society is becoming increasingly fragmented, less clear cut, and boundaries between friendship, family and other forms of relationships are becoming increasingly blurred.

The broad definition of the family found in public surveys is in accordance with the life course perspectives which elaborate the importance of time, context, process and meaning on human development and family life, so that the family can be perceived of as a micro-social group within a macro social context – a 'collection of individuals with shared history who interact within ever-changing social contexts across ever increasing time and space' (Bengston and Allen 1993, 470). Ageing and life transitions are thus continuous processes that are experienced throughout family life. At the same time, comprehending the family crucially involves examining the meeting point of social and historical factors across the generations (Elder 1985; Hareven 1996).

In their contribution to exploring such complexities, Price et al. (2000) take a life course approach to family life – including parent–child, sibling relationships and marriage relationships – stressing the diversity represented in contemporary families as they respond and adapt to changes and transitions in family relationships during the life course. Here is recognition that diversity impacts all stages of family life over time, including how relationships may radically alter. Nonetheless, while the family would seem to increasingly be subject to change, dislocation and discontinuities over the life course, they do not necessarily suggest that linked lives by way of multi-generational bonds have inevitably been undermined (Bengston 2001).

Evidence of the intricacy of family life even within the delimited period of emerging adulthood has been spelt out by Schoen and her associates (2007), who have surveyed the vast variety of experiences of women's family transitions into adulthood in the USA – up to age 24. Using Add Health surveys, they found that only a third of all women marry, and a fifth of those marriages dissolve before age 24. Three out of eight women had a first birth, with a notable majority of those births outside of marriage (66 per cent for whites, 96 per cent for blacks and 72 per cent for Mexican Americans). Cohabitation was the most popular union, with nearly 60 per cent of women cohabiting at least once by age 24. The researchers summarise the family and relationship experience of women up to this age in terms of four categories, each accounting for roughly a quarter of all women: those who remain single non-parents; early marriers, women whose marriage is not preceded by a first birth; those who become single parents; and those who cohabit at least once, but who do not marry or have a birth by age 24. These variations prove that the strictly ordered transitions of the mid-twentieth century have virtually disappeared and have been replaced by a variety of paths into adulthood.

SUMMARY

One of the principal insights which Sociology provides into the variety of relationships considered above is that they are a social product created by societal needs and reflect cultural trajectories, whether friendships or more intimate relationships, according to time and place. Today, some cherished institutions such as marriage and the family unit which historically channelled relationships and constrained sexuality – uniting it to reproductive functions – are clearly being undermined and numerous alternatives present themselves. Whether single parenthood, cohabitation or any other variation to the family are for the long-term benefit of society remains to be seen.

Founded on recent trends, some predictions for the future may be conjectured. Divorce rates are likely to remain high and underscore public debates about the health of family life. It is clear that in the West governments recognise the variety and consequences of diverse forms of relationships, as evident in the rights of sexual minorities and provisions for single parenthood. However, many people continue to give priority to an ethic of the importance of marriage and family life – a normalisation which has become more prevalent by policies around mainstreaming the nuclear family, inclusion, community-based services, and parental rights and responsibilities. Yet, it is unlikely that marriage will regain the durability that it sustained before the 1960s, so that divorce and relationship breakdowns now mark one of the main discontinuities in adult life.

Family life in the twenty-first century will undoubtedly continue to be highly variable. This represents new conceptions of family relations as a matter of choice concomitant with late/postmodernity. There have now emerged new, flexible, highly individualistic and sexually variant relationship patterns (Cancian 1987). An optimistic view of the future is one which predicts that relationships will emerge where adult men and women are equal and interdependent; their child-raising is altogether part of a more egalitarian and democratic arrangement, where sexuality and love become more 'plastic', diffuse and open. These are all relationships of choice, closely allied to individualism, and may forge a kinship arrangement that some sociologists term the 'postmodern family' (Stacey 1996, 8). Whatever its precise designation, it is one whose precise structure is unpredictable and part of a broader context of relationships where alternatives to marriage present themselves.

Clearly, transformations in the family have stimulated a great deal of debate in the realm of politics and social policy. For some with informed opinions these changes amount to a disaster; to others they mark social progress, bringing individualism and the end of patriarchy and restrictive gender roles, as well as enhancing a culture where choice is of paramount importance. Whatever the merits behind changes in the nature of relationships and the family and attitudes towards sexuality, their increasing diversity and exposure to choice has considerable impact on the life course in terms of risks and discontinuities, alongside increasing opportunity and challenges across the generations.

FURTHER READING

Adelman, M. (2000) *Midlife Lesbian Relations: Friends, Lovers, Children and Parents*, New York: Routledge.

Ahrons, C. (2007) 'Family Ties After Divorce: Long-Term Implications for Children', *Family Process*, 46(1): 53–65.

Arber, S. and Marsh, C. (eds.) (1992) *Families and Households: Divisions and Change*, Basingstoke: Palgrave Macmillan.

Celello, K. (2009) *Making Marriage Work: A History of Marriage and Divorce in the Twentieth-Century United States*, Chapel Hill, NC: University of North Carolina Press.

Chambers, D. (2012) *A Sociology of Family Life: Change and Diversity in Intimate Relations*, Cambridge: Polity Press.

Coltrane, S. and Ishii-Kuntz, M. (1992) 'Men's Housework: A Life Course Perspective', *Journal of Marriage and the Family*, 54(1): 43–58.

Denick, L. (1989) 'Growing Up in the Post-Modern Age: On the Child's Situation in the Modern Family, and on the Position of the Family in the Modern Welfare State', *Acta Sociologica*, 32(2): 155–80.

Duncan, S. and Phillips, M. (2008) 'New Families? Tradition and Change in Partnering and Relationships', *British Social Attitudes 2007/8*, London: NatCen, Sage.

Duncan, S. and Phillips, M. (2010) 'People Who Live Apart Together (LATs) – How Different Are They?', *The Sociological Review*, 58(1): 112–34.

Elkind, D. (1992) *The Post-modern Family, A New Imbalance,* New York: Knopf.

Gillis, J. (2002) 'Our Imagined Families: The Myths and Rituals We Live By', *The Emory Center For Myth and Ritual In American Life,* working paper no. 7: 1–20.

Goldscheider, F. and Sassler, S. (2006) 'Creating Stepfamilies: Integrating Children Into the Study of Union Formation', *Journal of Marriage and Family*, 68(2): 275–91.

Goldstein, J. and Kenny, C. (2001) 'Marriage Delayed or Marriage Forgone? New Cohort Forecasts of First Marriage for U.S. Women', *American Sociological Review*, 66(4): 506–19.

Guldner, G. (2003) *Long Distance Relationships: The Complete Guide*, Corona, CA: J. F. Milne Publications.

Jamieson, L. (1998) *Intimacy: Personal Relationships in Modern Society*, Cambridge and Oxford: Polity Press and Blackwell.

Kiernan, K. (1999) 'Cohabitation in Western Europe', *Population Trends*, 96(Summer): 25–32.

Kennedy, S. and Bumpass, L. (2008) 'Cohabitation and Children's Living Arrangements: New Estimates from the United States', *Demographic Research*, 19(47): 1663–92.

Lauer, R. and Lauer, J. (1994) *Marriage and Family: The Quest for Intimacy*, Madison: Brown & Benchmark.

Mitchell, B. (2000) 'The Refilled "Nest": Debunking the Myth of Families in Crisis', in E. Gee and G. Gutman (ed.), *The Overselling of Population Aging: Apocalyptic Demography, Intergenerational Challenges, and Social Policy*, Toronto: Oxford University Press.

Musick, K. (2007) 'Cohabitation, Nonmarital Childbearing, and the Marriage Process', *Demographic Research*, 16(9): 249–86.

Niehuis, S. and Reifman, A. and Lee, K-H. (2015) 'Disillusionment in Cohabiting and Married Couples: A National Study', *Journal of Family Issues*,36(August): 951–73.

Pilcher, J. (2000) '"Change Slow A-Coming": Domestic Divisions of Labour in the Twentieth Century', *Work, Employment and Society*, 14(4): 771–80.

Pilcher, J., Williams, J. and Pole, C. (2003) 'Rethinking Adulthood: Families, Transitions and Social Change', *Sociological Research Online*, 8(4).

Roseneil, S. (2006) 'On Not Living with a Partner: Unpicking Coupledom and Cohabitation', *Sociological Research Online,* 11(3).

Stacey, J. (1990) *Brave New Families,* New York: Basic Books.

Sweeney, M. (2010) 'Remarriage and Stepfamilies: Strategic Sites for Family Scholarship in the 21st Century', *Journal of Marriage and Family*, 72(3): 667–84.

Vaughan, D. (1986) *Uncoupling – Turning Points in Intimate Relationships*, Oxford University Press.

Wilcox, W. (2011) *Why Marriage Matters: Thirty Conclusions from the Social Sciences,* 3rd edition, New York: Institute for American Values.

Williams, K. and Umberson, D. (2004) 'Marital Status, Marital Transitions, and Health: A Gendered Life Course Perspective', *Journal of Health and Social Behavior*, 45(1): 81–98.

Chapter 10

Constructing mid-life

Fundamental to sociological focus on the subject of mid-life is the conviction that it serves as an exemplary example of the social construction of a specific 'phase' or 'transition' in the life course. Undoubtedly, Western culture has impacted and shaped popular views of mid-life – assuming early adulthood is a relatively stable and tranquil period following the trials and tribulations of youth and that mid-life heralds the distressing decline of old age which invariably follows. Put otherwise, common-sense discourse typically focuses on mid-life as a climacteric or 'crucial period' perceived as a juncture between physical and mental maturity and then deterioration in later life. Such assumptions are perennially enforced by the medical gaze, which continues to problematise mid-life and the alleged 'crisis' that attends its. Infused by the interests of the pharmaceutical industries, mid-life is regularly approached as a list of medical complaints, some of which at least are understood to be 'curable'.

Cultural perceptions have also spawned the view that mid-life is the 'half way stage' of the life course, inevitably generating a realisation that time is 'running out' or 'the best years are behind'. More sophisticated appraisals may include notions of a process of intensive 'transition' of the self, including a re-evaluation of life values and goals. If so, late/postmodernity may enhance this reflexive re-orientation, encouraging planning for the 'second half' of life and bringing a realisation that death is an inevitable future event which has to be come to terms with in the present. At the same time, late/postmodernist accounts point to how some of the common assumptions and perceptions regarding mid-life are plausibly beginning to be eroded, allowing mid-life identity to undergo a fresh appraisal. This is understood to be at least partly due to growing optimistic views forged by aspects of choice in terms of lifestyle and self-actualisation, so that in the consumer society it may now be possible to talk of a plurality of mid-lifestyles. Such developments, however, do not distract from the cultural forces, including academic appraisals, which continue to shape perceptions of mid-life. These themes will constitute the subject matter of this chapter.

HISTORICAL AND CROSS-CULTURAL PERSPECTIVES

One means of substantiating the tendency for 'mid-life' to be singled out as a particularly significant phase of life with distinctive attributes and maladies is to embrace historical and cross-cultural comparisons. In the first instance, it may be observed that even in Western societies notions of a mid-life 'crisis' are notably absent from the pages of history narratives. Certainly, the common picture that mid-life is practically synonymous with the so-called physiological change in life experienced by women, which is challenging at best and a curse at worse, are scarcely evident. There is little to suggest that a change in reproductive capacities – the 'handicap' of menopause, accompanied by 'unwanted' emotional and psychological baggage which is assumed to occur – is of major concern. While it may be true that women have been 'absent from history' in that their life experiences are rarely recorded, it is clear that the life expectancy for females (and males) was little more than what is designated as mid-life today, where reaching 40 years old was regarded as an achievement. For many women, life was little more than a cycle of pregnancy and childbirth, quickly followed by 'old age' and death. This invariably raises the question of precisely which years constitute 'mid-life' today, at a time when life expectancy continues to increase. As the life span lengthens into the 80s and 90s in Western societies, the onset of mid-life may be more adequately viewed as commencing in the early 50s, in contrast to the cultural belief that it commences in the late 30s or early 40s.

Anthropological and cross-cultural research reinforces the realisation that the dominant Western view of mid-life is distinctly unique. Not all cultures respond to the mid-life transition (if it is a 'transition') by designating it as a 'crisis', in part because of their more positive perceptions of ageing. In many non-Western cultures, ageing is connected with life experience, wisdom and, thus, a positive social status, rather than some form of 'crisis' (Menon 2001). This compares starkly to Western culture, where ageing is often associated with gradual decrepitude, disability and dependency. It follows that the notion of a 'mid-life crisis' is invariably more ubiquitous in the West, given it suggests that ageing requires a process of adaptation.

Even amongst technologically advanced societies, the perceived meaning and 'symptoms' of mid-life seemingly vary considerably. Lambley (1995, 9–11) provides the example of Japan. The modern industrialised nation is in many respects comparable to the societies of the West, with similar economic values and not dissimilar standards of living. 'Mid-life', especially amongst women, does not display the same meaning in Japan, where it continues to be regarded as marking the commencement of maturity rather than merely the onset of old age. Until they have reached the age of 50, Japanese men and women are not generally considered as fully mature. Although the cessation of menstruation in Japanese women is seen as part of the 'change of life', it fails to be attributed the same implications which it assumes in the West. Even the symptoms reported are apparently different. Hot flushes – the single most frequently reported complaint amongst Western females – are uncommonly highlighted by Japanese women during menopause, whereas others, notably constipation and diarrhoea, are familiarly accounted conditions.

Neither are attitudes towards mid-life, conceived in terms of the stage of menopause for women, by any means uniform among Western societies. One cross-national study in Europe (Komesaroff et al. 1997), for example, discovered that over half the women surveyed found the menopause psychologically distressing. Yet, while two-thirds of French and UK females experience menopause in this way, it did not appear to be the case with German women, amongst whom fewer than half had found it particularly arduous. Sharon Wray's research (2007) similarly draws attention to the significance of ethnic and cultural diversity even within the Western setting regarding how mid-life is experienced and enacted. In short, Wray suggests that extant theorising tended to overlook the complex meanings attached to mid-life, especially by women, and how these meanings are often bound up with past and current ethnic and cultural belief systems and values which are not structured around Western concerns and priorities. Moreover, wealth and education apparently impact women at this stage of life, as they do during earlier years on the life course. Thus, more affluent and better-educated women tend to report fewer physical and psychological problems associated with the menopause, suggesting that it is essentially accumulated detrimental social conditions which contribute to encounters of the middle-age phase of life (Lambley 1995, 10).

A MID-LIFE CRISIS?

While notions of a 'crisis' enthuse popular perceptions of mid-life, such a condition could be little more than a cluster of unfavourable factors which converge at a particular time of life. One such factor highlighted by Robert Atchley (1988) is that 'middle-age' (ages 40–55) may frequently be the period of life when a person initially becomes aware of the fact that s/he is ageing; a time when the person recognises a reduction in energy and often begins to favour less strenuous activities which also precipitate psychological adjustment. What has been questioned nonetheless is whether mid-life, however it is defined, invariably means a decline in physical health and cognitive abilities. For instance, Sherry Willis (1999) established that verbal and numerical ability, reasoning and verbal memory, may in fact improve by mid-life. The only ability she found to decline between 25 years old and mid-life was perceptual speed – the ability to quickly and accurately perform tasks. Conversely, the cognitive capabilities of people in mid-life may well be above what they were in young adulthood.

More broadly, academic research since the 1980s has tended to reject the notion of a mid-life 'crisis' as a phase of life that most adults invariably pass through, although it has not entirely disappeared from the radar and continues to frame research. In one analysis (Lachman and James 1997) fewer than 10 per cent of people in the USA were found to have a psychological crisis due to their age or ageing. Rather, it is a particular personality type and a history of psychological problems which predispose some individuals towards a conventional mid-life crisis. Further research has produced mixed and even contradictory findings. Whereas Levinson (1977) found that 80 per cent of middle-aged participants reported experiencing a crisis and Ciernia (1995) discovered that 70 per cent of men in mid-life claimed to have experienced such an occurrence (Shek 1996), other researchers have failed to replicate such findings (e.g. Whitbourne 2009).

The question as to whether or not there is truly a psychological phenomenon which may be described as a mid-life 'crisis' now tends to be addressed through recent research attempting to identify it as a construct in the mind of the researcher and not a series of tangible negative experiences. Moreover, identified changes in personality are just as likely to occur throughout the adult years with no specific 'peak' in general distress or psychosocial 'crisis' in mid-life (Whitbourne et al. 2009). Indeed, Costa and McCrae (1980) found that, while some people were likely to experience a number of 'crises' in mid-life related to problems encountered during significant life events, generally they were just as likely to experience such crises in their 20s and 30s. Hence, these experiences were not somehow unique to mid-life.

There are other foundations to prevailing conceptions of a mid-life crisis. Works such as that of Kastenbaum (1971) indicated that perceptions of mid-life were informed by views suggesting that it was a fairly clear and pre-dictable 'stage of life', where a 'crisis' was informed by profound personal changes; one where people believed their work career had more or less reached a plateau, and where children had left home to lead their own lives and retirement loomed. Many of such changes appeared to be bound up with principal processes of modernity. In particular, these assumptions of mid-life were a product of the emergence of a new and distinctly bounded period between the completion of child-raising and retirement from work.

Mid-life is also associated with a time of life when parents or other older people close to the individual die – reminding him/her of a limited time-span and their own mortality – and thus constitute 'mortality markers'. An integral aspect of such recognition of ageing is what has come to be known as changing 'time perspectives' (Atchley 1988). It thus follows that the older person in later life avoids thought of the future because of the limited time left and instead dwells on the past, their achievements and failures. For the middle-aged, changing 'time perspectives' amounts to a greater conscious-ness of the time they have left to live rather than the time since birth (Karp and Yoels 1982, 81).

Criticism of the notion of a mid-life 'crisis' has invariably led to evaluation or modification of the concept. Wethington (2000) advances the view that it may be worth considering mid-life 'crisis' and mid-life 'transition' not as alternative definitions of this period of life but as points on a continuum over a fairly contracted period of time. Thus it is conceivable that the feel-ings associated with some form of mid-life 'crisis' are a necessary impetus for transitions to life's next chapter, that is, later life. Wethington concludes that academic studies have found on average only 10–26 per cent of adults over 40 report having a mid-life crisis, inviting proposals that it may be more appropriate to speak of a mid-life 'transition'. Both terms imply change, but change probably need not imply crisis.

Where does the varied evidence above leave the understanding that mid-life amounts merely to a social construct which entails some form of 'crisis'? One of the most insightful accounts from this perspective comes from the work of Margaret Gullette, who designates the social construct of mid-life as 'middle ageism', which results from the way culture perceives ageing and in such a way as to generate a form of social exclusion. Gullette, while not denying the ageing process, insists that age and ageing is a complex, inter-sectional social and psychological construction and a set of mediated rela-tionships among individuals located at different phases of the life course. In short, an 'ideology of ageing' is often coded into a narrative structure that associates ageing with inevitable decline and decay. This permits Gullette to utilise alternative terms which are void of ageist connotations such as 'ageing-past-youth', 'ageing-into-the-middle years' and 'ageing-into-old age' (Gullette 1997, 3–44).

Subjective views

While the writings of those such as Gullette point to notions of a mid-life 'crisis' as constituting a range of ideas relating to ageing, research around the subject of mid-life also emphasises how it is perceived by those within this phase of life, with evidence implying that individuals are often influenced by wider cultural understandings. An early study by Bernice Neugarten (1971) focused on how people came to 'know' they were middle-aged, based on detailed interviews of several dozen middle-class people. Her data indicated that individuals who subjectively viewed mid-life as having special charac-teristics which distinguish it from other 'stages' of life seemed not to have internalised the chronological passage of time but rather the social mean-ings given to being middle-aged. In regard to perceptions of mid-life, the majority of interviewees in Neugarten's research had come to accept the cul-tural significance of signs of bodily ageing, alterations in the family structure and changes in the state of career as collectively indicating its onset. Perhaps of greatest importance was recognition of being located between genera-tions. In short, an awareness of a position bridging two age groups: of their parents and of their children. This was an awareness, asserted Neugarten, of feeling less involved with their children, while identifying more with their parents.

Wethington's research (2000) suggests that regardless of academic decon-structions of 'mid-life', a popular perception of mid-life crisis remains. This seems due to the fact that, when asked, people use a much broader defin-ition of mid-life crisis than researchers. For those surveyed, the term connotes personal turmoil and sudden changes (for men it is often a metaphor for phys-ical or psychological changes). Moreover, Alwin and Levenson (2001) opine that notions of a mid-life are transmitted particularly by one generation: middle-aged Baby Boomers. It is this generation – one exposed to psychothera-peutic discourses and narratives of self-improvement – which most commonly utilise the term 'mid-life crisis' and do so to describe nearly any setback driven by significant life events, including those related to career or family life.

THE 'PROBLEM' WITH MID-LIFE

Popular notions of a mid-life 'crisis' beg the question as to precisely from where they have emerged. Clearly, it has several origins, many of which are associated with the medicalisation of a particular phase of life. One root is the theoretical frameworks or 'models' that tended to pathologise what has come to be known as 'mid-life'. Initially influential for the framing of mid-life and its perceived problematic characteristics are the writings of Sigmund Freud, who insisted it was the time of middle-age in which fears of inevitable death invariably arose. Prevalent too has been Jungian theory (although Carl Jung himself never referred to a mid-life 'crisis'). Central to Jung's thinking was that mid-life connects with increasing 'individuation', which involves a re-evaluation of self-actualisation, along with a self-awareness that contains a number of contradictions and which, in turn, generates confusion over a person's life and goals and could constitute a 'crisis' expressed in behaviour patterns (Jung 1971).

This kind of supposition was integrated into Erik Erikson's (1963) model, in which middle adulthood was viewed as life's seventh stage – middle adulthood – whereby individuals attempt to find new meaning and purpose to their existence; raising profound questions which may lead to what is now comprehended as a mid-life crisis. Certainly, Erikson's influential concepts of 'generativity' versus 'stagnation' resonated with notions of such a crisis. The former connected with a stage of life in which a person begins to appreciate his/her mortality and the imperative of being entrusted to improving the lives of future generations to come. Stagnation is the lack of psychological development and the abandonment of helping the wider community at a time when a person is barely able to aid their own family. Those who experience stagnation subsequently fail to partake in the growth of either themselves or others.

Developing the ideas of Jung, Myers-Briggs (1998) established a 'personality model' which tended to be underscored by 'stages' of changes of identity in mid-life. According to this model the process of journeying through various stages was likely to engender personal doubts about the self. Such doubts were said to generate a sense of failure and questions about life itself, perhaps accompanied by boredom; physical and psychological symptoms of exhaustion; irritability; dependency on alcohol, drugs and food; decreased sexual drive; significantly decreased or increased ambition, reflection on past relationships and personal/professional decisions; restlessness; and a strong desire to forge change without an apparent sense of direction. While these might occur 'naturally', they may also be impacted by life change: events or loss such as divorce, death of a parent or additional 'significant others', changes in work situation, the birth of grandchildren, a decrease in social networks, age related illness and a sense of transition which may be overwhelming. Practically all of these negative 'symptoms' have fed into popular discourses which surround mid-life.

In his 1965 article 'Death and the Midlife Crisis', psychologist Elliot Jaques apparently first coined the term 'mid-life crisis'. Here the emphasis was on a developmental life period (typically commencing between the ages of 30 and 40 years old and extending to the early 60s) when an individual came to realise their own mortality and how much time they may have left to live; to consider future autonomy; and analyse their past and capabilities. Jaques saw mid-life as analogous to being at the top of the 'hill' (thus the popular adage of being 'over the hill'). Implicit in this view was that mid-life was a developmental stage of maturation and adaption constituting part of the process of ageing itself – a transition which might hasten a 'crisis', especially when accompanied by a realisation that the end of life is inevitable. This idea too has clearly come to have popular currency. Indeed, Blanchflower and Oswald (2008) have found that the notion of a 'dip' (or 'slump') in mid-life is increasingly accepted by people worldwide as this Western cultural idea globally spreads.

Integral to psychological reductionism is that the mid-life transition, often accompanied by some form of 'crisis', was experienced differently by individuals, especially men and women and such a possibility will be discussed shortly. What may however be concluded at this juncture is that despite the impact of a wide range of theorising around the subject of mid-life, much has failed to show that the mid-life 'crisis' is a universal experience, or even a real condition at all. Nonetheless, perhaps the ultimate 'proof' of the social construction of mid-life comes from a scrutiny of the way that it has become increasingly medicalised in various respects through a numbers of 'symptoms' associated with ageing, especially for women, notably those experiencing the menopause.

The 'pathology' of menopause

The so-called mid-life climacteric in women has long been regarded differently from that of men. This is perhaps inevitable given women have traditionally been thought to display a contrasting psychological as well as physiological nature compared to men, based on broader common-sense beliefs regarding their reproductive system. One legacy of this is an almost Western cultural preoccupation with the womb, which has often been blamed for a good deal of what men do not understand about the behaviour of women. Above all, it has been held responsible for a broad scope of female emotional 'problems' (emblematic of this negative view of the reproductive system is that the term 'hysteria' derives from the ancient Greek word for 'womb' [hysteria]).

Such discourse surrounding the womb has endured throughout the centuries and was to eventually surface with the hegemonic nature of the medical profession, with wide-ranging implications. In Western societies, under the auspices of the profession, menopause came to be viewed as something of a mixed blessing for women. On the one hand, it was understood as a time when a woman was exempt from her natural reproductive functions and perceived related emotions. On the other hand, it was evidence that her period of fertility was over and this had implications for her social purpose, status and femininity.

In the early medical writings mid-life was increasingly designated as a 'problem' and the great majority of so-called health difficulties were seen as connected to a woman's reproductive system. In the eighteenth century, there were periodic references to the familiar symptoms which are today associated with the menopause. John Leake, an English physician, wrote in one of the earliest published medical textbooks (1777) that women during mid-life sometimes experienced headaches, dizziness, chronic pains and a range of 'female' hysterical disorders. Leake was also one of the first to refer to the association between the appearance of chronic disease and the loss of menstruation, and this helped to bring about the widespread assumption that physical as well as emotional problems occurred at about the same time. It was not, however, until the nineteenth century that doctors typically came to be convinced there was something more than mere 'hysteria' happening during the mid-life of a woman.

With reference to this medicalised context, Gannon (1996) explains how, in the past, mid-life might have been concerned with age-related physical deterioration, such as diminished energy and cardio-vascular changes, which have become redefined as part of the 'menopausal syndrome'. This involved the transformation of menopause from a predictable, expected and normal life event to a progressive 'disease' with manifestations in every sphere of life consistent with sexual and, indeed, medical politics – defining and pathologising women according to their reproductive status as bio-logically disadvantaged. Putting things in perspective, Gannon (1996, 68) writes

.... a woman's menopausal status has become a crucial component of her identity. In many disciplines, a woman's career, roles, and accomplishments, and lifestyles are being reconstructed within a hormonal paradigm.

While the medical profession in the Western world once held the conventional view that little of medical interest occurred during the menopause, in France, in the early nineteenth century, medical reports surfaced describing a 'menopausal syndrome' that required treatment. By the mid-century, European and North American doctors followed suit, and medicalisation of the mid-life period began in earnest. The association of organic pathology and emotional problems with the menopause slowly gained popularity in medical circles as the nineteenth century progressed. Two broad medical approaches to mid-life emerged, the gynaecological and psychiatric.

Gynaecologists, seeking to understand the workings of the womb from an early stage, focused on the role played by the ovaries and hormones in the female reproductive cycle and purported that 'problems' encountered by women in mid-life were largely due to changes in these. Typifying this development was the fact that at least one school of gynaecological thought regarded the menopause as a mid-life 'disease'. However, it was not until the 1960s that effective hormone-enhancing medications became available, but once they were, they aided the near monopoly of gynaecological interpretations of the menopause.

Psychiatry, on the other hand, arose almost entirely out of the hegemony acquired by the medical profession to deal with those deemed to be psychologically disturbed, and this played a major part in the theories which were to be developed about mid-life, with much focus on assumptions regarding mid-life problems and their alleged prevalence in menopausal women. As the profession turned its attention to the subject, a possible link to the more extreme forms of mental instability became increasingly acceptable. Continuing in currency throughout the twentieth century was the view that the menopause amounted to an important medical and psychological issue. It was deduced that during the menopause women experience the almost compulsory symptoms of hot flushes, depression, headaches and dizziness – all of which could be put down to hormonal changes (typically associated with the drop in oestrogen and the effects of testosterone).

The second half of the twentieth century saw the growth of the 'psycho-analytical revolution', generated by Freud, Jung and others, and its belief that practically all human ailments could be reduced to psychological factors. Evidence suggests the influence of psychoanalysis on public opinion and discourse in respect of the female menopause has been even more important than the contributions of gynaecology. Part of the growth of this medical specialism was due to the fact that psychoanalytic thought influenced public thinking and penetrated more areas of society than those of the other professions, impacting upon a whole range of non-medical groups, especially those in the cultural sphere such as writers, artists and film-makers.

By way of critiquing these medical developments Judd et al. (2012) have scrutinised cross-sectional and longitudinal studies over the three decades previously to consider what evidence exists to support the proposals that depression in mid-life women occurs as a biological response to hormonal change and is so dominant that all middle-aged women should be routinely screened for depression. They suggest the evidence reveals that depressive symptoms have no major diagnostic significance, and even when they are severe they do not always reflect some depressive syndrome. Put succinctly, there is no clear evidence that depressive disorders occur more commonly in association with the menopause. Rather, it appears the true extent of disorder is similar to that at other periods in a woman's reproductive life. Although depressive symptoms are common at this time, data does not support the call for screening of all women for depression during menopause.

Conversely, the evidence confirms that, rather than female health being impacted by factors associated with mid-life, this phase of life may be influenced by the culmination of life events in earlier life. Hughes and Waite (2009) have shown how long-term effects of the history of marriage, divorce and widowhood can impact experiences of mid-life for women and their health: chronic conditions, mobility limitations, self-rated health and depressive symptoms. This research study found that the experience of marital disruption damages health, with the effects still evident years later; among the currently married, those who have ever been divorced show worse health on all dimensions. This is especially so for those who do not remarry, are divorced or are widowed, given that they are more prone to chronic conditions and mobility limitations.

Similarly, McMunn et al. (2006) have investigated mid-life women and the connection between earlier social roles and health in regard to employment and parenthood. This was undertaken by examining a sample of women derived from a national UK cohort born in 1946 and their self-reported health at age 54, alongside work and family role measures at ages 26, 36, 43 and 53, as well as a sample with a valid body mass index at the same age. Women who occupied multiple roles over the long term reported relatively good health at age 54, and this was not explained by early health levels. Women with weak long term ties to the labour market were more likely to be obese at age 53 and tended to be home-makers. Such findings indicate that mid-life in various respects is engendered or at least experienced through the prism of gender, and it is this tendency that will now be further considered. However, accounts are not without recognition that much research has been based upon the experiences and cultural perceptions of heterosexual women. In this respect, Cole and Rothblum (1991) have drawn attention to the tendency of research to ignore the experiences of lesbian women in mid-life; this is inclined to reflect the heterosexist and pathological bias to be found in the scientific literature on menopause.

WOMEN'S 'EXPERIENCE'

Consideration of women's experiences in mid-life may call upon various indices of evidential negative consequences, many of which connect with broader gender stereotypes and roles. In Western societies perceptions of the ageing body have implications for the individual's social identity and social status, and the physical changes which take place at mid-life are culturally evaluated as signifiers of age (Hepworth and Featherstone 1980). The cultural stress placed upon the requirement to look young and attractive may impact in a derogative way for women and help shape mid-life as some kind of 'crisis' point. Neither is the overarching shadow of medicalising processes entirely absent, and it is observable in popular conceptions of the 'biological clock ticking away', which transforms women from fertile into infertile females. The repercussions for women's self-appraisal could be severe given the confluence of culturally proscribed perceptions of the decline in beauty, sexuality, fertility and all that counts as femininity. Accompanying these appraisals are additional social constructs related to gender roles, most notably ascribed domestic responsibilities in later life, which, in turn, have led to assumptions that it is women who have to make the greatest adaptations during mid-life.

Much by way of such cultural evaluations were uncovered in early sociological works on the subject. Nowak (1977), for instance, found that a person's attitude towards their body varies according to their age and that such attitudes are linked to levels of concern about physical attractiveness.

This pre-occupation with attractiveness was discovered to continue well into the mid-life period. During this stage women appeared to be far more likely to express a 'below-average body' image than men of the same age. Nowak found that the mid-life period, and particularly the years between 45 and 55, is a time in which women exhibit a greater concern with facial attractiveness and youthfulness than at any other point in their lives.

Family responsibilities prescribed to women in mid-life have been found to negate the choices and greater freedom that mid-lifestyles are supposed to often afford. Older mothers frequently continue to shoulder the burden of domestic labour and house work. They still have to deal with demands from grown-up children and are more likely to be responsible for dependent older relatives. The fact that gendered multiple roles carry on into mid-life may be evidenced in different ways. Hislop and Arber's (2003) work on women's sleep patterns, which draws upon empirical data from focus groups and 'sleep diaries', shows that sleep is a socially patterned phenomenon which reflects the gendered nature of women's roles and responsibilities. For many women in mid-life, the reality of sleep patterns is one of disruption, where their sleep needs are compromised by unpaid physical and emotional labour associated with family duties and obligations

It is also evident that women experience mid-life in different ways, responding to the so-called challenges of mid-life as a result of a range of factors. Indicative of this is Daly's interview of 150 women in the USA regarding the way they encountered mid-life (Daly 1997). The respondents fell into three categories. A small minority claimed to be 'gliding through mid-life'. Nearly two dozen felt 'besieged by problems'. The great majority (105 women), however, were 'battling through problems', suggesting that the alleged difficulties were far from insurmountable. While Daly's study indicated there was nothing deterministic about women's experience of mid-life, it also provided evidence of how this stage of life was circumvented by medical processes and discourse and that women had not infrequently internalised the language of 'crisis'. Interview findings showed that women's perceptions often concentrated on the 'problems' of menopause, ageing processes, domestic responsibilities and accompanying references to such treatments as tranquillisers and hormone therapy.

MEN'S 'EXPERIENCE'

Much of the discussion above has related to perceptions and experiences of women in mid-life. In recent years more has been made of men's encounter

of middle adulthood. Again, there is evidence of this stage of life being popularly associated with 'crisis' and a range of psychological problems. These
'problems' have, as with women, been associated with a number of factors.
In recent years there has been a discernible developing discourse around
the so-called male menopause, although such a notion is by no means new
(Hepworth and Featherstone 1985). Recent notions tend, however, to be
based upon research into men's hormone levels and the 'andropause' – the
consequences of which are supposed to be manifest in irritability and depression, among other negative signs, which overlap with notions of a male mid-
life 'crisis'. The medical evidence produced is that testosterone levels may
fall, while too much testosterone present may be in a form which cannot be
used by the body. Vitality ebbs, fatigue and weariness are understood to be
commonplace and, together with depression, loss of libido and irritability,
are the apparent hallmarks of the andropause mood. Unlike the equivalent
menopausal condition in women, the existence of the male counterpart has
by no means yet received full endorsement and remains an area of contention within the medical profession.

While the 'discovery' of the male menopause to some extent marks the
extension of medical interests into the male mid-life domain, there is also
the cultural baggage of mid-life, where men supposedly 'go off the rails' as
if being distracted from the main trajectory of the life course. Clearly there
is much which is engendered here. While women's menopausal state may
be perceived as a hindrance to herself and those around her, popularised
views of men's 'crisis' is often couched in frivolous terms, articulating a
kind of mid-life 'laddish' disposition or return to adolescence. Moreover,
physical decline is commonly perceived as a challenging experience for
many men and signifies significant counterpoints to women's experience of
ageing, since it connects the masculine body with weakness, dependency
and passivity – all the supposedly 'feminine' qualities they have spent a life-
time attempting to deflect. Thus the common notion of decline in sexual
desire, illness and injury means a renegotiation of dominant, heterosexual
masculine identities.

Despite this parallel with the female 'crisis', men, if not ascribed some
kind of fresh attractiveness in their maturity, provide a stark counterpoint
to perceptions of women: men being perceived as likely to embark on extra-
marital affairs in the need to stave off the effects of ageing and 'prove something to themselves'. If media reports are to be believed, the increasing
incidence of such affairs and a growing divorce rate among mid-life men
can be blamed on the extensive use of Viagra. The same drug may also have

had the effect of medicalising 'dysfunctional' sexuality among older men. In this respect, Barbara Marshall (2002) argues that ideas about 'healthy ageing' suggest 'normal' sexual functioning. In fact, Viagra has become yet another site to amplify cultural expectations of gender through notions of male heterosexual 'performance'.

Does something which might be referred to as a mid-life 'crisis' exist among men at all? Hermans and Oles' (1999) study of middle-aged men in Poland explored the specific personal meanings related to mid-life attributed by a sample of men and excavated familiar cultural idioms. Mid-life 'crisis' was described by the men as a process of intensive transition of the self, including the re-interpretation of time perspective, re-evaluation of life values and aims, confrontation with death as a personal event in the future and planning of the second half of life. Three groups, one 'high in mid-life crisis', one 'medium', and one 'low' crisis, were compared. It was found that the high crisis group displayed a lower level of affect referring to self-enhancement, a lower level of positive affect and a higher level of negative affect than both other groups. The high crisis group showed a greater level of negative affect than positive affect for personal meanings referring to the future, but not for personal meanings referring to the past and the present.

Alwin and Levenson (2001) maintain that, given the bulk of the data, it is likely that for most men mid-life can in fact be a time of achievement and satisfaction. For a certain proportion of men, however, the passage seems far from smooth. Indeed, they found a similar pattern when they reviewed research on what are commonly thought to be major life events which amounted to triggers for women's mid-life crisis such as children leaving home and the 'sandwich' of caring for both parents and children. Like most women, men navigated those periods without a traumatic psychological 'crisis'.

Conversely, drawing on data from a study of 150 families, Margaret Huyck (1999) considered factors that put men at risk of stress and depression at mid-life. Huyck found that men's vulnerability is related to what she calls 'gender expansion', which occurs as men become more nurturing and women more assertive at mid-life. Men who perceived their mothers as strong and domineering and their fathers as weak and ineffectual suffer when they and their wives undergo this shift. Men make what Huyck calls 'unconscious and fanciful' projections that they will end up like their fathers and their wives like their mothers. The result is psychological distress. Despite this kind of evidence, what constitutes a 'crisis' may be little more than an emotional response to a multitude of 'stresses', including an unhappy marriage, disappointment in career and financial problems. Vivian Diller (2011) argues that, similar to middle-aged women, there can be a cumulative effect of such stresses, but these may occur at different ages and stages of life but particularly impact males. Diller proposes reconstituting the 'mid-life crisis' as the 'the emerging maturity crisis' that arises from a number of culminating 'stressors'. The significance of these stressors will now be considered.

Life 'stressors'

Rebecca Clay (2003) argues that day-to-day stressors are likely to add up to and be thought of as a 'crisis', but, in reality, it is simply an 'overload' of life events and problems at a particular phase of life. Mid-life can be understood as a time when different 'stressors' impact, but Clay found the effects on men and women to be different. A man's mid-life 'overload' is more likely to be caused by work issues; the woman's counterpoint informed by personal evaluations of their roles. Women often experience multiple stressors because of their simultaneous roles as wives, mothers, employees, daughters, etc..

Clay suggests that many middle-aged adults experience major life events that can cause a period of psychological stress or depression, such as the death of a loved one, or a career setback. However, reiterating the discussion above, those events could have happened earlier or later in life, making them a 'crisis' of sorts, but not necessarily a mid-life one. Fifteen per cent of middle-aged adults in Clay's study experienced this type of mid-life turmoil. Moreover, being of a lower educational status is related to feeling stressors to a greater degree than those of a higher education level during mid-life.

Brim and associates (2004) come to a similar conclusion. Day-to-day stressors, including conflict with a partner and work deadlines, give a more accurate depiction of well-being than such rare life events as divorce or a loved one's death that most researchers stress. While younger adults experience these day-to-day stressors more frequently, Almeida (2009) has found that mid-life adults experience more 'overload' stressors which amount to juggling too many activities at one time. The study also revealed gender differences. Mid-life women experience more 'crossover' stressors derived from multiple domains like work and family than their male counterparts and report higher levels of distress as a result. Socioeconomic status also seemingly makes a difference. In a study by Almeida and colleagues (2009) it was discerned that while mid-life people with lower educational status report the same number of stressors as those with higher educational status, they were more likely to rate stressors as more severe. Day-to-day stress does not add up to a mid-life crisis, however. In fact, these stressors may even have a positive effect. The reason why mid-life people have these stressors is that they actually have more control over their lives than earlier and later in life and describe these stressors, often, in terms of meeting challenges in a positive way.

THE 'NEW' MID-LIFE

There is a measure of evidence which suggests that in late/postmodernity the way individuals think about and negotiate mid-life is undergoing significant change, thus further pointing to the social construction of this phase of life. A common theme in much of the relevant literature is one addressing the major cultural trajectories in which the body and bodily change is perceived and that this is intrinsically linked with the way the ageing process is appraised. Nonetheless, this may merely amount to a cultural re-construction of mid-life as a more positive stage of life militating against fairly deterministic roles and fatalistic viewpoints. Again, such a development may entail a measure of medicalised psychotherapeutic discourse which has taken a different trajectory. The publication *Psychology Today* in taking a positive view of mid-life suggests that:

> The symptoms are not physically based: you can maintain an active sex life, keep fit and enjoy yourself as you mature. Below are some tips for middle-aged adults focusing on healthy lifestyles.... Explore, accept and share your feelings; allow yourself to reflect about your life regularly; devote extra time to your partner and rekindle your relationship; set new goals and develop new hobbies; travel; volunteer; devote special time to your children; take care of your mental health (join a group or seek out a therapist if necessary).

This new, more positive direction has been described by Lambley (1995) as a means of coping by individuals trying to remake self-identity. Much amounts to an attempt to establish one's personality against social stereotypes and how society at large sees the ageing process. Such a response can be seen as a counterpoint to the rebellious nature of the adolescent years and constitutes a means of dealing with mid-life changes and new challenges. At the same time, it also amounts to an attempt to challenge the status quo and cherished assumptions about mid-life (Komesaroff et al. 1997, 9).

As life-expectancy increases, mid-life arguably becomes more significant. Now there is almost as much time to live after the mid-life period as there was before it. This is comparable to the nineteenth century, in which the life expectancy for a man was under 45 years. Hence the present popular adage that 'life now begins at 60' (rather than 40). Some mid-lifers may choose to change their careers or become active in aspects of life which may be new to them, such as enhancing fitness levels, or perhaps try to reduce the effects of ageing. They may now have access to resources offered by consumer society such as body creams, face-lifts, spare-part surgery and other items constituting part of a vast commercial industry.

According to Powell and Biggs (2000), the use of new technologies to modify the appearance of ageing identity exemplifies the postmodern condition. It is the more affluent mid-life people who can partake of this development. To paraphrase Morris (1998), new technologies hold out the promise of 'utopian bodies' or perfect bodies. Indeed, Haraway's (2000) reference to cyborgic fusion of biological and machine entities has been taken up by postmodern gerontology. The list of technologies available extends beyond traditional conceptualisations of the body to include virtual identities created by and reflected in the growing number of 'silver surfers' using the internet as a free-floating form of identity management (Powell and Biggs 2002). Thus Featherstone and Wernick (1995, 3) claim that it is possible to 're-code the body' itself, since biomedical and information technologies make available the capacity to alter not just the meaning but also the very material infrastructure of the body. Bodies can be re-shaped, remade, fused with machines and empowered through technological devices and extensions.

In the media there is now much talk about finding ways of restoring the vigour of youth, especially in men. Today, it appears to be more acceptable that middle-aged people will try to put the 'biological clock' back if they have the time and money to make the effort. Such an attempt to retain youth is increasingly accepted as legitimate. The media is in constant pursuit of representing middle-aged people in a fresh light. This age group is now being portrayed in more affirmative ways by celebrity culture and celebrity figures who are seen as 'ageless'. Such positive attitudes may be indicators of wider social change: while many conventional age-related roles have become increasingly flexible and no longer subject to the conforming social pressures associated with past generations, individual choice as to whether or not to assume these roles has also come to the fore. Thus mid-life people will consciously negotiate mid-life in a reflexive way.

Gullette (1997) has pointed out that much of the relevant literature draws attention especially to the Baby Boomer generation – those born in the 1950s and 1960s – as open to the possibility of change despite the fact they carry notions of a 'mid-life' crisis. Whitbourne and Willis (2006) note that this is the largest cohort ever to enter middle age in Western society, and they represent approximately one-third of the total population in the USA. Baby Boomers continue to exert a powerful impact on the media, fiction, movies and even popular music, just as they were an imposing force in society from the time of their entry into youth. The Baby Boomers have reached mid-life in a culture of relativism, choice and lifestyle preferences. These are people who are aware that they have another 30–40 years of life-expectancy ahead of them. They may see a practically endless future rather than the beginning of the end. Subsequent generations, after the Baby Boomers, have grown up in a late/postmodernist culture with its preoccupation with personal growth and change. Thus, it is possible that the trend for trying to stay young for as long as possible will continue to proliferate. People will thus attempt to redefine the meaning of middle and later life, taking part in a variety of active creative leisure pursuits. Others may simply opt to 'grow old disgracefully'.

Whitbourne and Willis (2006) argue that those now in mid-life tend to be closely linked to increasing dependence on rewarding interpersonal relationships, with interaction with teenage children as the point of reference rather than association with parents. This may involve exposure to new values and fashions and stimulate self-awareness and identification with youth rather than old age and, indeed, a nostalgic yearning by mid-lifers for their own youth. In investigating this development, Paul Hodkinson (2011), via exploring the continuing involvement in youth music and style cultures of older participants in the case of the Goth scene, notes how mid-lifers relate to the youth cultures to which they once belonged. While these adults are obliged to reconcile material, domestic and physical elements of developing adult lives, they may still attempt to retain their music and style culture as a collective experience. Similarly, Hodkinson and Bennett (2013) in their edited volume have explored what happens to punks, clubbers, Goths, riot girls, soulies, break-dancers and queer-scene participants as they become older. For decades, research on 'spectacular' youth cultures were comprehended as adolescent phenomena and assumed that involvement ceased with the onset of adulthood. In an age of increasingly complex life trajectories, those who embraced such youth cultures continue to participate in them to one degree or another into adulthood and middle-age.

SUMMARY

This chapter has attempted to overview how mid-life, as a supposedly distinctive phase of the life-course, has been socially constructed according to time and place. It has traced how mid-life has conventionally been perceived as accompanied by a 'crisis' which is understood to have various dimensions, at least according to cultural understandings, gender constructs, and medical and pathologising discourses. The chapter has attempted to show that if a 'crisis' does occur at mid-life then it may prove to be little more than the phase of the life course when a number of subjectively perceived 'turning points' occur (between 45–64) (Cappeliez et al. 2008).

The chapter concluded by noting how mid-life is perceived as undergoing transformations often informed by major components of late/postmodernity. Cultural perceptions are now more positive and more optimistic, and writings on the subject found in a range of disciplines appear to embrace a 'progress narrative' of mid-life as a way out of the binary between 'positive ageing' and the previous 'decline narrative' (Gullette 1997, 3–44). Yet conceptions of mid-life are not just a reflection of cultural change. Lachman and James (1997) comment that the age boundaries for mid-life are now fuzzy, with no clear demarcation. Those between the ages of 40 and 60 are typically considered to be middle-aged, but there is at least a 10-year range on either side of this spectrum, so that it is not uncommon for some to consider middle age to begin at 30 and end at 75. This age range, along with other numerous factors which generate a variety of mid-life styles, implies that this phase of life can take numerous trajectories (Lachman and James 1997).

Given the diversity in mid-life and disintegrated norms and roles associated with it, the question may have become 'has middle age been abolished?' The answer is probably 'not yet'. It is likely to be the case that perceptions of mid-life are still accompanied by various permutations, usually negative and forged by cultural trajectories and the processes of medicalisation. In fact, in a youth-orientated society, being middle aged still means being older, if not yet elderly and subject to what Gullette (1997, 46) refers to as 'the master narrative of ageing', which has negative connotations. It is this cultural narrative which will also provide a major focus of the next chapter, which is concerned with exploring later life.

FURTHER READING

Becker, D. (2006) 'Therapy for the Middle-Aged: The Relevance of Existential Issues', *American Journal of Psychotherapy*, 60(1): 87–99.

Biggs, S. (1997) 'Choosing Not to be Old? Masks, Bodies and Identity Management in Later Life', *Ageing and Society*, 17(5): 553–70.

Farrell, M. and Rosenberg, S. (eds.) (1981) *Men at Midlife*, Boston, MA: Auburn House.

Featherstone, M. and Hepworth, M. (1996) 'The Midlifestyle of "George and Lynne": Notes on a Popular Strip', in M. Featherstone, M. Hepworth and B. Turner (eds.), *The Body: Social Process and Cultural Theory*, London: Sage.

Freund, A. and Ritter, J. (2009) 'Midlife Crisis: A Debate', *Gerontology*, 55(5): 582–91.

Gannon, L. (1996) *Women and Ageing: Transcending the Myths*, Routledge: London.

Graefe, D. and Lichter, D. (2007) 'When Unwed Mothers Marry: The Marital and Cohabiting Partners of Midlife Women', *Journal of Family Issues*, 28(5): 595–622.

Gullette, M. (1998) 'Midlife Discourses in the Twentieth-Century United States: An Essay on the Sexuality, Ideology, and Politics of 'Middle Ageism', in R. Shweder (ed.), *Welcome to Middle Age! (and Other Cultural Fictions)*, Chicago: University of Chicago Press.

———. (1997) *Declining to Decline: Cultural Combat and the Politics of the Midlife* (Age Studies), Charlottesville, VA: University of Virginia Press.

Hepworth, M. (1987) 'The Midlife Phase', in G. Cohen (ed.), *Social Change and the Life Course*, London: Tavistock.

———. (1999) 'In Defiance of an Ageing Culture', *Ageing and Society*, 19(1): 139–48.

———. (2000) *Stories of Ageing*, Buckingham and Philadelphia: Open University Press.

Hughes, M. and Waite, L. (2009) 'Marital Biography and Health at Mid-Life', *Journal of Health and Social Behavior*, 50(3): 344–58.

Kruger, A. (1994) 'The Mid-life Transition: Crisis or Chimera?', *Psychological Reports*, 75(3): 1299–305.

Lachman, E. (2004) 'Development in Midlife', *Annual Review of Psychology*, 55(1): 305–31.

Marshall, B. (2002) '"Hard Science": Gendered Constructions of Sexual Dysfunction in the "Viagra Age"', *Sexualities*, 5(2): 131–58.

McAdams, D. (1994) 'Can Personality Change? Levels of Stability and Growth in Personality Across the Lifespan', in T. Heatherton and J. Weinberger (eds.), *Can Personality Change?*, Washington DC: American Psychological Association Press.

———. (1996) 'Narrating the Self in Adulthood', in J. Birren, G. Kenyon and J.-E. Ruth (eds.), *Aging and Biography: Explorations in Adult Development*, New York: Springer.

Mitchell, B. and Lovegreen, L. (2009) 'The Empty Nest Syndrome in Midlife Families: A Multimethod Exploration of Parental Gender Differences and Cultural Dynamics', *Journal of Family Issues*, 30(2): 1651–70.

Newton, N. and Stewart, A. (2010) 'The Middle Ages: Change in Women's Personalities and Social Roles', *Psychology of Women Quarterly*, 34(1): 75–84.

Oles, P. (1999) 'Towards a Psychological Model of Midlife Crisis', *Psychological Reports*, 84 (3, pt. 2): 1059–69.

Samuels, S. (1997) 'Midlife Crisis: Helping Patients Cope with Stress, Anxiety, and Depression', *Geriatrics*, 52(7): 55–56; 59–63.

Seibold, C., Richards, L. and Simon, D. (1994), 'Feminist Method and Qualitative Research About Midlife,' *Journal of Advanced Nursing*, 19(2): 394–402.

Twigg, J. (2007) 'Clothing, Age and the Body: A Critical Review', *Ageing and Society*, 27(2): 285–305.

Woods, N., Fugate, A. and Mitchell, E. (1997) 'Women's Images of Midlife: Observations from the Seattle Midlife Women's Health Study', *Health Care for Women International*, 18(5): 439–53.

———. (2002) 'Patterns of Depressed Mood Across the Menopausal Transition: Approaches to Studying Patterns in Longitudinal Data', *Acta Obstetricia et Gynecologia Scandinavica*, 81(7): 623–32.

Chapter 11

Ageing and later life

While this penultimate chapter considers ageing and later life, it is largely misleading to bring these two themes together for discussion, since they by no means converge. Ageing is a life-long process. Nonetheless, the themes of ageing, and indeed imminent death, are commonly associated in the Western world with the principal trajectory of the later years of life. For that reason, this chapter is at least partly concerned with how popularised notions of ageing and later life are constructed in contemporary societies, although it will be acknowledged that, as with other aspects of the life course, there are continuities to be observed, not least the impact of structured inequality and additional demographic variables. Change is also evident – change generated by late/postmodernity, which offers new perceptions of ageing and later life that are in keeping with a distinctive cultural milieu.

THE AGEING PROCESS

A popularly held view, as explored in the previous chapter, is that the ageing process takes off in earnest during the mid-life period and invariably precipitates decline. This is a misnomer in the sense that ageing begins at the very height of physical and mental fitness. Many medical theories regarding ageing abound, although, as Rosenfeld (1985) suggests, they tend to fall into two broad categories. First, there are those which conjecture that the important factor is 'wear and tear' on the body over time, causing it to break down and rendering age essentially a 'natural' process. Put succinctly, over time the body loses some of its ability to recognise and counter disease-causing agents and may even assail healthy cells, resulting in autoimmune disorders such as rheumatoid arthritis. A second set of theories advance an analogy of a 'biological clock' ticking away. This suggests that, as with other living species, humans have a genetic clock within them that is programmed to determine the manner and time at which they 'naturally' age and die.

That ageing is related to inevitable decline is, it would seem, very much a medical construct. It is one which tends to stress the interaction of various genetic and other biological factors alongside social-psychological dimensions, including anxieties generated by simply growing older. Enforcing this emphasis is the medical concept of 'primary ageing' and 'secondary ageing'. The former is understood to occur over time and has certain distinguishing features or particular 'visual signs of ageing' (Rexbye and Povlsen 2007): the skin will become darker and less elastic, the hair turns grey, wrinkles appear, loss of height and weight occur and so on. This is assumed to bring an inevitable linear, overall decline in strength and vitality, as well as other physical symptoms such as a decrease in the number of nerve cells in the skin, deficiency in sight and hearing, stiffening of joints and a greater vulnerability to chronic illnesses like arthritis and diabetes.

What the medical profession commonly designates 'secondary' or 'premature' ageing is generally attributed to environmental considerations. Here, by way of illustration, we can note Rosenfeld's findings (1985) of the factors which would seem to hold up the ageing process and hence extend life among certain peoples in the world. Rosenfeld observes that the greatest longevity is to be found among a number of communities living in economically underdeveloped mountain tribes. This includes the Vilcabambans of Ecuador, the Hunzas on the border of China and Pakistan and the Abkhasians in the Russian Caucasus. Whether the life-span of these peoples is due to genetics is not known. What is clear, however, is such tribes live a slow-paced rural life at high altitudes; work and exercise regularly even at old age; and embrace a simple diet which is practically vegetarian, sugar-free and includes large amounts of fruits, vegetables and yogurt, and consume fewer calories than North Americans and West Europeans. By contrast, in other 'developing' countries inadequate diet, stress, poverty, adverse working or living conditions, or for women experiences of pregnancy and childbirth, can all hasten the ageing process and ensures living to 40 years might be regarded as 'old'.

SOCIAL PERCEPTIONS OF OLD AGE

While not doubting the impact of environmental factors on the ageing process and the life-span, ageing has a further social element in that how it is formulated and culturally perceived remains in accordance with an infinite number of features. This is particularly so in the context of the later stages of life. In the West, so Cowgill and Holmes (1972) opine, there have been several simultaneous processes operating since the middle of the nineteenth century when the development of modernity transformed the status of the elderly to one that was lowly: the rise of modern medicine contributed to increasing life expectancy; modern economic technology limited employment opportunities among older workers; urbanisation attracted rural youth to the cities – breaking down the extended family; and mass education and literacy undermined the mystique associated with age.

If 'old age' is designated as a clear 'stage' of the life course, it is one open to a degree of negotiation given the difficulty in fixing a precise time at which it commences. Nonetheless, negative connotations remain, including notions that later life is a period of loss and deterioration (Baltes et al. 1980); a time for settling unresolved issues and preparing for death (Erikson 1998); and at best, as a point in time for focusing on achievements in early life to compensate for failures and losses (Baltes and Baltes 1996). This tendency is at least partly due to a unique Western cultural directive which places a great deal of emphasis on the virtues of being young – shaping self-perceptions and experiences of old age: frustration, fear and self-doubt (Hamel 1990).

It may well be that the contemporary Western cultural value placed on youthfulness and looking and behaving 'young' is increasingly amplified. If Bauman (2000) is correct regarding the main features of what he designates 'liquid modernity', contemporary society is particularly perturbed by signs of ageing. A culture which stresses the freedom of the individual to forge personal, physical and social transformation is certain to look negatively on the inevitable process of ageing. Put otherwise, 'old age' suggests a one-way direction of travel, offering little time or space for change.

Much of such Western perceptions of ageing are in contrast with other cultures both past and present. As examined throughout the early chapters of this volume, in pre-industrial communities the elderly may achieve a high level of status in recognition of past social roles and for the wealth of experience and knowledge that can be passed on to later generations over which they retain authority. For example, in the case of rural China strong affection and respect for the elderly still remain and they continue to maintain considerable control over the social and economic lives of their adult children, while in their later years they would expect to be supported and cared for by them.

This is in stark distinction with Western societies, where later life is the only stage of life with systematic social losses rather than gains (Rostow 1974, 148).

The cultural convention is to expect that for the elderly the major tasks in life, such as pursuing a career and raising a family, are accomplished. Thus an older person's responsibilities decline, whereas dependency on others, because of reduced income or physical and mental infirmities may increase. Subsequently, his/her roles are typically expected to be limited to retirement, widowhood, an aged-dependent or the chronically ill person – scarcely socially valued or conferred high status. A number of these themes will be re-joined in this chapter.

DISENGAGEMENT

Andrew Blakie (1999, 59–60) maintains that in the case of the UK the social construction of ageing passed through three stages in the twentieth century, and these developments were largely connected with the matter of social disengagement. To begin with, the first half of the century witnessed the emergence of retirement as a common experience. Second, this form of disengagement culminated in its mid-century institutionalisation through state pension support. Nonetheless, since the late 1960s, an increasing fragmentation became evident, both as regards the time in which people left work and in ways they spent their time thereafter, in a phase of the life course when life-expectancy was increasingly extended.

The simple explanation for the creation of a retirement 'period' is that advanced technology reduces the need for the labour force to work literally for life, while placing a premium on current skills implies the older worker has to give way to the younger. By contrast to these developments in the West, in Majority World societies which depend on the labour of all, male and female alike, no state benefit support for older people exists; most work until they are physically incapable of doing so and are dependent on younger family members.

In terms of a sociological framework applied to the understood social and economic necessity of retirement, the earliest formulation was that commonly designated as 'disengagement theory'. Cumming and Henry's (1961) theoretical paradigm is perhaps the best known and most critiqued, since it tends to enforce a rather negative picture of the social positioning of older people. The theory contends that disengagement for the aged is socially and psychologically functional and a natural part of the ageing process. Thus, ageing has certain fixed repercussions which, in turn, account for the reasons why the elderly become socially marginalised. It is a theory which implies that the major social passage in later life is associated with 'loss', whether one of social role, status or income.

Disengagement theory assumes that biological ageing is a more or less straightforward process, and a detachment of older people from the workforce is not only constructive, since their 'disengagement' gives way to younger people in the occupational sphere, but there is also the additional advantage that older people with diminished capabilities invariably welcome the opportunity for more leisure time and the freedom from the pressures of employment. There is a psychological dimension too. As people age, their most basic socio-psychological requirements change from active involvement to inactive contemplation about the meaning of life in the face of impending death.

Despite modifications, a number of far-reaching critiques have undermined the disengagement theory – many of which connect with a measure of changing conceptions of ageing. First, it largely fails to recognise that many older people may not wish to disengage from productive roles, since this includes loss of social prestige and brings social isolation. Second, a comprehensive system of disengagement would have to take into account widely different abilities of older people, and the passage into later life may take various trajectories. Third, in practical terms those who were previously lower paid workers cannot always readily disengage from employment because they do not enjoy sufficient financial security to do so. Conversely, retirement means the financial care of people by the state who might better be able to provide for themselves. This is particularly so in an ageing society, where governments are increasingly concerned with how such a large portion of the population can be economically supported. Finally, it is possible to argue that the older individual's contribution to society is hugely underestimated, especially because they take part in such unpaid work as childcare or perhaps opt to undertake a voluntary charity capacity and similar activities.

A further critique of the disengagement theory is that retirement is not a simple stage of adaptation but rather has both positive and negative consequences. Thus Atchley (1988) identifies various possible phases of retirement: the 'honeymoon' phase that is marked by euphoria, since it may be possible to engage with activities s/he 'never had time for before'. This phase requires money and good health. Other retired people will take a different trajectory and move instantly to 'an immediate retirement routine' which in all probability stabilises over time and involves scheduled activities at a regulated pace that will likely turn into a more or less permanent lifestyle. Still others will see retirement as a 'rest and relaxation' phase consisting of a very low level of activity. Many may initially adopt this but become disenchanted with such a lifestyle and subsequently seek to be become more active.

After experiencing one of these three phases during the initial retirement, according to Atchley, movement to other phases is likely. Some older people edge into a 'disenchantment phase' as they discover retirement does not live up to expectations. Another possibility is a 're-orientation' phase in which retired persons change their approach to retirement. They may become increasingly involved with friends and family, after initially pursuing their interests more or less on their own. Nonetheless, eventually the great majority of retired persons enter into the phase of 'routine', in which they know what it is they want and are able to do – a set of stable activities often constituting a particular lifestyle. Finally, they may adopt a 'termination phase' and return to the employment they left in one capacity or another, or commence a new one because of many of the benefits of working: financial, social engagement or a sense of worth.

Recent trends in retirement

A further critique of the disengagement theory is that there is now no standard age at which people retire in Western societies – suggesting the complexity of contemporary economic life. In such nations there is little consensus as to when a person should retire, and, indeed, mandatory retirement has been challenged by discourses related to the right to work and equality of opportunity. Recognised retirement ages were initially reduced in some countries and this was partly connected to the growth of unemployment, allowing perhaps a greater guarantee of work for younger generations. Certainly, the number of people working into their 60s continued to decline at the end of the twentieth century. According to *Social Trends* (1997, 27), the percentage of men in the UK over 65 years old still in paid employment had diminished from 66 per cent in 1961 to 7 per cent in 1992. However, as a result of policies encouraging older people to work longer and financially support themselves in later life in order to address economic dependency on the state, the UK statutory age of retirement of 65 was abolished in 2011.

Alternatively, some older people may decide to disengage from employment at an earlier age. Much may relate to economic factors which cut across the life course as one linear, ordered process. Thus, the occupational structuring of 'retired' people has been greatly complicated by early retirement for those who can afford it, voluntary severance, 'retirement at 50' and a 'no jobs for life' culture of Western societies, while contractual employment agreements might include 'the rules of the job' that stipulate time of retirement and length of service. Early retirement in this respect is essentially a system under which employees are allowed to retire, with employers providing supplemental pension payments sufficient to sustain it at an adequate level until the retiree becomes old enough to collect a state pension.

The evidence suggests that the age of retirement in the future will probably become increasingly flexible. In all possibility, there will be phased retirement consisting of reduced work schedules, prorated salaries and varying health and benefit services. In so far as the individual has a choice, many factors may be influential, including whether or not a person is self-employed, demands of the family, pre-retirement planning and the desire for leisure. Others reasons include savings, fitness and finding work too difficult or challenging – possibly in the light of rapid technological change. This is likely to see older people adopt different approaches to dealing with the flexibility that is now offered. All of this may imply that older people will be closer to the social, cultural and economic mainstream of society than ever before. However, Mallier and Shafto (1994) maintain that the issue of retirement and the rise in proportion of the population who are still active after ceasing full-time employment – in their 'Third Age' (discussed later) – raises a range of questions, including what the social role of this age category should ideally be.

Certainly, there is little doubt that the age of retirement is intrinsically linked to the subject of inequalities in later life. In middle-class and professional sectors, there has arisen a new younger 'retired' constituency, which, in turn, has proved to be a significant consumer grouping in the organisation of pensions, insurances and spending. It is a constituency that has the wealth accumulated throughout life to allow a greater participation in developing 'leisure worlds'. It is not surprising, then, that the perception of wealthier people as 'retired' has produced a range of niche-marketing consumer literature, including popular publications specialising in retirement planning. It follows that, since the 1990s, there has been a vast interest in postmodern perspectives of age and ageing identity underpinned by discourses of 'better lifestyles' and increased leisure opportunities for older people due to healthier environmental conditions and growing use of bio-technologies to facilitate the longevity of human experiences (e.g. Blakie 1999; Powell and Biggs 2000).

ACTIVITY THEORY

Activity theory (alternatively known as 'the implicit theory of ageing') emerged in response to disengagement theory and gained greater credence given the evidence of the complex nature of later life. The theory was initially advanced by Robert Havighurst (1961), who argued that older people did not necessarily have to disengage from society on all fronts and could still continue to perform constructive social roles. The theory was built upon by others including Bernice Neugarten (1971) who argued life satisfaction in later life rested on active maintenance of personal relationships and wider social involvement. The facts suggested that the 'young old' (in their 60s) were indeed frequently active and socially engaged. This approach also highlighted social diversity among older people by way of class, gender, ethnicity and marital status. Such theories clearly challenged stereotypes about ageing and pointed towards notions of 'positive ageing'.

A modification of activity is 'continuity theory', which posits that not infrequently older people adapt or sustain similar activities, relationships and their sense of self they did in their earlier years, despite changing physical, cognitive and social status (Maddox 1968). This they do by retaining their lifestyle through adopting strategies connected to their past experiences (Nimrod and Kleiber 2007). In addition, studies on positive ageing relate to human resources accumulated throughout the years, enabling growth and development that continues until the end of life (Gergen and Gergen 2003). There is even evidence that late-life negative events, such as widowhood, may eventually generate opportunities to provide an incentive to create new positive meanings in life (Koren and Lowenstein 2008).

'Positive ageing'

'Positive ageing' is a concept that has increasingly come to enjoy common currency, generating a whole commercial industry and range of voluntary organisations. The focus is typically on advancing (typically for those over 50) a 'design for a life course' approach to promote affirmative emotional states, optimal cognitive functioning, and enabling people to prepare and plan for later life. Essentially, 'positive ageing' is a philosophy advancing a positive view advocating keeping fit and healthy, enjoying a good quality of life and engaging fully in social activities, and cultivating a sense of control of one's life and relationships despite the changes which later life brings. In total, it amounts to an ethic insisting ageing should be recognised as an integral part of the life course that should be socially valued.

Fernandez-Ballesteros (2011) upholds the view that 'positive ageing' and other related terms (optimal, healthy, successful, active, productive ageing) are, however, essentially medicalised concepts, most of them operationally described by a broad set of bio-psycho-social factors, as well as subjective viewpoints which may be culturally influenced. This subjective aspect has been explored by Ming-Lin Chong et al. (2006) who studied middle-aged and older people within the urban Chinese population in Hong Kong. Among the themes which emerged with those interviewed in relation to views of 'positive ageing' were that it comprised good health, positive life attitudes, engagement with an activity or with society, promoting family and inter-personal relationships, and building up financial resources. While such aspirations may seem beneficial, Kotter-Grühn and Hess (2012) discovered that the activation of positive age stereotypes does not necessarily positively influence self-perceptions of ageing. On the contrary, and paradoxically, priming middle-aged and older adults in good health with positive age stereotypes tended to make those surveyed feel older and more negative about their own capabilities.

THE THIRD AGE

Notions of 'positive ageing' have increasingly become associated with the so-called Third Age. One repercussion of increasing life-expectancy is the breakdown of familiar age categorisations, subsequently complicating views of ageing, the identity of older people, and they open new possibilities of self-enhancement. Similarly, it brings changing perceptions of retirement as being the primary 'cut off' point which signifies an induction or rites of passage into 'old age'. There are now several new broadly recognised distinctions: between the so-called Third Age (50–74 yeen years) – a period of life often free from parenting and paid work when a more active, independent life is achieved – and a 'fourth age' – an age of eventual dependency. This permits the further drawing of a division between the younger elderly (65–75 years) – individuals who may enjoy good health and financial security, are typically autonomous, possibly living as part of a couple – and the 'older elderly' (75–85 years) who become increasingly dependent on others because of both health and financial problems. The former is an ever-growing sector – adding to the complicated definition of what constitutes 'mid-life' as distinct from 'the elderly'. All these divergent ways of grouping older people nonetheless suggest a move from periods of increased activity and autonomy to one of growing dependency.

Peter Laslett (1987) was probably the first to speak of the Third Age as part of a 'New Division of the life course'. First, he conjectured, there is an era of dependence, socialisation, immaturity and education associated with the early years of life. Second, there is an era of independence, maturity and responsibility, of earning and financial saving. Third, there may be an era of freedom and personal fulfilment. Fourth, there is a period of final dependence and decrepitude. The emergence of the Third Age, according to Laslett, coincided with demographic changes where over half of those aged 25 can now expect to reach at least 70 years. The advent of the Third Age also converged with a point where post-industrial nations switched into ageing societies characterised by high numbers of men in retirement (the figure for women being difficult to compute and not strictly comparable, because of the prevalence of interrupted paid work).

Silva (2008) takes a rather different view in exploring the historical emergence of conceptions of the Third Age as an identity category linked to the process of ageing. As an age category, 'old age' has its roots mainly in medical knowledge, specialised in the study of the aged body, and the onset of retirement. The category of the Third Age arose as a result of a complex combination of factors such as medical and social knowledge – especially advocatory discourses of social gerontology, the specialisation of management agents for ageing, political movements and economic interests spawned by the consumer culture, which have all transformed the process of contemporary ageing. The importance of the latter is also stressed by Blakie (1999, 59, 72), who notes that many in the Third Age may be free to engage in a period of self-realisation and perhaps economic and political empowerment, although those reaching the Third Age at this point in time are very different from previous age cohorts. They were raised in an age of prosperity and experienced the emergence of the consumer culture – one which has created more disposable income that tends to be spent on leisure products and pursuits which enhance personal lifestyles.

THE FOURTH AGE

Western cultural negativity surrounding perceptions of later life is at least partly attributed to acute 'problems' associated with 'real' or 'deep' old age, what has been reconfigured as a less negatively implied 'Fourth Age'. In respect of those 75 years old and over, in contrast to other stages of life, old age is frequently appraised as an unpleasant period with a higher probability of loneliness, boredom and loss of self-esteem. Moreover, physical and mental infirmities and the reality of being fatigued, in poor health and less able to cope with everyday problems – all set in a framework of the recognition of impending death – may produce issues related to adjustment and depression for the elderly.

Higgs and Gilleard (2015), taking a global and historical approach, argue that the Fourth Age is in some ways different and in other ways similar to conventional models of old age. The Fourth Age now embodies the most feared and marginalised aspect of later life. It constitutes a 'social imaginary' shaped and maintained by cultural and political discourses and practices related to the fragmentation of 'old age'. Essentially, it emerges from the institutionalisation of the infirmities of later life set against the appearance of a Third-Age culture that negates past representations of ageing. Within this perspective, the Fourth Age can be understood by examining not the experience itself, but its impact on the discourses that surround and orientate themselves to it.

It may well be that the major development regarding older people over recent decades is that the evasion of old age can apparently be accomplished through a range of youth-preserving techniques and lifestyles, so that it might be difficult to gauge when 'real' old age sets in. Blakie (1999, 194–96), however, notes the difficulty in transferring from the Third to the Fourth Age. In terms of self-perception, transference may be negative and involve infantisation, stigmatisation and institutionalisation. Indeed, Blakie maintains that Western society is facing a cultural dilemma in relation to the very old. To talk of the 'end of old age' is to go too far. Yet, he suggests, a postmodern impasse has arrived where there are no coherent guidelines how the end of life is confronted. Certainly, there is no positive image of later life which can prepare adequately for decline and death (Blakie 1999, 210–11).

The Fourth Age clearly implies dependency and reliance on the care of others, and this connects with various issues related to the lowly status of those in deep old age. Although a sensitive subject, Yates (1986) draws attention to cases of abuse of older people in care in a domestic setting. Often the causes of abuse lies in the stress of caring – financially and emotionally – for ageing parents, perhaps at a time that children are also being cared for. Abuse appears to be most common where the stresses are greatest: in families with a very old person suffering from serious health problems which bring overwhelming demands and tensions. There has been a general lack of reliable data in this area and it is often argued that the absence is a reflection of the low priority given to work associated with older people. Research suggests that between 3 and 4 per cent of elderly people (mainly women) suffer serious maltreatment each year, and three times as many sustain abuse at some point (Whittaker 1997). However, it is probable that as the proportion of elderly people rises, so does the incidence of abuse (Holmstrom 1994). Alternatively, care for the elderly is increasingly in an

Table 11.1 Changes in the Resident Care Home Population Aged 65 and Over in England and Wales, 2001 to 2011

Age	Resident care home population, 2001	Proportion of usual resident population, 2001 (%)	Resident care home population, 2011	Proportion of usual resident population, 2011 (%)	Change in resident care home population between 2001 and 2011 (%)	Change in usual resident population between 2001 and 2011 (%)
65 and over	290,000	3.5	291,000	3.2	0.3	11.0
65–74	29,000	0.7	31,000	0.6	5.1	11.1
75–84	97,000	3.3	88,000	2.8	-9.2	6.2
85 and over	164,000	16.2	172,000	13.7	5.1	23.9

Source: Office of National Statistics, licensed under the Open Government License v.3.

institutional setting. Artazcos and Rueda (2007) report the significance of this in focusing on the analysis of gender inequalities in health, because gender is closely associated with entry into residential care. As older women live longer than their male counterparts, they are less likely to have a spouse to provide informal care when they become disabled and are therefore more likely to enter a residential environment (the topic of increasing institutionalisation of later life is re-joined in the final chapter).

THE SELF IN OLD AGE

Although the interest in the construction of self and identity throughout the life course has enjoyed something of a resurgence in recent years, largely through postmodernist theorising, the topic still remains somewhat neglected in reference to older people and the impact of actual or perceived ageing on understandings of the self. There are, however, a number of important studies that directly or indirectly throw light on how older people view themselves.

Influential in this respect is the notion of the 'mask of ageing' (Featherstone and Hepworth 1991, 148), which denotes a clear distinction between the self and the body. The ageing body in the mirror is not a reflection of the self the older person sees. Rather, the visible body 'masks' the unseen self inside. The mask is essentially an image, one which reflects the tension between the public appearance and the private feelings within, as well as recognition of the cultural stigma around ageing. Moreover, it is evidence of the postmodern attempt to undermine traditional age-related categories and tensions connected to personal identity, resistance to ageist stereotypes and the challenge to cultural images of ageing. And, these tendencies interface with the powers of self-expression and deepest emotions of older people (Hepworth 2000, 28).

Rostow (1974), in an early study, found that a low feeling of self-worth and well-being among older people was widespread, and this tended to reduce them to a low status age-set which had limited interaction with younger generations. Such evidence points towards a negative perception of self because of the way contemporary society constructs and frames old age. To some extent, for Rostow, this results from previous statutory retirement, which constituted a major status passage in an individual's life course and perceptions of old age precipitated by popular notions equating the ageing process with inevitable decline. For the most part, this status passage brought with it a loss of prestige, privileges and power, not to mention income. On retiring, the individual departs from his/her familiar environment of employment, in which roles, functions and personal relationships associated with work are typically well-established. Thus, for older people, the bases of identity and self-worth are derived from the private sphere – family, leisure and the commitment to clubs and associations. Here, some older people can actively seek to meet others, develop a sense of belonging and reappraise themselves through new challenges which plausibly had positive or negative consequences.

Positive and negative self-appraisals were also discerned by Neugarten (1971), who conjectured that there are three smaller subgroups in the older population whose sense of self is adversely affected. The first constituency developed a 'disintegrated' or 'disorganised' personality as a result of finding it extremely arduous to come to terms with later life. Above all, there is a frequent sense of despair to the extent of very older people 'giving up' and becoming passive residents of hospitals or nursing homes. A second group displayed 'passive-dependent personalities'. These older people have little confidence in their own abilities to cope on a day-to-day basis – sometimes seeking help even if they do not necessarily require it. Their social withdrawal tends to mean that their level of life satisfaction remains relatively low. A third category, 'defended personalities', live independently but fear growing older, fight to stay youthful and physically fit, but in doing so frequently set unrealistic standards which, in turn, may engender stress and disappointment. The majority of Neugarten's subjects, however, fared far better, displaying what she called 'integrated personalities'. Their success lay in retaining their personal dignity, self-confidence and optimism, while accepting that growing old was inevitable.

A further relevant study is that of Preston and Guidiken (1996), which compared the attitudes of retired and non-retired older people and discovered no significant differences between the two groups in terms of life satisfaction. In a subsequent study, Preston (1996) found older people felt more positive about themselves than previously assumed. There may be important variables, however, since Preston discovered that those who reported more chronic health disorders and more incapacity due to illness displayed a greater tendency to think of themselves as being 'old' than those who reported no such problems.

In yet another example of research related to how older people perceive themselves, Kaufman (1978) found that they do not necessarily slip into some 'old age identity' which brings a deterministic change in the perceptions of self. Rather, the self is 'ageless'. Older people expressed a personal identity that had maintained continuity over the life-span, regardless of the physical and social changes associated with old age. That is, they define themselves as being essentially the same person they were when younger: they had simply grown old. Kaufman argues that in later life one is not a different person even if some personality traits become more pronounced. Furthermore, those interviewed often regarded themselves as much younger than they really were. Thus, biological ageing and how people are expected to think and act do not necessarily coincide.

Later studies focused upon identity in terms of major demographic divisions and differing life experiences among older people. One core theme has been that of gender, typified by the work of Arber and Ginn (1991), who claim that because women's value in particular is exercised in the awareness of a loss of a youthful appearance, that brings social devaluation, which is exploited by pressures of the 'cosmeticization' industry. Additional research by Orth et al. (nd) presents a longitudinal study of a sample of adults in the USA. They found that self-esteem rises steadily as people age but starts declining around the time of retirement. Subjects were also asked about their ethnicity, education, income, work and relationships. On average, women had lower self-esteem than men throughout most of adulthood, but self-esteem levels converged as men and women reached their 80s and

90s. Blacks and whites had similar self-esteem levels throughout young adulthood and middle age. In later life, average self-esteem among blacks dropped much more sharply than among whites. Education, income, health and employment status all had some effect on the self-esteem trajectories, especially as people aged.

RELATIONSHIPS

Biographical approaches to later life tend to show that older people do not journey the life course alone but are embedded in wider family networks and partnerships, even if these relationships may undergo significant changes. This area has spurred significant research in recent years; a fair few studies of which point to the richness of individual relational experiences of older people and the multi-faceted nature of their personalities. A number of findings may be considered here.

As a result of divorce and rising proportions of those who have not married, in recent decades a large proportion of older adults are single. Among men, this increase results primarily from a doubling of the proportion who never married, whereas for older women the growth is largely because of divorce (Cooney and Dunne 2001). Divorced and widowed men are more likely to remarry than their female counterparts (Ahrons 2007), further diminishing the pool of mates available for unattached older women. Using data from the 2000 USA census, Calasanti and Kiecolt (2007) found that at age 65 and older 73 per cent of the men were married, compared with only 43 per cent of women, reflecting the tendency for women to marry men somewhat older than themselves.

There is some evidence that the interactions of older couples are less emotional but more affectionate than the interactions of middle-aged couples, suggesting a greater need for companionship in later life (Cartensen et al. 2003). A measure of research suggests that older husbands are more likely to name their spouse as a primary confidant than are older wives. These results imply that men may be relatively more dependent on marriage for interpersonal involvement and intimacy in later life than are women (Tower and Kasl 1996).

Other studies have focused on how aspects of wider social change impact on marriage. Chaya Foren (2011) engages with debates around continuity and discontinuity using the experiences of older persons living in second couplehood in old age, a phenomenon which is emerging due to the wish for companionship following widowhood or divorce against a background of increasing life expectancy. Couplehood fulfils needs such as friend-ship, intimacy, sexuality, love, compassion, emotional support and mutual assistance. These needs may not necessarily be fulfilled through marriage. Cohabitation among the older population in the USA is most heavily concen-trated among those aged 51 to 59 and the previously married (Brown and et al. 2012), compared to only 1 per cent of men and 0.5 per cent of women age 65 and older (Calasanti and Kiecolt 2007). Yet as the population ages, the proportion of older cohabiting adults is likely to increase. Sassler (2010) also refers to generational cohort effects, especially as the Baby Boom gen-eration matures into retirement. For this generation, remarriage rates will probably remain low, but various factors – increased life expectancy, good health, and the rise in internet dating and retirement communities – will undoubtedly change the partnership options available to older adults.

Sexuality

Negative connotations of later life are perhaps exemplified by cultural atti-tudes towards older people and sexuality – sexuality being an important aspect of relationships and identity. Here there is a contrast between outlooks in the West and more 'simple' societies. For example, amongst the Kaliau of Papua New Guinea there is no expectation that during later life women will end their sexual activity. Indeed, sexual activity is encouraged for older people as an effective way to maintain a sense of self and personhood. Thus, the majority of older individuals endeavour to maintain and demonstrate their status as an active elder and sexual individual.

By comparison, contemporary culture in the West is pre-occupied by the subject of sex but finds the thought of sexual relations for the eld-erly repulsive. Sexually active older men are often depicted as lewd and reprehensible, while sexuality in older women, according to Barash's analysis (1983), is popularly perceived as humorous at best. This may be why there has been very little literature produced, at least until rela-tively recently, focusing on the sexuality of older men and women. What has been unearthed by research findings confirms that older males take longer to become sexually aroused and reach orgasm, while the latency period between intercourse takes longer. It is assumed that older women lose their sex drive, with accompanying reduction in physical sensations which may well have begun with the menopause. Nonetheless, the evi-dence proves that the reality is they do not lose the ability or desire to have sexual intercourse.

Laura Clarke (2006) builds upon studies which show rates of sexual activity do in fact decline over the life course, as individuals experience marital transitions and the loss of partners, health problems and decreased sexual interest. Clarke compares and contrasts earlier and later-life sexual experiences and examines the changing meanings older women ascribe to sexuality over the life course. Her data from a study involving 24 women aged 52 to 90 who were remarried after age 50 illuminate a shift, as individuals age, from an emphasis on the importance of sexual intercourse and passion to a greater valuing of companionship, affection and intimacy. Further studies of the sexual activity of older adults also report that unmarried women are less likely than men to partake of an intimate relationship (e.g. Lindau et al. 2007).

As noted by Heaphy et al. (2003), in-depth discussion of older lesbian and gay lives is strikingly absent from the sociological literature, especially in relation to later life. Nonetheless, they present findings of sexual minority women and men in the UK aged 50 and over, suggesting that there are specific implications that non-heterosexuality has for patterns of living and to broader developments in social and cultural life than for ageing more generally. They indicate how sexuality, gender and age interact in complex ways to influence these matters, while older people will probably have experienced a life-time of discrimination and marginalisation before the arrival of more tolerant cultural attitudes. Thus older gay and lesbian people in later life are likely to reconfigure life-long experiences and give distinct meanings to their ageing, gender and sexuality. In addition, one LGBT advocacy organisation for older people (SAGE) identifies social isolation as a primary source of the lack of well-being. This is especially acute for those living alone (many of whom are estranged from their biological families because of their sexual orientation) which is twice that of the general population. They are twice as likely to be single, and 3 to 4 times less likely to have children.

Grandparenting

The emphasis in performing a constructive social role and sense of identity in later life has often been associated with grandparenting in terms of childcare and enhancing close connections and continuity over the generations. While grandparenting is often portrayed by the media as associated with being old, it is increasingly the case that grandparenthood is occurring among middle-aged segments of the population. From the 1970s studies indicated around 20 per cent of grandparents assume this role somewhere between the ages of 31 and 46 with another 44 per cent having adopted grandparenthood between the ages of 47 and 54. It is evident, then, that early marriage, earlier childbirth and longer life expectancy are producing grandparents at a younger age. In this regard, Lillian Troll and her associates (1979) maintained that as parents come to anticipate becoming grandparents, seeing it as a natural part of the life course, they found themselves in a social role bridging middle and later life. Some men discovered that they were grandfathers while still in the work force, and women increasingly became grandmothers during the period when they re-entered the workforce after a long absence due to child-raising activities.

Neugarten (1973) found with a sample of grandparents in 70 middleclass families that there were varied meanings associated with the role. The findings related to those who were middle-aged as well as those in older age categories. Comments of these respondents suggested several different responses to grandparenthood. First, there is what Neugarten and Weinstein (1964) refer to as 'biological renewal' and/or 'biological continuity', where grandchildren provide the opportunity to 'feel young again'. Here emotional self-fulfilment is discovered in the chance to be 'a better parent', as if it were the second time around, while the role is enhanced as a 'resource person' in providing financial aid and care giving. There are, in addition, 'vicarious accomplishments' which denote the possibility of reliving, through the grandchildren, frustrated ambitions: an opportunity to 'aggrandise the ego'. Alternatively, there may be 'feelings of remoteness' – a sense that some people have of restricted involvement in the lives of their grandchildren and little in terms of a relationship with them.

Research also throws light on the possibility that a certain ambiguity also informs contemporary grandparenthood, and this is partly due to the absence of clearly defined norms on the one hand and changes in family structures on the other. Hearn (1995, 102) sees this as particularly the case with men, where the relative 'invisibility' of grandfatherhood prevails since the role is rarely talked about and when it is, it is often through allusions, caricatures or humour. This ambiguity in the grandparent role is also compounded by step-grandfathering, an increasing phenomenon with the rates of re-marriage and the growth of re-constituted families, where there are few socially specified roles or norms to structure relationships.

Social networks

Partnerships and grandparenting are only part of the network in which older people are embedded. While aspects of consumption plausibly bring a greater connectivity with mainstream society, lack of geographical and social mobility may still forge social age-sets and generational-sets, whereby older people are separated off into networks comprising those who are younger and closer to the child-raising age. Thus, a number of sociological accounts have argued that older people form themselves into a subculture with its own distinctive norms, values and lifestyles. Here a distinct age group is viewed as based around a sense of common life and generational experiences enforced through frequent interaction with peers, reinforced by how younger generations perceive older people. The growing size of the aged as a social category, alongside increasing segregation into retirement communities and retirement practices, may well have helped the forging of such a distinct subculture.

Robert Atchley (1988) observes that Rostow's (1974) argument concerning society failing to socialise the elderly adequately for participation in a particular role of 'old person' is not a wholly accurate description of their role relationships. Atchley points out that older people usually associate on a daily basis primarily with people they know. Typically, they continue to function in their usual roles in the family and network of friends. Thus, most roles older people play are those they have been socialised into over an appreciable length of time.

Bernard et al.'s research (1995), however, points towards both continuities and change in the family and community life of older people. While those among a number of ethnic minorities, such as older Bangladeshi people, are part of flourishing family networks, whites typically have only one child living close by, with others dispersed. Nonetheless, when white older people were asked to name who is important to them, most identified kin as being the main group with whom reciprocal relations were maintained. Above all, relationships with their own children appeared to be the cornerstone of social integration. Therefore, those who are significant to older individuals in terms of interaction are people of their own age, plus their own children. Fewer than one in five of those interviewed placed themselves within a network which stretched beyond two generations. Another observation concerned the vital role older people play within the helping network and reciprocal nature of these intergenerational ties. Older people continued to see themselves as playing a supportive role to family and friends, notably in areas such as confiding in personal problems and giving advice on health. Bernard et al. conclude that intergenerational support is crucial to the present-day family and community life of older people. They are not being abandoned wholesale by their families, neither are they falling victim to extensive conflict between generations.

For those void of a constructive family life and networks, social isolation may be an unwelcome predicament for older people, but one exacerbated by some recent developments related to an increased life-span. Disengagement from the employment sphere may mean separation from friends and work-mates, while illness could reduce the opportunity for contact. The death of a partner may leave the older person on their own without the companion-ship they relied on for many years. Thus nearly half of those over 80 years old may find themselves living on their own (Walker and Maltby 1997, 13), with profound implications for their physical and mental health (Cornwall and Waite 2009). However, this is not to imply total isolation, and often the most important regular source of contact for the older individuals are adult children and grandchildren – either by living near to them or what might be referred to as 'intimacy at a distance': communication by phone or other forms of distant communication.

At least one study has found that almost three-quarters of widows and widowers cited loneliness as their most serious problem, and it is they who must often rebuild their lives at this late stage (Lund 1989). As with prac-tically everything associated with later life, social isolation is strongly influ-enced by factors related to gender (Arber and Ginn 1995). The problem of social isolation, then, falls most heavily on women, who typically out-live their husbands. Over 40 per cent of older women (especially the 'older elderly') live alone, compared to 16 per cent of older men. Bereaved older males, however, may face specific challenges. Studies of elderly men have long noted a high rate of mortality in the months following the death of their wives – perhaps indicating once again who it is that benefits in prac-tical terms from partnerships (e.g. Parkes et al. 1969). Finally, a recent devel-opment appears to be the increase in social isolation as a result of marital breakdown and divorce. The UK Family Policy Studies Centre (2009) has predicted that older people are increasingly isolated and lonely due to the rise in divorce. According to Social Trends (2002), the number of divorced people living on their own expected in 2025 will be 20 per cent, six times that of 1990.

THE PERSEVERANCE OF INEQUALITIES IN OLD AGE

It is evident from the discussion above that progressing into later life consti-tutes a form of social inequality based on the process of ageing itself. Thus Phillipson (1998) insists that, despite a recognition of new life styles and consumerism, in globalised late-modern societies it remains vital to retain a strong focus on the 'traditional' concerns of social exclusion and social inequality that may be observed in later life. Despite the apparent improvement of the economic position of contingents of older people, one enhanced by opportunities to partake of the consumer society, a high level of discrimination or ageism would still seem to be evident in Western societies despite age discrimination being taken seriously by governments. Ageism may be evident in the subtle form of infantilisation (as when people speak to the elderly with a condescending tone, as if they were children) (Kalish 1979). Terms such as 'the elderly', 'the old' or 'OAPs' (old age pensioners) both depersonalise and stigmatise the people to whom they refer.

Gerontologists increasingly use a life course perspective to understand how old age is shaped by events experienced earlier in life (Brown et al. 2005; Ferraro and Shippee 2009). This includes how economic disadvantages which have impacted throughout life are translated into negative consequences in later life. This tendency may enhance those disadvantages which are automatically brought about by retirement, since it traditionally means a loss of income for most people: the average income for families in which at least one member is 65 or older is only half the average wage for the UK as a whole. The decline in the value of savings and pensions suggests the worst-off are often the very old (Vincent 1996, 23–24). Thus, there is a systematic curve which indicates that income starts low in early life, increases until middle-age and then declines through later years. Later statistics showed mixed findings. A report issued by the UK Office for National Statistics found that the average disposable income of retired households was over two and a half times higher in real terms in 2010–11 than in 1977. By comparison, people of working age saw their income grow just two-fold over the same period. On the other hand, two reports (Kotecha et al. 2013; Department for Work and Pensions 2015) indicated that more than half (of all those of state pension age) did not report any level of material deprivation. However, 40 per cent reported they lacked up to three of the fifteen items considered to be an indication of such deprivation (for example, being able to go on a holiday, or see friends and family regularly). These contrasting statistics suggest major divisions among older people in terms of income and wealth. In turn, they indicate levels of social exclusion – the denial of full access to opportunities and resources deemed the right of the adult population at large in a consumer society.

Differing life trajectories and life events, varying levels of wealth, education and health all ensure older people do not constitute a homogenous age group. Heterogeniety and diversity is also evident in the varied experiences of different age cohorts. This is particularly important given that what constitutes 'the elderly' spans across an ever-expanding number of years. Riley (1987) thus insists the assumption that age cohorts share similar experiences and perspectives is flawed. Rather, they can be impacted by the differing life resources accumulated during their life course and the economic or cultural capital (including wealth and education) as well as social capital (such as family support) previously available to them. Furthermore, the longer a person lives, the greater the exposure to factors affecting experiences of ageing.

Differences of occupational reward, ethnicity and gender splinter older people as they do younger generations. Those in higher social classes largely have far more economic security, greater access to top medical care and more options for personal satisfaction, which clearly impact opportunities, lifestyles and meaningful choices. Such inequality is far from new. As early as the 1960s, Titmus (1962) referred to the 'two nations of old age' and stressed the wide variety of income among the over 65s. The variables Titmus identified as important were related not only to social class but also to gender: the 'haves' being the younger elderly – 60–75 year-olds, they were more likely to be middle-class, male, married; the 'have nots' were likely to be those over 75-years old, who were working-class, female, single, the divorced or widowed.

Today in the UK, 15 per cent of older people live below the poverty line – one of the largest groups in poverty, since they rely solely on state pensions. Occupational status determines conditions in later life, since it allows resources such as savings and investments, as do occupational pension. Indeed, for the more affluent, later life is not a period of impoverishment, pessimism or despair. There is a growing segment of older people that is frequently referred to as 'woopies', well-off older persons, who enjoy an abundant and fruitful lifestyle from the Third through to the Fourth Age. Hence, they are likely to have a higher standard of health well into old age and experience, for better or worse, a greater life-longevity. On the other hand, as Phillipson (1982) points out, the retirement experience for some older people is linked to the timing of economic reduction of wages, and enforced withdrawal from work has made many older people in the UK financially insecure. Moreover, governments may help construct the social marginality of older people in key areas such as welfare delivery. For Phillipson (1998), inequalities in the allocation of resources for older people should also take into account political circumstances and the distribution of power within society, rather than in terms of individual variation.

Gender and ethnicity

As already tentatively explored, gender divisions in later life also have considerable significance and may cut across the variable of class. For quite some time the subject of ageing was a neglected area of feminist scholarship. However, works such as that of Calasanti and Slevin (2006) have increasing explored how feminist studies have shown how gender shapes the lives of older women as well as men. They also consider how gendered power relations interface with race and ethnicity, class and sexual orientation.

Women have greater life-expectancy than men in the majority of Western societies and, as already noted, are thus more likely to live alone. This is a tendency generally referred to as 'the feminisation of old age'. Since the 1990s in the UK the ratio of men to women in the 60–64 age group has been about 50:50; at ages 65–69 the ratio is 47 males to 53 females; at ages 70–74 there are 44 males to 56 females; and at age 75 and over the ratio is approximately 38 males to 62 females. Women are also more inclined to be subject to higher rates of poverty: 38 per cent of women and 24 per cent of men over 65 years live on the poverty line. Some 77 per cent of carers of the elderly at home are women, and around 66 per cent are over the age of 55.

Throughout Europe, at least, a major source of income for older people is a pension. Generally, this is a two-tier system: public and private (usually an occupational pension). The latter is much more easily available to men, once again reinforcing the weaker position of women in later life. The woes for older women do not stop here, however. More health problems inflict the older elderly, those past the age of 75 years. Because women typically live longer than men do, it follows that it is they who will spend more years suffering from chronic diseases and the need for support from other people in daily living.

A report for the Joseph Rowntree Foundation (2002) suggests that early retirement in their 50s or redundancy frequently mean that some people, both men and women in the UK, will spend later life in poverty, although this may vary considerably among occupational groups such as clerical or sales, skilled crafts and personal or protective services. Bardasi and Jenkins (2002), who researched the report, argue that reduced opportunities for a mass savings and pension entitlement were unlikely to have been the only reason some stopped work in their 50s. Many of the men affected may also have been low earners within their occupational group and, as such, more likely to lose their jobs. The financial implications are consequently likely to be felt in later life.

There exists an ethnic dimension to later life as well, especially where ethnic minority populations display a younger age structure, largely reflecting the history of immigration in the UK and other Western countries, particularly those migrating in the 1950s and 1960s. Some 25 per cent of the black Caribbean and 47 per cent of the Pakistani and Bangladeshi population in the UK in subsequent generations were under 15 years of age, compared to 21 per cent of whites. Only 3 per cent of the ethnic minority population are aged 65 and over, compared to 17 per cent of whites. However, the proportion of older people from ethnic minorities has invariably increased as its population itself ages. This might more than hint that their life experiences and opportunities will converge with those of the majority population. However, for some ethnic groups ageing is compounded by what might be referred to as the 'triple jeopardy' of being old, non-white and poor, to which can be added aspects of gender inequality. Ethnic minorities are also likely to experience vast differences of health, environment and income in comparison to the white population, where lack of accumulated resources during the earlier life course has a significant impact in later life.

The relationship between age and ethnicity remains an under-researched area. Certainly, there are often major differences in the 'ageing experience' between ethnic groups, for example, in self-identity, morale, life-satisfaction and standards of living. Thus, Blakemore and Boneham (1993) maintain that there is the danger of generalising about ethnic groups, such as the insistence that Asian extended families are more likely to have caring family networks responsible for older people. Nonetheless, they conjecture that the situation of older people in ethnic groups can be divided into three categories. First, the 'Self-Reliant Pioneer' – older people in minority ethnic groups who are influenced more by their roles and position in their own communities than by mainstream norms and expectations. The position of older people in the country of origin will be replicated as far as possible, for example, in terms of status and extended family ties. A second category is, the 'Gradually Adjusting Migrant', who makes certain adaptations to the 'role' of old age in common with mainstream society. This suggests a partial social integration. Third, there is the 'Passive Victim' – those who are part of a minority that feel discriminated against because they are both old and members of an ethnic community.

SUMMARY

The picture drawn of later life in this chapter displays extraordinary complexity in life experiences and trajectories – one where in contemporary Western societies there are observably both changes and continuities. Continuity is observable in that, despite philosophies of 'positive' ageing, the process of and location of people in 'later life' still retains stereotypes and negative popular appraisals. Moreover, continuities remain significant, with the impact of demographic variables such as class, ethnicity and gender, not to mention the significance of accumulated educational benefits, wealth and impact, all of which still inform life chances, experiences and perceptions of the self in later years of the life course. When all the vital factors are considered, later life experiences in late/post modernity are increasingly fragmented. On the 'plus' side, today's older people have generally benefited from higher levels of education and economic position. They are larger in number than in the past, and therefore hold the potential of constituting a major economic, social and political force which may constitute a counterpoint to their conventional lowly status.

FURTHER READING

Altman, A. and Ashner, L. (2007) *Sexuality in Mid-Life and Beyond*, Boston: Harvard Medical School.

Arber, S. and Cooper, H. (1999) 'Gender Differences in Health in Later Life: The New Paradox', *Social Science and Medicine*, 48(1): 861–76.

Biggs, S. (1993) *Understanding Ageing*, Milton Keynes: OUP.

Bullington, J. (2006) 'Body and Self: A Phenomenological Study on the Ageing Body and Identity', *Medical Humanities*, 32(1): 25–31.

Cacioppo, J., Hughes, M., Waite, L., Hawkley, L. and Thisted, R. (2006) 'Loneliness as a Specific Risk Factor for Depressive Symptoms: Cross-sectional and Longitudinal Analyses', *Psychology and Aging*, 21(1): 140–51.

Conrad, S. (1992) 'Old Age in the Modern and Postmodern Western World', in T. Cole (ed.), *Handbook of the Humanities and Ageing*, New York: Springer.

Erber, J. (2010) *Aging and Older Adulthood*, Chichester, UK/Malden, MA: Wiley-Blackwell.

Featherstone, M. and Hepworth, M. (1986) 'New Lifestyles in Old Age?', in C. Phillipson, M. Bernard and P. Strang (eds.), *Dependency and Interdependency in Old Age: Theoretical Perspectives and Policy Alternatives*, London: Croom Helm.

Featherstone, M. and Wernick, A. (1995) *Images of Ageing*, London: Routledge.

Gee, E. (1991) 'The Transition to Grandmotherhood: A Quantitative Study', *Canadian Journal on Aging*, 10(3): 254–70.

Ginn, J. and Arber, S. (2000) 'Ethnic Inequality in Later Life: Variation in Financial Circumstances by Gender and Ethnic Group', *Education and Aging*, 15(1): 65–83.

Goodman, A. and Greaves, E. (2010) 'Cohabitation, Marriage and Child outcomes', Nuffield Foundation, www.ifs.org.uk/comms/comm114.pdf, accessed 3 June 2015.

Hank, K. and Buber, I. (2009) 'Grandparents Caring for their Grandchildren: Findings From the 2004 Survey of Health, Ageing, and Retirement in Europe', *Journal of Family*, 30(1): 53–73.

Hareven, T. (ed.) (1996) *Aging and Generational Relations: Life Course and Cross-Cultural Perspectives*, New York: Aldine de Gruyter.

Hockey, J. and James, A. (1993) *Growing Up and Growing Old: Ageing and Dependency in the Life Course,* London: Sage.

Nazroo, J. (2006) 'Ethnicity and Old Age', in J. Vincent, C. Phillipson and M. Downs (eds.), *The Futures of Old Age,* UK: Sage.

Phillipson, C. and Biggs, S. (1998) 'Modernity and Identity: Themes and Perspectives in the Study of Older Adults', *Journal of Aging and Identity*, 3(1): 11–23.

Quadagno, J. (2007) *Aging and The Life Course: An Introduction to Social Gerontology*, 4th edn., McGraw-Hill Humanities/Social Sciences/Languages.

Stoller, E. and Gibson, R. (2000) *Worlds of Difference: Inequality in the Aging Experience*, Thousand Oaks, CA: Pine Forge Press.

Turner, B. (1995) 'Ageing and Identity', in M. Featherstone and A. Wernick (eds.), *Images of Ageing,* London: Routledge.

Chapter 12

End of life, death and dying

While it may be inappropriate to discuss death in the same breath as ageing, Western culture tends uniquely to bring together these themes: death is viewed as the climax of the ageing process. Most deaths now occur not among the young but among the old. Death, thus postponed through high life expectancy, takes on new meanings for both the individual and the wider social world. The almost taken-for-granted assumption is to live into old age, allowing an anticipation of the possibilities, constraints and risks involved. What is given far less consideration is the end of life. Indeed, Western societies have become in a sense death-denying: while the limit of life-expectancy is forever being driven upwards, perhaps thoughts of death are pushed ever more to the recesses of consciousness. While many older people invariably anticipate their own deaths with legal and financial planning, death itself may be something that they prefer not to envisage.

As Mellor and Shilling (1993) point out, almost reflecting the Western cultural neglect of the subject of death, Sociology has conventionally been concerned with problems of life rather than its end. Given that death is an essential feature of the human condition, to neglect death is to ignore one of the few universal parameters in which social and individual experiences are constructed. Acknowledging this neglected area of death, as well as the course of dying, John Riley (1983) points to the growing range of literature offered by different disciplines and perspectives, including Sociology: dying as a social process; dying trajectories; attitudes toward death; and the potential impact of such 'stressors' which might enhance the possibility of premature death – retirement, residential relocation and economic change; the meaning of loss by death to surviving 'significant others', widowhood and bereavement and grief.

The emphasis of sociological inquiries in particular, Riley notes, can be summarised as attempting to examine the norms and social structures that aid in defining and managing dying and the consequences of death. He also points to a number of key questions emerging in Western societies, including: will socialisation for death become routine?; will euthanasia become more acceptable?; will innovating patterns of bereavement emerge?; and will environments for the terminally ill be increasingly institutionalised? A number of these themes will inform this final chapter. However, in keeping with the principal aims of the volume, an emphasis will be on the changes and continuities to be found in late/postmodernity regarding trends and perceptions of death which have fed into what might be termed the social construction of death.

The moment of death

While death is the end of life and the termination of the life course, it begs a definition. That accepted by Western culture generally conforms to medical scientific frameworks which, nonetheless, have changed over time. Today, death is generally regarded in the medical sphere as amounting to physiological death which constitutes a 'process' rather than a single event – a definition which has arisen from the recognition that the criteria previously regarded as specifying death may now be reversed either 'naturally' or a result of medical intervention. The medical measurement now generally focuses on 'vital signs', which are integral to the 'process' of 'clinical death' (which frequently departs from 'legal death', which demands formal documental confirmation).

As medical knowledge progresses, a precise definition of death becomes increasingly more problematic. Currently doctors and coroners typically refer to 'brain death' or 'biological death' to confirm the cessation of life. The former relates to the permanent end of human consciousness. This definition has, however, been questioned on the grounds that other 'vital signs' might be evident among patients, including evidence of the functioning of circulation and respiration, excretion wastes, healing wounds, combating infections and even – in the case of a pregnant woman – the gestation of foetuses. From these complexities arise a number of ethical questions including what, if any, forms of euthanasia are permissible and the decision to terminate life by switching off life support systems. Such ethical concerns will be addressed below.

Death trajectories

While Western culture may associate death with old age, and this remains a realistic assumption in advanced societies, the two do not always necessarily converge. The significance of the timing and cause of death as a part of a death 'trajectory' or 'pattern of dying' is largely attributed to the work of Glasner and Strauss (1965), which focused on how the demise of human life involved contrasting causes and conditions. The subject attracted subsequent sociological interest, since patterns of disease and other causes of death invariably impact not only the lives of the patients but also their families and relationships as well as clinicians. All of these parties are inevitably obliged to prepare for the death of an individual psychologically, including how death is perceived, and in practical terms of care, depending on what has come to be termed 'duration' and 'shape'. The former refers to the length of time a patient has to live – other than instant death – ranging from days to years. Put succinctly, 'duration' amounts to the time between the onset of dying and the arrival of death. This allows levels of predictability: whether death is expected and when. 'Shape' describes how that duration may then be mapped out or graphed and otherwise termed 'the course of dying'. Collectively 'duration' and 'shape' constitute the 'death course' and its consequences, which will depend upon the diagnosis of the patient and anticipated trajectory. Thus end-of-life plans may vary considerably.

Common death trajectories might be said to be of three forms. First, sudden death occurs without warning and is typified by accidents, heart failure or stroke. This category does not, however, exclude death as a result of chronic illnesses where sudden 'unexpected' death can be anticipated. However, from the perspective of the patient and family, if they are unaware of this risk, death will come without warning. Second, a trajectory founded upon a steady decline in health status over time with an inevitable decline towards death. This will depend upon the nature of the chronic illness. Several types of cancer (pancreatic, lung, stomach) are typical examples where the duration from diagnosis to death is measured in weeks to months, while for other chronic illnesses, such as Alzheimer's, the diagnosis of death foresees that it will take place over a much longer period of time. Each type permits a time duration for the patient and their 'significant others' to come to terms with and prepare for death. Third, trajectories might be based on chronic illnesses with a gradually declining slope and periods of acute crises, where after each crisis the patient's quality of life drops even further. Chronic lung disease, congestive heart failure and terminal stage liver disease are examples of this pattern, one which may lead both the patient and family to be convinced that the next episode will not be survived.

CAUSES OF DEATH

The changing perceptions of death in Western societies (considered below) have clearly been accompanied by the changing causes of death. Over the last century and a half, improved sanitary conditions in particular, and environmental conditions in general, have not only prolonged life but brought a drastic reduction in death caused by infections and parasites. In 1900, the leading causes of death throughout industrialising nations were pneumonia, tuberculosis, diarrhoea, cholera and related diseases. None of these are listed among the five leading causes of death in developed countries at the current time. Today, almost 70 per cent of all deaths are a result of heart disease, cancer and strokes. By contrast, many of the causes of death are related to the so-called diseases of affluence resulting from stress, fatty 'fast food' diets, alcohol consumption, smoking and obesity. To illustrate these developments we may note the *Historical Statistics of the United States* (1983), which showed diseases of the heart and cancer malignancies as by far the major causes of death compared to 1900, where pneumonia, influenza and tuberculosis were the predominant killers. The 'diseases of affluence', then, have become the new 'risks'.

Control over many causes of mortality, particularly among the young, largely explains why old age is linked to death. Fewer children die at birth, and accidents and disease now take a smaller toll among adults. Except during times of war or catastrophe, premature death has come to be viewed as an extraordinary event. In 1995, 85 per cent of the population in Western societies died after the age of 55. By this time, death and old age became largely fused. Although most retired people can now look forward to an increasing life-span, growing old cannot now be separated from eventual physical decline and ultimate death. Thus the largest unifying cause of death in the developed world is biological ageing, leading to various complications known as 'age-associated disease'. Of the roughly 150,000 people who die each day across the world, about two-thirds die of age-related causes. In post-industrialised nations, the proportion is much higher, approaching 90 per cent (De Grey 2007). In high-income and middle-income countries, nearly half up to more than two-thirds of all people live beyond the age of 70 and predominantly die of chronic diseases. In low-income countries, where less than one in five people reach the age of 70, and more than a third of all deaths are among children under 15, people predominantly die of infectious diseases. This is all in marked contrast to the past, where, in circa 1900, some one-third of all deaths in Europe occurred before the age of 5, another third took place before the age of 55 and the remaining third died in what was then defined as old age.

Table 12.1 Major Causes of Death in England & Wales, 2010

Cause of death	male	female	2010 total	Rate per 100,000 pop	% change, 2009–10
All causes, all ages	237,916	255,326	493,242	892.90	0.39
All causes, ages under 28 days	1,184	964	2,148		−4.58
All causes, ages 28 days and over	236,732	254,362	491,094		0.41
Circulatory diseases	77,260	80,824	158,084	286.17	−1.06
Cancers and neoplasms	74,267	67,179	141,446	256.05	0.68
Respiratory diseases	31,563	35,713	67,276	121.79	−0.42
Digestive diseases	12,164	13,498	25,662	46.46	1.71
Mental and behavioural disorders	6,299	13,617	19,916	36.05	10.52
Death not caused by disease	10,545	6,656	17,201	31.14	−3.79
Diseases of the nervous system	8,551	9,932	18,483	33.46	6.18
Genitourinary diseases	4,893	7,513	12,406	22.46	3.40
Other causes	2,534	7,334	9,868	17.86	6.76
Endocrine, nutritional and metabolic diseases	3,232	3,953	7,185	13.01	0.87

Source: Annual Mortality Statistics, Office for National Statistics, licensed under the Open Government License v.30, as presented by the Guardian Newspaper, Mortality statistics Guardian, Simon Rogers, 28 October, 2011.

THE SOCIAL SIGNIFICANCE OF DEATH

Whatever the cause of death, how societies perceive and deal with the event varies as much as the way they construct other significant events of life. Hence, there are infinite variations by which death has been perceived and the meaning attributed to it throughout human history, and perceptions and meanings differ considerably between cultures today. The cultural prism through which Western societies view death is in many respects quite distinct and can be compared to many developing countries, where death is a familiarity and is, in short, a part of life. Where life-expectancy is low and infant mortality is high, death is a common aspect of daily existence, especially where resources are scarce.

Throughout most of history, confronting the reality of death has been part of the human condition. It was rarely assumed that a new-born child would necessarily live for very long: a fact that frequently led parents to delay naming a child until it had survived for a year or two. For those who lived through infancy, illness prompted by poor nutrition, accidents and natural disasters, such as drought or famine, combined to make life precarious. In times of great need death was often deliberate, the result of a strategy to protect the community by sacrificing a group's less productive members, namely the practice of infanticide and geronticide. If death was routine, it was also readily accepted and this is historically evidenced by Medieval Christianity, which assured the European populace that death fitted into the divine plan for the human race.

Irrespective of the degree of familiarity with death, its occurrence has a social relevance, although there are considerable cultural variations as to its significance. Maurice Halbwachs (1930), a student of Emile Durkheim, was one of the first to study the social relevance of death, stressing the fact that it must be comprehended and appraised within the environment of wider social relationships. This was certainly so in 'traditional' societies where the broader social context and extended kinship networks were significant. To illustrate this point, Halbwachs distinguished between 'physical death' and 'social death'. The former refers to the medical definition of death: simply, the human body ceases to biologically function. The latter denotes the social consequence of death. Life may have been extinguished, but the social implications remain. This is starkly seen in the example of Malaya, where death is a 'process' in the sense that it amounts to a series of ceremonies marking the slow transition from the 'living world' to the after-life. Due to a very hot climate the deceased is buried within a short period of time. This represents 'physical death'. A few days later the body is exhumed and a funeral ceremony takes place in which friends and relatives say a final 'goodbye' to the dead. This constitutes 'social death'.

There is an implicit meaning here that the deceased is still part of continuing social relations for an appreciable period of time. The dead are not easily forgotten, since they were, and remain for a short while, an integral and significant element of the lives of those left behind, as well as probably once fulfilling various important social roles. Frequently, this signifies that relatives and, in the case of small-scale pre-industrial societies, entire communities have to deal with psychological and practical problems left in the wake of the death of a social member. This is why most cultures have elaborate funeral ceremonies and an accompanying period of mourning which symbolise the fact that society slowly withdraws from the dead over a time of transition until the memory of that person diminishes and the implications of the loss of an individual gradually recede.

WESTERN PERCEPTIONS OF DEATH

According to Freud (1938), all societies display a collective subconscious fear of death. The corpse, in particular, is a thing of taboo: a dread of touching that which is perceived to be in an 'unclean' condition. More broadly, death undermines 'ontological security'– the stable mental state derived from a sense of continuity in respect of events of life which bring an impression of order and continuity for individual and social experiences, giving meaning to human existence.

Western society, however, appears to have a heightened aversion to death. In the midst of plenty in the consumer culture of late/postmodernity, death is hidden and excluded from everyday experience. For a society preoccupied with health, choice of alternatives and human potential, death is a subject infrequently discussed. At the same time, however, there is what may be referred to as 'celluloid death'. In other words, death is often presented to a mass audience in popular fiction, magazines, the cinema, simulated computer games or, alternatively, the 'real' death seen in news clips. Death, then, is frequently 'invented' or constitutes death in another part of the world, channelled through contemporary images which do not tangibly touch the public gaze beyond media portrayals.

At the same time, in Western societies the death of the individual is also of less and less social significance in the sense that Halbwachs understood: death is largely anonymous. This stands in marked contrast with the past. Aries (1973) notes how once in Europe the dead were often buried together in unmarked graves. Later burial was undertaken in individual plots with inscriptions etched on the tombstone detailing who was buried on the site and the years in which they lived. These plots were to be found in church graveyards, with the church itself forging an integral part of social life. The need to indicate who was buried where was initiated to remind the living, whereas in the past it would have been common knowledge to the people of the village, who were well aware of the generations that went before them. This indicated the importance of wider kinship and social relationships, as well as the low level of geographical mobility. Today, the dead are generally disposed of by cremation – their ashes interned in the gardens of crematoriums which are frequently to be found on the outskirts of towns and cities, thus signifying that death is very much out of sight, out of mind. Moreover, in modern industrial society, as Aries (1973) and others have shown, death is feared all the more because it makes life seem meaningless in a largely secular culture, where beliefs in the after-life are on the decline. Death, then, generates a range of anxieties, and where this is perhaps most in evident in the Western cultural setting is in responses to the death of a child. In a culture where longevity is viewed almost as a right, the death of a child is often viewed as almost unimaginable.

THE MEDICALISATION OF DEATH

In contemporary societies, the process of dying has largely been removed from everyday experience and taken into specialised institutions (hospitals or nursing homes) to be supervised by professional personnel and managed by appropriate technologies (there are alternatives to dying in hospital, and programmes have been designed for the care of the terminally ill, but these are relatively recent innovations). Other institutions such as the hospice have long catered for the needs of the terminally ill and dying. In the hospital or similar institution the dying are isolated from the rest of society. This reverses the social processes evident in the past: thus, typically, society will retire from the individual before they die, rather than afterwards – the typical pattern to be found in pre-industrial societies. Consequently, older adults may approach the end of their own lives and that of their age peers with more fear and distress than the elderly in societies where people directly observe death and where dying is more readily discussed.

Since old age and death, as with birth, take place increasingly within the context of the institutional setting, it is clear that the medical profession has now come to have an almost complete hegemony in overseeing the great milestones of life. Ivan Illich (1969), in his work *Medical Nemesis,* lamented this development, arguing that the nineteenth century saw a shift from death as the domain of the church to the domain of medicine. The doctor took the place of the priest at the bedside; religion was usurped by science. Death, according to Illich, had also lost its 'human' dimension. The dying are rarely surrounded in their last days by the people they know and love. They may be obliged to take pain-killing drugs and have little idea what is happening to them: while medicine eases the process of death, it denies it as part of the human experience of life.

Institutionalisation of later life and dying

Before the first decades of the twentieth century, most people in Western countries died in their own homes, surrounded by family and comforted by clergy, neighbours and doctors making house calls. By the mid-twentieth century, half of all Americans died in a hospital. By the start of the twenty-first century, only about 20 to 25 per cent of people in developed countries died outside of a medical institution (Ahmad and O'Mahony 2005; Nuland 1994). The shift away from dying at home towards dying in a professionalised medical environment could only add to the phenomenon of 'invisible death'.

The institutionalisation of death is invariably linked to the formal health care of those in later life. Uppal et al.'s (1995) findings suggested that predictors of nursing home placement are mainly based on underlying cognitive and/or functional impairment, and associated lack of support and assistance in daily living. Social and medical services in Western societies tend to be subdivided into services for children, services for adults and services for the elderly. 'Deep' old age is not, however, given the same status in these services as earlier adulthood. To some extent this is a result of infantisation, that is, the perception of the elderly as inevitably returning to a child-like state but at the same time having little time to live with subsequent low quality of life (Hockey and James 1993, 131, 172–73). This is a process built into the medical model of ageing. In later life 'post-adults' are perceived as returning to a subordinate child-like location, while in the health-care system patients are frequently discriminated against by being denied operations and transplants which would prolong their lives in favour of transplants for the young. Over several decades in the Western world, the national health resources directed towards older people have failed to rise in proportion to their number. Moreover, geriatric patients are not treated as a priority, while geriatric nursing has a relatively low status. As much can be said of care for the dying.

There is also a gender dimension to be considered. In the UK, 25 per cent of men are more likely to die in their own homes compared to women (19 per cent) and women are almost twice as likely to die in 'communal institutions', which includes nursing and residential homes (Luppa et al. 1998). This is partly a product of the greater life-longevity of women. Clearly, there is little research into the experiences of dying in communal institutions, where the majority of women over 85 will see out their lives. However, among the observations made by Field et al. (1997) is that women's self-identity is put at greater risk than men's once they become dependent upon the care of others within the institutional setting.

PRESERVING LIFE AND END OF LIFE DECISIONS

In medicine, nursing and allied health professions end-of-life supervision refers to health care, not only of patients in the final hours or days of life, but more broadly care of all those with a terminal illness or terminal condition that has become advanced, progressive and incurable. End-of-life care requires a range of decisions, including questions of palliative care, patients' right to self-determination (of treatment and/or life), medical experimentation, the ethics and negotiation of hazardous and even routine medical interventions, and the ethics and effectiveness even of continued routine medical interventions, as well as matters of the allocation of resources in hospitals and national medical systems. Such decisions are informed both by technical, medical considerations and economic factors as well as bioethics. In addition, end-of-life treatments are subject to considerations of patient autonomy and the rights of their families in determining when to pursue aggressive treatment or withdraw life support.

Exemplifying some of the more optimistic re-evaluations of medicine is the growing assumption that ageing and thus 'decline' may be a process that can be modified if not reversed. Life extension science (also known as 'anti-ageing medicine'), indefinite life extension, experimental gerontology and biomedical gerontology, amounts to the study of slowing down or reversing the process to extend both the maximum and average life-span, with advocates believing that future breakthroughs in tissue rejuvenation, stem cells, regenerative medicine, molecular repair, pharmaceuticals and organ replacement, such as with artificial organs, may eventually enable humans to have indefinite life-spans through complete rejuvenation to a healthy youthful condition.

If Western societies are increasingly death-defying, this defying aspect may not only include the application of medication in aiding longer life but also the development of 'spare part' surgery and what has come to be known as 'regenerative medicine', concerned with the process of replacing, engineering or regenerating human cells, tissues or organs to restore or establish normal functioning. This field holds the promise of engineering damaged tissues and organs via stimulating the body's own repair mechanisms to functionally heal previously irreparable tissues or organs. Regenerative medicine refers to a group of biomedical approaches to clinical therapies that may involve the use of stem cells. Relatedly, it has included the transplant of *in vitro* grown organs and tissues (or tissue engineering).

While these processes may constitute medical 'advances', Parry et al. (2015) have pulled attention to how the fields of medicine and healthcare are being radically transformed by new biotechnologies, creating, in the process, a genuinely globalised sphere of biomedical production and consumption. This emerging market is characterised by the circulation of bodily materials (tissues, organs and bio-information), patients and expertise across what traditionally have been relatively secure ontological and geographical borders. Ethical questions are thus raised in relation to bodies crossing borders, whether this exacerbates existing health inequalities and how these circulations impact on healthcare services, and whether these developments should be regulated.

In terms of life longevity, scientists such as Rudman and his colleagues (1990) have produced a measure of evidence suggesting that the development of the human growth hormone could restrict the effects of ageing. It follows that life expectancy could increase and that subsequently there may be the liberty to choose, by the claimed advances of medical science, to live longer with an average life-span perhaps feasibly increasing in the future to around 110 years old. If so, then an older but fitter population remains plausible. Nonetheless, the implication of such a development is not one that has been seriously pondered inasmuch as the 'advance' of science may be ahead of both cultural expectations and social policy considerations around ageing.

Important ethical questions, in some cases, are raised about extending life – perhaps unnecessarily. At the same time, medically speaking, a low priority is given to the elderly and the dying. This apparent contradiction is at least partly evident in the debate surrounding euthanasia. At the present time euthanasia is illegal in the great majority of Western countries. Should it become legal, the processes would undoubtedly be overviewed by the medical profession. Such a development may still be a long way off, however. Euthanasia is legal in Holland, and several states in the USA have presented (unsuccessful) challenges to constitutional law against euthanasia. Thus, the culture of choice is not currently extended to the voluntary ending of life – freely chosen by the individual. Nonetheless, legal proscriptions have not prevented the growth of so-called end-of-life clinics such as Dignitas, a Swiss organisation based in Zurich, established for those with terminal illness and severe physical and mental illnesses who wish to die. This process of what amounts to voluntary death is assisted by qualified doctors and nurses, who have aided over 1000 people on the proviso they are of sound judgement and submit to an in-depth medical report, prepared by a psychiatrist, which establishes the patient's condition.

Those who call for a legalisation of euthanasia argue that it is a fundamental human right to die when one wishes to, and to prevent human suffering and a condition of life which has little or no quality. This was exemplified by the case of Diane Pretty, a terminally ill woman in the UK who fought a legal challenge to establish a 'right' to so-called assisted-suicide, but lost her appeal to the House of Lords in 2001. Her argument, and others like her, was that the experience of life was so unbearable under the weight of terminal illness that death would be a welcome relief. The rhetoric surrounding such cases indicates that those who oppose euthanasia do so on two broad grounds: moral and utilitarian. The moral view is largely taken by religious groups who believe that it is morally wrong to take life under any circumstances. These constituencies often refer to the 'right to life' and see euthanasia as an issue often spoken in the same breath with the subject of abortion – that the unborn as well as the elderly and disabled have a right to life. Others argue that voluntary euthanasia is the 'thin end of the wedge' and would eventually lead to compulsory euthanasia for those with terminal medical conditions or who could not be easily looked after. And, moreover, that 'official' euthanasia would become the norm under the power of the medical profession, thus further extending the medicalisation of life course events.

COPING WITH DEATH

Coping with death has various dynamics. In Western societies, the connectiveness of old age with death in variable raises issues for those in later life and may impact a sense of identity for those with few years left to live and the 'impending horizon' of the prospect of death (Bullington 2006). A discernible 'cycle of grieving' on news that death is likely is now well-established, with varieties of models derived from that initially developed by the Kübler-Ross model (1969), which postulates a series of emotional stages experienced by those diagnosed as terminally ill: denial; anger ('why me?', 'how can this happen to me?', 'who is to blame?'); bargaining (with God or human agencies in exchange for a reformed lifestyle), depression and finally acceptance.

Death, as acknowledged above, challenges the meaning of life and frailty of human existence. Around this challenge has developed 'meaning management theory', indicating that human reactions to death are complex, multi-faceted and dynamic, initially associated with Paul Wong's (1987–88) work. Wong's 'Death Attitude Profile' identified three types of death acceptances as 'neutral', 'approach' and 'escape' acceptances, each of which are rooted in the bases of death anxiety. The ten meanings he proposes are finality, uncertainty, annihilation, ultimate loss, life flow disruption, leaving loved ones, pain and loneliness, prematurity and violence of death, failure of life work completion, judgement and retribution. Later theories took an existential approach, with theorists such as Rollo May (1996), who stressed the individual's personality as being governed by the continuous choices and decisions in relation to the realities of life and death. Another approach is the 'regret theory', which was introduced by Tomer and Eliason (1996). The main focus of the theory is to consider the way people evaluate the quality and/or worth of their lives. The possibility of death usually makes people more anxious if they feel that they have not and cannot accomplish any positive task in the life that they are living.

It is during the years of young adulthood (20 to 40 years of age) that death anxiety apparently most often begins to become prevalent. However, during the next phase of life, the middle-age adult years (40–64 years of age), death anxiety peaks at its highest levels when in comparison to all other age ranges throughout the life-span. Levels of death anxiety then slump off in the later years of adulthood (65 years of age and older), which is rather unexpected given the negative connotations younger adults have about older people and the ageing process, and that later life brings the prospect of death ever closer (Kurlychek and Trenner 1982).

While these above theories and studies are largely concerned with psychological aspects of the meaning of death, sociological approaches typified by that of Giddens (1991a) focus on the relationship between self-identity and the experience of death in the social context of late-modernity, where its organisation and encounters are increasingly privatised. For Giddens, this has acquired particular significance as a result of three central characteristics of the contemporary West: the growing role played by the reflexive re-ordering of biographical narratives in the construction of self-identity; the increased identification of the self with the body; and the decline of the sacred. This is not to argue, maintains Giddens, that people lack survival strategies when dealing with death, but that these strategies become increasingly precarious and problematic.

Mourning and grief

Given cultural perceptions of death in the secular societies of the West, where a religious perception of the world is in demise, 'supernatural' explanations for the causes of death likewise decline. One of the consequences is that in a culture where a religious worldview has experienced demise, satisfactory ontological answers as to why death occurs cannot always be provided at a meaningful level. At the same time, funerals and mourning, which often give expression to religious sentiment, are often inadequate, rushed events. Thus, Tony Walter (1994) paints a gloomy picture of the way in which death is dealt with in Western societies. Funerals are often brief, staid, unemotional affairs that leave little time for meaningful mourning. Given the decline of after-life beliefs, there has been, Walter suggests, an 'eclipse of eternity'. For that reason, the 'alternative' funeral, like the 'alternative' wedding is in vogue – often providing the meaning and significance woefully missing from the standard funeral and, more often than not, void of religious trappings. Hence, the funeral, as with so much else in a culture of choice, is open to personal preferences and self-expression.

This is all in stark contrast to pre-industrial societies, many of which appear to deal more effectively with the psychological problems generated by death. Malinowski's (1954) work with the people of the Trobriand Islands showed religion was particularly significant during certain times, in particular, situations of individual emotional stress that threatened collective solidarity and sentiment. For Malinowski, anxiety and tension tended to disrupt social life. Contexts which produced these emotions included crises such as birth, puberty, marriage and death. He noticed that in all pre-industrial societies life crises are surrounded with religious ritual. Death was the most disruptive of these events, since it severed strong personal attachments and thwarted people's future plans. This is why Malinowski regarded the ability to deal with the problems associated with death as probably the main source of religious belief. Thus, through funeral ceremonies belief in immortality can be expressed, in a sense denying the fact of death itself and thus comforting the bereaved. Indeed, bereavement signifies a particular type of discontinuity. Death means the cessation of someone's life and the end of the relationships that the deceased shared with others. Moreover, it brings a unique form of psychological challenge since death is final.

Individuals must deal with their grief and societies in various ways and various degrees permit expressions of mourning. Yet, mourning is clearly expressed contrastingly in different cultural contexts. In the contemporary cultural environment where death is rarely spoken of immediate relatives, and even more distant friends and associates, may be ill-prepared to express their own emotions of a loss at any stage of life. Embarrassment or fear of saying something inappropriate may mean people disassociating themselves from the death or distancing themselves from close relatives. The resulting isolation of the family may therefore add to the grief that is experienced. The inability to deal with death, however, is also related to wider processes of mourning. Here, there is a noteworthy comparison of Western societies with other cultures, especially in preindustrial societies where funerals are of considerable importance.

This final rite of passage in the life course amounts to a ceremony that has both a psychological and social function in providing a ritual which expresses solidarity and a set of beliefs about the after-life. There may be religious significance and taboo status attached to this transition from one social status to another: from the living to the dead. It is perhaps death which constitutes the most profound 'life crisis' – generating an uncertainty and demanding significant psychological adjustment for those who are left to come to terms with it. For instance, people in the UK are not prone to wearing their emotions 'on their sleeves' and are expected to bear suffering with 'a stiff upper lip'. This emotional reserve leads to a unique way of dealing with grief, perhaps resulting from the desire not to break down in front of children. Much may be derived from a desire to protect the child from pain or the belief that the young are incapable of experiencing grief. Such reserve is not necessarily to be welcomed. However it is interpreted, according to Gorer (1965), the holding back of grief, the forbidding of its public manifestation, the obligation to suffer alone and secretly, have further aggravated the trauma stemming from the loss of a dear one.

It may now be possible to speak of a postmodern approach to mourning. In short, there is a culture of grief which accepts that containing emotion works for some people, while expressing feeling is relevant for others. This is an approach which refuses to judge whether forgetting or remembering the dead is the healthier option. Rather ironically, suggests Walter, people do not know how to utilise their new-found freedom of expressing grief. There are all kinds of dilemmas. For instance, individuals may choose to grieve in private, but it is not always clear to others they know that this is the case (Walter 1999a, 141).

After-life beliefs

In much the same way as there are changing attitudes to mourning, after-life beliefs say something about recent cultural changes and shifting values in contemporary societies. The *European Values Survey* of 1981 and 1990 asked respondents whether they believed in life after death, and found those answering 'yes' constituted around 40 per cent of the sample: this figure has changed little over subsequent decades. However, surveys also contained more specific questions about what the after-life was supposed to actually entail. For example, it showed that whereas belief in heaven remained fairly buoyant (at around 30–50 per cent), belief in hell had definitely gone out of fashion (at around 15–25 per cent).

The *European Values Survey* data indicated that those who believe in an after-life tend to be religious according to other measurements. This is almost certainly the major single reason why the USA and Europe are so far out of line with each other on after-life beliefs: Europe is, by and large, a much more secular continent than North America. The other factor very clearly associated with after-life belief is gender: up to twice as many women as men say they believe in some kind of after-life (Davies 1997). Belief in an after-life may possibly also be related to stages in the life course. In the 1970s, Witzel (1975) conducted research in which he found far higher levels of belief in an after-life among those on their deathbeds than a control group of seriously but not fatally ill patients. Insofar as older people typically have higher levels of belief in a life after death, it is not clear whether this is because they have lived longer and are nearer death or because they were brought up in a more religious era.

Douglas Davies (1997) has identified five options of a possible after-life which respondents in the UK find fairly easy to choose between. In his study of 1603 individuals he identified the following distribution of beliefs: that nothing happens, we come to the end of life (29 per cent); our soul passes on to another world (43 per cent); our bodies await a resurrection (8 per cent); we come back as something or someone else (12 per cent); trust in God, all is in his hands (22 per cent). In Davies' survey 12 per cent of respondents appeared to believe in reincarnation, a belief traditionally alien to Western culture.

Other research has put such belief as high as 20 per cent when respondents answered 'yes' to the question 'Do you believe in reincarnation?'. In this case the pollsters presented those asked with the option of replying 'yes', 'no', or 'don't know' (Gallop and Proctor 1982, 137–38). Walter and Waterhouse (1998) found in their survey that those in the UK who answered the question 'yes' to whether they believe in reincarnation far outnumber those who belong to such religions as Hinduism, Sikhism and Buddhism which formally teach reincarnation or rebirth. Reincarnation, therefore, is not in most Western societies part of a well-established and communally held folk-religion. This means belief in reincarnation is not something that has been formally codified by the respondent's own culture and religion. These ideas are scarcely sophisticated and rarely seem to originate clearly in any world religion. Walter and Waterhouse also argue that after-life beliefs are becoming semi-detached from other religious beliefs and almost entirely detached from morality; hence there is no overriding fear of hell in retribution for actions in this life. In turn, this implies a choice and convergence of religious ideas which more than hint at the primary motifs of a pick 'n mix postmodernity.

Walter maintains that despite secularisation belief in an after-life remains buoyant. But for many people this belief is a tentative one, and the content of the after-life remains vague. For a fair number of young adults, it may be the case that they are refusing to rule out an after-life, although they would not go so far as to say they positively believe one actually exists. It is a generation which finds itself in the culture of relativism that is associated with postmodernity, one which does not trust religion but also no longer has faith in science and thus keeps an open mind on life after death (Walter 1999b).

SUMMARY

This chapter has explored various themes related to death. What might be concluded? It may well be that as the proportion of women and men in old age increases, it can be expected the culture of late/postmodernity will become more comfortable with the reality of death. Yet profound difficulty in coming to terms with human morality and inevitable death remains. As Cole notes (1993, 239), to negotiate the later stage of life 'successfully' is to fail to deliberately accommodate death and dying as anything other than sudden and painless death, and ambiguities and uncertainties are apparent in the emergent culture. Much in this respect is in stark contrast to how death has been perceived and socially constructed in human history. How death is approached, then, as the close of life, displays many of the changes and continuities evident throughout the contemporary life course at the beginning of the twenty-first century.

FURTHER READING

Cole, D. (1992) 'The Reversibility of Death', *Journal of Medical Ethics*, 18(1): 26–30.

Corr, C. and Corr, M. (2012) *Death & Dying, Life & Living,* seventh edition, Belmont, CA: Wadworth Publishing.

Dickenson, G. and Leming, M. (2013) *Annual Editions: Dying, Death, and Bereavement,* 14th Edition, New York: McGraw-Hill Education.

Erikson, E. (1998) *The Life Cycle Completed*, New York: Norton.

Gerstorf, D., Ram, N., Lindenberger, U. and Smith, J. (2013) 'Age and Time-to-Death Trajectories of Change in Indicators of Cognitive, Sensory, Physical, Health, Social, and Self-Related Functions', *Developmental Psychology,* 49(10): 1805–21.

Hockey, J., Katz, J. and Small, N. (eds.) (2001) *Grief, Mourning and Death Ritual.* Buckingham: Open University Press.

Howarth, G. (2007) *Death and Dying: A Sociological Introduction,* Oxford: Wiley.

Kearl, M. (1989) *Endings: A Sociology of Death and Dying: A Sociology of Death and Dying,* Oxford: Oxford University Press.

McNamara, B. (2001) *Fragile Lives*: *Death, Dying and Care,* Buckingham: Open University Press.

Miller, F. (2009) 'Death and Organ Donation: Back to the Future', *Journal of Medical Ethics,* 35(10): 616–20.

Penrod, J., Hupcey, J., Baney, B. and Loeb, S. (2010) 'End-of-Life Caregiving Trajectories', *Clinical Nursing Research,* 20(1): 7–24.

Tomer, A. (1992) 'Attitudes Toward Death in Adult Life-Theoretical Perspectives', *Death Studies,* 16, 475–506.

Walter, T. (1994) *The Eclipse of Eternity: Religion and Death in the Modern Era,* Basingstoke: Palgrave Macmillan.

———. (2006) 'Funerals: The Emerging Culture of Choice', in *A Good Funeral, vol. 14,* Solihull: Foundation of Lady Katherine Leveson, (Leveson Papers).

———. (2007) 'Modern Grief, Postmodern Grief', *International Review of Sociology,* 17 (1): 123–34.

———. (2012) 'Why Different Countries Manage Death Differently: A Comparative Analysis of Modern Urban Societies', *British Journal of Sociology,* 63 (1): 123–45.

References

Abrams, M. (1995) *The Teenage Consumer*, London: Routledge & Keegan Paul.

Acheson, D. (1998) *Inequalities in Health: Report of an iIdependent Inquiry*, London: HMSO.

Ahmad, S. and O'Mahony, M. (2005) 'Where Older People Die: A Retrospective Population-Based Study', *Quarterly Journal of Medicine*, 98(12): 865–70.

Ahrons, C. (2007) 'Family Ties After Divorce', *Family Process*, 46(1): 53–65.

Akande, A. (1994) 'The Glass Ceiling: Women and Mentoring in Management and Business', *Employee Counselling Today*, 6(1): 21–28.

Alan Guttmacher Institute (2010) *U.S. Teenage Pregnancies, Births and Abortions: National and State Trends and Trends by Race and Ethnicity*, New York: Alan Guttmacher Institute, accessed 11 May 2011.

———. (2012) 'Induced Abortion in the United States', www.guttmacher.org/pubs/fb_induced_abortion.html, accessed 17 September 2014.

Albee, G. (1982) 'The Politics of Nature and Nurture', *American Journal of Community Psychology*, 10(1): 1–36.

Alexander, C. (2006) *The Asian Gang: Ethnicity, Identity, Masculinity*, Oxford: Berg.

Allan, G. and Crow, G. (2001) *Families, Households and Society*, Basingstoke: Palgrave Macmillan.

Allan, G., Hawker, S. and Crow, G. (2001) 'Family Diversity and Change in Britain and Western Europe', *Journal of Family Issues*, 22(7): 819–37.

Allat, P., Keil, T., Bryman, A. and Bytheway, B. (eds.) (1987) *Women and the Life Cycle: Transitions and Turning Points, Explorations in Sociology*, Basingstoke: Palgrave Macmillan.

Almeida, D. (2009) 'Ask the Brains: Is Midlife Crisis a Myth?', *Scientific American MIND Magazine*, 27 January.

Almeida, D. and Wong, J. (2009) 'Life Transition and Stress: A Life Course Perspective on Daily Stress Processes', in G. Elder and J. Ziele (eds.), *The Craft of Life Course Research*, New York: Guilford Press.

Alwin, D., Hofer, S. and McCammon, R. (2006) 'Modeling the Effects of Time: Integrating Demographic and Developmental Perspectives', in R. Binstock and L. George (eds.), *Handbook of Aging and the Social Sciences*, New York: Academic Press.

Alwin, D. and Levenson, M. (2001) 'Stress, Coping, and Health at Midlife: A Developmental Perspective', in M. Lachman (ed.), *Handbook of Midlife Development*, New York: John Wiley.

Alwin D. and McCammon R. (2003) 'Generations, Cohorts and Social Change', in J. Mortimer and M. Shanahan (eds.), *Handbook of the Life Course*, New York: Kluwer Academic/Plenum.

Amit-Talai, V. and Wulff, H. (1995) *Cross-Cultural Studies of Contemporary Youth*, London and New York: Routledge.

Anderson, P. (1993) *Women and Unemployment: A Case Study of Women's Experiences of Unemployment in Glasgow*, PhD thesis, University of Warwick.

Anderson, W. and O'Hara, M. (1991) 'Welcome to the Postmodern World', *Networker*, September/October.

Arai, S. and Pedlar, A. (2003) 'Moving Beyond Individualism in Leisure Theory: A Critical Analysis of Concepts of Community and Social Engagement', *Leisure Studies*, 22(3): 185–202.

Arber, S. and Ginn J. (eds.) (1995) *Connecting Gender and Ageing: A Sociological Approach*, Buckingham: Open University Press.

Aries, P. (1965) *Centuries of Childhood*, London: Cape.

———. (1973) *Western Attitudes Towards Death: From the Middle Ages to the Present*, Baltimore, MD: Johns Hopkins Press.

Armstrong, E. (2003) *Conceiving Risk, Bearing Responsibility: Fetal Alcohol Syndrome and the Diagnosis of Moral Disorder*, Baltimore: Johns Hopkins University Press.

Arnett J. (2000) 'Emerging Adulthood - A Theory of Development From the Late Teens Through the Twenties', *American Psychologist*, 55(5): 469–80.

Arnett, J., Kloep, M., Hendry, L. and Janner, J. (2011) *Debating Emerging Adulthood: Stages or Process*, New York: Oxford University Press.

Arriaga, X. (2001) 'The Ups and Downs of Dating: Fluctuations in Satisfaction in Newly-Formed Romantic Relationships', *Journal of Personality and Social Psychology*, 80(5): 754–65.

Arriaga, X., Reed, J., Goodfriend, W. and Agnew, R. (2006) 'Relationship Perceptions and Persistance: Do Fluctuations in Perceived Partner Commitment Undermine Dating Relationships?', *Journal of Personality and Social Psychology*, 91(6): 1045–65.

Artazcos, L. and Rueda, S. (2007) 'Social Inequalities in Health Among the Elderly: A Challenge for Public Health', *Research Journal of Epidemiology Community Health,* 61(6): 466–67.

Assiter, A. (1996) *Enlightened Women: Modernist Feminism in a Postmodern Age*, London: Routledge.

Atchley, R. (1988) *The Sociology of Retirement*, Cambridge, MA: Shenkman.

Atkinson, J. (1985) 'The Changing Corporation', in D. Clutterbuck (ed.), *New Patterns of Work*, Aldershot: Gower.

Attias-Donfurt, C. and Arber, S. (2000) 'Equality and Solidarity Across the Generations', in C. Attias-Donfurt and S. Arber (eds.), *The Myth of Generational Conflict*, London: Routledge.

Attwood, F. (2006) 'Sexed Up: Theorizing the Sexualization of Culture', *Sexualities*, 9(1): 77–94.

Ball, S., Bowe, R. and Gerwitz, S. (1994) 'Market Forces and Parental Choice', in S. Tomlinson (eds.), *Educational Reform and Its Consequences*, London: IPPR/Rivers Omran Press.

Baltes, M. and Baltes, P. (1996) *The Psychology of the Control of Ageing*, Hillsdale, NJ: Eerlbuam.

Baltes, P., Reese, H. and Lipsitt, L. (1980) 'Life-Span Developmental Psychology', *Annual Review of Psychology*, 35(1): 65–110.

Bandura, A. (2002) 'Growing Primacy of Human Agency in Adaptation and Change in the Electronic Era', *European Psychologist, 7(1)*: 2–16.

———. (2006) 'Toward a Psychology of Human Agency', *Perspectives on Psychological Science,* 1(2): 164–80.

Banks, F., Daugherty, R. and Williams, M. (1992) *Continuing the Education Debate*, London: Cassell.

Baos, G. (1996) *The Cult of Childhood*, London: Warburg Institute.

Barash, D. (1983) *Ageing: An Exploration,* Seattle, WA: University of Washington Press.

Bardasi, E. and Jenkins, S. (2002) 'Risks of Old-Age Poverty for Those Retiring Early are Strongly Linked to Occupation', 29 April, Joseph Rowntree Foundation, www.jrf.org.uk/publications/work-history-and-income-later-life, accessed 4 April 2003.

Baudrillard, J. (1983) *Selected Writings,* Cambridge: Polity Press.

Bauman, Z. (1992) 'Is There a Postmodern Sociology?', *Theory, Culture and Society*, 5(2): 217–37.

———. (2000) *Liquid Modernity*, Cambridge: Polity Press.

———. (2001) *Liquid Love: On the Frailty of Human Bonds*, Cambridge: Polity Press.

———. (2011) *Collateral Damage: Social Inequalities in a Global Age*, Oxford: Wiley.

Beck, U. (1992) *Risk Society: Towards a New Modernity*, London: Sage.

Beck, U. and Beck-Gernsheim, E. (1996) *The Normal Chaos of Love*, Cambridge: Polity Press.

———. (2013) *Distant Love*, Oxford: Wiley.

Beck, U., Brater, M. and Jürgen, H. (1980) *Home: Sociology of Work and Occupations. Basics, Problem Areas, Research Results*, Verlag: Rowohlt.

Beechy, V. (1983) 'Women in Production', in A. Kuhn and A. Wolpse (eds.), *Feminism and Materialism*, London: Routledge & Kegan Paul.

Beidelman, T. (1966) 'The Ox and Nuer Sacrifice', *Man*, Series 1(4): 453–67.

Bell, D. and Blanchflower, D. (2010) 'UK Unemployment in the Great Recession', *National Institute Economic Review*, 214(1): 5161.

Bengston, L. (2001) 'Beyond the Nuclear Family: The Increasing Importance of Multi-Generational Bonds', *Journal of Marriage and the Family*, 63(1): 1–16.

Bengston, V. and Allen, K. (1993) 'The Life Course Perspective Applied to Families Over Time', in P. Boss, W. Doherty, R. Larossa, W. Schumm, and S. Steinmetz (eds.), *Sourcebook of Family Theories and Methods: A Contextual Approach*, New York: Plenum.

Bennett, F. (2014) 'Gender and Poverty in the UK: Inside the Household and Across the Life Course', 50.50 Inclusive Democracy, https://www.opendemocracy.net/5050/fran-bennett/gender-and-poverty-in-uk-inside-household-and-across-life-course, accessed 15 November 2014.

Bernard, M., Phillips, J., Phillipson, C. and Ogg, J. (1995) 'Family and Community Life of Older People', in S. Arber and J. Attias-Donfurt (eds.), *Connecting Gender and Ageing: A Sociological Approach*, Buckingham: Open University Press.

Bernstein, B. (1975) 'On the Classification and Framing of Education Knowledge', *Class Codes and Control*, vol.13, London: Routledge & Kegan Paul.

Besbrode, E. (2001) *Daily Telegraph*, 4th March.

Bjorklund, B. and Bee, H. (2008) *Journey of Adulthood*, New York: Pearson.

Blackwell D. and Lichter D. (2004) 'Homogamy Among Dating, Cohabiting, and Married Couples', *Sociological Quarterly*, 45(4): 719–37.

Blackenhorn, K. (1995) *Fatherless America*, Seattle, WA: University of Washington Press.

Blakemore, K. and Boneham, M. (1993) *Age, Race and Ethnicity. A Comparative Approach*, Buckingham: Open University Press.

Blakie, A. (1999) *Ageing and Popular Culture*, Cambridge: Cambridge University Press.

Blanchflower, D. and Oswald, A. (2008) 'Is Well-being U-Shaped Over the Life Cycle?', *Social Science and Medicine*, 69(4): 1733–49.

Blatterer, H. (2007) 'Reconceptualizing an Uncontested Category', *Current Sociology*, 55(6): 771–92.

Boulton, M. (1983) *On Being a Mother*, London: Tavistock.

Bourdieu, P. (1977) *Outline of a Theory of Practice*, Cambridge: Cambridge University Press.

Bowlby, J. (1944) 'Forty-Four Juvenile Thieves: Their Characters and Home Life', *International Journal of Psychoanalysis*, 25(19–52): 107–27.

———. (1969) *Attachment and Loss: Vol. 1. Loss*, New York: Basic Books.

Bradley, H. (1996) *Fractured Identities: Changing Patterns of Inequality*, Cambridge: Polity Press.

Brake, M. (1985) *Comparative Youth Culture: The Sociology of Youth Culture and Youth Subcultures in America, Britain and Canada*, Routledge: New York.

Branem, A. and Nilsen, A. (2002) 'Young People's Time Perspectives: From Youth to Adulthood', *Sociology*, 36(3): 513–57.

Brauer, J. and De Coster, S. (2015) 'Social Relationships and Delinquency: Revisiting Parent and Peer Influence During Adolescence', *Youth & Society*, 47(3): 374–94.

Bretherton, I. (1997) 'Bowlby's Legacy to Developmental Psychology', *Child Psychiatry and Human Development*, 28(1): 33–43.

Brim, O., Ryff, C. and Kessler, R. (2004) *How Healthy Are We?: A National Study of Well-being at Midlife*, Chicago: University of Chicago Press.

Brinkman, B., Rabenstein, K., Rosén, L. and Zimmerman, T. (2012) 'Children's Gender Identity Development: A Dynamic Negotiation between Conformity and Resiliency', *Youth and Society*, 65(5): 344–55.

Brown, L., Bulanda, J. and Lee, G. (2012) 'Transitions Into and Out of Cohabitation in Later Life', *Journal of Marriage and Family*, 74(4): 774–93.

Brown, S, Lamming, R., Bessant, J. and Jones, P., (2005) Strategic Operations Management, 2nd ed, Oxford: Butterworth Heinmann.

Brown, S., Van Hook J. and Glick, J. (2008) 'Generational Differences in Cohabitation and Marriage in the U.S.', *Population Research and Policy Review*, 27(5): 531–50.

Bullington, J. (2006) 'Body and Self: A Phenomenological Study on the Ageing Body and Identity', *British Medical Journal*, 32(1): 25–31.

Burgess, E. and Locke, H. (1953) *The Family: From Institution to Companionship*, New York: American Book Co.

Burgoyne, J. and D. Clark (1984) *Making a Go of It: Stepfamilies in Sheffield*, London, Routledge.

Busfield, J. and Paddon, M. (1977) *Thinking About Children: Sociology and Fertility in Post-War England*, Cambridge: Cambridge University Press.

Bryman, A. (1995) *Disney and His Worlds*, London: Routledge.

Byrne, A. and Carr, D. (2005) 'Caught in the Cultural Lag: The Stigma of Singlehood', *Psychological Inquiry*, 16(2): 84–91.

Calasanti T. and Kiecolt, K. (2007) 'Diversity Among Late-Life Couples', *Generations: Journal of the American Society on Aging*, 31(3): 10–17.

Calasanti, T. and Slevin, K. (2006) 'Introduction', in T. Calasanti and K. Slevin (eds.), *Age Matters: Re-aligning Feminist Theory*, New York: Routledge.

Campbell, L., Simpson, J., Boldry, J. and Rubin, H. (2010) 'Trust, Variability in Relationship Evaluations, and Relationship Progress', *Journal of Personal and Social Psychology*, 99(1): 14–31.

Cancian, F. (1987) *Love in America: Gender and Self Development*, Cambridge: Cambridge University Press.

Cappeliez, P., Beaupré, M. and Robitaille, R. (2008) 'Characteristics and Impact of Life Turning Points for Older Adults', *Ageing International*, 32(1): 54–64.

Cashmore, E. (1985) 'Rewriting the Script', *New Society*, 4, December: 7–8.

Castells, M. (1989) *The Information City*, Oxford: Blackwell.

———. (1996) The Rise of the Network Society, *The Information Age: Economy, Society and Culture Vol. I*, Cambridge, MA and Oxford: Blackwell.

———. (1997) *The Power of Identity, The Information Age: Economy, Society and Culture, Vol. II*, Cambridge, MA and Oxford: Blackwell.

Centers for Disease Control and Preventions, 'Health Statistics (2010) 'Marriage and Cohabitation in the United States: A Statistical Portrait Based on Cycle 6

(2002) of the National Survey of Family Growth', Vital and Health Studies series 23: 8, www.cdc.gov/nchs/data/series/sr_23/sr23_028.pdf, accessed 2 April 2014.

Centers for Disease Control and Preventions' Health Statistics (2012), 'Mortality in the United States', NCHS Data Brief, Number 168, Jiaquan Xu, M., Kenneth D., Kochanek, M., Sherry L, Murphy, B. and Arias, E. www.cdc.gov/nchs/data/databriefs/db168.htm, accessed 3 May 2015.

Centers for Disease Control and Prevention National Center (2013) 'Statistic Life Experience at Birth, 65, and 75, by Sex, Race, and Hispanic origin: United States selected years 1900–2010', Health United States, http://search.aol.co.uk/aol/search?q=university%20of%20the%20west%20of%20england&s_it=keyword_rollover&ie=UTF-8&VR=4086, accessed 19 June 2015.

Centers for Disease Control and Prevention, 'National Marriage and Divorce Rate Trends', www.cdc.gov/nchs/nvss/marriage_divorce_tables.htm, accessed 1 June 2016.

Center for the Study of Long Term Relationships (2005) 'Long Distance Relationship Frequently Asked Questions', www.longdistancerelationships.net/faqs.htm, accessed 24 July 2015.

Chamberlain, G. (2006) 'British Maternal Mortality in the 19th and Early 20th Centuries', *Journal of the Royal Society of Medicine*, 99(11): 559–63.

Chan, S. and Chan, K-W. (2011) 'Adolescents' Susceptibility to Peer Pressure: Relations to Parent–Adolescent Relationship and Adolescents' Emotional Autonomy From Parents', *Youth & Society,* 45(2): 286–302.

Cherlin, A. (2004) 'The Deinstitutionalizing of American Marriage', *Journal of Marriage and Family*, 66(4): 848–62.

Cherry, A. and Dillon, M. (2009) 'Teenage Pregnancy', Oxford Biographies, http://search.aol.co.uk/aol/search?q=Cherry%20%282009%29%20teeage%20pregnancy&s_it=keyword_rollover&ie=UTF-8&VR=4086, accessed 11 June 2012.

Chervenak, F. and McCullough, L. (2005) 'An Ethical Critique of Boutique Fetal Imaging: A Case for the Medicalization of Fetal Imaging', *Ultrasound in Obstetrics & Gynecology,* 192(1): 31–33.

———. (2005) 'An Ethical Critique of Boutique Fetal Imaging: A Case for the Medicalization of Fetal Imaging', *American Journal of Obstetrics and Gynecology,* 194(5): 31–33.

Chester, R. (1985) 'The Rise of the Neo-Conventional Family', *New Society* (May): 14–17.

Child Action Poverty Group (2013) 'Child Poverty Facts & Figures', www.cpag.org.uk/child-poverty-facts-and-figures, accessed 27 August 2015.

Chirumbolo, A. and Hellgren, J. (2013) 'Individual and Organizational Consequences of Job Insecurity: A European Study', *Economic and Industrial Democracy*, 24(2): 217–40.

Ciernia, J. (1995) 'Midlife Crisis in Men: Affective Organization of Personal Meanings', *Human Relations*, 52(11): 1403–26.

Claessens, A. and Ryan, R. (2003) 'Associations Between Family Structure Changes and Children's Behavior Problems: The Moderating Effects of Timing and Marital Birth', *Developmental Psychology*, 49(7): 1219–31.

Clark, J. and Critcher, C. (1985) *The Devil Makes Work: Leisure in Contemporary Britain*, Basingstoke: Palgrave Macmillan.

Clarke, L. (2006) 'Older Women and Sexuality: Experiences in Marital Relationships Across the Life Course', *Canadian Journal of Aging*, 25(2): 129–40.

Clay, R (2003) 'Researchers Replace Midlife Myths with Facts', *American Psychological Association*, 34(4): 36, www.apa.org/monitor/apr03/researchers. asp, accessed 23 March 2005.

Cohen, S. (1971) *Images of Deviance*, Harmondsworth: Penguin.

———. (1985) *Visions of Social Control: Crime, Punishment and Classification*, Cambridge: Polity Press.

Coker, T., Elliott, M., Kanouse, D., Grunbaum, J., Schwebel, D., Gilliland, M., Tortolero, S., Peskin, M. and Schuster, M. (2009) 'Perceived Racial/Ethnic Discrimination Among Fifth-Grade Students and Its Association With Mental Health', *American Journal of Public Health*, 99(5): 878–84.

Cole, D. (1993) 'Statutory Definitions of Death and The Management of Terminally Ill Patients Who May Become Organ Donars After Death', *Kennedy Institute of Ethics Journal*, 3(2): 145–55.

Cole, E. and Rothblum, E. (1991) 'Lesbian Sex At Menopause: As Good Or As Better As Ever', in B. Sang, J. Warshow and A. Smith (eds.), *Lesbians At Midlife: The Creative Transition*, San Francisco: Spinster Book Co.

Collishaw, S., Maughan, B., Goodman, R. and Pickles. A. (2004) 'Time Trends in Adolescent Mental Health', *Journal of Child Psychology Psychiatry*, 45(8): 1350–62.

Combi, C. (2015) *Generation Z: Their Voices, Their Lives,* London: Cornerstone.

Cooney, T. and Dunne, K. (2001) 'Intimate Relationships in Later Life: Current Realities, Future Prospects', *Journal of Family Issues*, 22(7): 838–58.

Cornwall, E. and Waite, L. (2009), 'Social Disconnectedness, Perceived Isolation, and Health among Older Adults', *Journal of Health and Social Behavior*, 50(1): 31–48.

Costa, P. and Macrae, R. (1980) 'Still Stable After All These Years: Personality as a Key to Some Issues in Adulthood and Old Age', in P. Baltes and G. Brim (eds.), *Life Span Behaviour,* New York: Academic.

Cote, E. and Allahar, A. (1996) *Generation on Hold: Coming of Age in the Late Twentieth Century*, New York: New York University Press.

Cowan, G. and Hoffman, C. (1986) 'Gender Stereotyping in Young Children: Evidence to Support a Concept-Learning Approach', *Sex Roles*, 14(3–4): 211–24.

Cowgill, D. and Holmes, L. (eds.) (1972) *Ageing and Modernization*, New York: Appleton-Century-Crofts.

Crawford, D., Jackson, E. and Godbey, G. (1991) 'A Hierarchical Model of Leisure Constraints', *Leisure Sciences*, 13(4): 309–19.

Crawford, R. (1980) *Healthism and the Medicalization of Everyday Life, Health,* 10(4): 401–20.

Croghan, R., Griffith, C. Hunter, J. and Phoenix, A. (2006) 'Style Failure: Consumption, Identity and Social Exclusion', *Journal of Youth Studies*, 9(4): 463–78.

Crompton, R. (1999) *Restructuring Gender*, Oxford: Oxford University Press.

Crooks, S., Pakulski, J. and Waters, M. (1992) 'A Hierarchal Model of Leisure Constraints', *Leisure Sciences*, 13(4): 309–19.

Crossley, M. (2007) 'Childbirth, Complications, and the Illusion of "Choice": A Case Study', *Feminism and Psychology*, 17(4): 543–63.

Crouch, S., Waters, E., McNair, R., Power J. and Davis, E. (2012) 'ACHESS – The Australian Study of Child Health in Same-Sex Families: Background Research, Design and Methodology', *Biomedicalcentral Public Health*, 12(1): 646, www.biomedcentral.com/1471-2458/12/646, accessed 19 April 2013.

Cumming, E. and Henry, W. (1961) *Growing Old: The Process of Disengagement*, New York: Basic Books.

Cunningham, H. (1995) *Children and Childhood in Western Society Since 1500*, London: Longman.

Dainton, M. (2000) 'Maintenance Behaviors, Expectations for Maintenance, and Satisfaction: Linking Comparison Levels to Relational Maintenance Strategies', *Journal of Social and Personal Relationships*, 17(6): 827–42.

Daly, J (1997) 'Facing Change', in P. Komesaroff, P. Rothfield and J. Daly (eds.), *Reinterpreting Menopause: Cultural and Philosophical Issues*, London: Routledge.

Davies, D. (1997) 'Contemporary Belief in Life After Death', in Jupp and T. Rogers (eds.), *Interpreting Death: Christian Theology and Pastoral Practice*, London: Cassell.

Davis-Floyd, R. (2004) *Birth as an American Rite of Passage*, 2nd edition, Berkeley, CA: University of California Press.

Deem, R. (ed.) (1980) *Schooling for Women's Work*, London: Routledge.

———. (1986) *All Work and No Play? The Sociology of Women and Leisure*, Milton Keynes: Open University Press.

De Grey, A. (2007) 'Life Span and Extension Research', *Studies in Ethics, Law, and Technology* 1 (1, Article 5), Methuselah Foundation, www.sens.org/files/pdf/ENHANCE-PP.pdf, accessed 13 January 2009.

Delcroix, C. (2000) 'The Transition of Life Stories from Ethnic Minority Fathers to Their Children', in S. Arber and J. Ginn (eds.), *Connecting Gender and Ageing: A Sociological Approach*, Buckingham: Open University Press.

Dellasega, C., Mastrian, K. (1995) 'The Process and Consequences of Institutionalising An Elder'. Western *Journal of Nursing Research*; 17: 123–140.

DeLucia, J. (1987) 'Gender Role Identity and Dating Behavior: What is the Relationship?', *Sex Roles*, 17(3): 153–61.

De Mauss, L. (1976) *The History of Childhood*, London: Souvenir Press.

Dennis, N. and Erdos, G. (1993) *Families Without Fatherhood*, London: Institute of Economic Affairs.

Department of National Statistics UK, (2013) 'Childhood, Infant and Prenatal Mortality in England and Wales, 2011', www.ons.gov.uk/ons/dcp171778_300596. pdf, accessed 12 September 2015.

Department of Work and Pensions (2015) 'Households Below Average Income: 1994/1995 to 2013/2014, https://www.gov.uk/government/statistics/households-below-average-income-19941995-to-20132014, accessed 20 June 2015.

Deutsch, N. and Theodorou, E. (2010) 'Aspiring, Consuming, Becoming: Youth Identity in a Culture of Consumption', *Youth & Society,* 4(2): 229–54.

Diller, V. (2011) 'Midlife Crisis: A Myth or a Reality in Search of a New Name?', *Psychology Today,* posted 7 April.

Dobash, S. and Dobash, S. (1980) *Violence Against Wives,* London: Open Books.

Doherty, M. (2009) 'When the Working Day is Through: The End of Work as Identity?', *Work Employment & Society,* 2(1): 84–101.

Douglas, J. (1964) *The Home and the School,* London: MacGibbon & Kee.

Douglas, M. (1966) *Purity and Danger,* London: Routledge.

Driver, S. (2008) *Queer Youth Cultures,* Albany, NY: University of New York Press.

Du Bois-Reymond, M. (1998) '"I Don't Want to Commit Myself Yet": Young People's Life Concepts', *Journal of Youth Studies,* 1(1): 63–79.

Duelli-Klein, R. (1989) *Infertility: Women Speak Out About Their Experiences of Reproductive Medicine,* London: Pandora.

Dunn, J. (2002) 'The Adjustment of Children in Stepfamilies: Lessons from Community Studies', *Child and Adolescent Mental Health,* 7(4): 154–61.

Edleson, J. (1999) 'Children's Witnessing of Adult Domestic Violence', *Journal of Interpersonal Violence,* 14(8): 839–70.

Eisenstadt, S. (1956) *From Generation to Generation,* Basingstoke: Collier-Macmillan.

Elder, G. (1974) *Children of the Great Depression: Social Change in Life Experience,* Chicago: University of Chicago Press.

———. (1985) *Life Course Dynamics,* Ithaca, NY: Cornell University Press.

———. (1994) 'Time, Human Agency, and Social Change: Perspectives on the Life Course', *Social Psychology Quarterly,* 57(1): 4–15.

———. (1998) 'The Life Course as Developmental Theory', *Child Development,* 69(1): 1–12.

Elder, G., Kirkpatrick Johnson, M. and R. Crosnoe (2003) 'The Emergence and Development of the Life Course Theory', in J. Mortimer and M. Shanahan (eds.), *Handbook of the Life Course* New York: Plenum.

Epstein, S. (2003) 'Sexualizing Governance and Medicalizing Identities', *Sexualities,* 6(2): 131–71.

Equality and Human Rights Commission, 'Sex and Power', www.equalityhuman-rights.com/about-us/our-work/key-projects/sex-and-power, accessed 3 January 2015.

Erikson, E. (1950) *Childhood and Society,* New York: Norton.

————. (1963) *Identity and the Life-Cycle,* London: Norton.

————. (1968) *Identity: Youth and Crisis,* New York, NY: Norton.

Ermisch, J. and Francesconi, M. (2002) 'Cohabitation in Great Britain: Not for Long, But Here to Stay', *Journal of the Royal Statistical Society*: Series A (Statistics in Society), 163(2): 153–71.

Esbensen, A.-A., Deschenes, E. and Winfree, L. (1999) 'Differences between Gang Girls and Gang Boys: Results from a Multisite Survey', *Youth & Society,* 31(1): 27–53.

Etaugh, C. and Liss, M. (1992) 'Home, School, and Playroom: Training Grounds for Adult Gender Roles', *Sex Roles,* 26 (3–4): 129–47.

Evans, M. (2003) *Love: An UnRomantic Discussion,* Oxford: Blackwell.

Evans, P. and Thane, T. (2012) *Sinners? Scroungers? Saints?: Unmarried Motherhood in Twentieth-Century England,* Oxford: Oxford University Press.

Eyde, D. and Lintner, V. (eds.) (1996) *Contemporary Europe,* Hemel Hempstead: Prentice Hall.

Fagin, L. and Little, M. (1984) *The Forsaken Families,* Harmondsworth: Penguin.

Family Policy Studies Centre (2009) 'The Older Generation: Caring for the Elderly', www.fpsc.org.uk/the-older-generation/, accessed 9 October 2013.

Featherstone, M. (1982) 'The Body in Consumer Culture', *Theory, Culture and Society,* 1(1): 18–33.

————. (1991) *Consumer Culture and Postmodernism,* London: Sage.

Featherstone, M. and Hepworth, M. (1991) 'The Mask of Ageing and the Postmodern Life Course', in M. Featherstone, M. Hepworth, and B. Turner (eds.), *The Body Process and Cultural Theory,* London: Sage.

Featherstone, M. and Wernick, A. (eds.) (1995) *Images of Ageing,* London: Routledge.

Federal Interagency Forum on Child and Family Statistics (2007), 'American Children: National Indicators of Well-being', www.childstats.gov/pdf/ac2007/ac_07.pdf, accessed 13 April 2012.

Fernandez-Ballesteros, R. (2011) 'Positive Ageing. Objective, Subjective, and Combined Outcomes', *Family Practice,* 10(4): 449–53.

Ferraro, K. and Shippee, T. (2009) 'Aging and Cumulative Inequality: How Does Inequality Get Under the Skin?', *Gerontologist,* 49(3): 333–43.

Ferreira, V. (2011) 'Becoming a Heavily Tattooed Young Body: From a Bodily Experience to a Body Project', *Youth & Society,* 46(3): 303–37.

Field, D., Hockey, J. and Small, N. (1997) *Death, Gender and Ethnicity,* London: Routledge.

Finn, L. (1998) 'It's for (Y)our Own Good: An Analysis of the Discourses Surrounding Mandatory, Unblinded HIV Testing and Newborns', *Journal of Medical Humanities,* 19(2–3): 133–62.

Foren, C. (2011) 'Continuity and Discontinuity: The Case of Second Couplehood in Old Age', The *Gerontologist,* http://gerontologist.oxfordjournals.org/content/early/2011/03/22/geront.gnr018.full.

Fowler, D. (1995) *The First Teenagers: The Lifestyle of Young Wage Earners in Interwar Britain*, The Woburn Press: London.

Freud, S. (1938) *Totem and Taboo*, Harmondsworth: Penguin.

Fruzzetti, L. (1982) 'Food and Worship Birth Rituals', *Journal of the Indian Anthropological Society*, 17(1): 13–31.

Funken, K. and Cooper, P. (eds.) (1995) *Old and New Poverty: The Challenge for Reform*, Buckinghamshire: Open University Press.

Furedi, F. (2001) *Paranoid Parenting: Why Ignoring the Experts May Be Best for Your Child,* London & New York; Continuum.

Furlong, A. and Cartmel F. (1997) 'Capitalism Without Classes', in A. Giddens (ed.), *Sociology: Introductory Readings*, Cambridge: Polity Press.

Gallop, C. and Proctor, W. (1982) *Adventures in Immortality*, New York: McGraw Hill.

Gannon, L. (1996) *Women and Ageing: Transcending the Myths*, London: Routledge.

Gergen. M. and Gergen, K. (2003) 'Positive Aging: Living Well is the Best Revenge', in J. Gubrium and A. Holstein (eds.), *Ways of Aging*, Malden, MA: Blackwell.

Ghail, M. (1995) *The Making of Men: Masculinities, Sexualities and Schooling*, Buckingham: Open University Press.

Giddens, A. (1991a) *Self-Identity. Self and Society in the Late Modern Age*, Cambridge: Polity Press.

———. (1991b) *The Consequences of Modernity*, Redwood, CA: Stanford University Press.

———. (1992) *The Transformation of Intimacy: Sexuality, Love and Eroticism in Modern Societies,* Stanford: Stanford University Press.

Giele, J. (1988) 'Gender and Sex Roles', in N. Smelser (ed.), *Handbook of Sociology*, Beverly Hills, CA: Sage Publications.

Giele, J. and Elder, G. (1998) *Methods of Life Course Research: Qualitative and Quantitative Approaches*, Thousand Oaks, CA: Sage.

Gilbert, D. (2007) *Stumbling on Happiness,* New York: Vintage Books.

Giroux, H. (1997) *Channel Surfing: Race Talk and The Destruction of Today's Youth*, Basingstoke: Palgrave Macmillan.

Glasner, B. and Strauss, A. (1965) *Awareness of Dying*, Chicago: Aldine.

Glendinning, E and Millar, J. (eds.) (1987) *Women and Poverty in Britain*, Brighton: Wheatsheaf.

Gluckman, M. (1963) *Essays in the Ritual of Social Relations*, Manchester: Manchester University Press.

Goetting, A. (1981) 'Divorce Outcome Research', *Journal of Family Issues*, 2(3): 350–78.

Goffman, E. (1967) *The Presentation of Self in Everyday Life*, Harmondsworth: Penguin.

Goldberg, S. and Lewis, M. (1972) 'Play Behaviour in the Infant: Early Sex Differences', in J. Bardwick (ed.), *Readings on the Psychology of Women*, New York: Harper & Row.

Golden, J. (2006) *Message in a Bottle: The Making of Fetal Alcohol Syndrome*, Cambridge, MA: Harvard University Press.

Goode, W. (1982) *The Family*, Englewood Cliffs, NJ: Prentice Hall.

Gorer, G. (1965) *Death, Grief, and Mourning in Contemporary Britain*, London: Cresset.

Gov.uk (nd) 'Parental Rights and Responsibilities', www.fnf.org.uk/law-and-information/parental-responsibility#faqnoanchor, accessed 3 April 2015.

Green, A., Hogarth, T. and Shackleton, R. (1990) *Long Distance Living: Dual Location Households,* Bristol: Policy Press.

Green, E., Hebron, S. and Woodward, D. (1990) *Women's Leisure. What Leisure?*, London: Palgrave Macmillan.

Greenfield, L. (2002) *Girl Culture*, San Francisco: Chronicle Books.

Griffin, C. (1985a) (ed.) *Typical Girls? Young Women from School to the Job Market*, London: Routledge & Kegan Paul.

———. (1985b) 'Adolescent Girls: Transitions From Girlfriends to Boyfriends', in C. Griffith (ed.), *'Typical Girls': Young Women From School to Job Market*, London: Routledge & Keegan Paul.

Grosswiler, P. (2010) *The Method is the Message: Rethinking McLuhan Through Critical Theory*, Bern: Peter Lang.

Guldner, G. (2003) *Long Distance Relationships: The Complete Guide*, Corona, CA: J. F. Milne Publications.

Gullette, M. (1997) *Declining to Decline: Cultural Combat and the Politics of the Midlife*, Age Studies, Charlottesville, VA: University of Virginia Press.

Guzzo, K. (2006) 'The Relationship Between Life Course Events and Union Formation', *Social Science Research*, 35(2): 384–08.

Gwartney-Gibbs P., Stockard, J. and Bohmer, S. (1987) 'Learning Courtship Aggression: The Influence of Parents, Peers, and Personal Experiences', *Family Relations: Journal of Applied Family & Child Studies,* 36(3): 276–82.

Habermas, J. (1984) *The Theory of Communicative Action,* vol. I: *Reason and the Rationalization of Society*, T. McCarthy (trans.), Boston: Beacon. [German, 1981, vol. 1].

Hagestad, G. (2003) 'Interdependent Lives and Relationships in Changing Times: A Life Course View of Families and Aging', in R. Settersten and J. Hendricks (eds.), *Invitation to the Life Course: Towards New Understandings of Later Life*, Amityville, NY: Baywood.

Hagestad, G. and Neugarten, B. (1985) 'Age and the Life Course', in R. Binstock and E. Shanas (eds.), *Handbook of Aging and the Social Sciences*, New York: van Nostrand Reinhold.

Haggard, L. and Williams, D. (1991) 'Self-Identity Benefits of Leisure Activities', in B. Driver, P. Brown and G. Peterson (eds.), *Benefits of Leisure*, Stage College, LA: Venturer Publishing.

Halbwachs, F. (1930) *Les Causes de Suicide*, Paris: Alcan.

Hall, S. and Jefferson, T. (eds.) (2006) *Resistance Through Rituals: Youth Subcultures in Post-War Britain*, London: Hutchinson.

Hamel, R. (1990) 'Raging Against Aging', *American Demographics*, 12(3): 42–45.

Hanson, M. and Lynch, E. (2013) *Understanding Families: Supportive Approaches to Diversity, Disability, and Risk* [online], second edition, London: Paul. H. Brookes Publishing Co.

Haque, A. (2013) 'Maintaining Trust in a Long Distance Relationship', *Expatriates Magazine*, 2(September): 21.

Haques, A. (2013) 'Maintaining Trust in a Long Distance Relationship', *Expatriates Magazine*, 2(September): 21.

Haraway, D. (2000) *A Cyborg Manifesto "Science, Technology and Socialist—Feminism in the Late Twentieth Century".* The Cybercultures Reader, Routledge: London.

Harden, A., Brunton, G., Fletcher, A., Oakley, A., Burchett, H. and Backhans, M. (2009) *Young People, Pregnancy and Social Exclusion: A Systematic Synthesis of Research Evidence to Identify Effective, Appropriate and Promising Approaches for Prevention and Support,* London: EPPI-Centre, Social Science Research Unit, Institute of Education, University of London.

Hareven, T. (ed.) (1996) *Aging and Generational Relations: Life Course and Cross-Cultural Perspectives*, New York: Aldine de Gruyter.

Hareven, T. and Trepagnier, B. (2008) *Families, History and Social Change: Life Course and Cross-Cultural Perspectives*, Boulder, CO: Westview Press.

Harvey, D. (1990) *The Condition of Postmodernity: An Enquiry into the Origins of Cultural Change*, Oxford: Wiley-Blackwell.

Havighurst, R. (1961) 'Successful Aging', *The Gerontologist*, 1(1): 8–13.

Hayman, S. (2001) *Moving On: Breaking Up Without Breaking Down*, New York: Vermillion.

Hayward, K. and Hobbs, D. (2007) 'Beyond the Binge in "Booze Britain": Market-Led Liminalization and the Spectacle of Binge Drinking', *The British Journal of Sociology*, 58(3): 437–56.

Heaphy, B. and Yip. A. (2006) 'Policy Implications of Ageing Sexualities', *Social Policy and Society*, 5(4): 443–51.

Heaphy, B., Yip, A. and Thompson, D. (2003) *Lesbian, Gay and Bisexual Lives Over 50*, Nottingham: York House Publications.

Hearn, J. (1995) 'Imagining the Aging of Men', in M. Featherstone and A. Wernick (ed.), *Images of Ageing,* London: Routledge.

Heidensohn, F. (1985) *Women and Crime*, London: Palgrave Macmillan.

Heinz, W. (2002) 'Transition Discontinuities and the Biographical Shaping of Early Work Careers', *Journal of Vocational Behavior*, 60(2): 220–40.

———. (2003) 'Combining Methods in Life-Course Research: A Mixed Blessing?'. in W. Heinz and V. Marshall (eds.), *Social Dynamics of the Life Course. Transitions, Institutions and Interrelations*, New York: Aldine de Gruyter.

Henwood, F. and Miles, I. (1987) 'Unemployment and the Sexual Division of Labour', in D. Fryer and P. Ullah (eds.), *Unemployed People*, Buckingham: Open University Press.

Hepworth, M. (2000) *Stories of Ageing,* Buckingham: Open University Press.

Hepworth, M. and M. Featherstone (1980) 'The Mid Life Phase', in G. Cohen (ed.), *Social Change and the Life Course*, London: Tavistock.

———. (1985) 'The History of the Male Menopause: 1848–1936', *Maturitas*, 7(3), 249–57.

Hetherington, M. and Kelly, J. (2002) *For Better or For Worse: Divorce Reconsidered*, New York : W.W. Norton

Her Majesty's Stationary Office Poverty Site (2010) www.poverty.org.uk/, accessed 22 July 2014.

Hermans, H. and Oles, P. (1999) 'Midlife Crisis in Men: Affective Organization of Personal Meanings', *Human Relations*, 52(11): 1403–26.

Hernandez, D. (2004) 'Demographic Change and the Life Circumstances of Immigrant Families', *Future of Children,* 14(2): 17–47.

Herrera, L., and Bayat, A. (2010) *Being Young and Muslim: New Cultural Politics in the Global South and North*, Oxford: Oxford University Press.

Hetherington, M. (1991) 'Coping With Family Transitions: Winners, Losers and Survivors', in M. Woodhead, P. Light and R. Carr (eds.), *Growing Up in a Changing Society,* London: Routledge.

Hetherington, M. & Kelly, J. (2002) *For Better or For Worse: Divorce Reconsidered*, New York: W.W. Norton.

Hetherington, M. and Kelly, J. (2003) *For Better or for Worse: Divorce Reconsidered,* New York: W. W. Norton & Company.

Hey, V. (1997) 'Even Sociologists Fall in Love: An Exploration in the Sociology of Emotion', *Sociology*, 27(2): 37–53.

Higa, D., Hoppe, M., Lindhorst, T., Mincer, S., Beadnell, B., Morrison, D., Wells, E., Todd, A. and Mountz, S. (2012) 'Negative and Positive Factors Associated With the Well-Being of Lesbian, Gay, Bisexual, Transgender, Queer, and Questioning (LGBTQ) Youth', *Youth & Society,* 46(5): 663–87.

Higgins, G., Piquero, N. and. Piquero, A. (2010) 'General Strain Theory, Peer Rejection, and Delinquency/Crime', *Youth & Society,* 43(4): 1272–97.

Higgs, P. and Gilleard, C. (2015) *Theorising the Fourth Age*, Basingstoke: Palgrave Macmillan.

Hill, J. (1977) *The Social and Psychological Impact of Unemployment*, London: Tavistock.

Hislop, J. and Arber, S. (2003) 'Sleepers Wake! The Gendered Nature of Sleep Disruption Among Mid-life Women', *Sociology* 37(4): 696–711.

Hockey, J. and James, A. (1993) *Growing Up and Growing Old. Ageing and Dependency in the Life Course,* London: Sage.

Hodkinson, P. (2011) 'Ageing in a Spectacular 'Youth Culture', *The British Journal of Sociology*, 62(2): 262–82.

Hodkinson, P. and Bennett, A. (2013) *Ageing and Youth Cultures: Music, Style and Identity*, London: Bloomsbury Publishing.

Holgate H., Evans R. and Yuen F. (2006) *Teenage Pregnancy and Parenthood: Global Perspectives, Issues and Interventions*, London: Routledge.

Holland, P., Berney, L., Blane, D., Smith, G., Gunnell, D. and Montgomery, S. (2000) 'Life Course Accumulation of Disadvantage: Childhood Health and Hazard Exposure During Adulthood', *Social Science & Medicine*, 50(9): 1285–95.

Holloway, S. and Valentine, G. (2000) 'Spatiality and the New Social Studies of Childhood', *Sociology*, 34(4): 763–83.

Holmes, J. and Kierman, K. (2010) *Fragile Families in the UK: Evidence from the Millennium Cohort Study*, draft version, University of Manchester and York, https://www.york.ac.uk/media/spsw/documents/research-and-publications/HolmesKiernan2010FragileFamiliesInTheUKMillenniumCohort.pdf, accessed 20 March 2011.

Holmstrom, D. (1994) 'Abuse of Elderly, Even by Adult Children, Gets More Attention and Official Concern', *Christian Science Monitor*, 29(July): 1.

Hubley, A. and Russell, L. (2009) 'Prediction of Subjective Age, Desired age, and Age Satisfaction in Older Adults: Do Some Health Dimensions Contribute More Than Others?', *International Journal of Behavioral Development*, 33(1): 12–21.

Hughes, M. and Waite, L. (2009) 'Marital Biography and Health at Mid-Life', *Journal of Health and Social Behavior*, 50(3): 344–58.

Huyck, M. (1999) *Handbook of Counseling and Psychotherapy with Older Adults*, New York: Wiley.

Hwang, C. (1989) 'The Changing Role of Swedish Fathers', in M. Lamb (ed.), *The Father's Role: Cross-Cultural Perspectives*, Hillsdale, NJ: Erlbaum.

Illich, I. (1975) *Medical Nemesis*, London: Calder & Boyars.

Innes, S. and Scott, G. (2003) "After I've Done the Mum Thing": Women, Care and Transitions', *Sociology Research Online*: 8(4).

Jackson, R. and Nesbitt, E. (1993) *Hindu Children in Britain,* Stoke-on-Trent: Trentham Books.

Jackson, S. and Scott, S. (2004) 'Anxiety, Excess and Desire: Antimonies of Sexuality in Late Modernity', *Sexualities,* 7(2): 233–48.

Jagger, E. (1993) 'Marketing Molly and Melville: Dating in a Postmodern, Consumer Society', *Sociology*, 35(1): 39–57.

Jameson, F. (1991) 'Postmodernism, or the Cultural Logic of Late Capitalism', in T. Docherty (ed.), *Postmodernism: A Reader*, New York: Harvester Wheatsheat.

Jamieson, L. (2011) 'Intimacy as a Concept: Explaining Social Change in the Context of Globalisation or Another Form of Ethnocentricism?', *Sociological Research Online*, 16(4), http://www.socresonline.org.uk/16/4/15.html, accessed 17 July 2012.

Jaques, E. (1965) 'Death and the Midlife Crisis', *International Journal of Psychoanalysis*, 46: 502–14.

Jeffrey, C. and Mcdowell, L. (2004) 'Youth in a Comparative Perspective: Global Change, Local Lives', *Youth & Society*, 36(2): 131–42.

Jeffries, M. (2011) *Thug Life: Race, Gender, and the Meaning of Hip-Hop*, Chicago: University of Chicago Press.

Jenks, C. (1996) *Childhood*, London: Routledge.

Johanson, R., Newburn, M. and Macfarlane, A. (2002) 'Has the Medicalisation of Childbirth Gone Too Far?', *British Medical Journal*, 324(7342): 892–95.

Jones, R., Dick, A., Coyl-Shephered, D. and Ogletree, M. (2012) 'Antecedents of the Male Adolescent Identity Crisis: Age, Grade, and Physical Development', *Youth Society*, 46(4): 443–59.

Joseph Rowntree Foundation (2002) 'Public Policy Initiatives For Older Workers', (P. Taylor), www.jrf.org.uk/publications/public-policy-initiatives-older-workers, accessed 27 May 2013.

Judd, F., Hickey, M. and Bryan, C. (2012) 'Depression and Midlife: Are We Overpathologising the Menopause?', *Journal of Affective Disorders,* 136(3): 199–211.

Jung, C. (1971) *Psychological Types* (Collected Works of C.G. Jung, Volume 6), Princeton, NJ: Princeton University Press.

Kalish, R. (1979) 'The New Ageism and the Failure Models: A Polemic', *The Gerontologist*, 19(4): 398–402.

Kalter (1990) *Growing Up With Divorce: Helping Your Child Avoid Immediate and Later Emotional Problems,* New York: Free Press.

Karp, D. and Yoel, C. (1982), 'The New Ageism and the Failure Models: A Polemic', *The Gerontologist*, 19(4), 398–402.

Kastenbaum, R. (1971) 'Age: Getting There', *Psychology Today*, 5(7), 53–54, 82–83.

Katz, S. (1995) 'Imagining the Life-Span. From Pre-modern Miracles to Post-Modern Fantasies', in M. Featherstone and A. Wernick (eds.), *Images of Ageing: Cultural Representations of Later Life*, New York: Routledge.

Kaufman, S. (1978) *The Ageless Self,* Madison, WI: University of Wisconsin Press.

Kidd, S., Eskenazi, B. and Wyrobek, A. (2001) 'Effects of Male Age on Semen Quality and Fertility: A Review of the Literature', *Fertility and Sterility*, 75(2): 237–48.

Kindon, D. (2001) *Too Much of a Good Thing*, Harvard, MA: Harvard University Press.

Kingston, B., Huizinga, D. and Elliott, D. (2009) 'Test of Social Disorganization Theory in High-Risk Urban Neighborhoods', *Youth & Society,* 41(1): 53–79.

Kirk, J. and Wall, C. (2012) 'When the Working Day is Through: The End of Work as Identity', *Work Employment & Society*, 23(1): 84–101.

Knopp, K, Rhoades, G., Stanley, S. and Markham, H. (2014) 'Stuck On You: How Dedication Moderates the Way Constraints Feel', *Journal of Social and Personal Relationship*, 32(1): 119–37.

Kohli, M. (1988) 'The World We Forgot: A Historical View of the Life Course', in V. Marshal (ed.), *Later Life: The Social Psychology of Ageing*, London: Sage.

Kohn, M. and Schooler, C. (1982) 'Jobs Conditions and Personality', *American Journal of Sociology*, 87(6): 39–65.

Komesaroff, A., Rothfield, P. and Daly J. (1997) (eds.) *Reinterpreting Menopause: Cultural and Philosophical Issues*, London: Routledge.

Koren, C. and Lowenstein, A. (2008) 'Late-Life Widowhood and Meaning in Life', *Ageing International*, 32(2): 140–55.

Kosten, P., Scheier, L. and Grenard, J. (2012) 'Latent Class Analysis of Peer Conformity: Who Is Yielding to Pressure and Why?', *Youth & Society*, 45(1): 565–90.

Kotecha, M., Arthur, S. and Coutinho, S. (2013) *Understanding the Relationship between Pensioner Poverty and Material Deprivation*, Research Report 827, Department for Work and Pensions.

Kotter-Grühn, D. and Hess, T. (2012) 'So You Think You Look Young?: Matching Adults' Subjective Ages With Age Estimations Provided By Young, Middle-Aged and Older Adults', *International Journal of Behavioral Development*, 36(2): 468–75.

Krahn, H., Howard, A. and Galambos, N. (2015) 'Exploring or Floundering? The Meaning of Employment and Educational Fluctuations in Emerging Adulthood', *Youth and Society*, 47(2): 245–66.

Kübler-Ross, E. (1969) *On Death and Dying. What the Dying Have to Teach Doctors, Nurses, Clergy and Their Own Families*, New York: Scribner.

Kuh, D., Head, J., Hardy, R., and Wadsworth, M. (1997) 'The Influence of Education and Family Background on Women's Earnings in Midlife: Evidence from a British National Birth Cohort Study', *British Journal of Sociology of Education*, 18(3): 385–405.

Kuhn, M. (1960) 'Self Attitudes by Age, Sex, and Professional Training', *Sociological Quarterly*, 1(1): 39–65.

Kukla, R. (2005) *Mass Hysteria: Medicine, Culture, and Mothers' Bodies*, Lanham, MD: Rowman & Littlefield.

Kurlychek, R. and Trenner, S. (1982) 'Accuracy of Perception and Attitude: An Intergenerational Investigation', *Perceptual and Motor Skill*, 54(1): 271–74.

Lachman, M. (2001) 'Introduction', in M. Lachman (ed.), *Handbook of Midlife Development*, New York: John Wiley and Sons.

Lachman, M. and James, J. (eds.) (1997) *Multiple Paths of Midlife Development*, Chicago: University of Chicago Press.

La Follette, M. (1996) *A Guide to Family Law,* London: Butterworth.

Laing, R. (1976) *The Politics of the Family*, Harmondsworth: Penguin.

Lamb, M. (ed.) (1987) 'Introduction', *The Father's Role: Cross-Cultural Perspectives*, Hilldale, NJ: Erlbaum.

Lambley, P. (1995) *The Middle-Aged Rebel: Responding to the Challenges of Midlife*, New York: Element Book.

Lancy, D. (2014) *The Anthropology of Childhood*: Cherubs, Chattel, Changelings, second edition, Cambridge: Cambridge University Press.

La Rossa, R. (1988) 'Fatherhood and Social Change', *Family Relations*, 37(4): 451–57.

Laslett, P. (1987) 'The Emergence of the Third Age', *Ageing and Society*, 7(2): 113–60.

Latouche, S. (1996) *The Westernization of the World: Significance, Scope and Limits of the Drive Towards Global Uniformity*, Oxford: Wiley.

Laumann-Billings, L. & Emery , R. (2000) 'Distress Among Young Adults From Divorced Families', *Journal of Family Psychology*, 14, 671–87.

Laurance, J. (1986) 'Unemployment: Health Hazards', *New Society*, 21 March: 23–26.

Leach, R. Phillipson, C. and Biggs, S. (2013) 'Baby Boomers, Consumption and Social Change: The Bridging Generation?', *International Review of Sociology*, 23(1): 104–22.

Lees, S. (1993) *Sugar and Spice: Sexuality and Adolescent Girls*, London: Penguin.

Leonard, D. (1980) *Sex and Generation: A Study of Courtship and Weddings*, London: Tavistock.

Leridon, H. (2004) 'Can Assisted Reproduction Technology Compensate for the Natural Decline in Fertility with Age? A Model Assessment', *Human Reproduction*, 19(7): 1548–53.

Levinson, D. (1977) 'The Mid-life Transition: A period in Adult Psychosocial Development', *Psychiatry, Journal for the Study of Interpersonal Processes*, 40(2): 99–112.

Levinson, D., Darrow. C, Klein, C., Levinson, M. and Braxton, B. (1978) *The Seasons of a Man's Life*, New York: Alfred A.Knopf.

Lewis, C. and Lamb, M. (2007) 'Understanding Fatherhood. A Review of Recent Research', Joseph Rowntree Foundation, www.jrf.org.uk/sites/files/jrf/under-standing-fatherhood.pdf, accessed 14 March 2013.

Lewontin, R. (1992) *Biology as Ideology: The Doctrine of DNA*, New York: Harper.

Li, Y. (2014) 'Understanding the Dynamics of Ethnic Identity and Inequality in the UK', Centre on Dynamics of Ethnicity, Economic and Social Research Council, www.esrc.ac.uk/my-esrc/grants/ES.K002198.1/outputs/Read/fc9cc967–5520-49e4-a0c7-8ea72d742f54, accessed 13 November 2014.

Lichter, D. and Qian Z. (2008) 'Serial Cohabitation and the Marital Life Course', *Journal of Marriage and Family*, 70(4): 861–78.

Lindau, S., Schumm, L., Laumanm, E., Levinson, W., Muircheartaigh and Waite, L. (2007) 'A Study of Sexuality and Health among Older Adults in the United States', *New England Journal of Medicine*, 23(8): 762–74.

Linn, M., Sandifer, R. and Stein, S. (1985) 'Effects of Unemployment on Mental and Physical Health', *American Journal of Public Health*, 75(5): 502–06.

Lund, D. (1989) 'Conclusions About Bereavement in Later Life and Implications for Interventions and Future Research', in D. Lund (ed.), *Older Bereaved Spouses: Research With Practical Implications*, London: Taylor-Francis-Hemisphere.

Lundy, A. and Rosenberg, J. (1987) 'Androgyny, Masculinity, and Self-esteem', *Social Behavior and Personality*, 15(1): 91–95.

Luppa, M., Luck, T., Weyerer, S., König, H-H., Brähler, E. and Riedel-Heller, S. (1998) 'Prediction of Institutionalization in the Elderly. A Systematic Review', *Journal of Aging Studies*, 12(2): 167–84.

Lynott, P. and Logue, P. (1993) 'The "Hurried Child": The Myth of the Lost Childhood on Contemporary Society', *Sociological Forum*, 8(3): 471–91.

Lyon, D. (2000) *Jesus in Disneyland: Religion in Postmodern Times*, Oxford: Polity.

Lyotard, J. (1984) *The Postmodern Condition: A Report*, Minneapolis, MN: Minnesota University Press.

MacDorman, M., Mathews, T. and Declercq, E. (2014) 'Trends in Out-of-Hospital Births in the United States, 1990–2012', *NCHS Data Brief*, 144, March, www.cdc.gov/nchs/data/databriefs/db144.htm, accessed 5 November 2015.

Macionis, J. and Plummer, K. (1997) *Sociology: A Global Introduction*, London: Prentice Hall.

Maddox, G. (1968) 'Persistence of Life Style Among the Elderly: A Longitudinal Study of Patterns of Social Activity in Relation to Life Satisfaction', in B. Neugarten (ed.), *Middle Age and Aging: A Reader in Social Psychology*, Chicago: University of Chicago Press.

Malinowski, A. (1954) *Magic, Science and Religion*, London: Souvenir Press.

Mallier, T. and Shafto, T. (1994) 'Flexible Retirement and the Third Age', *International Journal of Manpower*, 15(1): 38–54.

Marshall, B. (2002) '"Hard Science": Gendered Constructions of Sexual Dysfunction in the "Viagra Age"', *Sexualities*, 5(2): 131–58.

Marshall, D. (2010) *Understanding Children as Consumers*, London: Sage.

Marsiglio, W. (ed.) (1995) *Fatherhood: Contemporary Theory, Research, and Social Policy*, Thousand Oaks: Sage.

Martens, L. (2000) *Exclusion and Inclusion: The Gender Composition of British and Dutch Work Forces*, Aldershot: Avebury.

Martin, C., Wood, C. and Little, J. (1990) 'The Development of Gender Stereotype Components', *Child Development*, 61(6): 1891–1904.

Martinson, A., Vaughn, M. and Scheartz, N. (2002) 'Women's Experience of Leisure: Implications for Design', *New Media & Society*, 4(1): 29–49.

Matza, D. (1964) *Delinquency and Drift*, New Jersey: Transaction Publishers.

May, R. (1996) *The Meaning of Anxiety*, New York: Norton.

Mayall B. (2002) *Towards a Sociology for Childhood: Thinking from Children's Lives*, Milton Keynes: Open University Press.

McCartan, K. (2010) 'Media Constructions and Reactions to, Paedophilia in Modern Society', in K. Harrison (ed.), Dealing with High-Risk Sex Offenders in the Community: Risk Management, Treatment and Social Responsibilities, Cullompton: Willan 248–68.

McClelland, A. (2000) *Impact of Poverty on Children*, Brotherhood Comment: Brotherhood of St. Lawrence.

McLuhan, M. (2003) [1964] *Understanding the Media: The Extensions of Man*, Berkeley, CA: Gingko Press.

McMunn, A., Bartley, M., Hardy, R. and Kuh, D. (2006) 'Life Course Social Roles and Women's Health in Mid-life: Causation or Selection', *Journal of Epidemiology Community Health*, 60(6): 484–89.

McRobbie, A. (1978) *Jackie, An Ideology of Adolescent Femininity*, Oxford: Oxford University Press.

McRobbie, A. and Garber, J. (1976) 'Girls and Subcultures', in S. Hall and T. Jefferson (eds.), *Resistance Through Rituals: Youth Subcultures in Post-War Britain*, London: Hutchinson.

Mead, M. (1931) *The Coming of Age in Samoa*, New York: Morrow.

Mellor, P. and Shilling, C. (1993) 'Modernity, Self-Identity and the Sequestration of Death', *Sociology*, 27(3): 411–31.

Menon, U. (2001) 'Middle Adulthood in Cultural Perspective: The Imagined and Experienced in Three Cultures', in M. Lachman (ed.), *Handbook of Midlife Development*, New York: John Wiley.

Mental Health Foundation, 'Work-Life Balance', www.mentalhealth.org.uk/help-information/mental-health-a-z/w/work-life-balance/, accessed 3 September 2015.

Merton, R. (1969) *Social Theory and Structure*, New York: Free Press.

Miller, A. and Sassler, S. (2012) 'The Construction of Gender Among Working-Class Cohabiting Couples', *Qualitative Sociology*, 35(4): 427–46.

Mills, C.W. (1951) *White Collar: The American Middle-Classes*, New York: Open University Press.

Mills, R. (2000) 'Perspectives of Childhood', in J. Mills and R. Mills (eds.), *Childhood Studies: A Reader in Perspectives of Childhood*, Routledge: London.

Mindful Charity (nd) Better Future for Children, www.healthinharmony.com/mindful-charity-launch-a-better-future-for-childrens-mental-health, accessed 12 September 2015.

Ming-Ling Chong, A., Woo, J. and Yui-Huen Kwan, A. (2006) 'Positive Ageing: The Views of Middle-Aged and Older Adults in Hong Kong', *Ageing and Society*, 26(2): 243–65.

Mitchell, B. (2003) 'Life Course Theory', International Encyclopedia of Marriage and Family, www.encyclopedia.com/doc/1G2-3406900275.html, accessed 4 June 2008.

Mizen, P. (2003) 'The Best Days of Your Life?: Youth, Policy and Blair's New Labour', *Critical Social Policy*, 23(4): 453–76.

Monea, E. and Sawhillin, I. (2009) 'Simulating the Effect of the "Great Recession" on Poverty', *Brookings*, 10 September.

Morgan, D. (1986) 'Gender', in R. Burgess (ed.), *Social Theory and the Family*, London: Routledge & Keegan Paul.

————. (2011) 'Locating "Family Practices"', *Sociological Research Online*, 16(4).

Morris, D. (1998) *Illness and Culture in the Postmodern Age*, London: University of California Press.

Muggleton, D. (2005) 'From Classlessness to Clubculture: A Genealogy of Post-War British Youth Cultural Analysis', *Young*, 13(2): 205–19.

Myers-Briggs, D. (1998) 'Adulthood's Ages and Stages', *Psychology*, 5: 196–97.

National Assessment of Educational Progress (2013) http://nces.ed.gov/nationsre portcard/subject/publications/main2013/pdf/2014451.pdf, accessed 4 September 2015.

National Center for Health Statistics (2002) 'Cohabitation, Marriage, Divorce and Remarriage in the United States', www.cdc.gov/nchs/data/series/sr_23/sr23_022. pdf, 4 September 2015.

Natcent Social Research (2014) 'Child Poverty Transitions: Exploring the Routes Into and Out of Poverty 2009 to 2012', https://www.gov.uk/government/uploads/ system/uploads/attachment_data/file/436482/rr900-child-poverty-transitions. pdf, accessed 18 May 2015.

National Health Service Pregnancy, UK, 'Birth and Beyond for Dads and Partners', www.nhs.uk/conditions/pregnancy-and-baby/pages/dad-to-be-pregnant-partner. aspx#close, accessed 14 June 2015.

NatCen Social Research (2014) 'Predicting Wellbeing', www.natcen.ac.uk/ media/205352/predictors-of-wellbeing.pdf, accessed 17 April 2015.

National Assessment of Educational Progress (2013) http://nces.ed.gov/nationsre portcard/subject/publications/main2013/pdf/2014451.pdf, accessed 20 August 2015.

National Marriage Project, Rutgers Universe (2002) http://nationalmarriagepro ject.org/wp-content/uploads/2013/01/ShouldWeLiveTogether.pdf, accessed 13 June 2015.

Nauright, J. and Chandler, T. (1997) *Making Men: Rugby and Masculine Identity*, London: Frank Cass.

Nayak, A. and Kehily, M. (2013) *Gender, Youth and Culture: Young Masculinities and Femininities*, Basingstoke: Palgrave Macmillan.

Negru, O. (2012) 'The Time of Your Life. Emerging Adulthood Characteristics in a Sample of Romanian High-School and University Students', *Cognition, Brain, Behavior. An Interdisciplinary Journal*, XVI(3): 357–67.

Neugarten, B. (1964) *Personality in Middle and Late Life*,

————. (1965) *Norms, Age Constraints, and Adult Socialization*, Glenview, IL: Scott: Foreman.

————. (1971) 'Growing Older With Me: The Best is Yet to Be', *Psychology Today*, 5(2): 45–8.

————. (1973) 'Personality and Aging', in J. Birren and K. Warner Schael (eds.), *Handbook of the Psychology of Aging*, New York: Uan Nostrand Reinhold.

Neugarten, B. and Weinstein, K. (1964) 'The Changing American Grandparent', *Journal of Marriage and the Family*, 26(8): 199–204.

Newman, K. and Aptekar, S. (2007) 'Sticking Around: Delayed Departure From Parental Nest in Western Europe', in S. Danziger and C. Rouse (eds.), *The Price of Independence: The Economics of Early Adulthood*, New York: Russell Sage.

Nimrod, G. and Kleiber D. (2007) 'Reconsidering Change and Continuity in Later Life: Toward an Innovation Theory of Successful Aging', *International Journal of Aging and Human Development*, 65(1): 1–22.

Nuland, S. (1994) *How We Die: Reflections on Life's Final Chapter*, New York: A.A. Knopf.

Oakley, A. (1980) *Women Confined: Towards a Sociology of Childbirth*, London: Robertson.

Office for National Statistics, 'Household Income and Expenditure'. www.ons.gov.uk/ons/taxonomy/index.html?nscl=Household+Income+and+Expenditure, accessed 13 July 2014.

Office for National Statistics (2013) 'Estimates of the Very Old (including Centenarians) for England and Wales, United Kingdom, 2002 to 2013', www.ons.gov.uk/ons/rel/mortality-ageing/estimates-of-the-very-old--including-centenarians-/2002---2013--england-and-wales--united-kingdom-/stb-2002-2013-estimates-of-the-very-old.html, accessed 19 June 2015.

Office of Population, Census and Surveys, (1990) 'Labour Force Survey', http://www.ons.gov.uk/ons/guide-method/method-quality/specific/labour-market/labour-market-statistics/volume-5---2009.pdf, accessed 20 September 2001.

O'Rand, A. (1996) 'The Precious and the Precocious: Understanding Cumulative Disadvantage and Cumulative Advantage over the Life Course', *The Gerontologist*, 36(2): 230–38.

Orlofsky, J. (1977) 'Sex Role Orientation, Identity Formation, and Self-esteem in College Men and Women', *Sex Roles,* 3(2): 561–74.

Orth, U., Trzesniewski, K. and Robins, R. (nd.) 'Self Esteem Development From Young Adulthood to Old Age, A Cohort-Sequential Longitudinal Study', *Personality Processes and Individual Differences*, www.apa.org/pubs/journals/releases/psp-98-4-645.pdf, accessed 23 February 2001.

Pahl, R. (1984) *Divisions of Labour,* Oxford: Blackwell.

Palmer, P., MacInnis, T. and Kenway, G. (2007) 'Monitoring Poverty and Social Exclusion', New Policy Institute, Joseph Rowntree Foundation.

Parker, S. (1973) *The Future of Work and Leisure*, Oxford: Blackwell.

Parkes, C., Benjamin, B. and Fitzgerald (1969) 'Broken Heart: A Statistical Study of Increased Mortality among Widowers', *British Medical Journal*, 1(5646): 740–43.

Parris, L., Varjas, K., Meyers, J. and Cutts, H. (2011) 'High School Students' Perceptions of Coping With Cyberbullying', *Youth & Society*, 44(2): 284–306.

Parry, B., Brown, T, and Dyck, I. (eds.) (2015) *The Global Circulation of Body Parts, Medical Tourists and Professionals*, Farnham: Ashgate.

Parsons, T. (1959) 'The Social Structure of the Family', in R. Anshen (ed.), *The Family: Its Function and Destiny*, New York: Harper & Row.

Patchin, J. and Hinduja, S. (2010) 'Cyberbullying and Self-Esteem', *Journal of School Health*, 80(12): 614–21.

Pearlin, L. and Skaff, M. (1996) 'Stress and the Life Course: A Paradigmatic Alliance', *The Gerontologist*, 36(1): 239–47.

Peguero, A. and. Williams, L. (2011) 'Racial and Ethnic Stereotypes and Bullying Victimization', *Youth & Society*, 45(4): 54–564.

Perrin, E. and Siegel, B. (2013) 'Promoting the Well-Being of Children Whose Parents Are Gay or Lesbian', *Pediatrics*, 131(4): 827–30.

Pew Internet & American Life Project (2004) 'The Internet and Daily Life: Many Americans Use the Internet in Everyday Activities, But Traditional Offline Habits Still Dominate', www.pewhispanic.org/topics/birth-rate-and-fertility/, accessed 5 September 2015.

Pew Research Centre (2002) 'Older Americans and the Internet', www.pewinternet. org/2004/03/28/older-americans-and-the-internet/, accessed 12 October 2012.

———. (2010) 'Birth Rate and Fertility', www.pewresearch.org/topics/birth-rate-and-fertility/, accessed 2 August 2015.

Phillipson, C. (1982) *Capitalism and the Construction of Old Age*, London: Palgrave Macmillan.

———. (1988) 'Challenging Dependency: Towards a New Social Work with Older People', in M. Langan and P. Lee (eds.), *Radical Social Work Today*, London: Unwin Hyman.

———. (1998) *Reconstructing Old Age*, London: Sage.

Phinney, J. (1996) 'When We Talk About American Ethnic Groups, What do We Mean?', *American Psychologist*, 51(9): 918–27.

Phoenix, A. (1991) *Motherhood, Meanings, Practices and Ideologies*, London: Sage.

Piaget, M. (1964) *The Early Growth of Logic in the Child*, London: Routledge and Kegan Paul.

Pilcher, J. (1995) *Age and Generation in Modern Britain*, Oxford: Oxford University Press.

———. (1996) 'Transitions to and From the Labour Market: Younger and Older People and Employment', *Work, Employment and Society*, 10(1): 161–73.

Pittman, J. and Blanchard, D. (1996) 'The Effects of Work History and Timing of Marriage on the Division of Household Labor: A Life Course Perspective', *Journal of Marriage and the Family*, 58(1): 78–90.

Polhemus, T. (ed.) (1978) *Social Aspects of the Human Body*, Harmondsworth: Penguin.

Pollert, A. (1988) 'Dismantling Flexibility', *Capitalism and Class*, 34: 23–44.

Pollock, L. (1983) *Forgotten Children: Parent-Child Relationships, 1500–1900* Cambridge: Cambridge University Press.

Popenoe, D. (1988) *Disturbing the Nest: Family Change and Decline in Modern Societies*, New York: Aldine.

Postman, N. (1996*) The Disappearance of Childhood,* London & New York: Aldine.

Poverty Site (2010) 'Poverty Indicators', www.poverty.org.uk/, accessed 3 September 2015.

Powell, J. and Biggs, S. (2000) 'Managing Old Age: The Disciplinary Web of Power, Surveillance and Normalisation', *Journal of Aging and Identity*, 5(1): 3–13.

Preston, C. (1968) 'Subjectively Perceived Agedness and Retirement', *Journal of Gerontology*, 23(2): 201–04.

Preston, C. and Gudiken, K. (1996) 'A Measure of Self-Perception Among Older People', *Journal of Gerontology*, 212: 63–7.

Price, S., McKenry, P. and Murphy, M. (eds.) (2000) *Families Across Time: A Life Course Perspective*, Los Angeles: Roxbury.

Quintana, S. (1998), 'Children's Development Understanding of Ethnicity and Race', *Applied & Preventative Psychology*, 7(1): 27–45.

Radcliffe-Browne, A. (1939) 'Religion and Society', in *Idem, Structure and Function in Primitive Society*, London: Cohen & West.

Rampton Committee (1977) *Report on The West Indian Community, the Commons Select Committee on Race Relations and Immigration*, London: Her Majesty's Stationery Office.

———. (1975) *Leisure and the Family Life Cycle*, London: Routledge.

Redhead, S. (1993) *Subcultures to Clubcultures: An Introduction to Popular Cultural Studies*, Oxford: Blackwell.

Reichenberg, A., Gross, R., Sanding, S. and Susser, E. (2012) 'Advancing Paternal and Maternal Age Are Both Important for Autism Risk', *American Journal of Public Health*, 100(5): 772–73.

Rex, J. (1970) *Race Relations in Sociological Theory*, London: Widenfeld & Nicolson.

Rexbye, H. and Povlsen, J. (2007) 'Visual Signs of Ageing: What are We Looking At?', *International Journal of Ageing and Later Life*, 2(1): 61–83.

Richardson, D. (1993) *Women, Mothering and Childrearing*, London: Palgrave Macmillan.

———. (2010) 'Youth Masculinities: Compelling Male Heterosexuality', *British Journal of Sociology*, 61(4): 737–56.

Riley, J. (1983) 'Dying and the Meanings of Death: Sociological Inquiries', *Annual Review of Sociology*, 9: 191–216.

Riley, M. (1987) 'On the Significance of Age in Sociology', *American Sociological Review*, 52: 1–14.

Ritzer, G. (1983) *The McDonaldization of Society*, Thousand Oaks, CA: Pine Forge Press.

Roberts, K. (1978) *Contemporary Society and the Growth of Leisure*, New York: Longman.

Roberts, K., Noble, M. and Duggan, J. (1989) *Youth Unemployment: An Old Problem or a New Life-style, Employment and Unemployment?*, Milton Keynes: Open University Press.

Robertson, J. (1996) 'Genetic Selection of Offspring Characteristics', *Boston University Law Review*, 76(3): 301–61.

Roche, J., Tucker, S., Thompson, R. and Flynn, R. (2004) *Youth in Society: Contemporary Theory, Policy and Practice*, Buckingham: Open University.

Rodgers, R. and White, J. (1993) 'Family Development Theory', in P. Boss, W. Doherty, R. Larossa, W. Schumm and S. Steinmetz (eds.), *Sourcebook of Family Theories and Methods: A Contextual Approach*, New York: Plenum.

Rohlfing, M. (1995) 'Doesn't Anyone Stay in One Place Anymore? An Exploration of the Understudied Phenomenon of Long-Distance Relationships', in J. Woods and S. Duck (eds.), *Understudied Relationships: Off the Beaten Track*, Thousand Oaks, CA: Sage, 173–96.

Rohrbach, L,. Sussman, S., Dent, C., and Sun, P. (2005), 'Tobacco, Alcohol, and Other Drug Use Among High-Risk Young People: A Five-Year Longitudinal Study From Adolescence to Emerging Adulthood', *Journal of Drug Issues*, 35(2): 333–55.

Rönkä, A., Oravala, S. and Pulkkinen, L. (2003) 'Turning Points in Adults' Lives: The Effects of Gender and the Amount of Choice', *Journal of Adult Development*, 10(3): 203–15.

Rosenfeld, A. (1985) 'Stretching the Span', *Wilson Quarterly*, 9(1): 96–107.

Rostow, I. (1974) *Socialization of the Aged*, New York: Free Press.

Rothschild, J. (2005) 'Introduction', in E. Parens, and A. Asch (eds.), *Prenatal Testing and Disability Rights*, Georgetown, Washington DC: Georgetown University Press.

Rowland, R. (1993) *Living Laboratories: Women and Reproductive Technologies*, Bloomington, IN: Indiana University Press.

Rubin, J., Provenzano, F. and Luria, Z. (1974) 'The Eye of the Beholder: Parents' Views On Sex of Newborns', *American Journal of Orthopsychiatry*, 44(4): 512–19.

Rubin, L. (1976) *Worlds of Pain: Life in the Working-Class Family*, New York: Basic Books.

Rudman, D., Fella, A. and Hoskotes, S. (1990) 'Effects of Human Growth Hormone in Men Over 60 Years Old', *New England Journal of Medicine*, 323(1): 1–6.

Rutter, M. (1972) *Maternal Deprivation Reassessed*, Harmondsworth: Penguin.

———. (1979) 'Maternal Deprivation 1972–78: New Findings, New Concepts, New Approaches', *Child Development*, 50(2): 283–305.

SAGE (nd) 'Social Isolation', www.sageusa.org, accessed 18 August 2000.

Sandel, M. (2012) *What Money Can't Buy: The Moral Limits of Markets*, Basingstoke: Palgrave Macmillan.

Sandler, L. (2013), Pew Research Centre, 'Having it All Without Having Children', http://time.com/241/having-it-all-without-having-children/, accessed 17 March 2014.

Santrock, J. (1994) *Child Development*, 6th ed, Madison: Brown & Benchmark.

Sassler, S. (2010) 'Partnering Across the Life Course: Sex, Relationships, and Mate Selection', *Journal of Marriage and Family*, 72(3): 557–75.

Sassler, S., Addo, F. and Hartmann, E. (2010) 'The Tempo of Relationship Progression Among Low-Income Couples', *Social Science Research*, 39(5): 831–44.

Sawchurch, A. (1995) 'From Gloom to Boom', in M. Featherstone and M. Wernick (eds.), *Images of Ageing*, London: Routledge, pp. 173–87.

Schoen, R., Landale, N., and Daniels, K. (2007) 'Family Transitions in Young Adulthood', *Demography*, 44(4): 807–20.

Schwartz, S., Côté, J. and Arnett, J. (2005) 'Identity and Agency in Emerging Adulthood: Two Developmental Routes in the Individualization Process', *Youth & Society*, 37(2): 201–29.

Schwartz, S., Zamboanga, B., Luyckx, K., Meca, A. and Ritiche, R. (2012) 'Identity in Emerging Adulthood: Renewing the Field and Looking Forward', *Emerging Adulthood*, 1(2): 96–113.

Scott, J. (1996) *Poverty and Wealth,* London: Longman.

Seider, S. (1989) *Rediscovering Masculinity*, London: Routledge.

Selwyn, J. (2000) 'Infancy', in M. Boushel, M. Fawcett and J. Selwyn (eds.), *Childhood: Principles and Reality*, Oxford: Blackwell.

Sennett, R. (1970) *The Uses of Disorder: Personal Identity and City Life*, New York: Knopf.

———. (2005) 'The Culture of Work', in C. Calhoun, C. Rojek, and B. Turner (eds.), *The Sage Handbook of Sociology*, Sage: London.

Settersten R., (2003) 'Propositions and Controversies in Life-Course Scholarship', in R. Settersten (ed.), *Invitation to the Life Course: Toward New Understandings of Later Life*, Amityville, NY: Baywood.

Settersten R. and Mayer, K (1997) 'The Measurement of Age, Age Structuring, and the Life Course', *Annual Review of Sociology*, 23(2): 33–61.

Settersten R., and Ray, B. (2010) 'What's Going On With Young People Today? The Long and Twisting Path to Adulthood', *The Future of Children*, 20(1): 19–41.

Shanir, B. (1992) 'Commitment and Leisure', *Sociological Perspectives*, 31: 238–58.

Sharpe, S. (1994) 'Great Expectations', *Everywoman*, December.

Shek, D. (1996) 'Middle Age', *Academic American Encyclopedia,* 13: 390–91. Danbury, CT: Grolier.

Shorter, E. (1975) *The Making of the Modern Family,* New York: Basic Books.

Silber, S. (1991) 'Effect of Age on Male Fertility', *Seminars in Reproductive Endocrinology*, 9(3), www.infertile.com/pdf_files/archive/1991_Chap_EffectAge Male.pdf.

Silva, R. (2008) 'The Old Age to Third Age: The Historical Course of the Identities Linked to the Process of Ageing', *História, Clènclas, Saúde – Manguinhos*, 5(1): 158–68.

Sinfield, R. (1981) *What Unemployment Means*, London: Martin Robertson.

Singh, G. (1993) *Coping with Two Cultures: British Asians and Indo-Canadian Adolescents*, Clevedon: Multilingual Matters.

Skellington, R. and Morris, P. (1998) *'Race' in Britain Today*, London: Sage.

Smart, C. and Neale, B. (2001) 'Constructing Post-Divorce Childhoods', in A. Giddens (eds.), *Sociology. Introductory Readings*, Oxford: Polity.

Smith, A. (1991) *National Identity*, London: Penguin.

———. (2011) 'Are You a Guilty Parent? Focus on the Process of Parenting Not the Outcome', *Psychology Today*, September, https://www.psychologytoday.com/blog/healthy-connections/201109/are-you-guilty-parent, accessed 2 April 2011.

Smock, P. (2004) 'The Wax and Wane of Marriage: Prospects for Marriage in the 21st Century', *Journal of Marriage and Family*, 66(4): 966–74.

Society for Menstrual Cycle Research (2012) 'The Medicalization of the Menstrual Cycle', http://menstruationresearch.org/wp-content/uploads/2009/07/Medicalization-of-the-Menstrual-Cycle.pdf , accessed 11 September 2015.

Social Trends (1997) 41, 'Labour Market', Office of National Statistics, accessed 8 August 2015.

Soler-i-Marti, R. (2015) 'Youth Political Involvement Update: Measuring the Role of Cause-Oriented Political Interest in Young People's Activism', *Journal of Youth Studies*, 18(3): 396–416.

Solomon Z., Helvitz, H, Zerach, G. (2009) 'Subjective Age, PTSD and Physical Health Among War Veterans', *Aging and Mental Health*, 13(3): 405–13.

Spates, J. (1983) 'The Sociology of Values', in R. Turner (ed.), *Annual Review of Sociology*, 9, Palo Alto, CA: Annual Reviews.

Spender, D. (1982) *Women of Ideas and What Man Has Done to Them: From Aphra Behm to Adrienne Rich*, London: Routledge.

Sprecher, S. (2001) 'Equity and Social Exchange in Dating Couples: Associations with Satisfaction, Commitment, and Stability', *Journal of Marriage and Family*, 63(3): 599–613.

Stacey, J. (1996) *In the Name of the Family: Rethinking Family Values in the Postmodern Age*, Boston, MA: Beacon Press.

Stafford, L., Kline, S., and Rankin, C. (2004) 'Married Individuals, Cohabitors, and Cohabitors Who Marry: A Longitudinal Study of Relational and Individual Well-being', *Journal of Social and Personal Relationships*, 21(2): 231–48.

Stanton-Salazar, R. (2011) 'A Social Capital Framework for the Study of Institutional Agents and Their Role in the Empowerment of Low-Status Students and Youth', *Youth and Society*, 43(3): 1066–1109.

Stanworth, M. (1983) *Gender and Schooling: A Study of Sexual Divisions in the Classroom*, London: Hutchinson.

————. (ed.) (1987) *Reproductive Technologies: Gender, Motherhood and Medicine*, Minneapolis, MN: University of Minnesota Press.

Steinberg, L. (1987) 'Single Parents, Stepparents, and the Susceptibility of Adolescents to Antisocial Peer Pressure', *Child Development*, 58(1): 269–75.

Stodolska, M. (2000) Changes in *Leisure Participation Patterns After Immigration, Leisure Sciences, 22*, 39–63.

Stodolska, P. (2013) 'Changes in Leisure Participation Patterns After Immigration', *Leisure Sciences*, 22: 39–63.

Storr, M. (1999) 'Postmodern BiSexuality', *Sexualities*, 2(3): 309–63.

Strauss, M. and Gelles, R. (1986) 'Societal Change and Change in Family Violence From 1975 to 1985 as Revealed in Two National Surveys', *Journal of Marriage and the Family*, 48(4): 465–79.

Stryker, S. (1987) 'Identity Theory: Developments and Extensions', in L. Yardley and T. Honess (eds.), *Self and Identity*, Chichester: John Wiley & Sons.

Sukarieh, M. and Tannock, S. (2014) *Youth Rising. The Politics of Youth in a Global Economy*, London: Routledge.

Swann Report (1985), *Education for All. Report of the Committee of Enquiry into the Education of Children from Ethnic Minority Groups*, London: Her Majesty's Stationery Office.

Tackey, N., Barnes, H. and Khambhaita (2011) 'Poverty, Ethnicity and Education', The Joseph Roundtree Foundation.

Tew, M. (1990) *Safer Childbirth? A Critical History of Maternity Care*, London: Chapman & Hall.

Thompson, R. and Amato, P. (eds.) (1999) *The Postdivorce Family: Children, Parenting, and Society*, London: Sage.

Thompson, R., Bell, R., Holland, J., Henderson, S., McGrellis, S. and Sharpes, S. (2002) 'Critical Moments: Choice, Chance and Opportunity in Young People's Narratives of Transition', *Sociology*, 36(2): 335–54.

Titmus, S. (1962) *The Two Nations of Old Age*, Basingstoke: Macmillan.

Tomer, A. and Eliason, G. (1996) 'Toward a Comprehensive Model of Death Anxiety', *Death Studies*, 20(4): 343–65.

Tomlinson, J. (1999) *Globalization and Culture*, Oxford: Polity Press.

Townsend, P. (1987) *Poverty and Labour in London*, London: Low Pay Unit.

Tower, R. and Kasl, S. (1996) 'Depressive Illness Across Older Spouses: Longitudinal Influences', *Psychology and Ageing*, 11: 683–97.

Troll, B. et al. (1997) *Looking Ahead*, Englewood Cliffs: Prentice Hall.

Uhlenberg-Mauve, P. (1969) 'A Study of Cohort Life Cycles: Cohorts of Native Born Massachusetts Women, 1830–1920', *Population Studies: A Journal of Demographics*, 13(3): 407–20.

Umberson, D., Crosnoe, R. and Reczek, C. (2010) 'Social Relationships and Health Behavior Across the Life Course', *Annual Review of Sociology*, 36: 139–57.

UNICEF (2014) 'Children of Recession: The Impact of the Economic Chris on Child Well being in Rich Countries', Innocenti Report Card 12, www.unicef-irc. org/publications/733, accessed 5 July 2015.

United States Department of Labor (2013) 'Leading Occupations', Women's Bureau, United States Department of Labor (2013) www.dol.gov/wb/stats/leadoccupations.htm, accessed 6 April 2014.

US Census Bureau (1983), Historical Statistics of the United States https://www.census.gov/prod/www/statistical_abstract.html, accessed 6 November 2002.

US Congressional Budget Office (2009) 'The Distribution of Household Income and Federal Taxes', 2008–2009, www.cbo.gov/sites/default/files/112th-congress-2011-2012/reports/43373-06-11-HouseholdIncomeandFedTaxes.pdf, accessed 2 April 2015.

van Dijk, M. (2012) *The Network Society,* London: Sage.

van Gennep, A. (1908) *Les Rites of Passage,* London: Routledge.

L. van Ijzendoorn & M. Tavecchio (1987) 'Perceived Security and Extension of the Child's Rearing Context: A Parent-Report Approach', in L. Tavecchio and M. Ijendoorn (eds.), *Attachment in Social Networks. Contributors to the Bowlby-Ainsworth Attachment Theory,* North-Holland: Elsevier Science Publishers.

Ventura, S. and Hamilton, B. (2009) 'U.S. Teenage Birth Rate Resumes Decline', Centres for Disease Control and Prevention, www.cdc.gov/nchs/data/databriefs/db58.htm, accessed 30 March 2009.

Vincent, J. (2003) *Old Age,* London: Routledge.

Waites, M. (2003) 'Equality at Last?: Homosexuality, Heterosexuality and the Age of Consent in the United Kingdom', *Sociology,* 37(4): 635–55.

Walker, A. and Maltby, T. (1997) *Ageing Europe,* Buckingham: Open University Press.

Waller, A. and Ragsdell, G. (2012) 'The Impact of E-mail on Work-Life Balance', *Aslib Journal of Information Management,* 64(2): www.emeraldinsight.com/doi/abs/10.1108/00012531211215178, accessed 7 January 2015.

Walls, N., Kane, S. and Wisneski, H. (2010) 'Gay—Straight Alliances and School Experiences of Sexual Minority Youth', *Youth & Society,* 41(3): 307–32.

Walter, T. (1994) *The Revival of Death,* London: Routledge.

———. (1999a) *On Bereavement: The Culture of Grief,* Buckingham: Open University Press.

———. (1999b) 'Popular Afterlife Beliefs in the Modern West', in P. Badman and C. Becker (eds.), *Death and Eternal Life in World Religions,* London: Paragon.

Walter, T. and Waterhouse, H. (1998) *The Meaning of Reincarnation in Contemporary England,* unpublished research paper.

Ward, J. (1976) *Social Reality for the Adolescent Girl,* Swansea: University of Swansea, Faculty of Education.

Warr, P., Banks. M. and Ullah, P. (1985) 'The Experience of Unemployment Among Black and White Urban Teengers', *British Journal of Psychology,* 76(1): 45–55.

Washbrook, J. and Waldfogel, E. (2008) *Early Years Policy*, London: Social Mobility and Education Policy.

Waters, M. (1995) *Globalization*, New York: Routledge.

Watson, S. and Gibson, K. (eds.) (1995) *Post-Modern Cities and Spaces*, Oxford: Blackwell.

Weeks, J. (1990) 'The Value of Difference', in J. Rutherford (ed.), *Identity*, London: Lawrence & Wishart.

'Wealth Inequality has widened along, racial, ethnic lines since end of Great Recession', Pew Research Centre, www.pewresearch.org/fact-tank/2014/12/12/racial-wealth-gap, accessed 24 June 2015.

Weaver, J. and Usher, J. (1997) 'How Motherhood Changes Life: A Discourse Analytic Study of Mothers With Young Children', *Journal of Reproductive and Infant Psychology*, 15(1): 51–68.

Weber, J. (2012) 'Becoming Teen Fathers: Stories of Teen Pregnancy, Responsibility, and Masculinity', *Gender & Society*, 26(6): 900–21.

Welch, M., Price, E. and Yankey, N. (2002) 'Moral Panic Over Youth Violence: Wilding and the Manufacture of Menace in the Media', *Youth & Society*, 34(1): 3–30.

Weston, K. (1991) *Families We Choose: Lesbians, Gays, Kinship*, New York: Columbia University Press.

Westwood, S. and Bhachu, P. (eds.) (1988) *Enterprising Women: Ethnicity, Economy and Gender Relations*, London: Routledge.

Wethington, E. (2000) 'Expecting Stress: Americans and the "Midlife Crisis"', *Motivation and Emotion*, 24(2): 85–103.

Whitbourne, S. (2010) *The Search for Fulfillment: Revolutionary New Research Reveals the Secret to Long-Term Happiness*, New York: Ballantine Books.

Whitbourne, S. and Willis, S. (2006) *Baby Boomers Grow Up: Contemporary Perspectives*, New York: Psychology Press.

Whitbourne, S., Sneed, J., and Sayer, A. (2009) 'Psychosocial Development from College Through Midlife: A 34-year Sequential Study', *Developmental Psychology*, 45(5), 1328–40.

Whiting, J., Kluckhohn, C. and Anthonu, A. (1958) 'The Function of Male Initiation Ceremonies at Puberty', in C. MacCoby et al. (eds.), *Readings in Social Psychology*, New York: Henry Holt.

Wiener, J. and Tilly, J. (2002) 'Population Ageing in the United States of America: Implications for Public Programmes', *Medicine & Health, International Journal of Epidemiology*, 31(4): 776–81.

Williams, T. and Sánchez, B. (2001) 'Identifying and Decreasing Barriers to Parent Involvement for Inner-City Parents', *Youth & Society,* 45(1): 54–74.

Williams, Z. (2014) *Bring it on, Babe: How to Have a Dudelike Baby*, London: Guardian Books.

Willis, P. (1977) *Leaning to Labour,* Farnborough: Saxon House.

Willis, S. (1999) *Life in the Middle,* New York: Academic Press.

Willmott, M. and Young, P. (1973) *The Symmetrical Family,* London: Routledge & Keegan Paul.

Winfree, L., Bächström, T. and Mays, G. (1994) 'Social Learning Theory, Self-Reported Delinquency, and Youth Gangs: A New Twist on a General Theory of Crime and Delinquency', *Youth & Society,* 26(2): 147–77.

Winn, M. (1983) *Children Without Childhood,* New York: Pantheon Books.

Witzel, L. (1975) 'Behaviour of the Dying Patient', *British Medical Journal,* 2(2): 73–90.

Wong, P. (1987–88) 'Death Attitudes Across the Life Span: The Development and Validation of the Death Attitude Profile (DAP), *Omega,* 18(2), www.drpaulwong.com/wp-content/uploads/2013/09/1987-Gesser-Wong-Reker-Death-Attitude-Profile.pdf, accessed 18 March 2002.

Woodman, D. and Wyn, J. (2014) *Youth and Generation: Rethinking Change and Inequality in the Lives of Young People,* London: Sage.

World Bank estimates derived from various sources including census reports, the United Nations Population Division's World Population Prospects, national statistical offices, household surveys conducted by national agencies, and ICF International, http://data.worldbank.org/indicator/SP.POP.DPND, accessed 8 June 2015.

Wray, S. (2007) 'Women Making Sense of Mid-Life: Ethnic and Cultural Diversity', *Journal of Aging Studies,* 21(1): 31–42.

Wright, E. O. (1979) *Class Structure and Income Determination,* New York: Academic Press.

Wyatt, G. (1997) *Stolen Women: Reclaiming Our Sexuality, Taking Back Our Lives,* New York: Wiley.

Wyness, M. (2000) *Contesting Childhood,* London: Falmer.

Wysocki, D. (1998) 'Let Your Fingers Do the Talking: Sex On An Adult Chat Line', *Sexualities,* 1(4): 425–52.

Yates, R. (1986) 'Self-Managed Teams: Innovation in Progress', *Business and Economics Quarterly,* Fall-Winter: 2–6.

Yeatman, A. (1994) *Postmodern Revisioning of the Political,* London: Routledge.

Yip, A. *(1999)* 'Same-Sex Couples: The Hidden Segment in the Study of Close Relationships', *Sociological Review,* 8(3): 30–33.

Yougov Rights and Responsibilities, https://www.gov.uk/parental-rights-responsibilities/what-is-parental-responsibility, Youth Justice Statistics for England and Wales 2012, accessed 18 May 2015.

Zogby (2009) 'American Attitudes Towards Muslims and Arabs', www.aaiusa.org/american-attitudes-toward-arabs-and-muslims-2014, accessed 13 September 2014.

Index